Blackstone's Police Manual

Crime

345

Blackstone's Police Manual

Volume 1

Crime

2011

Paul Connor

Cert Ed, LLB

Consultant Editor: Paul Connor

OXFORD

UNIVERSITY PRESS

OXFORD
UNIVERSITY PRESS

Great Clarendon Street, Oxford OX2 6DP

Oxford University Press is a department of the University of Oxford.
It furthers the University's objective of excellence in research, scholarship,
and education by publishing worldwide in

Oxford New York

Auckland Cape Town Dar es Salaam Hong Kong Karachi
Kuala Lumpur Madrid Melbourne Mexico City Nairobi
New Delhi Shanghai Taipei Toronto

With offices in

Argentina Austria Brazil Chile Czech Republic France Greece
Guatemala Hungary Italy Japan Poland Portugal Singapore
South Korea Switzerland Thailand Turkey Ukraine Vietnam

Published in the United States
by Oxford University Press Inc., New York

First published 1998
Thirteenth edition published 2010

British Library Cataloguing in Publication Data

Data available

Library of Congress Cataloging in Publication Data

Data available

Typeset by Laserwords Private Limited, Chennai, India
Printed in Italy
on acid-free paper by
L.E.G.O.S.p.A.

ISBN 978-0-19-959120-6

10 9 8 7 6 5 4 3 2 1

Foreword for 2011
Blackstone's Police Manuals

The role of a police officer has become more technical and more demanding over the last decades. To be properly qualified as a frontline officer, particularly a frontline supervisor and manager, there is a huge quantity of law, legal precedent and its interpretation that is required. Unlike a barrister, solicitor or judge, who have the books to hand or a website one click away with their mouse, a police officer frequently has to make crucial legal decisions with partial knowledge of all the facts, the pressure of time and events and the presence of a none-too-cooperative citizen. It is a testimony to the training that officers receive that they get the decisions right most of the time.

However, the training is crucially dependent on the quality of the training materials. These manuals are the product of a partnership between the National Policing Improvement Agency and Blackstone's. The NPIA has a key role in promoting learning and the development of leadership in policing. It is building on more than two decades of national expertise in supporting learning for police officers, and now has responsibility for improving every aspect of learning in policing from recruit training to the most senior ranks. Alongside Blackstone's we are committed to ensuring that the public is served by qualified, well-trained and well-led officers and police staff. These manuals are a key part of that mission.

Peter Neyroud QPM
Chief Constable and Chief Executive of the
National Policing Improvement Agency

Preface

Many readers of the Blackstone's Police Manuals are studying for promotion examinations, either to the rank of sergeant or inspector. They may have been informed that the Manuals are overcomplicated and contain unnecessary detail; this is anything but the case. The Manuals aim to bridge the gap between the practical and theoretical worlds of policing, of the law in practice and the letter of the law. Whilst it is conceded that the law is sometimes complicated, this fact alone is not reason enough to prevent its reproduction or discussion. The law is sometimes complex because, of course, it deals with complex situations. How these Manuals differ to the standard approach taken to such issues is to provide the reader with numerous examples and pragmatic explanations, particularly in the 'Keynote' sections, of the law in action. This enables practically-minded individuals to make the connection between the law on the streets and the law as it is applied and interpreted by the courts.

All the Manuals include explanatory keynotes and case law examples, providing clear and incisive analysis of important areas. As well as covering basic law and procedure they take full account of the PACE Codes of Practice and Human Rights implications. They can also be used as a training resource for police probationers, special constables and PCSOs, or as an invaluable reference tool for police staff of all ranks and positions.

Oxford University Press are always happy to receive any useful written feedback from any reader on the content and style of the Manual, especially from those involved in or with the criminal justice system. Please email this address with any comments or queries: police.uk@oup.com.

The law is stated as at 1 June 2010.

Acknowledgements

Blackstone's Police Manuals have become a firmly established 'household name' in the context of police law, particularly to candidates studying for the sergeants' or inspectors' OSPRE Part I examinations.

The production of the Manuals could not be accomplished without the professional participation of a great many people in a variety of capacities.

Many thanks to the production, editorial and marketing team at Oxford University Press, particularly Peter Daniell and Stuart Johnson.

Thanks must also go to the team of legal checkers and the staff of the National Policing Improvement Agency for their work in reviewing the 2011 editions.

And last but by no means least I thank my wife, whose continued whole-hearted support and understanding for me and my work has been, and continues to be, the primary reason you are reading these words.

Paul Connor

Contents

Contents

Contents

Table of Cases

Table of Statutes

Table of Secondary Legislation

Table of Codes of Practice

Table of Home Office Circulars

Table of International Treaties and Conventions

Table of European Law

How to use this Manual

Volume numbers for the Manuals

The 2010 Blackstone's Police Manuals each have a volume number as follows:

Volume 1: *Crime*
Volume 2: *Evidence and Procedure*
Volume 3: *Road Policing*
Volume 4: *General Police Duties*

The first digit of each paragraph number in the text of the Manuals denotes the Manual number. For example, paragraph 2.3 is chapter 3 of the *Evidence and Procedure* Manual and 4.3 is chapter 3 of the *General Police Duties* Manual.

All index entries and references in the Tables of Legislation and the Table of Cases, etc. refer to paragraph numbers instead of page numbers, making information easier to find.

Length of sentence for an offence

Where a length of sentence for an offence is stated in this Manual, please note that the number of months or years stated is the maximum number and will not be exceeded.

OSPRE® Rules and Syllabus Information

The rules and syllabus for the OSPRE® system are defined within the OSPRE® Rules & Syllabus document published by the National Policing Improvement Agency (NPIA) Examinations and Assessment on behalf of the Police Promotions Examination Board (PPEB). The Rules & Syllabus document is published annually each September, and applies to all OSPRE® assessments scheduled for the calendar year following its publication. For example, the September 2007 Rules & Syllabus document would apply to all OSPRE® Part I and Part II assessments held during 2009.

The document provides details of the law and procedure to be tested within the OSPRE® Part I examinations, information on the Part II assessment, and also outlines the rules underpinning the OSPRE® system.

All candidates who are taking an OSPRE® Part I examination or Part II assessment are strongly encouraged to familiarise themselves with the Rules & Syllabus document during their preparation. The OSPRE® Part I rules also apply to candidates who take the Part I examination and then go on to apply for their force's work-based assessment promotion trials.

The document can be downloaded from the Recruitment, Assessment & Selection Section of the NPIA website, which can be found at www.npia.police.uk. Electronic versions are also supplied to all force OSPRE® contacts.

If you have any problems obtaining the Rules & Syllabus document from the above source, please email the OSPRE® Candidate Administration Team at:

exams.ospre@npia.pnn.police.uk

Usually, no further updates to the Rules & Syllabus document will be issued during its year-long lifespan. However, in exceptional circumstances, the NPIA (on behalf of the PPEB) reserves the right to issue an amended syllabus prior to the next scheduled annual publication date.

For example, a major change to a key area of legislation or procedure (e.g. the Codes of Practice) during the lifespan of the current Rules & Syllabus document would render a significant part of the current syllabus content obsolete. In such circumstances, it may be necessary for an update to the syllabus to be issued, which would provide guidance to candidates on any additional material which would be examinable within their Part I.

In such circumstances, an update to the Rules & Syllabus document would be made available through the NPIA website, and would be distributed to all force OSPRE® contacts. The NPIA will ensure that any syllabus update is distributed well in advance of the examination date, to ensure that candidates have sufficient time to familiarise themselves with any additional examinable material. Where possible, any additional study materials would be provided to candidates free of charge.

Please note that syllabus updates will only be made in *exceptional* circumstances, an update will not be made for every change to legislation included within the syllabus. For further guidance on this issue, candidates are advised to regularly check the NPIA website, or consult their force OSPRE® contact, during their preparation period.

1.1 State of Mind

1.1.1 Introduction

The starting point of any analysis of the law begins with an examination of *mens rea* (state of mind) and *actus reus* (criminal conduct). This is because these concepts are fundamental to an understanding of all offences and the idea of criminal liability generally.

There is a cardinal rule in the criminal law of England and Wales that acts alone cannot amount to a crime unless they are accompanied by a 'guilty mind' or '*mens rea*'.

The key to proving *mens rea* in any criminal charge is to show that a defendant had *the required state of mind at the required time*. If you are going to do that, you need to know what the relevant state of mind for the offence is.

1.1.2 Strict Liability

Some criminal offences are said to be offences of 'strict liability'. This expression generally means that there is little to prove beyond the act itself and that the state of mind of the defendant is immaterial. However, in most cases it is more accurate to say that there is no need to prove *mens rea* in relation to one particular aspect of the criminal activity or behaviour. There have been isolated instances in which the courts have held that an offence does not require any *mens rea* to be proved. An example relates to the offence of driving with excess alcohol, contrary to the Road Traffic Act 1988, s. 5 (**see Road Policing, chapter 3.5**), which was stated in *DPP v H* [1997] 1 WLR 1406 not to require proof of any *mens rea*.

In some other, albeit rare, cases absolute liability is imposed, reducing even further the burden on the prosecution.

Situations where strict or absolute liability is imposed are usually to enforce statutory regulation (e.g. road traffic offences), particularly where there is some social danger or concern presented by the proscribed behaviour. So, where a defendant was charged with possessing a 'prohibited' weapon (**see General Police Duties, chapter 4.14**) the court held that it did not matter whether he *knew* he had the weapon—a CS gas canister—in order to prove 'possession' (*R v Bradish* [1990] 1 QB 981).

Some other offences such as public nuisance at common law require only strict liability in relation to some elements of the criminal conduct (**see General Police Duties, chapter 4.9**).

As a general rule, however, there is a presumption that *mens rea* is required for a criminal offence unless parliament clearly indicates otherwise (see *B (A Minor) v DPP* [2000] 2 WLR 452). This rule should be borne in mind, not only when approaching the rest of the material in this Manual, but also when considering criminal law in general.

1.1.3 States of Mind

Criminal offences generally can be classified in terms of the level of *mens rea* required. These are discussed below.

1.1.3.1 Offences Requiring a Particular *Mens Rea*

These are often referred to as crimes of *specific* intent or *basic* intent, a distinction which is important when considering defences.

Crimes of specific intent are only committed where the defendant is shown to have had a particular intention to bring about a specific consequence at the time of the criminal act. Murder is such a crime, requiring proof of an intention to kill or seriously injure. Other examples would be offences such as:

- wounding or inflicting grievous bodily harm *with intent* (Offences Against the Person Act 1861, s. 18);
- burglary (Theft Act 1968, s. 9(1)(a));
- blackmail (Theft Act 1968, s. 21);
- robbery (Theft Act 1968, s. 8);
- contamination of goods (Public Order Act 1986, s. 38(1)).

The common feature with all of these offences is that the *intention* of the offender is critical—without that intent, the offence does not exist.

Other criminal offences require no further proof of anything other than a basic intention to bring about the given circumstances.

Whereas an offence of burglary under s. 9(1)(a) of the Theft Act 1968 requires proof of the specific intent described above, burglary under s. 9(1)(b) simply requires proof that the person entered the building/part of a building as a trespasser and that he/she went on to commit one of the prohibited acts (theft/attempted theft; inflicting/attempting to inflict grievous bodily harm). Other examples would be offences such as:

- manslaughter;
- maliciously wounding or inflicting grievous bodily harm (Offences Against the Person Act 1861, s. 20);
- assault occasioning actual bodily harm (Offences Against the Person Act 1861, s. 47);

The important difference between offences of specific and those requiring only basic intent is that, in the case of the latter type of offence, *recklessness* will often be enough to satisfy the mental element.

1.1.3.2 Negligence

Negligence is generally concerned with the defendant's compliance with the standards of reasonableness of ordinary people. Like strict liability, the concept of negligence focuses on the consequences of the defendant's conduct rather than demanding proof of a particular state of mind at the time. Unlike strict liability, negligence still ascribes some notion of 'fault' or 'blame' to the defendant who must be shown to have acted in a way that runs contrary to the expectations of the reasonable person.

The most important criminal offence that can be committed by negligence is manslaughter (manslaughter by gross negligence), which is also one of the only offences to include specific reference—at common law—to the word 'negligence'. Other offences that can be committed by negligence do not usually contain the word itself but attract that test in relation to the mental element. Good examples are offences involving the standard of driving.

1.1.4 Statutory Expressions

Statutory offences use a number of different terms to describe the respective states of mind which must be proved. The more common expressions are:

- intent
- recklessness
- wilfully
- dishonestly.

These have been developed through our common law system and now have the following meanings:

1.1.4.1 Intent

Like many other concepts of *mens rea* 'intention' is not defined by any statute. If a defendant intends something to happen, he/she wishes to bring about certain consequences. In some offences, say burglary under s. 9(1)(a) of the Theft Act 1968, the defendant's *intention* may be very clear; he/she may enter a house as a trespasser *intending* to steal property inside. Provided there is enough admissible evidence (e.g. the possession of articles for use in the theft or perhaps an admission by the defendant), this element of the defendant's intention is relatively straightforward.

However, there will often be consequences following from a defendant's actions that he/she did not *intend* to happen. An example might be where, in the above burglary, it was late at night and the householder came across the burglar and suffered a heart attack as a result of the shock. In such an event it would be reasonable to suggest that it was the defendant's behaviour or actions that had brought about the victim's heart attack (**see chapter 1.2**). The defendant, however, may well argue that, although he/she intended to break in and steal, there had never been any *intention* of harming or frightening the occupant. At this point you might well say that the defendant should have thought about that before breaking into someone else's house in the middle of the night. This then brings in the concept of *foresight*, a concept that has caused the courts considerable difficulty over the years—for a number of reasons.

First, there is the Criminal Justice Act 1967 which says (under s. 8) that a court/jury, in determining whether a person has committed an offence:

(a) shall not be bound in law to infer that he intended or foresaw a result of his actions by reason only of its being a natural and probable consequence of those actions; but

(b) shall decide whether he did intend or foresee that result by reference to all the evidence, drawing such inferences from the evidence as appear proper in the circumstances.

Secondly, there is the body of case law which has developed around the area of 'probability', culminating in two cases in the House of Lords (*R* v *Moloney* [1985] AC 905 and *R* v *Hancock* [1986] AC 455). Following those cases it is now settled that foresight of the probability of a consequence *does not amount to an intention to bring that consequence about, but may be evidence of it*.

In other words, you cannot claim that a defendant *intended* a consequence of his/her behaviour simply because it was virtually certain to occur. What you can do is to put evidence of the defendant's foresight of that probability before a court, which may infer an intention from it. In proving such a point the argument would go like this:

- at the time of the criminal act there was a *probability* of a consequence;
- the greater the probability, the more likely it is that the defendant *foresaw* that consequence;

- if the defendant foresaw that consequence, the more likely it is that the defendant *intended* it to happen.

Whether or not a defendant intended a particular consequence will be a question of fact left to the jury (or magistrate(s) where appropriate). Most of the problematic cases in this area have arisen in relation to murder (**see chapter 1.5**). In such circumstances, where death or serious bodily harm was a *virtual certainty* from the defendant's actions and he/she had appreciated that to be the case, the jury *may* infer that the defendant intended to bring about such consequences (*R v Nedrick* [1986] 1 WLR 1025). Therefore, where the defendant threw a three-month-old baby down onto a hard surface in a fit of rage, the jury *might* have inferred both that death/serious bodily harm was a virtual certainty from the defendant's actions and that he must have appreciated that to be the case; they should therefore have been directed by the trial judge accordingly (*R v Woollin* [1999] 1 AC 82).

Finally, the relevant intent may have been formed, not of the defendant's own volition, but influenced in some way by other external factors. An example is where the defendant's thinking is affected by duress (as to which **see para. 1.4.6**).

1.1.4.2 Recklessness

The concept itself goes beyond a statutory expression and has probably become more important in proving criminal offences than the concept of 'intent' above as proof of recklessness is often enough to fulfil the requirement of *mens rea* (although not in offences requiring 'dishonesty'—**see chapter 1.13**).

KEYNOTE

Following decades of complex differences between objective and subjective recklessness (the former applying only to a very limited number of offences), the law was eventually clarified so that the standard approach to dealing with the term 'recklessness' will be that 'subjective recklessness' is the order of the day.

An advantage of recklessness over intention is that the former is easier to prove by the attendant circumstances; a disadvantage is the different elements attributed to the word 'reckless' by different courts considering different offences.

EXAMPLE

Consider a schoolgirl who throws a stone into a neighbour's garden, breaking the glass of a greenhouse window. She tells you that she was only 'having a laugh' and did not stop to think of what damage might be caused by the stone. Does the fact that she gave no thought to the consequences of her actions make her 'reckless' or blameless? Had she stopped to think about the possible consequences, would she have seen the risk? Does that matter?

If some reasonable person walking past at the time had seen her about to throw the stone, would that person have realised the possible risk? What if the person walking past had been another schoolgirl of the same age and understanding as the one who threw the stone?

Are all these questions relevant in determining recklessness?

Taking the last question first, yes—some of the above deliberations can be relevant, in deciding, the liability of the defendant.

In addition, the word 'recklessness' is *applied* in different ways to different offences.

Take the example of assault occasioning actual bodily harm (**see chapter 1.8**). In such an offence recklessness can suffice in proving the mental element (*R* v *Venna* [1976] QB 421). But recklessness as to what? The defendant may have been reckless as to the assault itself and/or to the *harm* that was actually caused *by* the assault. The courts have held that assault occasioning actual bodily harm only requires proof of recklessness *as to the assault* and there is no need to show that the defendant was reckless as to the extent of the harm caused by his/her assault (see *R* v *Savage* [1992] 1 AC 699).

In offences of criminal damage (**see chapter 1.15**), the concept of 'objective' recklessness caused problems for the courts. In such cases, so-called Caldwell recklessness (from the House of Lords decision in *Metropolitan Police Commissioner* v *Caldwell* [1982] AC 341) applied. This gave rise to difficulties of proof where the defendant failed to consider an *obvious* risk and then went on to damage property. In those cases a defendant was not allowed to claim to have had no *mens rea* simply because he/she had not thought the matter through and if the prosecution showed that the relevant risk (in our schoolgirl example above, the risk to property) would have been apparent to a reasonable person, it was not necessary to show that the defendant realised that risk. Of course if a defendant *did* in fact see the risk then clearly this strengthens the prosecution's case in any event. But this notion of obvious risk presented some real problems in practice, for instance, where the defendant, because of his/her mental condition or personal attributes, would not have been able to appreciate the risk *even if he/she had stopped to consider the consequences*. This meant that a defendant could be held criminally liable for the consequences of his/her actions even where he/she could not have foreseen those consequences and the strict application of the rule resulted in some 'harsh' decisions (*Elliot* v *C* [1983] 1 WLR 939; *R* v *R* (*Stephen Malcolm*) (1984) 79 Cr App R 334). The abolition of the old *doli incapax* rule (**see para. 1.4.10**) meant that, where objective recklessness was the appropriate test—e.g. manslaughter and criminal damage—children who were incapable of appreciating the risks arising from their actions could still be found guilty. Similarly, adults whose mental characteristics prevent them from appreciating the risks created by their behaviour were not able to raise those characteristics as a defence to charges requiring objective recklessness.

Although this type of recklessness was generally confined to offences under the Criminal Damage Act 1971, it still caused concern among practitioners and academics alike. It was a criminal damage case involving children, who did not think that their actions would lead to the ultimately disastrous consequences, that changed the law. In *R* v *G & R* [2003] UKHL 50, the House of Lords decided that the former *Caldwell* decision should be departed from and that recklessness in criminal damage matters should be viewed subjectively (**see para. 1.14.2.8**).

Whilst the House of Lords has concluded (*R* v *Reid* [1992] 1 WLR 793) that the word reckless may not have exactly the same meaning in all statutory provisions, in offences that can be committed 'recklessly' the test will be *subjective*.

The requirements of subjective recklessness can be found in the case of *R* v *Cunningham* [1957] 2 QB 396 and are satisfied in situations where the defendant foresees the consequences of his/her actions as being probable or even possible. In cases requiring subjective recklessness, the fact that the consequences *ought to have been foreseen* by the defendant will not be enough. The most important group of offences where this will be the case is those requiring 'malice' under the Offences Against the Person Act 1861 (**see chapters 1.8 and 1.9**). In such cases the term 'malice' is misleading. What the prosecution will need to show is that the defendant either intended to do harm to the victim or that he/she *foresaw that harm* (though not the extent of that harm) *may be caused but nevertheless went on to take that risk* (*R* v *Savage* [1992] 1 AC 699).

A good operational example of these issues in action can be seen in *D v DPP* [2005] EWHC 967. In that case a police officer attending a domestic incident arrested a man in order to prevent a breach of the peace. During a subsequent struggle the defendant bit the officer on the hand. The magistrates' court convicted the defendant of assaulting the officer in the execution of his duty (**see para. 1.8.3.3**) on the basis that the biting of the officer had been 'reckless'. The defendant appealed, arguing that a bite could not be reckless; either it was deliberate or it was accidental. The Divisional Court dismissed the appeal and held that the test of recklessness in this case involved the defendant having foreseen the risk that the victim would be subjected to unlawful force and having gone on to take the risk. While the case endorses the view that there can be a reckless 'battery' (**see para. 1.8.2.2**) the facts of it are not so convincing as, say, an occasion where the defendant causes injury by thrashing his arms around to avoid being handcuffed or by attempting to throw away some property during an arrest.

1.1.4.3 Wilfully

This term implies that a defendant must be shown to have desired the consequences of his/her actions or at least to have foreseen them (subjective recklessness). The term 'wilfully' however is *not* restricted to such occasions and has been taken to include *objective* (*Caldwell*) recklessness (*R v Sheppard* [1981] AC 394; *R v Newington* (1990) 91 Cr App R 247).

'Wilful' can also mean simply that an action was voluntary, that is, it describes the criminal conduct (*actus reus*) rather than the state of mind (*mens rea*).

1.1.4.4 Dishonestly

The concept of 'dishonesty' is of great importance to a number of mainstream offences, including theft and fraud. In proving many of the offences under the Theft Acts 1968 and 1978 you will need to show that the defendant acted dishonestly. This expression is defined for certain purposes within the 1968 Act itself. However, it has also been extended by common law decisions of the courts and it is critical, in dealing with offences requiring proof of dishonesty, that you identify the nature of the state of mind required and the ways in which it can be proved/disproved. For a full discussion of this concept, **see chapter 1.13**.

1.1.5 Transferred Malice

The state of mind required for one offence can, on occasions, be 'transferred' from the original target or victim to another. Known generally as the doctrine of 'transferred malice' because it originates from a case involving malicious wounding (**see chapter 1.8**), the doctrine only operates if the crime *remains the same*. In other words, a defendant cannot be convicted if he acted with the *mens rea* for one offence but commits the *actus reus* of another offence. For example, in the original case (*R v Latimer* (1886) 17 QBD 359) the defendant lashed out with his belt at one person but missed, striking a third party instead. As it was proved that the defendant had the required *mens rea* when he swung the belt, the court held that the same *mens rea* could support a charge of wounding against any other victim injured by the same act. If the *nature of the offence* changes, then the doctrine will not operate. Therefore if a defendant is shown to have thrown a rock at a crowd of people intending to injure one of them, the *mens rea* required for that offence cannot be 'transferred' to an offence of criminal damage if the rock misses them and breaks a window instead. The House of Lords has acknowledged that this doctrine is somewhat arbitrary and is an exception to the general principles of law (*Attorney-General's Reference (No. 3 of 1994)* [1998] AC 245).

The issue of transferred *mens rea* (which is really what this doctrine amounts to) can be important in relation to the liability of accessories (as to which, **see chapter 1.2**). If the principal's intentions are to be extended to an accessory, it must be shown that those intentions were either contemplated and accepted by that person at the time of the offence, or that they were 'transferred' by this doctrine.

....

EXAMPLE

A person (X) encourages another (Y) to assault Z. Y decides to attack a different person instead. X will not be liable for that assault because it was not contemplated or agreed by X. If, however, in trying to assault Z, Y happens to injure a third person inadvertently, the doctrine of 'transferred malice' may result in X being liable for those injuries even though X had no wish for that person to be so injured.

....

1.2 | Criminal Conduct

1.2.1 Introduction

Having considered the concepts relating to state of mind, the next key element is that of the criminal conduct. Many statutory offences spell out exactly the sort of behaviour that will attract liability, but there are some important general rules that also need to be considered.

For a person to be found guilty of a criminal offence you must show that they:

- acted in a particular way
- failed to act in a particular way (omissions) or
- brought about a state of affairs.

Known as the *actus reus*, this essential characteristic of any offence is the behavioural element.

1.2.2 *Actus Reus*

Mens rea is what a defendant must have had; *actus reus* is what a defendant must have done—or failed to do.

When proving the required *actus reus* you must show:

- that the defendant's conduct was voluntary and
- that it occurred while the defendant still had the requisite *mens rea*.

1.2.2.1 Voluntary Act

Other than in the few specific instances where an 'omission' will suffice, you must generally show that a defendant acted 'voluntarily', that is, by the operation of his/her own free will.

If a person is shoved into a shop window, he/she cannot be said to have damaged it for the purposes of criminal liability, even though he/she was the immediate physical cause of the damage. Similarly, if a person was standing in front of a window waiting to break it and someone came up and pushed that person into the window, the presence of the requisite *mens rea* would still not be enough to attract criminal liability for the resultant damage. In each case, the person being pushed could not be said to be acting of his/her own volition in breaking the window and therefore could not perform the required *actus reus*.

This aspect of voluntariness becomes important, not just when considering offences committed under physical compulsion, but also where the defendant has lost control of his/her own physical actions. Reflexive actions are generally not classed as being willed or voluntary, hence the (limited) availability of the 'defence' of automatism (**see chapter 1.4**).

Likewise, the *unexpected* onset of a sudden physical impairment (such as severe cramp when driving; actions when sleepwalking) can also render any linked actions 'involuntary'.

If the onset of the impairment could reasonably have been foreseen or anticipated (e.g. where someone is prone to blackouts) the defendant's actions may be said to have been willed in the respect that he/she could have prevented the loss of control or at least avoided the situation (e.g. driving) which allowed the consequences to come about.

1.2.2.2 Coincidence with *Mens Rea*

Generally it must be shown that the defendant had the requisite *mens rea* at the time of carrying out the *actus reus*. However, there is no need for that 'state of mind' to remain unchanged throughout the entire commission of the offence. If a person (X) poisons another (Y) intending to kill Y at the time, it will not alter X's criminal liability if X changes his mind immediately after giving the poison or even if X does everything he can to halt its effects (see *R v Jakeman* (1983) 76 Cr App R 223).

Conversely, if the *actus reus* is a continuing act, as 'appropriation' is (**see chapter 1.13**), it may begin without any particular *mens rea* at the start but the required 'state of mind' may come later while the *actus reus* is still continuing. If this happens, whereby the *mens rea* 'catches up' with the *actus reus*, the offence is complete.

This principle can be seen in the offence of rape. The sexual intercourse may be consensual at the time it starts but, if that consent is later withdrawn, any continued intercourse will amount to an offence (*Kaitamaki v The Queen* [1985] AC 147).

A further illustration can be found in a case where a motorist was being directed to pull his car over to the kerb by a police officer. In doing so, the motorist inadvertently drove onto the officer's foot. Having no *mens rea* at the time of driving onto the officer's foot, the defendant was not at that point guilty of battery. However, once the situation was pointed out to him, the fact that he left the car where it was (the *actus reus*) was then joined by the appropriate *mens rea* and he was convicted of assault (*Fagan v Metropolitan Police Commissioner* [1969] 1 QB 439).

1.2.3 Omissions

Criminal conduct is most often associated with *actions*: damaging or stealing property, injuring or deceiving others, but occasionally liability is brought about by a failure to act.

Most of the occasions where failure or omission will attract liability are where a *duty to act* has been created. Such a duty can arise from a number of circumstances, the main ones being:

D The creation of a Dangerous situation by the defendant. See, for example, *R v Miller* [1983] 2 AC 161 where the defendant, having accidentally started a fire in a house, moved to another room taking no action to counteract the danger he had created.

U Under statute, contract or a person's public 'office'. Examples would be where a police officer failed to intervene to prevent an assault (*R v Dytham* [1979] QB 722) or where a crossing keeper omitted to close the gates at a level crossing and a person was subsequently killed by a train (*R v Pittwood* (1902) 19 TLR 37).

T Where the defendant has Taken it upon himself/herself to carry out a duty and then fails to do so. Such a duty was taken up by the defendant in *R v Stone* [1977] QB 354 when she accepted a duty to care for her partner's mentally-ill sister who subsequently died.

Y In circumstances where the defendant is in a parental relationship with a child or a Young person, i.e. an obligation exists for the parent to look after the health and welfare of the child.

Whether or not there is a sufficient proximity between the defendant and the victim brought about by a duty to act will be a question of law (see generally *R v Singh* [1999] Crim LR 582 and *R v Khan* [1998] Crim LR 830). A graphic example of where such a duty can be created by the defendant is in the case of a lorry driver smuggling illegal immigrants in the back of his vehicle (*R v Wacker* [2002] EWCA Crim 1944).

In such situations there may be a *duty* to act. Having established such a duty, you must also show that the defendant has *voluntarily* omitted to act as required or that he/she has not done enough to discharge that duty. If a defendant is unable to act (e.g. because someone else has stopped them) or is incapable of doing more because of their own personal limitations, the *actus reus* will *not* have been made out (see *R v Reid* [1992] 1 WLR 793).

Some statutory offences are specifically worded to remove any doubt as to whether they can be committed by omission as well as by a positive act (e.g. torture under the Criminal Justice Act 1988, s. 134, **see para. 1.9.2**). Other offences have been held by the courts to be capable of commission by both positive acts and by omission (e.g. false accounting under the Theft Act 1968, s. 17, **see chapter 1.14**).

The distinction between acts and omissions was considered by the High Court in a case concerning withholding medical treatment from chronically ill patients (*NHS Trust A v M* [2001] 2 WLR 942). For a discussion of this case, **see General Police Duties, chapter 4.5**.

1.2.4 Causal Link or Chain of Causation

Once the *actus reus* has been proved, you must then show a *causal link* between it and the relevant consequences. That is, you must prove that the consequences would not have happened 'but for' the defendant's act or omission.

In a case of simple criminal damage it may be relatively straightforward to prove this causal link: a defendant throws a brick at a window; the window would not have broken 'but for' the defendant's conduct. Where the link becomes more difficult to prove is when the defendant's behaviour triggers other events or aggravates existing circumstances. For example, in *R v McKechnie* [1992] Crim LR 194 the defendant attacked the victim, who was already suffering from a serious ulcer, causing him brain damage. The brain damage prevented doctors from operating on the ulcer which eventually ruptured, killing the victim. The Court of Appeal, upholding the conviction for manslaughter, held that the defendant's criminal conduct had made a significant contribution to the victim's death even though the untreated ulcer was the actual cause of death. In some cases a significant delay can occur between the acts which put in train the criminal consequences. An example is where a defendant transported an accomplice to a place near to the victim's house some 13 hours before the accomplice shot and killed the victim. Despite the delay and despite the fact the accomplice had not fully made up his mind about the proposed shooting at the time he was dropped off by the defendant, there was no intervening event that diverted or hindered the planned murder—*R v Bryce* [2004] EWCA Crim 1231.

In a case which had similar facts to our 'simple damage' example above, the defendant entered the house after throwing the brick through the window. Although the defendant did not attack the occupant, an 87-year-old who died of a heart attack some hours later, the Court of Appeal accepted that there could have been a causal link between the defendant's behaviour and the death of the victim. If so, a charge of manslaughter would be appropriate (*R v Watson* [1989] 1 WLR 684).

1.2.5 Intervening Act

The causal link can be broken by a new intervening act provided that the 'new' act is 'free, deliberate and informed' (*R v Latif* [1996] 1 WLR 104).

If a drug dealer supplies drugs to another person who then kills himself/herself by overdose, the dealer cannot, without more, be said to have *caused* the death. Death would have been brought about by the deliberate exercise of free will by the user. This approach was reaffirmed in *R v Kennedy* [2007] UKHL 38 (**see chapter 1.5**). The supplier is unlikely to be held liable for *causing* death in such a case unless he/she actually takes a more active part in the administering of the drug (see *R v Dias* [2001] EWCA Crim 2986).

If the medical treatment which a victim is given results in their ultimate death, the treatment itself will not normally be regarded as a 'new' intervening act (*R v Smith* [1959] 2 QB 35). However, in *R v Jordan* (1956) 40 Cr App R 152, where the defendant had stabbed the deceased, it was held that death could not be attributed to the defendant. In this case the actual cause of death had been the administration of a drug (terramycin) after the deceased had shown he was intolerant to it (treatment described as 'palpably wrong' by the court) and when his original wound had nearly healed. *R v Jordan* has been described as a very particular case, depending on its exact facts. The basic rule is that an intervening act will not generally break the causal link/chain of causation.

There is also a rule which says defendants must 'take their victims as they find them'. This means that if the victim has a particular characteristic—such as a very thin skull or a very nervous disposition—which makes the consequences of an act against them much more acute, that is the defendant's bad luck. Such characteristics (e.g., where an assault victim died after refusing a blood transfusion on religious grounds (*R v Blaue* [1975] 1 WLR 1411)) will not break the causal link.

Actions by the victim will sometimes be significant in the chain of causation such as where a victim of a sexual assault was injured when jumping from her assailant's car (*R v Roberts* (1972) 56 Cr App R 95). Where such actions take place, the victim's behaviour will not necessarily be regarded as introducing a new intervening act. If the victim's actions are those which might reasonably be anticipated from any victim in such a situation, there will be no new and intervening act and the defendant will be responsible for the consequences flowing from them. If, however, the victim's actions are done entirely of his/her own volition or where those actions are, in the words of Stuart-Smith LJ 'daft' (see *R v Williams* [1992] 1 WLR 380), they *will* amount to a new intervening act and the defendant cannot be held responsible for them.

1.2.6 Principals and Accessories

Once you have established the criminal conduct and the required state of mind, you must identify what degree of involvement the defendant had.

There are two ways of attracting criminal liability for an offence: either as a *principal* or an *accessory* (accessories can also be referred to as *secondary parties*).

A principal offender is one whose conduct has met all the requirements of the particular offence. An accessory is someone who helped in or brought about the commission of the offence. If an accessory 'aids, abets, counsels or procures' the commission of an offence, he/she will be treated by a court in the same way as a principal offender for an indictable offence (Accessories and Abettors Act 1861, s. 8) or for a summary offence (Magistrates'

Courts Act 1980, s. 44). The expression 'aid, abet, counsel and procure' is generally used in its entirety when charging a defendant, without separating out the particular element that applies. Generally speaking, the expressions mean as follows:

- aiding = giving help, support or assistance
- abetting = inciting, instigating or encouraging.

Each of these would usually involve the presence of the secondary party at the scene (unless, for example, part of some pre-arranged plan):

- counselling = advising or instructing
- procuring = bringing about.

These last two activities would generally be expected to take place before the commission of the offence. These are purely guides by which to separate the elements of this concept and will not necessarily apply in all cases. However, if you are trying to show that a defendant *procured* an offence you must show a causal link between his/her conduct and the offence (*Attorney-General's Reference (No. 1 of 1975)* [1975] QB 773). 'Counselling' an offence requires no causal link (*R v Calhaem* [1985] QB 808). As long as the principal offender is aware of the 'counsellor's' advice or encouragement, the latter will be guilty as an accessory, even if the principal would have committed the offence anyway (*Attorney-General v Able* [1984] QB 795). If an accessory is present at the scene of a crime when it is committed, his/her presence may amount to encouragement which would support a charge of aiding or abetting if he/she was there as part of an agreement in respect of the principal offence. This would not be the case if a person was simply passing by and watched the offence. It is not an offence to do so as the ordinary citizen is not under a duty to prevent an offence occurring and failing to do so will not create liability as an accomplice (see *R v Coney* (1882) 8 QBD 534).

1.2.6.1 State of Mind for Accessories

Generally, the state of mind (*mens rea*) which is needed to convict an accessory is: 'proof of intention to aid as well as of knowledge of the circumstances' (*National Coal Board v Gamble* [1959] 1 QB 11 at p. 20). The *minimum* state of mind required of an accessory to an offence is set out in *Johnson v Youden* [1950] 1 KB 544. In that case the court held that, before anyone can be convicted of aiding and abetting an offence, he/she must at least know the essential matters that constitute that offence. Therefore the accessory to an offence of drink/driving (**see Road Policing, chapter 3.5**) must at least have been aware that the 'principal' (the driver) had been drinking (see *Smith v Mellors and Soar* (1987) 84 Cr App R 279).

There must also be a further mental element, namely an intention to aid the principal. Whether there was such an intention to aid the principal is a question of fact to be decided in the particular circumstances of each case. An example of such a case can be seen in *Gillick v West Norfolk & Wisbech Area Health Authority* [1986] AC 112. The case concerned the question as to whether a doctor who prescribed a contraceptive pill for a girl under the age of 16 could be charged with being an accessory to an offence by the girl's partner of having unlawful sexual intercourse (as to which, **see chapter 1.10**).

You can see from this requirement that the wider notions of recklessness and negligence are not enough to convict an accessory.

Occasionally statutes will make specific provision for the state of mind and/or the conduct of accessories and principals. An example can be found in s. 7 of the Protection from Harassment Act 1997 (**see General Police Duties, chapter 4.9**).

Joint Enterprise

A joint criminal enterprise exists where two (or more) people embark on the commission of an offence by one or both (or all) of them. It is a joint enterprise because all the parties have a common goal—that an offence will be committed.

KEYNOTE

As the parties to a joint enterprise share a combined purpose, each would be liable for the consequences of the actions of the other in the pursuit of their joint enterprise (but see below for such liability when the nature of the offence changes). This is the case even if the consequences of the joint enterprise are a result of a mistake. For example, two offenders (A and B) agree to carry out a burglary on a particular house. Offender A leads the way but makes an error in trying to identify the house and mistakenly breaks into the wrong house. The fact that the mistake has been made by offender A will not prevent offender B being guilty as an accomplice to the burglary offence.

What happens when one party to the joint enterprise goes beyond that which was agreed or contemplated by the other?

....

EXAMPLE

Two men (A and B) agree to carry out an offence of theft. During the course of the offence, the owner of the property subject of the offence appears and tries to prevent the offence taking place. Offender A produces a flick-knife and stabs the victim, causing grievous bodily harm. Offender B had no idea whatsoever that offender A had a flick-knife and had never even contemplated the use of violence during the theft offence.

....

The actions of offender A are a clear departure from the nature and type of crime that was envisaged by offender B who did not know that A possessed a flick-knife; it is an act so fundamentally different from that originally contemplated by B that B is most unlikely to be liable for the injuries caused to the victim (see *R v Anderson* [1966] 2 QB 110).

The situation would alter if offender B knew that offender A possessed the flick-knife. Here, offender B could be convicted of a wounding offence if he had contemplated as a real possibility that offender A might commit the wounding offence but nevertheless still took part in the theft.

This line of thinking is also relevant when considering the liability of a joint enterprise offender when a death has taken place. In *R v Powell* [1999] 1 AC 1, two defendants accompanied a third defendant to a drug dealer's house to buy drugs. When the drug dealer came to the door he was shot. It was unclear who had fired the fatal shot but the prosecution argued that, if the third defendant had done so, then the first two defendants were guilty of murder because they knew that the third defendant was armed with a gun. The first two defendants were convicted of murder. They appealed but the House of Lords dismissed the appeal holding that where one party (D) to a joint enterprise to commit an offence foresees as a real possibility that another party (E) may, in the course of it do an act, with the requisite *mens rea*, constituting another offence (and E does so), D is liable for that offence. This is the case even if D has not expressly or tacitly agreed to that offence, and even though he expressly forbids it. This approach was re-affirmed in the more recent case of *R v Rahman* [2008] UKHL 45 where the House of Lords considered an appeal by a group of men who chased and attacked their victim with weapons including baseball bats, iron bars and knives. The victim died from two stab wounds to his back. There was no evidence that the appellants inflicted the fatal injuries; the participant who did probably escaped arrest but this did not prevent the defendants being convicted for their part in the joint enterprise. The House of Lords ruled that where a defendant was involved in a joint enterprise which resulted in murder, that defendant only had to foresee what his associate might do, not what he specifically intended to do, to be guilty of murder as an accessory. The defendants knew they were taking part in a joint attack with the purpose of causing serious injury, in which one or more of the participants was armed with a knife. Obviously, those participants would not have had a knife unless they were prepared to use it in the attack, a fact the defendants must have realised when they joined the attack. Killing due to the use of the knife could not be regarded as a complete departure from what the defendants contemplated as being involved in the common design.

What of the situation where the accessory or secondary party is not present during the substantive offence? In such circumstances involved in the example above, the position can be summarised as follows:

> Where the principal (P) relies on acts of the accessory (D) which assist him/her in the preliminary stages of a crime later committed in D's absence, it is necessary to prove *intentional assistance by D* in acts which D knew were steps taken by P towards the commission of the crime. Therefore the prosecution must prove:
>
> - an act done by D;
> - which *in fact* assisted the later commission of the offence;
> - that D did the act deliberately realising that it was capable of assisting the offence;
> - that D, at the time of doing the act, contemplated the commission of the offence by P, (e.g. he/she foresaw it as a real or substantial risk or real possibility); and
> - that when doing the act D intended to assist P.
>
> (see *R* v *Bryce* [2004] EWCA Crim 1231).

Another practical consideration arises, not from the absence of the accessory, but the failure to trace the *principal*.

If the principal cannot be traced or identified, the accessory may still be liable (see *Hui Chi-ming* v *The Queen* [1992] 1 AC 34). Similarly, an accessory may be convicted of procuring an offence even though the principal is acquitted or has a valid defence for his/her actions. The reasoning for this would seem to be that the principal often supplies the *actus reus* for the accessory's offence. If the accessory also has the required *mens rea*, the offence will be complete and should not be affected by the fact that there is some circumstance or characteristic preventing the principal from being prosecuted.

Additionally, if the accessory had some responsibility and the actual ability to control the actions of the principal, his/her failure to do so may attract liability (e.g. a driving instructor who fails to prevent a learner driver from driving without due care and attention (*Rubie* v *Faulkner* [1940] 1KB 571)).

It is possible for an accomplice to change his/her mind before the criminal act is carried out. However, the exact requirements of making an effective 'withdrawal' before any liability is incurred is unclear. Evidence such as how far the proposed plan had already proceeded before the withdrawal and the amount and nature of any help or encouragement already given by the accessory will be very relevant. Simply fleeing at the last moment because someone was approaching would generally not be enough. In the absence of some overwhelming supervening event, an accessory can only avoid liability for assistance rendered to the principal offender towards the commission of the crime by acting in a way that amounts to the *countermanding* of any earlier assistance such as a withdrawal from the common purpose. Repentance alone, unsupported by any action taken to demonstrate withdrawal, will not be enough (see e.g. *R* v *Becerra* (1975) 62 Cr App R 212 and *R* v *Mitchell* (1999) 163 JP 75).

A person whom the law is intended to protect from certain types of offence cannot be an accessory to such offences committed against them. For example, a girl under 16 years of age is protected (by the Sexual Offences Act 2003 (**see chapter 1.10**)) from people having sexual intercourse with her. If a 15-year-old girl allows someone to have sexual intercourse with her she cannot be charged as an accessory to the offence (*R* v *Tyrrell* [1894] 1 QB 710).

1.2.7 Corporate Liability

Companies which are 'legally incorporated' have a legal personality of their own, that is they can own property, employ people and bring law suits: they can therefore commit offences. There are many difficulties associated with proving and punishing criminal conduct by companies. However, companies have been prosecuted for offences of strict liability (*Alphacell Ltd* v *Woodward* [1972] AC 824); offences requiring *mens rea* (*Tesco Supermarkets Ltd* v *Nattrass* [1972] AC 153); and offences of being an 'accessory' (*R* v *Robert Millar (Contractors) Ltd* [1970] 2 QB 54—aiding and abetting the causing of death by reckless (now dangerous) driving). There are occasions where the courts will accept that the knowledge of certain employees will be extended to the company (see e.g. *Tesco Stores Ltd* v *Brent London Borough Council* [1993] 1 WLR 1037).

Clearly there are some offences that would be conceptually impossible for a legal corporation to commit (e.g. some sexual offences) but, given that companies can be guilty as accessories (see *Robert Millar* above), they may well be capable of aiding and abetting such offences even though they could not commit the offence as a principal.

A company (OLL Ltd) has also been convicted, along with its Managing Director, of manslaughter (following the school canoeing tragedy at Lyme Bay in 1994) (*R* v *Kite* [1996] 2 Cr App R (S) 295). Companies can now be prosecuted for such offences under the terms of the Corporate Manslaughter and Corporate Homicide Act 2007 (**see chapter 1.5**).

1.2.8 Vicarious Liability

The general principle in criminal law is that liability is *personal*. There are, however, occasions where liability can be transmitted *vicariously* to another.

The most frequent occasions are cases where a statutory duty is breached by an employee in the course of his/her employment (see e.g. *National Rivers Authority* v *Alfred McAlpine Homes (East) Ltd* [1994] 4 All ER 286), or where a duty is placed upon a particular individual such as a licensee who delegates some of his/her functions to another (**see General Police Duties, chapter 4.9**). The purpose behind this concept is generally to prevent individuals or organisations from evading liability by getting others to carry out unlawful activities on their behalf. A common law exception to the rule that liability at criminal law is personal can be found in the offence of public nuisance (as to which, **see General Police Duties, chapter 4.9**).

Incomplete Offences and Police Investigations

1.3.1 Introduction

There are circumstances where defendants are interrupted or frustrated in their efforts to commit an offence. Such circumstances might come about as a result of police intervention (e.g. where intelligence suggests that a serious offence is to take place on a given date) or as a result of things not going as the defendants had hoped (e.g. the property which they intended to steal not being where they thought it was). In these and other cases several general offences, often called inchoate or incomplete offences, may be used to ensure that the defendant's conduct does not go unpunished.

It should be noted that most incomplete offences *cannot* be mixed, and that most *cannot* be attempted. For instance, you *cannot* conspire to aid and abet, neither can you attempt to conspire. There are, as ever, limited exceptions to this rule.

1.3.2 Encouraging or Assisting Crime

The common law offence of inciting an offence was abolished by the Serious Crime Act 2007. Incitement was replaced by the offences under ss. 44, 45 and 46 of the Act.

KEYNOTE

Readers should note that any references in existing legislation to the common law offence of incitement are to be read as references to the offences in ss. 44, 45 and 46, i.e. to be read as 'encouraging or assisting an offence'.

OFFENCE: **Intentionally Encouraging or Assisting an Offence—*Serious Crime Act 2007, s. 44***

• Triable in the same way as the anticipated offence • Where the anticipated offence is murder the offence is punishable by life imprisonment • In any other case a person is liable to any penalty for which he would be liable on conviction of the anticipated offence

The Serious Crime Act 2007, s. 44 states:

(1) A person commits an offence if—
    (a) he does an act capable of encouraging or assisting in the commission of an offence; and
    (b) he intends to encourage or assist its commission
(2) But he is not to be taken to have intended to encourage or assist the commission of an offence merely because such encouragement or assistance was a foreseeable consequence of his act.

OFFENCE: **Encouraging or Assisting an Offence believing it will be committed—*Serious Crime Act 2007, s. 45***

> • Triable in the same way as the anticipated offence • Where the anticipated offence is murder the offence is punishable by life imprisonment • In any other case a person is liable to any penalty for which he would be liable on conviction of the anticipated offence

The Serious Crime Act 2007, s. 45 states:

> A person commits an offence if—
> (a) he does an act capable of encouraging or assisting in the commission of an offence; and
> (b) he believes—
> > (i) that the offence will be committed; and
> > (ii) that his act will encourage or assist its commission.

OFFENCE: **Encouraging or Assisting Offences believing one or more will be committed—*Serious Crime Act 2007, s. 46***

> • Triable on Indictment • Where the reference offence is murder the offence is punishable with life imprisonment • In any other case a person is liable to any penalty for which he would be liable on conviction of the reference offence

The Serious Crime Act 2007, s. 46 states:

> (1) A person commits an offence if—
> (a) he does an act capable of encouraging or assisting the commission of one or more of a number of offences: and
> (b) he believes—
> > (i) that one or more of those offences will be committed (but has no belief as to which); and
> > (ii) that his act will encourage or assist the commission of one or more of them.
> (2) It is immaterial for the purposes of subsection (1)(b)(ii) whether a person has any belief as to which offence will be encouraged or assisted.

General Points

Section 47 of the Act sets out what needs to be proved in order to establish guilt for each of the above offences.

Section 49(1) of the Act states that offences can be committed regardless of whether or not the encouragement or assistance has the effect which the defendant intended or believed it would have.

....

EXAMPLE

D, a dentist, wishes to sexually assault his patients whilst they are unconscious under anaesthetic. To do so D will need the co-operation of his assistant, V. D puts his idea to V while they are having a drink in a pub, intending to encourage V to take part in the offences. V is outraged and wants nothing to do with D's plan. In this situation, the fact that V is not remotely interested in D's plan and is not encouraged to take part in it will not alter the fact that D has committed an offence under s. 44 of the Act.

....

A person can be convicted of more than one of these offences (ss. 44, 45 or 46) in relation to the same act (s. 49(3)).

Section 50 of the Act sets out that it will be a defence to the offences under sections 44, 45 and 46 if the person charged with those offences acted reasonably, that is in the circumstances he was aware of, or in the circumstances he reasonably believed existed, it was reasonable for him to act as he did.

Section 51 limits the liability of the offence by setting out in statute the common law exception established in the case of *R* v *Tyrrell* [1894] 1 QB 710. A person cannot be guilty of the offences in sections 44, 45 and 46 if, in relation to an offence that is a 'protective' offence, the person who does the act capable of encouraging or assisting that offence falls within the category of persons that offence was designed to protect and would be considered as the victim.

....

EXAMPLE

D is a 12-year-old girl and encourages P, a 40-year-old man to have sex with her. P does not attempt to have sex with D. D cannot be liable of encouraging or assisting child rape despite the fact that it is her intent that P has sexual intercourse with a child under 13 (child rape) because she would be considered the 'victim' of that offence had it taken place, and the offence of child rape was enacted to protect children under the age of 13.

....

The offences under sections 44, 45 and 46 do not apply to the offence of corporate manslaughter. This means an individual cannot be guilty of an offence of encouraging or assisting the offence of corporate manslaughter (s. 62 of the Act).

1.3.3 Conspiracy

Conspiracies can be divided into statutory and common law conspiracies.

1.3.3.1 Statutory Conspiracy

OFFENCE: **Statutory Conspiracy—*Criminal Law Act 1977, s. 1***
- Triable on indictment • Where conspiracy is to commit murder, an offence punishable by life imprisonment or any indictable offence punishable with imprisonment where no maximum term is specified—life imprisonment
- In other cases, sentence is the same as for completed offence

The Criminal Law Act 1977, s. 1 states:

(1) Subject to the following provisions of this Part of this Act, if a person agrees with any other person or persons that a course of conduct will be pursued which, if the agreement is carried out in accordance with their intentions, either—
   (a) will necessarily amount to or involve the commission of any offence or offences by one or more of the parties to the agreement; or
   (b) would do so but for the existence of facts which render the commission of the offence or any of the offences impossible,
   he is guilty of conspiracy to commit the offence or offences in question.

KEYNOTE

A charge of conspiracy can be brought in respect of an agreement to commit indictable or summary offences. Conspiracy is triable only on indictment even if it relates to a summary offence (in which case the consent of the DPP will be required). Offences of conspiracy are committed at the time of the agreement, therefore it is immaterial whether or not the substantive offence is ever carried out.

Agreeing with Another

For there to be a conspiracy there must be an agreement. Therefore there must be at least two people involved. Each conspirator must be aware of the overall common purpose to which they all attach themselves. If one conspirator enters into *separate* agreements with different people, each agreement is a separate conspiracy (*R v Griffiths* [1966] 1 QB 589).

A person can be convicted of conspiracy even if the actual identity of the other conspirators is unknown (as to the affect of the acquittal of one party to a conspiracy on the other parties, see the Criminal Law Act 1977, s. 5(8)).

A defendant cannot be convicted of a statutory conspiracy if the only other party to the agreement is:

- his/her spouse (or civil partner)
- a person under 10 years of age
- the intended victim (Criminal Law Act 1977, s. 2(2))

A husband and wife can both be convicted of a statutory conspiracy if they conspire with a third party (not falling into the above categories) (*R v Chrastny* [1991] 1 WLR 1381). A person is not guilty of statutory conspiracy if the only other person with whom he agrees is his civil partner. A civil partnership is a same-sex partnership registered under the Civil Partnership Act 2004. The 'end product' of the agreement must be the commission of an offence by *one or more of the parties to the agreement*. Once agreed upon, any failure to bring about the end result or an abandoning of the agreement altogether will not prevent the statutory conspiracy being committed. An agreement to aid and abet an offence of conspiracy is not, in law, capable of constituting a statutory conspiracy under s. 1(1) of the Criminal Law Act 1977 (*R v Kenning* [2008] EWCA Crim 1534).

Note that if an agreement to commit a *summary offence which is not punishable by imprisonment* is made in contemplation or furtherance of a trade dispute, it must be disregarded (Trade Union and Labour Relations (Consolidation) Act 1992, s. 242).

1.3.3.2 Common Law Conspiracies

OFFENCE: **Conspiracy to Defraud—*Common Law***
- Triable on indictment • Ten years' imprisonment and/or a fine

Conspiracy to defraud involves:

> ... an agreement by two or more [persons] by dishonesty to deprive a person of something which is his or to which he is or would or might be entitled [or] an agreement by two or more by dishonesty to injure some proprietary right [of the victim]...

(*Scott* v *Metropolitan Police Commissioner* [1975] AC 819).

(See also *Blackstone's Criminal Practice 2010*, para. A6.48.)

KEYNOTE

This offence has been endorsed by senior judges as representing an effective—if not *the* most effective—means of dealing with multiple defendants engaged in a fraudulent course of conduct.

The common law offence of conspiracy to defraud can be divided into two main types. The first is contained in the case of *Scott* above, the second involves a dishonest agreement to *deceive* another into acting in a way that is contrary to his/her duty (see *Wai Yu-Tsang* v *The Queen* [1992] 1 AC 269).

Although the requirement for an agreement between at least two people is the same, this offence is broader than statutory conspiracy. There is no requirement to prove that the end result would amount to the commission of *an offence*, simply that it would result in depriving a person of something under the specified conditions or in injuring his/her proprietary right.

You must show *intent* to defraud a victim (*R* v *Hollinshead* [1985] AC 975).

You must also show that a defendant was dishonest as set out in *R* v *Ghosh* [1982] QB 1053 (see para. 1.13.2.2.).

Clearly there will be circumstances where the defendant's behaviour will amount to both a statutory conspiracy and a conspiracy to defraud. The Criminal Justice Act 1987, s. 12 makes provision for such circumstances and allows the prosecution to choose which charge to prefer.

Examples of common law conspiracies to defraud include:

- Buffet car staff selling their own home-made sandwiches on British Rail trains thereby depriving the company of the opportunity to sell their own products (*R* v *Cooke* [1986] AC 909).
- Directors agreeing to conceal details of a bank's trading losses from its shareholders (*Wai Yu-Tsang* above).
- Making unauthorised copies of commercial films for sale (*Scott* above).

A further example can be found in *R* v *Hussain* [2005] EWCA Crim 1866 where the defendant pleaded guilty to conspiracy to defraud after a widespread abuse of the postal voting system. In that case the defendant, an official Labour party candidate, collected uncompleted postal votes from households and completed them in his own favour.

1.3.4 Attempts

The Criminal Attempts Act 1981, s. 1 states:

(1) If, with intent to commit an offence to which this section applies, a person does an act which is more than merely preparatory to the commission of the offence, he is guilty of attempting to commit the offence.

...

(2) A person may be guilty of attempting to commit an offence to which this section applies even though the facts are such that the commission of the offence is impossible.

(3) In any case where—

(a) apart from this subsection a person's intention would not be regarded as having amounted to an intent to commit an offence; but

(b) if the facts of the case had been as he believed them to be, his intention would be so regarded,

then, for the purposes of subsection (1) above, he shall be regarded as having had an intent to commit that offence.

(4) This section applies to any offence which, if it were completed, would be triable in England and Wales as an indictable offence, other than—

(a) conspiracy (at common law or under section 1 of the Criminal Law Act 1977 or any other enactment);

(b) aiding, abetting, counselling, procuring or suborning the commission of an offence;

(ba) an offence under section 2(1) of the Suicide Act (c 60) (encouraging or assisting suicide);

(c) offences under section 4(1) (assisting offenders) or 5(1) (accepting or agreeing to accept consideration for not disclosing information about a relevant offence) of the Criminal Law Act 1967.

KEYNOTE

Most attempts at committing criminal offences will be governed by s. 1. Although some statutory exceptions apply, the sentence generally for such attempts will be:

- for murder—life imprisonment
- for indictable offences—the same maximum penalty as the substantive offence
- for either way offences—the same maximum penalty as the substantive offence *when tried summarily*.

If the attempted offence is triable summarily only, it cannot be an offence under s. 1. However, if the only reason the substantive offence is triable summarily is because of a statutory limit imposed in some cases (e.g. criminal damage to property of a low value) the offence can be attempted (**see chapter 1.15**). Some offences include an element of attempt (e.g. drink drive offences—**see Road Policing, chapter 3.5**).

If the offence attempted is triable only on indictment, the attempt will be triable only on indictment. Similarly, if the offence attempted is an 'either way' offence, so too will the attempt be triable either way (s. 4(1)).

Many other statutory offences contain references to 'attempts', including:

- Theft Act 1968, s. 9(1)(b) (burglary)
- Firearms Act 1968, s. 17 (using firearm to resist arrest)

Section 3 of the Criminal Attempts Act 1981 deals with such statutory provisions and they will generally be governed by the same principles as those set out here.

More than Merely Preparatory

A defendant's actions must be shown to have gone beyond mere preparation towards the commission of the substantive offence. Whether the defendant did or did not go beyond that point will be a question of fact for the jury/magistrate(s). There is no specific formula used by the courts in interpreting this requirement. An example of where the defendant was held to have done no more than merely preparatory acts was *R* v *Bowles* [2004] EWCA Crim 1608. In that case the defendant had been convicted of several offences involving dishonesty against an elderly neighbour. The neighbour's long-standing will left her estate to charity but, following his arrest, police officers searched the defendant's premises and found a new will, fully complete except for the signature. The defendant and his wife were named as the main beneficiaries and were to inherit the neighbour's house. Although the defendant's son was said to have been heard making reference to the fact that he was going to inherit the house, the 'new' will had been drafted over six months earlier and there was no evidence of any steps to have it executed, nor was there any evidence of it being used. On this basis the Court of Appeal held that the making of the will was no more than merely preparatory and the defendant's conviction for attempting to make a false instrument (as to which **see para. 1.14.11.4**) was quashed. Courts have accepted an approach of questioning whether the defendant had 'embarked on the crime proper' (*R* v *Gullefer* [1990] 1 WLR 1063) but there is no requirement for him/her to have passed a point of no return leading to the commission of the substantive offence. However, to prove an 'attempt' you must show an *intention* on the part of the defendant to commit the substantive offence.

This requirement means that a higher level or degree of *mens rea* may be required to prove an attempt than for the substantive offence. For instance, nothing less than an *intent* to kill can support a charge of attempted murder (*R* v *Whybrow* (1951) 35 Cr App R 141), while in proving the substantive offence, an intention to cause grievous bodily harm will suffice. A defendant's intention may be *conditional*, that is, he/she may only intend to steal from a house if something worth stealing is later found inside. The conditional nature of this intention will not generally prevent the charge of attempt being brought and the defendant's intentions will, in accordance with s. 1(3) above, be judged *on the facts as he/she believed them to be*.

Although 'intent to commit' the offence is required under s. 1(1), there are occasions where a state of mind that falls short of such a precise intention may suffice. For instance, in cases of attempted rape (**see chapter 1.10**) the courts have accepted that recklessness as to whether the victim is consenting was (under the earlier sexual offences legislation) sufficient *mens rea* for attempted rape because it is sufficient for the substantive offence (*R* v *Khan* [1990] 1 WLR 813).

In proving an 'attempt' it is enough to show that a defendant was in one of the states of mind required for the substantive offence and that he/she did his/her best, so far as he/she was able, to do what was necessary for the commission of the full offence (*Attorney-General's Reference (No. 3 of 1992)* [1994] 1 WLR 409).

1.3.4.1 Interfering with Vehicles

OFFENCE: **Interfering with Vehicles—*Criminal Attempts Act 1981, s. 9***

- Triable summarily • Three months' imprisonment and/or a fine

The Criminal Attempts Act 1981, s. 9 states:

(1) A person is guilty of the offence of vehicle interference if he interferes with a motor vehicle or trailer or with anything carried in or on a motor vehicle or trailer with the intention that an offence specified in subsection (2) below shall be committed by himself or some other person.

(2) The offences mentioned in subsection (1) above are—
   (a) theft of the motor vehicle or trailer or part of it;
   (b) theft of anything carried in or on the motor vehicle or trailer; and
   (c) an offence under section 12(1) of the Theft Act 1968 (taking and driving away without consent);

   and, if it is shown that a person accused of an offence under this section intended that one of those offences should be committed, it is immaterial that it cannot be shown which it was.

(3)–(4) ...

(5) In this section 'motor vehicle' and 'trailer' have the meanings assigned to them by section 185(1) of the Road Traffic Act 1988.

KEYNOTE

The term 'interference' is not defined by the Criminal Attempts Act 1981. This offence is one of specific intent and you must prove that the defendant interfered with the vehicle, etc. with one of the intentions listed—(note, however, that it is not necessary to show which *particular* intention).

For the definitions of motor vehicle and trailer, see Road Policing, chapter 3.1.

The above offence is a specified offence for the purposes of the Vehicles (Crime) Act 2001, s. 3(4)(b) (as to which, see Road Policing).

1.3.5 Impossibility

Practical difficulties have arisen where, despite the best (or worst) efforts of the defendant, his/her ultimate intention has been impossible (such as trying to extract cocaine from a powder which is, unknown to the defendant, only talc). Impossibility is now far clearer following the Criminal Attempts Act 1981 and its interpretation through the courts. It differs however in some incomplete offences.

EXAMPLE

Taking an example of someone who tries to handle goods which are not in fact stolen, the following rules would apply:

- A defendant could *not* be guilty of encouraging another, nor of common law conspiracy to defraud in these circumstances. The *physical* impossibility of what they sought to do would preclude such a charge.
- A defendant *could* be guilty of a statutory conspiracy with another to handle 'stolen' goods and also of attempting to handle 'stolen' goods under these circumstances. The physical impossibility would not prelude such charges as a result of the Criminal Attempts Act 1981 and the House of Lords' decision in *R* v *Shivpuri* [1987] AC 1. The only form of impossibility which would preclude liability under the Criminal Attempts Act 1981 or for a statutory conspiracy would be the *legal* impossibility.

1.3.6 Inter-relationship and Police Operations

The issues of involvement of a police officer in an incomplete offence *are* of practical relevance to police officers particularly in the area of covert operations. Is it a conspiracy if one of the conspirators is an undercover police officer?

1.3.6.1 Entrapment and Undercover Operations

One of the arguments that is often raised by defendants who are caught by undercover officers is that they were induced or pressurised into committing the offence by the officers and that, as a result, either they should not be prosecuted or the evidence of the officer(s) should be excluded.

In *R* v *Loosely; Attorney-General's Reference (No. 3) of 2000* [2001] UKHL 53, the House of Lords took the chance to set out in detail the legal position in relation to these issues. Their lordships held that it is both unfair and an abuse of process if a person is incited (the predecessor of encouraging or assisting an offence) or pressurised by an undercover officer into committing a crime which the person would otherwise not have committed. If, however, the police officer(s) did no more than present a person with an 'unexceptional opportunity' to commit a criminal offence and the person took that opportunity, this would not amount to such an abuse of process.

This point was reinforced in *R v Jones (Ian Anthony)* [2007] EWCA Crim 1118 where the defendant appealed against a conviction of attempting to incite a child under 13 years old into penetrative sexual activity contrary to s. 8 of the Sexual Offences Act 2003. One of the defendant's grounds for appeal was that during the investigation he had been entrapped by the police who had deceived him into believing he was communicating with a real child and that no offence would have been committed otherwise. His appeal was dismissed, with the court stating that it was clear from the defendant's conduct that he was looking for opportunities to incite a child to penetrative sexual activity. The police did not incite nor instigate a crime but merely provided the opportunity for the defendant to commit a similar offence and provide evidence for a conviction. The offence was not instigated by the police but by the defendant's own actions.

1.3.6.2 Entrapment

In *Edwards* v *United Kingdom* (2005) 40 EHRR 24, the European Court of Human Rights restated the rights of defendants who are to be prosecuted on the basis of evidence obtained by undercover officers and, once again, highlighted the tensions between protecting the sensitive sources of that evidence while affording the defendant a fair trial.

- As a starting point—it is not acceptable for the 'State' (police officers or other agents) to lure its citizens into committing acts that are against the law and then to prosecute those citizens for doing so—this amounts to entrapment, a misuse of power and abuse of the courts' process.
- If police officers acted only as 'detectives' and 'passive observers' of criminal activity that was to take place anyway, there would be no real problem in drawing the line between what is allowable and what is not.
- However, some offences need a degree of active involvement by the police if those offences are to be successfully prosecuted. In such cases the police officers themselves become the reporters and witnesses of the offence as well as the investigators.
- The yardstick for judging the activities of the police in this regard is to ask whether the officers' conduct preceding the offence was no more than might have been expected from others in the circumstances. That is, did they do no more than give the defendant the 'unexceptional opportunity' to commit a crime as described above? If the answer is 'yes', the consequences below are not relevant. If the answer is 'no', there are several potential consequences for any subsequent trial.

The trial judge's task in such cases is to distinguish between legitimate crime detection and illegitimate crime creation (*R v Byrne* [2003] EWCA Crim 1073).

- The greater the inducement or persistence by the officers—the more readily the courts will conclude that they have overstepped the line.
- The greater the degree of intrusiveness into the 'target's' life—the closer the courts will scrutinise the 'proportionality' of the operation.
- The courts will also look at the defendant's personal circumstances including his/her vulnerability and experience. What might be insignificant in terms of an inducement to one person may not be seen as so insignificant in relation to another.

The consequences are as follows:

- Courts have a general discretion to exclude evidence under the Police and Criminal Evidence Act 1984, s.78 (**see Evidence and Procedure, chapter 2.8**).
- Courts also have a common law power to stay (discontinue) proceedings and order the release of a defendant where it becomes apparent that there has been a serious abuse

of power by the State (R v *Horseferry Road Magistrates' Court, ex parte Bennett* [1994] 1 AC 42).

- Courts also have a general duty to consider the fairness of any defendant's trial under Article 6 of the European Convention on Human Rights (**see General Police Duties, chapter 4.5**). However, it should be noted that violations of Article 8 (right to privacy) will not by themselves usually give rise to exclusion of any evidence obtained as a result (*PG* v *United Kingdom* 46 EHRR 51).

The use of informants in this area is particularly hazardous and may invite suggestions that the police did more than present the defendant with an unexceptional opportunity to commit their crimes. Where participating informants are involved, the same legal principles apply but the issues become far more complicated and policy regarding 'participating informant' status will be crucial. This is an area in which the expertise of the CPS will be needed from a very early stage.

What of the situation where, rather than approaching others, an undercover police officer is approached to take part in a proposed offence? There are several types of situation where this may occur.

In relation to this activity, there is no need for the person encouraged to have any intention of going on to commit the offence. The Divisional Court has held that there is no requirement for 'parity of *mens rea*' between the parties (*DPP* v *Armstrong* [2000] Crim LR 379). In that case the defendant had approached an undercover police officer asking him to supply child pornography. At his trial, the defendant argued that, as the officer in reality had no intention of supplying the pornography, there was no offence of incitement. On appeal by the prosecutor, the Divisional Court held that incitement, like conspiracies and attempts, was an auxiliary offence where criminal liability was attributed to the defendant where the full offence had not been committed. Consequently the intent of the person incited was irrelevant. The court also held that the issue of impossibility did not arise in circumstances such as Armstrong's because it had been 'possible' for the officer to supply the material.

A further situation involving police operations is where a defendant enters into an agreement with another person to commit an offence but that other person is in fact a police officer. Under normal circumstances, forming an agreement with another person to carry out an offence is a conspiracy. If, however, one of only two conspirators is an undercover officer who has no intention of going through with the agreement, there is a strong argument that there can be no 'true' conspiracy as the only other person had no intention of going through with the plan (see the comments of Lord Griffiths in *Yip Chiu-Cheung* v *The Queen* [1995] 1 AC 111). In conspiracies, the intention of at least two parties *is* the basis of the whole offence. In cases where the only other 'conspirator' is a police officer, encouraging an offence may be a more appropriate charge.

Making *an offer* which amounts *in itself* to a criminal offence (e.g. an offer to supply a controlled drug, **see chapter 1.6**) to an undercover officer may still amount to the offence and a defendant cannot claim that the offer was not 'real' because of the identity of the recipient (see *R* v *Kray* (1998) 10 November, unreported).

1.4 | General Defences

1.4.1 Introduction

'General defences' in criminal law are concerned with cases where the prosecution are unable to prove all elements beyond reasonable doubt because of some specific characteristics of the defendant or circumstances of a particular offence. This failure may come about at trial but will often be apparent at the evidence-gathering stage of a proposed prosecution. Police officers need to be aware of any defences that a person may have in answer to a criminal charge as:

- they have a duty to investigate crime *impartially and fairly*—if there is evidence that supports a person's defence, the police officer should be collecting it in the same way as evidence of the offence itself—it is not their job just to collect the evidence that proves someone *did* do something wrong;
- the police will need to be able to deal with any likely defences when they interview the accused person.

Some offences have particular defences attached to them (e.g. criminal damage), others exist only in relation to murder. These defences are discussed in the relevant chapters. This chapter is concerned with 'general defences', that is, those circumstances which may negate a conviction or even the bringing of a charge for a number of different offences.

1.4.2 Automatism

Strictly speaking, automatism is not a 'defence'; it is an absence of a fundamental requirement for any criminal offence, namely the 'criminal conduct' (*actus reus*). In **chapter 1.2** we considered the need for criminal conduct to be *voluntary* and *willed*. It therefore follows that, if a defendant has total loss of control over his/her actions, he/she cannot be held liable for those actions and provided the loss of control is *total*, there may be grounds to claim a defence of automatism. The best example of this defence is one where a swarm of bees flies into a car causing a reflex action by the driver resulting in an accident. As the driver's actions were involuntary, and not sufficient to support a criminal charge, the defence of automatism would be available. Other examples might include a person inadvertently dropping and damaging property when suddenly seized by cramp or discharging a firearm as a result of an irresistible bout of sneezing.

If the loss of control is brought about by voluntary intoxication or by insanity, the defence becomes narrower (**see paras 1.4.3 and 1.4.4**).

1.4.3 Intoxication: Voluntary or Involuntary

There is no general defence of intoxication. If there were, a high proportion of criminal behaviour would clearly go unpunished. What intoxication does is potentially remove the necessary *mens rea* required for a defendant to commit an offence. There are some statutory offences where specific provision is made for drunkenness (e.g. the Public Order Act 1986, **see General Police Duties, chapter 4.12**).

Intoxication can be divided into two categories; voluntary intoxication (you got yourself in that condition) and involuntary intoxication (you are not responsible for getting in that condition). The distinction between the two types of intoxication is important when considering whether the offence the defendant is alleged to have committed is one of 'specific' or 'basic' intent (these terms were discussed at **para. 1.1.3**).

Where an offence is a specific intent offence, such as murder or theft, a defendant who was voluntarily intoxicated at the time the offence was committed may be able to show that he/she was so intoxicated that he/she was incapable of forming the *mens rea* required for the offence. An individual who is voluntarily intoxicated *would not* be able to say this if accused of an offence of basic intent as the courts have accepted that a defendant is still capable of forming basic intent even when completely inebriated (see *DPP* v *Majewski* [1977] AC 443).

Where the offence is a basic intent offence, such as s. 47 assault, a defendant who was involuntarily intoxicated (perhaps because his/her drink had been spiked) at the time of the offence may be able to say that he/she lacked the *mens rea* for that basic intent offence.

KEYNOTE

Therefore, voluntary intoxication can be raised in answer to a charge of an offence of specific intent but not basic intent; involuntary intoxication can be raised in answer to a charge of both specific *and* basic intent.

If a defendant simply misjudges the amount or strength of intoxicants which he/she takes, this will not be regarded as involuntary intoxication and the restrictions discussed below will apply (*R* v *Allen* [1988] Crim LR 698). Similarly, if the defendant can be shown to have actually formed the required *mens rea* necessary for the offence, intoxication (voluntary or involuntary) will not be available as a drunken intent is still an 'intent' (*R* v *Kingston* [1995] 2 AC 355).

The source of the intoxication can be drink or drugs. In the latter case, however, the courts will consider the known effects of the drug in deciding whether or not the defendant had formed the required degree of *mens rea*; the characteristics of the drugs will also be relevant in determining whether the defendant behaved recklessly in taking them.

Where the defendant forms a 'mistaken belief' based on the fact that he/she is intoxicated and not thinking straight, that belief may sometimes be raised as a defence. In cases of criminal damage where a defendant has mistakenly believed that the property being damaged is his/her own property, and that mistaken belief has arisen from the defendant's intoxicated state, the courts have accepted the defence under s. 5 of the Criminal Damage Act 1971 (*Jaggard* v *Dickinson* [1981] QB 527) (**see chapter 1.15**). However, this appears to be confined to the wording of that particular statute and the courts have refused to accept similar defences of mistaken, drunken belief (see *R* v *O'Grady* [1987] QB 995 where a defendant charged with murder could not rely on a mistake induced by his own voluntary intoxication and claim 'self-defence'), or where the defendant mistakenly believed that the victim of a rape was consenting to sexual intercourse. The Court of Appeal has confirmed that the decision in *O'Grady* also applies to manslaughter—*R* v *Hatton* (2006) 1 Cr App R 16.

One further qualification is that if a defendant becomes intoxicated in order to gain false courage to go and commit a crime, he/she will not be able to claim a defence of intoxication *even if the crime is one of specific intent*. This is because he/she has already formed the intent required and the intoxication is merely a means of plucking up 'Dutch' courage to carry it out (*Attorney-General for Northern Ireland* v *Gallagher* [1963] AC 349).

1.4.4 Insanity

There is a rebuttable presumption in law that all people are sane. Where a person wishes to raise insanity as a defence, the burden of proof (on a balance of probabilities) rests with the defendant.

If a defendant claims to have been 'insane' at the time of the offence (to attract an acquittal in a summary trial or an order of the court when tried on indictment), that claim will be judged against the M'Naghten rules. The rules (*M'Naghten's Case* (1843) 10 Cl & F 200) state:

> ... to establish a defence on the ground of insanity, it must be clearly proved that, at the time of the committing of the act, the party accused was labouring under such a defect of reason, from disease of the mind, as not to know the nature and quality of the act he was doing; or, if he did know it, that he did not know he was doing what was wrong.

The question of whether the defendant's attributes or condition amount to a 'disease of the mind' is a question of law and not a question of medical opinion (*R* v *Sullivan* [1984] AC 156).

An epileptic fit and a hypoglycaemic episode in a diabetic have both been deemed to be similar to insanity in respect of a defence to a criminal charge and therefore the M'Naghten rules above should be applied (*Sullivan* and *R* v *Quick* [1973] QB 910).

A special verdict of 'not guilty by reason of insanity' is provided by the Trial of Lunatics Act 1883 if the defence is successful.

1.4.5 Inadvertence and Mistake

There are occasions where a defendant makes a mistake about some circumstance or consequence but claims that a defendant 'made a mistake' or did something 'inadvertently' will only be an effective defence if they negate the *mens rea* for that offence. Therefore, if someone picks up another person's shopping at a supermarket till or wanders out of a shop with something they have yet to pay for, their mistake or inadvertence, in each case, might negative any *mens rea* of 'dishonesty' (**see chapter 1.13**). As the requirement for the *mens rea* in such a case is *subjective* then the defendant's mistake or inadvertence will be judged subjectively. The same will generally be true for offences requiring subjective recklessness. It does not matter whether the mistake was 'reasonable' (*DPP* v *Morgan* [1976] AC 182). The appropriate test is whether the defendant's mistaken belief was an honest and genuine one. There are occasions where a genuine mistake on the part of the defendant may amount to a defence.

In *R* v *Lee* [2000] Crim LR 991, a case arising from an assault on two arresting police officers, the Court of Appeal reviewed the law in this area, reaffirming the following points:

- A genuine or honest mistake could provide a defence to many criminal offences requiring a particular state of mind, including assault with intent to resist arrest (*R* v *Brightling* [1991] Crim LR 364).
- A defence of mistake had to involve a mistake of fact, not a mistake of law (see below).
- People under arrest are not entitled to form their own view as to the lawfulness of that arrest. They have a duty to comply with the police and hear the details of the charge against them (*R* v *Bentley* (1850) 4 Cox CC 406).
- Belief in one's own innocence, however genuine or honestly held, cannot afford a defence to a charge of assault with intent to resist arrest under s. 38 of the Offences Against the Person Act 1861 (as to which, **see chapter 1.8**).

A defendant attempted to argue that his honest and reasonable mistake as to the *facts* of his arrest (as opposed to the law) after he was lawfully arrested for a public order offence was different from the decision in *Lee*. The Divisional Court did not agree with him (see *Hewitt* v *DPP* [2002] EWHC 2801 (QB)).

In relation to offences involving negligence, inadvertence would clearly not amount to a defence and any 'mistake' would generally need to be shown to be a reasonable one.

Generally, it is no defence to claim a mistake as to the law because all people are presumed to know the law once it is made. With statutory instruments a defendant can show that the instrument in question was not in force at the time of the offence or that the behaviour that it sought to control was beyond the powers (*ultra vires*) of that instrument.

There is one particular example, however, where a mistaken belief in the legal position is specifically provided for in a criminal offence. This is where a person appropriates property in the belief that he/she has a legal right to deprive another person of it under s. 2 of the Theft Act 1968 (**see chapter 1.13**).

1.4.6 Duress

Where a person is threatened with death or serious physical injury unless he/she carries out a criminal act, he/she may have a defence of *duress* (see *R* v *Graham* [1982] 1 WLR 294). The threat of serious physical injury does not appear to include serious *psychological* injury (see *R* v *Baker* [1997] Crim LR 497). Where relevant intent is an essential ingredient of the offence, the defendant might claim that he/she only formed that intent as a result of duress (e.g. an intent to supply controlled drugs—**see para. 1.6.5.2**). However, unless it is shown that the intent had—or could have—been formed *only* by reason of that duress (e.g. the duress was the only thing causing the defendant to form that intent), the defence will fail (see *R* v *Fisher* [2004] EWCA Crim 1190).

It would seem that the threat need not be made solely to the person who goes on to commit the relevant offence and there are authorities to suggest that threats of death/serious harm to loved ones may allow a defence of duress (see *Blackstone's Criminal Practice 2010*, section A3.22).

KEYNOTE

The defence is not available in respect of an offence of murder (*R* v *Howe* [1987] AC 417) or attempted murder (*R* v *Gotts* [1992] 2 AC 412), as a principal or secondary offender. It is, however, available in other offences even in offences of strict liability (*Eden DC* v *Braid* [1998] COD 259—taxi driver threatened and forced to carry excessive number of people in breach of his licensing conditions).

There are several key elements to this defence:

- the threat must have driven the defendant to commit the offence;
- the defendant must have acted as a sober and reasonable person sharing his/her characteristics would have done;
- the threatened injury must be anticipated at or near the time of the offence (i.e. not sometime in the distant future).

The anticipated death or serious physical injury must be *imminent* (i.e. liable to happen soon); the threat need not be one of *immediate* (i.e. there and then) death or serious physical injury.

Duress is not available as a defence if it is proved that the defendant failed to take advantage of an opportunity to neutralise the effects of the threat (perhaps by escaping from it or reporting the matter to the authorities), which a reasonable person of a similar sort to the defendant would have taken in his position. A good example of this approach is the case of *R* v *Heath* [2000] Crim LR 109, where the defendant alleged that he had been pressurised into transporting drugs. Because the defendant had more than one safe avenue of escape (going to the police, which he did not do because he was scared and because he was a drug addict, and going to his parents in Scotland, which he did not do because he did not want them to know about the position he was in) the defence failed. Whether a defendant could be expected to take such an opportunity of rendering the threat ineffective, e.g. by seeking police protection, will be a matter for the jury. Therefore, a defendant who is ordered to steal from a shop in 24 hours' time or suffer a serious physical injury for failing to do so might be unable to utilise the defence as a jury may consider the defendant had ample opportunity to take evasive action and avoid the threat.

If a defendant knowingly exposes himself/herself to a risk of such a threat of death or serious physical injury, he/she cannot then claim duress as a defence. For instance, if a person joins a violent gang or an active terrorist organisation, he/she cannot then claim duress as a defence to any crimes he/she may go on to commit under threat of death or serious injury from another member or rival of that organisation (see *R* v *Sharp* [1987] QB 853). However, if the purpose of the organisation or gang is not predominantly violent or dangerous (e.g. a gang of shoplifters) then the defence of duress *may* be available in relation to offences committed while under threat of death or serious physical injury from other gang members (*R* v *Shepherd* (1987) 86 Cr App R 47).

The above issues can be seen in action in the House of Lords' decision in *R* v *Hasan* [2005] UKHL 22. In that case the defendant had been convicted of aggravated burglary and raised the defence of duress. He claimed that a drug dealer (associated with the defendant) who was known for his use of violence had threatened to injure him and his family if he did not carry out the burglary. The prosecution argued that he should have foreseen the risk of being compelled to commit criminal offences by his association with violent criminals and further, that remarks made 'off the record' in a later interview showed that any threats had not been made until after the burglary. The House of Lords held that the defence of duress is excluded when, as a result of the defendant's voluntary association with others engaged in criminal activity, he or she foresaw or ought reasonably to have foreseen the risk of being subjected to any compulsion by threats of violence. However, the law of duress does not require there to have been foresight of coercion to commit crimes *of the kind with which the defendant is charged*. The test should be an objective one of what the defendant in all the circumstances and knowing what he or she did, ought reasonably to have foreseen. The general policy behind the law here was to discourage association with known criminals, and the courts should be slow to excuse the criminal conduct of those who did so.

1.4.6.1 Marital Coercion

Closely linked to the defence of duress is the defence of 'marital coercion' whereby a *wife* charged with any offence other than treason or murder, may raise the defence that she committed the offence in the presence and under the coercion of her husband (see the Criminal Justice Act 1925, s. 47 and *R v Shortland* [1996] 1 Cr App R 116).

1.4.7 Duress of Circumstances

There may be times when circumstances leave the defendant no real alternative but to commit an offence. If a doctor is suddenly called upon to use his/her car to get someone to hospital for emergency treatment then those circumstances may provide a defence for driving while disqualified (see e.g. *R v Martin* [1989] 1 All ER 652). Similarly, threats of immediate violence may allow a defence of duress of circumstances for someone who drives dangerously in order to escape the threat (*R v Willer* (1986) 83 Cr App R 225). In such cases the court will consider the reasonableness of the defendant's behaviour in light of the prevailing circumstances. If the defendant commits a very serious offence in order to avoid very minor or trivial consequences then this defence is unlikely to be available.

Although it was said for a long time that there was no defence of 'necessity' in the law of England and Wales, there is now authority for this defence, albeit in very narrow circumstances (*R v A (Children) (Conjoined Twins: Surgical Separation)* [2001] 2 WLR 480).

This type of duress should be distinguished from that at **para. 1.4.6**. There the duress comes from a threat made to the defendant compelling him/her to commit an offence: a gun to the head type of situation where one person says to another *'Do this or else...'*. With duress of circumstances, there is no such threat being made. Rather there is a threatening situation or set of circumstances from which the defendant wishes to escape and, in so doing, feels impelled to commit an offence as the lesser of two present evils. Here the threat is 'situational' and the defendant feels *'If I don't do this, then I will suffer death or serious physical injury...'*. A good example is in *R v Willer* (1986) 83 Cr App R 225 where the defendant, while in his car, feared he would be attacked by a gang of youths and drove across a shopping precinct in order to avoid the assault. In answer to a charge of what was then 'reckless' (now 'dangerous', **see Road Policing, chapter 3.2**) driving, the defendant raised the defence of duress of circumstances.

This growing defence was examined by the Court of Appeal in a case where someone jumped onto the bonnet of the car that the appellant was driving. The appellant drove for some distance with the man on the bonnet of the car, braking after a short time to go over a speed ramp. The man fell from the bonnet and the appellant drove on, running the man over and causing him grievous bodily harm (as to which, **see chapter 1.8**). In determining whether or not the defence of 'duress of circumstances' was available, the court held that the jury must ask two questions in relation to the appellant:

- Was he (or might he have been) impelled to act as he did because, as a result of what he reasonably believed, he had good cause to fear he would suffer death or serious injury if he did not do so?

- If so, would a sober person of reasonable firmness and sharing the same characteristics, have responded to the situation in the way that he did?

If each question were answered with a 'yes', the defence would be made out (*R* v *Cairns* [1999] 2 Cr App R 137).

The important aspect to this defence then is that it will only avail the defendant as long as he/she is acting under compulsion of the prevailing circumstances when committing the offence. It appears that the defendant need only hold an *honest* belief that those circumstances exist without necessarily having *reasonable grounds* for that belief (see *DPP* v *Rogers* [1998] Crim LR 202) and there is no need for the threat to be 'real'. There is certainly no need for the threat (perceived threat) to amount to a criminal offence and the Court of Appeal has accepted the possibility of a 'duress of circumstances' defence being applicable where a defendant acts in fear of the consequences of declaring war on Iraq (see *R* v *Jones (Margaret)* [2004] EWCA Crim 1981). However, the defendant's actions in order to avoid that perceived threatening situation must be reasonable and in proportion to the threat presented. Therefore defendant(s) in situation(s) like *Willer* and *Cairns* would not be able to claim duress of circumstances if they drove at their victims repeatedly until all had been injured to a point whereby they no longer posed a threat.

An attempt to extend the defence was made in *R* v *Altham* [2006] EWCA Crim 7, where the defendant had been charged with possessing a controlled drug (cannabis). The defendant appealed against his conviction and argued that he needed to smoke the drug to ease the pain he suffered as a consequence of injuries he had received in a car accident. It was argued that the defence of duress of circumstances should be open to the defendant on the basis that he was suffering serious physical harm. This was countered by the prosecution who argued that pain can never amount to serious physical harm. The appeal was dismissed and the court stated that the defence could not be available in this type of circumstance because it would allow unlawful activity to be undertaken and it would be in direct conflict with the purpose and effect of the intention of the Misuse of Drugs Act 1971.

It seems that, apart from the offence of murder or attempted murder (or treason), the defence is available against any other charge (including hijacking, *R* v *Abdul-Hussain* [1999] Crim LR 570).

1.4.8 Defence of Self, Others or Property

There are circumstances where the use of force against person or property will be permissible. This aspect of criminal law has attracted a great deal of interest as a result of several widely reported court cases. Clarification of the law has come in the form of s. 76 of the Criminal Justice and Immigration Act 2008 which provides a gloss on the common law of self-defence and the defences provided by s. 3(1) of the Criminal Law Act 1967, which relate to the use of force in the prevention of crime or making an arrest. Section 76 aims to improve understanding of the practical application of these areas of law using elements of case law to illustrate how the defence operates. It does not change the current test that allows the use of reasonable force.

1.4.8.1 The Use of Force

When a defendant is charged with an offence he/she may seek to rely on the common law defence of self-defence or the defence provided by s. 3(1) of the Criminal Law Act 1967.

The Criminal Law Act 1967, s. 3(1) states:

A person may use such force as is reasonable in the circumstances in the prevention of crime or in effecting or assisting in the lawful arrest of offenders or suspected offenders or of persons unlawfully at large.

It is to these potential defences that s. 76 of the Criminal Justice and Immigration Act 2008 applies, in particular to the question as to whether the degree of force used by the defendant was reasonable in the circumstances. The 'degree of force' means the type and amount of force used. Of significant importance is the fact that s. 76(10)(b) resolves the question as to whether reasonable force in self-defence would include acting in the defence of another person—it does.

The question whether the degree of force used by the defendant was reasonable in the circumstances is to be decided by reference to the circumstances *as the defendant believed them to be* (s. 76(3)). If the defendant claims to have held a particular belief as regards the existence of any circumstances, the reasonableness or otherwise of that belief is relevant to the question whether the defendant genuinely held it. If it is determined that the defendant did genuinely hold the belief the defendant is entitled to rely on it even if the belief was mistaken or, if it was mistaken, the mistake was a reasonable one to have made.

EXAMPLE

X has a long and violent history and has been convicted of several wounding offences involving the use of a knife. In a totally unprovoked attack, X attacks Y in a pub by punching Y in the face. Y is aware of X's violent past and after being punched, Y sees X's hand move towards the inside of his jacket. Y genuinely believes that X is going to stab him and so grabs hold of a chair and smashes it against X's arm, breaking X's arm in the process. X was not going to stab Y as he did not have a knife.

In the above example, Y reacted to the circumstances as he believed them to be. The reasonableness of Y's belief is relevant in deciding whether or not Y actually held the belief. If the court accepted Y held the belief, the fact that X did not have a knife and was not going to stab Y (a mistake by Y) will not affect Y's ability to utilise the defence.

The situation would be different if Y had got himself drunk and, simply seeing X walk into the pub, mistakenly thought X was going to stab him. This is because s. 76(5) would not enable Y to rely on any mistaken belief due to intoxication that was voluntarily induced.

Section 76(6) adds that the degree of force used by the defendant is not to be regarded as reasonable in the circumstances as the defendant believed them to be if it was disproportionate in those circumstances.

In deciding whether or not the degree of force used was reasonable in the circumstances, s. 76(7) requires certain considerations to be taken into account:

- that a person acting for a legitimate purpose (the purposes of the defences to which s. 76 applies) may not be able to weigh to a nicety the exact measure of any necessary action; and
- that evidence of a person's having only done what the person honestly and instinctively thought was necessary for a legitimate purpose constitutes strong evidence that only reasonable action was taken by that person for that purpose.

This does not prevent other matters from being taken into account where they are relevant in deciding whether the degree of force used was reasonable in the circumstances.

KEYNOTE

Section 76 retains a single test for self-defence and the prevention of crime (or the making of an arrest) which can be applied in each of these contexts. The law has been developed in line with case law regarding self-defence and the use of force, most notably the case of *Palmer* v *The Queen* [1971] AC 814. The defence will be available to a person if he/she honestly believed it was necessary to use force and if the degree of force used was not disproportionate in the circumstances as he/she viewed them. The section reaffirms that a person who uses force is to be judged on the basis of the circumstances as he/she perceived them, that in the heat of the moment he/she will not be expected to have judged exactly what action was called for, and that a degree of latitude may be given to a person who only did what he/she honestly and instinctively thought was necessary. A defendant is entitled to have his/her actions judged on the basis of his/her view of the facts as he/she honestly believed them to be.

Where such a defence is raised in relation to taking someone's life, the provisions of Article 2 of the European Convention on Human Rights will apply. The requirements of Article 2 are more stringent than under s. 3(1) of the Criminal Law Act 1967 and s. 76 of the Criminal Justice and Immigration Act 2008. Under Article 2, the test will be whether the force used was no more than *absolutely necessary* and lethal force will be 'absolutely necessary' only if it is strictly proportionate to the legitimate purpose being pursued. In order to meet those criteria, regard will be had to:

- the nature of the aim being pursued;
- the inherent dangers to life and limb from the situation;
- the degree of risk to life presented by the amount of force employed.

The only circumstances in which lethal force might be permissible here are where the defendant was acting:

- in defence of any person from unlawful violence;
- in order to effect a lawful arrest or to prevent the escape of a person lawfully detained;
- in action lawfully taken for the purpose of quelling a riot or insurrection.

It is important to note that the taking of life *in order to prevent crime* is not mentioned in Article 2.

1.4.8.2 Defence of Property

Section 3(1) of the Criminal Law Act 1967 states reasonable force may be used in the prevention of crime. Therefore, if a person is acting in order to prevent a crime against his/her property, it follows that force can be used to protect property. Whether such force is reasonable or not will be subject to the requirements of s. 76 of the Criminal Justice and Immigration Act 2008. However, it might be somewhat problematic (if not impossible) to reconcile reasonable force to protect property with the taking of a person's life. It is likely that such lethal force would fall foul of s. 76(6) which states that if the force used is disproportionate then it will not be regarded as being reasonable in the circumstances. Allied to this is the fact that Article 2 of the European Convention on Human Rights does not support the taking of life in the defence of property and it can be seen that such a defence is highly likely to fail.

1.4.9 Police Officers

When using force against others, police officers will be criminally liable for any assaults they commit, in the same way as any other person. Assaults in such circumstances can be seen by the courts as a breach of public trust and, as such, any harm done is not only done to the victim, but to society's confidence in its public services. This approach can be seen in a case involving assaults by prison officers on a prisoner in their charge (*R v Fryer* [2002] EWCA Crim 825). In *Fryer* the Court of Appeal also took account of the relevant ranks and seniority of the officers when passing sentence.

However, just as the same offences and sentences will apply, similarly, the same general *defences* will potentially be available to the officer. One specific issue that can often arise where force is used by a police officer is the technique employed by the officer in applying force or striking someone. This may consist of a particular technique that the officer has been trained to use—either with some form of weapon such as a baton, or without, such as a hand or knee strike. The issue of whether a particular technique is a 'proper' or 'recognised' one is not the same as the question of the *lawfulness* of any force used on that occasion. Clearly the controlled use of a technique in which an officer has been trained may help a court in determining the issue of the lawfulness or otherwise of the use of force. So too will any training that the officer has (or has not) received in relation to the use of force and personal protection. However, there are times when using an 'authorised technique' will nevertheless be unlawful; conversely there will be circumstances in which the use of an improvised strike or use of an object may be lawful. All will turn on the circumstances of the case.

1.4.10 Infancy

Children under the age of 10 are *irrebuttably* presumed to be incapable of criminal responsibility (*doli incapax*) by virtue of s. 50 of the Children and Young Persons Act 1933.

1.5 | Homicide

1.5.1 Introduction

Homicide covers not only the offences of murder and manslaughter, but also other occasions where a person causes, or is involved in, the death of another. The common law which has grown up around the subject of homicide is important, not only because of the gravity of the offences themselves, but also because the cases have defined a number of key issues in criminal law which are applicable to many other offences.

In all cases of homicide the general criminal conduct (*actus reus*) is the same—the killing of another person.

Many assaults can turn into homicides simply by the consequent and causally-connected death of the victim. For this reason, it is necessary that police officers have at least a general understanding of the key concepts.

1.5.2 Murder

OFFENCE: **Murder—*Common Law***
  • Life imprisonment (mandatory)

Murder is committed when a person unlawfully kills another human being under the Queen's Peace, with malice aforethought.

KEYNOTE

A conviction for murder carries a mandatory sentence of life imprisonment (in the case of a defendant who is under 18, 'detention at Her Majesty's pleasure': Powers of Criminal Courts (Sentencing) Act 2000, s. 90).

'Unlawful killing' means actively causing the death of another without justification and includes occasions where someone fails to act after creating a situation of danger (see chapter 1.2).

'Another human being' includes a baby who has been born alive and has an existence independent of its mother. 'Existence independent of mother' means that the child is fully expelled from the womb—it is not necessary that the umbilical cord has been cut. If a person injures a baby while it is in its mother's womb and it subsequently dies from those injuries *after being born*, it may be appropriate to bring a charge of murder. If the defendant intended only to cause serious injury to the mother, that intention cannot support a charge of *murder* in respect of the baby if it goes on to die after being born alive. It may, however, support a charge of *manslaughter*. This liability is clear from the House of Lords' ruling in *Attorney-General's Reference (No. 3 of 1994)* [1998] AC 245. The House of Lords ruled that the doctrine of 'transferred malice' does not fully apply in cases of unborn children (*in utero*) and therefore any liability

---

of the defendant for the subsequent death of a child that he/she injured before it was born alive will depend on the defendant's intentions at the time of causing the injury.

'Under the Queen's Peace' appears to exclude deaths caused during the legitimate prosecution of warfare (see the War Crimes Act 1991). Under the provisions of the Offences Against the Person Act 1861 any British citizen who commits a murder anywhere in the world may be tried in England or Wales.

It should be noted that the only state of mind or *mens rea* that will support a charge of attempted murder is an *intention to kill*. Nothing less will suffice.

Where a charge of murder is brought there may be specific restrictions on the applicability of a defence that might otherwise be available. For example, a claim of self-defence based on a mistake arising out of voluntary drunkenness will not be allowed in a prosecution for murder (or manslaughter)—see para. 1.4.3.

1.5.2.1 Malice Aforethought

After the cases of *R* v *Moloney* [1985] AC 905 and *R* v *Hancock* [1986] AC 455, the *mens rea* required for murder is an intention:

- to kill, or
- to cause grievous bodily harm.

Murder is therefore a crime of 'specific intent'.

The term 'malice aforethought' is often associated with some form of premeditation; this is not required.

1.5.2.2 Year and a Day

Since the Law Reform (Year and a Day Rule) Act 1996 there is no longer a need to show that a victim died within a year and a day of the defendant's actions (s. 1).

If a victim of an alleged murder dies *more than three years after receiving their injury* then the consent of the Attorney-General (or Solicitor-General) is needed before bringing a prosecution (s. 2(2)(b)). That consent is also needed if the defendant has already been convicted of an offence committed under the circumstances connected with the death (s. 2(2)(a)).

1.5.3 Special Defences

As a conviction for murder leaves a judge no discretion in sentencing a defendant, a number of 'special defences' developed around the offence (diminished responsibility, provocation and suicide pact)—these are dealt with in the Homicide Act 1957. Rather than securing an acquittal, they allow for a conviction of 'voluntary manslaughter' instead of murder. As these Manuals go to press, those 'special defences' still exist but on October 4th 2010, SI 816/2010 brings into force sections 52 to 57 of the Coroners and Justice Act 2009 which will amend the 'special defence' of diminished responsibility and remove provocation as a 'special defence' and replace it with the partial defence of 'loss of control'. To make this Manual as relevant and current as possible, the law relating to 'special defences' is given as it will be from the implementation of SI 816/2010. On 4th October 2010. It should be noted that the 'special defence' of suicide pact remains unaltered.

1.5.3.1   Diminished Responsibility

The Homicide Act 1957, s. 2 states:

(1) A person ('D') who kills or is a party to a killing of another is not to be convicted of murder if D was suffering from an abnormality of mental functioning which—

    (a) arose from a recognised medical condition,

    (b) substantially impaired D's ability to do one or more of the things mentioned in subsection (1A), and

    (c) provides an explanation for D's acts and omissions in doing or being party to the killing.

(1A) Those things are—

    (a) to understand the nature of D's conduct;

    (b) to form rational judgement

    (c) to exercise self-control.

(1B) For the purposes of subsection (1)(c), an abnormality of mental functioning provides an explanation for D's conduct if it causes, or is a significant contributory factor in causing, D to carry out that conduct.

(2) On a charge of murder, it shall be for the defence to prove that the person charged is by virtue of this section not liable to be convicted of murder.

(3) A person who but for this section would be liable, whether as principal or as accessory, to be convicted of murder shall be liable instead to be convicted of manslaughter.

(4) The fact that one party to a killing is by virtue of this section not liable to be convicted of murder shall not affect the question whether the killing amounted to murder in the case of any other party to it.

KEYNOTE

The 'special defence' of diminished responsibility is altered by s. 52 of the Coroners and Justice Act 2009 which replaced the definition of the partial defence of diminished responsibility with a modernised definition (s. 2(1), (1A) and 1(B)) based on the concept of 'an abnormality of mental functioning' arising from a 'recognised medical condition'. The new definition requires that the abnormality *substantially* impaired the defendant's ability to do one (or more) of three things and also provides that the defendant's abnormality of mental functioning should be of at least a significant contributory factor in causing the defendant's acts or omissions. The abnormality must arise from a *recognised medical condition*. 'Abnormality of mind' has been held to be 'a state of mind so different from that of ordinary human beings that the reasonable man would term it abnormal' (*R* v *Byrne* [1960] 2 QB 396). This includes the mental inability to exert control over one's behaviour and to form rational judgement.

'Impairment of mental responsibility'—this impairment must be 'substantial'. Whether or not that is the case will be a question of fact for the jury to decide. Minor lapses of lucidity will not be enough. There may be any number of causes of the 'abnormality' of the mind. Examples accepted by the courts to date have included post-natal depression and pre-menstrual symptoms (*R* v *Reynolds* [1988] Crim LR 679) and 'battered wives' syndrome' (*R* v *Hobson* [1998] 1 Cr App R 31). A further example arose in the case of *R* v *Dietschmann* [2003] UKHL 10 where the House of Lords accepted that a mental abnormality caused by a grief reaction to the recent death of an aunt with whom the defendant had had a physical relationship could suffice. In that case their lordships went on to hold that there is no requirement to show that the 'abnormality of mind' was the *sole* cause of the defendant's acts in committing the killing.

The burden of proving these features lies with the defence and the standard required is one of a balance of probabilities.

1.5.3.2   **Loss of Control**

The Coroners and Justice Act 2009, s. 54 states:

(1) Where a person ('D') kills or is a party to the killing of another ('V'), D is not to be convicted of murder if—
    (a) D's acts and omissions in doing or being a party to the killing resulted from D's loss of self-control,
    (b) the loss of self-control had a qualifying trigger, and
    (c) a person of D's sex and age, with a normal degree of tolerance and self-restraint and in the circumstances of D, might have reacted in the same or in a similar way to D.

(2) For the purposes of subsection (1)(a), it does not matter whether or not the loss of control was sudden.

(3) In subsection (1)(c) the reference to 'the circumstances of D' is a reference to all of D's circumstances other than those whose only relevance to D's conduct is that they bear on D's general capacity for tolerance or self-restraint.

(4) Subsection (1) does not apply if, in doing or being a party to the killing, D acted in a considered desire for revenge.

(5) On a charge of murder, if sufficient evidence is adduced to raise an issue with respect to the defence under subsection (1), the jury must assume that the defence is satisfied unless the prosecution proves beyond reasonable doubt that it is not.

(6) For the purposes of subsection (5), sufficient evidence is adduced to raise an issue with respect to the defence if evidence is adduced on which, in the opinion of the trial judge, a jury, properly directed, could reasonably conclude that the defence might apply.

(7) A person who, but for this section, would be liable to be convicted of murder is liable instead to be convicted of manslaughter.

(8) The fact that one party to a killing is by virtue of this section not liable to be convicted of murder does not affect the question whether the killing amounted to murder in the case of any other party to it.

KEYNOTE

Section 54 replaces the old 'special defence' of provocation which is abolished (by virtue of s. 56 of the Coroners and Justice Act 2009).

Section 54 sets out the criteria which need to be met in order for the new partial defence of loss of self-control to be successful, those being:

- the defendant's conduct resulted from a loss of self-control,
- the loss of self-control had a qualifying trigger (which is defined in section 55—see below), and
- a person of the defendant's sex and age with an ordinary level of tolerance and self-restraint and in the circumstances of the defendant might have acted in the same or similar way to the defendant.

Section 54(2) clarifies that the loss of control *need not be sudden*. Under the previous partial defence of provocation, the courts had held that the loss of self-control must be sudden. Case law developed over time to the effect that the partial defence might still apply though where there was a delay between the provocative incident and the killing. Although subsection (2) in the new partial defence makes clear that *it is not a requirement* for the new partial defence that the loss of self control be sudden, it will remain open for the judge (in deciding whether to leave the defence to the jury) and the jury (in determining whether the killing did in fact result from a loss of self-control and whether the other aspects of the partial defence are satisfied) to take into account any delay between a relevant incident and the killing.

Section 54(3) supplements subsection (1)(c) by clarifying that the reference to the defendant's circumstances in that subsection means all of those circumstances except those whose only relevance to the defendant's conduct is that they impact upon the defendant's general level of tolerance and self-restraint. Thus, a defendant's history of abuse at the hands of the victim could be taken into account in deciding whether an ordinary person might have acted as the defendant did, whereas the defendant's generally short temper could not. Consequently, when applying the test in subsection (1)(c) the jury will consider whether a person of the defendant's sex and age with an ordinary level of tolerance and self-restraint and in the defendant's specific circumstances (in the sense described earlier in this paragraph) might have acted as the defendant did.

Those acting in a considered desire for revenge cannot rely on the partial defence, even if they lose self-control as a result of a qualifying trigger.

Qualifying Trigger

Section 55 of the Coroners and Justice act 2009, explains the phrase 'qualifying trigger' mentioned in s. 54(1)(b). The defendant's loss of self-control must be attributable to:

- *The defendant's fear of serious violence from the victim against the defendant or another identified person.* This will be a subjective test and the defendant will need to show that he or she lost self-control because of a genuine fear of serious violence, whether or not the fear was in fact reasonable. The fear of serious violence needs to be in respect of violence against the defendant or against another identified person. For example, the fear of serious violence could be in respect of a child or other relative of the defendant, but it could not be a fear that the victim would in the future use serious violence against people generally.
- *To a thing or things done or said (or both) which constituted circumstances of an extremely grave character and caused the defendant to have a justifiable sense of being seriously wronged.* Whether a defendant's sense of being seriously wronged is justifiable will be an objective question for a jury to determine. This sets a very high threshold for the circumstances in which a partial defence is available where a person loses self-control in response to words or actions. The effect is to substantially narrow the potential availability of a partial defence in cases where a loss of control is attributable to things done or said compared to the current partial defence of provocation (where no threshold exists in relation to the provoking circumstances).
- A combination of the above two factors.

Section 55(6) states that in determining whether a loss of self-control had a qualifying trigger:

- the defendant's fear of serious violence is to be disregarded to the extent that it was caused by a thing which the defendant incited to be done or said for the purpose of providing an excuse to use violence;
- a sense of being seriously wronged by a thing done or said is not justifiable if the defendant incited the thing to be done or said for the purpose of providing an excuse to use violence;
- the fact that a thing done or said constituted sexual infidelity is to be disregarded.

1.5.3.3 Suicide Pact

The Homicide Act 1957, s. 4 states:

> (1) It shall be manslaughter, and shall not be murder, for a person acting in pursuance of a suicide pact between him and another to kill the other or be a party to the other being killed by a third person.

KEYNOTE

The *defendant* must show that:

- a suicide pact had been made, and
- he/she had the intention of dying at the time the killing took place.

'Suicide pact' is defined by the Homicide Act 1957, s. 4(3) as:

a common agreement between two or more persons having for its object the death of all of them, whether or not each is to take his own life, but nothing done by a person who enters into a suicide pact shall be treated as done by him in pursuance of the pact unless it is done while he has the settled intention of dying in pursuance of the pact.

1.5.4 Manslaughter

This subject is divided into two classifications—voluntary and involuntary manslaughter.

The three sets of circumstances where 'special defences' may reduce a murder charge to one of manslaughter make up one type or classification of the offence (*voluntary* manslaughter). They have been covered in **paras 1.5.3.1 to 1.5.3.3** above. In that sense, voluntary manslaughter is more a finding by a court than an offence with which someone can be charged. The second classification (*involuntary* manslaughter) occurs where the defendant causes the death of another but is not shown to have had the required *mens rea* for murder.

As with murder, a defendant on a charge of manslaughter cannot rely on a mistake induced by their own voluntary intoxication in claiming self-defence.

OFFENCE: **Manslaughter—*Common Law***
- Triable on indictment • Life imprisonment

KEYNOTE

Manslaughter, like murder, is the unlawful killing of another human being. What it does not require is the intention to kill or to cause grievous bodily harm.

The second classification of manslaughter, that is, those cases which do not involve the 'special defences' under the Homicide Act 1957, can be separated into occasions where a defendant:

- kills another by an *unlawful act* which was *likely to cause bodily harm*, or
- kills another by *gross negligence*.

1.5.4.1 Manslaughter by Unlawful Act

In order to prove manslaughter by an unlawful act (constructive manslaughter), you must prove:

- An unlawful act by the defendant, that is, an act which is *unlawful in itself*, irrespective of the fact that it ultimately results in someone's death. The act must be *inherently* unlawful. An act that only becomes unlawful by virtue of the way in which it is carried out will not be enough. A good example is 'driving'. Driving is clearly not an inherently unlawful act but becomes so if done dangerously or carelessly on a road or public place. Therefore if someone drives dangerously and thereby causes the death of another, the act of driving—albeit carried out in a way that attracts criminal liability—is *not* an 'unlawful act' for the purposes of constructive manslaughter (see *Andrews v DPP* [1937] AC 576). This is one reason why there are statutory offences addressing most instances of death that are caused by poor standards of driving. The act need not be directed or aimed at anyone and can include acts committed against or towards property (*R v Goodfellow* (1986) 83 Cr App R 23).

Generally, if the actions of the victim break the chain of causation between the defendant's unlawful act and the cause of death, the defendant will not be responsible for the death of that victim (**see chapter 1.2**).

This is why drug dealers who supply controlled drugs cannot generally be held liable for the ultimate deaths of their 'victims' (See *R v Dalby* [1982] 1 WLR 621 and *R v Armstrong* [1989] Crim LR 149). This view was affirmed in the case of *R v Kennedy* [2007] UKHL 38. The circumstances of the case were that the defendant had prepared a dose of heroin for the deceased and had given the syringe to the deceased before leaving the room they were both in. The deceased injected the drug and as a result died. The House of Lords ruled that a supplier of a drug is not guilty of manslaughter where the deceased freely and voluntarily self-administered the drug. Therefore a supplier of a drug is unlikely to be convicted of an offence of manslaughter unless he/she has done far more than just supply the drug.

An *omission* to do something will not suffice. Any unlawful killing caused by an omission would either come under the circumstances outlined in **chapter 1.2** or under those required to prove gross negligence.

- That *the act* involved a risk of somebody being harmed. That risk will be judged *objectively*, that is: would the risk be apparent to a reasonable and sober person watching the act? (See *R v Church* [1966] 1 QB 59.) Such acts might include dropping a paving stone off a bridge into the path of a train (*DPP v Newbury* [1977] AC 500), setting fire to your house (*Goodfellow* above) or firing a gun at police officers and then holding someone else in front of you when the officers return fire (*R v Pagett* (1983) 76 Cr App R 279). 'Harm' must be physical; the risk of emotional or psychological harm does not appear to be enough (see *R v Dawson* (1985) 81 Cr App R 150). In *R v C* [2006] EWCA Crim 17 the deceased—aged 15—had been out walking with friends and had met the defendants who had been drinking alcohol all afternoon. The defendants were verbally abusive and threatening to the deceased and her group. One defendant punched one of the deceased's group and another attacked the deceased herself, pulling her hair back and punching her in the face. Two boys intervened and stopped the attack, at which point the deceased ran off but collapsed and died later that night. The medical evidence showed that, unknown to her doctors or her family, the deceased had a severely diseased heart, and that she might not have died had she not been running.

  On appeal it was held that the manslaughter charge (of which the first defendant was convicted) should have been withdrawn from the jury. Although the attack was unpleasant and accompanied by bullying, any injuries caused had been slight. None of the defendants had intended to cause really serious harm to any of the victims and they did not intend that the deceased should die. The Court of Appeal reiterated the general principle that a person who inflicts a slight injury that unforeseeably leads to the death of the victim nevertheless commits manslaughter (per *R v Church* [1966] 1 QB 59). However, to hold the defendants liable for the deceased's death in the circumstances of this case would have involved an 'unwarranted extension of the law'. The court observed that the law of unlawful act manslaughter required the commission of an unlawful act which was recognised, by a sober and reasonable person, as being dangerous and likely to subject the victim to the risk of some physical harm which in turn caused their death. In the instant case the only act committed against the deceased that was 'dangerous' was the assault and the physical harm resulting from it did not cause her death.

- That the defendant had the required *mens rea* for the relevant 'unlawful act' (e.g. for an assault or criminal damage) which led to the death of a victim. If he/she did not have that *mens rea*, the offence of manslaughter will not be made out. See, for example, *R v Lamb* [1967] 2 QB 981 where the defendant pretended to fire a revolver at his friend. Although the defendant believed that the weapon would not fire, the chamber containing a bullet moved round to the firing pin and the defendant's friend was killed. Lamb was charged with manslaughter by unlawful act (the unlawful act being assault) but it could not be proved that Lamb had the *mens rea* required (an intent or recklessness to cause a person to apprehend immediate unlawful violence) for an assault (**see chapter 1.8**) and his conviction for manslaughter was quashed.

If a defendant uses a motor vehicle as a means to commit an 'unlawful act' (e.g. an assault) then he/she can be charged with manslaughter as long as the 'act' goes beyond poor driving. The CPS has published a policy document which sets out the way in which it will deal with cases of bad driving. Unlawful act manslaughter will be considered the most appropriate charge when there is evidence to prove that the vehicle was used as an instrument of attack (but where the necessary intent for murder was absent), or to cause fright, and death resulted. There are, however, reasons of policy (see *R v Lawrence* [1982] AC 510) why, in all but the most deliberate of cases, the offences under the Road Traffic Act 1988 should be used (**see Road Policing, chapter 3.2**).

1.5.4.2 Manslaughter by Gross Negligence

Manslaughter is the only criminal offence at common law capable of being committed by negligence. The degree of that negligence has been the source of considerable debate over the years and particular problems have arisen in trying to distinguish the level of negligence required for manslaughter and that required to prove 'recklessness'.

A charge of manslaughter may be brought where a person, by an instance of *gross negligence*, has brought about the death of another. The ingredients of this offence were reviewed and re-stated by the Court of Appeal and essentially consist of death resulting from a negligent breach of a duty of care owed by the defendant to the victim in circumstances so reprehensible as to amount to gross negligence (*R v Misra and Srivastava* [2004] EWCA Crim 2375). The most difficult task in defining the degree of negligence that will qualify as 'gross' falls to the trial judge when he/she addresses the jury. Whether a defendant's conduct will amount to gross negligence is a question of fact for the jury to decide in the light of all the evidence (*R v Bateman* (1925) 19 Cr App R 8).

Although the lack of clarity around this offence has resulted in its being challenged under the European Convention on Human Rights, the Court of Appeal has held that its ingredients are sufficiently certain for those purposes (*R v Misra and Srivastava*). What is clear from the decided cases is that civil liability, although a starting point for establishing the breach of a duty of care, is not enough to amount to 'gross negligence', neither is objective 'recklessness' (*R v Adomako* [1995] 1 AC 171).

The test in *Adomako* as summarised by Lord Mackay seems to provide the leading authority on the area. Lord Mackay put the test for the jury as being: '. . . whether, having regard to the risk of death involved, the conduct of the defendant was so bad in all the circumstances as to amount in their judgment to a criminal act or omission'.

Note that it is no longer possible to bring proceedings for gross negligence manslaughter against a company or other organisation to which the offence under the Corporate Manslaughter and Corporate Homicide Act 2007 applies (s. 20 of the Corporate Manslaughter and Corporate Homicide Act 2007).

1.5.4.3   Corporate Manslaughter and Corporate Homicide Act 2007

While most of the Act has been brought into force, it is of particular relevance to police officers (especially custody officers) to note that the provisions contained in the Act in respect of deaths in custody are not scheduled to be implemented until April 2011.

OFFENCE: **Corporate Manslaughter—*Corporate Manslaughter and Corporate Homicide Act 2007, s.1***
- Triable on indictment • Unlimited fine

The Corporate Manslaughter and Corporate Homicide Act 2007, s. 1 states:

(1) An organisation to which this section applies is guilty of an offence if the way in which its activities are managed or organised—
   (a) causes a person's death, and
   (b) amounts to a gross breach of a relevant duty of care owed by the organisation to the deceased.

KEYNOTE

The offence is concerned with the way in which an organisation's activities were managed or organised. Under this test, the courts will examine management systems and practices across the organisation, and whether the adequate standard of care was applied to the fatal activity.

The threshold for the offence is gross negligence. The way in which the activities were managed or organised must have fallen far below what could reasonably have been expected.

The failure to manage or organise activities properly must have caused the victim's death.

A duty of care is an obligation that an organisation has to take reasonable steps to protect a person's safety. These duties exist, for example, in respect of the systems of work and equipment used by employees, the condition of worksites and other premises occupied by an organisation and in relation to products or services supplied to customers. The duty must be a *relevant* one. Relevant duties are set out in s. 2 of the Act and include:

- Employer and occupier duties
- Duties connected to:
  - Supplying goods and services
  - Commercial activities
  - Construction and maintenance work
  - Using or keeping plant, vehicles or other things
- Duties relating to holding a person in custody (bearing in mind that this part of the Act is not yet in force)

In relation to policing and law enforcement in the Act, there are some exceptions to the relevant duty of care obligation (s. 5 of the Act), these are in:

- Operations for dealing with terrorism, civil unrest or serious disorder, that involve the carrying on of policing or law-enforcement activities where officers or employees of the public authority in question come under attack, or face the threat of attack or violent resistance, in the course of the operations
- Activities carried out in preparation for, or directly in support of, such operations as above
- Training of a hazardous nature or training carried out in a hazardous way in order to improve or maintain the effectiveness of officers or employees of the public authority with respect to such operations as above

Police services and authorities are still subject to the Act and could be prosecuted in matters where death relates to the organisation's responsibility *as an employer* (or to others working for the organisation) or as *an occupier of premises.*

The Corporate Manslaughter and Corporate Homicide Act 2007, s. 1 states:

(2) The organisations to which this section applies are—
   (a) a corporation;
   (b) a department or other body listed in Schedule 1;
   (c) a police force;
   (d) a partnership or trade union or employers' association, that is an employer.

KEYNOTE

The Act applies to:

- Companies incorporated under companies legislation or overseas
- Other corporations including:
   ♦ Public bodies incorporated by statute such as local authorities, NHS bodies and a wide range of non-departmental public bodies
   ♦ Organisations incorporated by Royal Charter
   ♦ Limited liability partnerships
- All other partnerships, and trade unions and employer's associations, if the organisation concerned is an employer
- Crown bodies such as government departments
- Police forces

Under the Act a corporation would include a police authority.

The offence is concerned with the corporate liability of the organisation itself and *does not apply* to individual directors, senior managers or other individuals. It is not possible to convict an individual of assisting or encouraging this offence (s. 18). This does not change the position that individuals can be prosecuted for the offence of gross negligence manslaughter.

The Corporate Manslaughter and Corporate Homicide Act 2007, s. 1 states:

(3) An organisation is guilty of an offence under this section only if the way in which its activities are managed or organised by its senior management is a substantial element in the breach referred to in subsection (1).

KEYNOTE

The term 'senior management' is defined in s. 1(4) of the Act to mean those persons who play a significant role in the management of the whole or of a substantial part of the organisation's activities. This covers those individuals in the direct chain of management as well as those in, for example, strategic or regulatory compliance roles.

The offence can be prosecuted if the harm resulting in death occurs in the United Kingdom, in the United Kingdom's territorial waters (for example, an incident involving commercial shipping or leisure craft), on a British ship, aircraft or hovercraft or on an oil rig or other offshore installation covered by UK criminal law.

Proceedings for an offence of corporate manslaughter may not be instituted in England and Wales without the consent of the DPP. An organisation that is guilty of the offence is liable on conviction on indictment to a fine (these fines are likely to run into many millions of pounds). The Act also provides for remedial orders (under s. 9) and publicity orders (under s. 10). A remedial order will force an organisation to address the cause of the fatal injury; publicity orders will require an organisation to publicise the fact of its conviction and certain details of the offence in a way specified by the court.

1.5.5 **Causing or Allowing the Death of a Child or Vulnerable Adult**

There is a specific offence to cater for circumstances where a relevant person causes or allows the death of a child or vulnerable adult. This offence came about as a result of the practical difficulties that arise where a child or other vulnerable person dies as a result of the unlawful act of one of several people but it cannot be shown which of them actually caused the death or allowed it to occur.

OFFENCE: **Causing or Allowing the Death of a Child or Vulnerable Adult—*Domestic Violence, Crime and Victims Act 2004, s. 5***

- Triable on indictment • 14 years' imprisonment

The Domestic Violence, Crime and Victims Act 2004, s. 5 states:

(1) A person ('D') is guilty of an offence if—
  (a) a child or vulnerable adult ('V') dies as a result of the unlawful act of a person who—
    (i) was a member of the same household as V, and
    (ii) had frequent contact with him,
  (b) D was such a person at the time of that act,
  (c) at that time there was a significant risk of serious physical harm being caused to V by the unlawful act of such a person, and
  (d) either D was the person whose act caused V's death or—
    (i) D was, or ought to have been, aware of the risk mentioned in paragraph (c),
    (ii) D failed to take such steps as he could reasonably have been expected to take to protect V from the risk, and
    (iii) the act occurred in circumstances of the kind that D foresaw or ought to have foreseen.

KEYNOTE

This offence has a number of key components that must be proved before it is made out.

First you must show that the victim was a child or vulnerable adult. 'Child' means a person under the age of 16 and 'vulnerable adult' means a person aged 16 or over whose ability to protect themselves from violence, abuse or neglect is significantly impaired through physical or mental disability or illness, through old age or otherwise (s. 5(6)).

It will then be necessary to prove that the victim died *as a result of the unlawful act* of a person who fits a number of criteria. For these purposes 'act' includes 'omissions' and an act or omission will generally only be 'unlawful' if it would have amounted to an offence (see s. 5(5) and (6)). The first criterion that must be shown to apply to the defendant is that, *at the time of the act* they were a member of the same household as the victim *and* had frequent contact with him or her. For these purposes a person will be a member of a particular household if they visit it so often and for such periods of time that it is reasonable to regard them as a member of it—even if they do not actually live there (s. 5(4)(a)). Where, as often happens, the victim lived in different households at different times, the 'same household' criterion will mean the household in which the victim was living at the time of the act that caused their death (s. 5(4)(b)).

Finally it must be shown that, at the time, there was a significant risk of serious physical harm being caused to the victim by the unlawful act of a person meeting these criteria. 'Serious harm' means grievous bodily harm for the purposes of the Offences against the Person Act 1861 (**see para. 1.8.6.2**).

Once these elements have been established, the offence is completed in one of two ways: directly (i.e. by the defendant's act causing the victim's death) or indirectly and the prosecution does not have to prove which alternative applies (see s. 5(2)). However, in cases where indirect causation is suspected, three further things must be shown, namely that:

(1) the defendant was (or ought to have been) aware of the risk of grievous bodily harm;

(2) the defendant failed to take such steps as he or she could reasonably have been expected to take to protect the victim from the risk; *and*

(3) the act occurred in the kind of circumstances that the defendant foresaw (or ought to have foreseen).

Unless the defendant is the mother or father of the victim (a) they cannot be charged with an offence under this section if they were under 16 at the time of the act and (b) restrictions will be made on what steps would have been reasonable for a defendant to have taken while under that age (see s. 5(3)).

1.5.6 Encouraging or Assisting Suicide

Although there are several generic defences (**see chapter 1.4**) as well as the specific defences to murder, there is no defence of 'mercy killing' or formal recognition of euthanasia under our current legal system. However, there is a specific offence of encouraging or assisting another to take their own life. This offence was previously referred to as 'aiding suicide' but has been amended by s. 59 of the Coroners and Justice Act 2009.

OFFENCE: **Encouraging or Assisting Suicide—*Suicide Act 1961, s. 2***
* Triable on indictment • 14 years' imprisonment

The Suicide Act 1961, s. 2 states:

(1) A person ('D') commits an offence if—
  (a) D does an act capable of encouraging or assisting the suicide or attempted suicide of another person, and
  (b) D's act was intended to encourage or assist suicide or an attempt at suicide.
(1A) The person referred to in subsection (1)(a) need not be a specific person (or class of persons) known to, or identified by, D.
(1B) D may commit an offence under this section whether or not a suicide, or an attempt at suicide, occurs.

KEYNOTE

This offence is an alternative verdict on a charge of murder/manslaughter (Suicide Act 1961, s. 2(2)). The person committing the offence need not know, or even be able to identify, the other person. So, for example, the author of a website promoting suicide who intends that one of more of his/her readers will commit suicide is guilty of an offence, even though he/she may never know the identity of those who access the website. The offence applies whether or not a person commits or attempts suicide.

1.5.6.1 Acts Capable of Encouraging or Assisting

The Suicide Act 1961, s. 2A states:

(1) If D arranges for a person ('D2') to do an act that is capable of encouraging or assisting the suicide or attempted suicide of another person and D2 does that act, D is also to be treated for the purposes of this Act as having done it.
(2) Where the facts are such that an act is not capable of encouraging or assisting suicide or attempted suicide, for the purposes of this Act it is to be treated as so capable if the act would have been so capable had the facts been as D believed them to be at the time of the act or had subsequent events happened in the manner D believed they would happen (or both).
(3) A reference in this Act to a person ('P') doing an act that is capable of encouraging the suicide or attempted suicide of another person includes a reference to P doing so by threatening another person or otherwise putting pressure on another person to commit or attempt suicide.

KEYNOTE

These are 'new' subsections inserted into the Suicide Act 1961 and elaborate on what constitutes an act capable of encouraging or assisting suicide.

Section 2A(1) creates a liability when a defendant arranges for another to encourage or assist suicide so that responsibility cannot be avoided by using a third party as a conduit to commit the offence. Note that that third party must actually do the 'act', i.e. he/she must encourage or assist the suicide.

Section 2A(2) has the effect that an act can be capable of encouraging or assisting suicide even if the circumstances are such that it was impossible for the act actually to encourage or assist suicide. An act is therefore treated as capable of encouraging and assisting suicide if it would have been so capable had the facts been as the defendant believed them to be at the time of the act (e.g. if pills provided with the intention that they will assist a person to commit suicide are thought to be lethal but are in fact harmless) or had subsequent events happened as the defendant believed they would (e.g. if lethal pills which were sent to a person with the intention that the person would use them to commit or attempt to commit suicide get lost in the post), or both.

Section 2A(3) clarifies that references to doing an act capable of encouraging or assisting another to commit or attempt suicide include a reference to doing so by threatening another person or otherwise putting pressure on another person to commit or attempt suicide.

An 'act' will include a course of conduct.

Providers of information society services (any service normally provided for remuneration, at a distance, by electronic means and at the individual request of a recipient of services) who are established in England, Wales or Northern Ireland are covered by the offence of encouraging or assisting suicide even when they are operating in other European Economic Area states (sch. 12 to the Coroners and Justice Act 2009). The schedule provides exemptions for internet service providers from the offence in limited circumstances, such as where they are acting as mere conduits for information that is capable, and provided with the intention, of encouraging or assisting suicide or are storing it as caches or hosts.

1.5.7 Solicitation of Murder

OFFENCE: **Encouraging Another to Murder—*Offences Against the Person Act 1861, s. 4***
- Triable on indictment • Life imprisonment

The Offences Against the Person Act 1861, s. 4 states:

> Whosoever shall solicit, encourage, persuade or endeavour to persuade, or shall propose to any person, to murder any other person, whether he be a subject of Her Majesty or not...shall be guilty of a misdemeanour...

KEYNOTE

This offence has received greater attention in recent years in the contexts of contract killings and terrorism. An example of the latter can be seen in the case of *R* v *El-Faisal* [2004] EWCA Crim 343 where the defendant, a minister of Islam, was convicted of this offence after creating audio tapes containing public speeches given by him encouraging the killing of non-believers.

The proposed victim may be outside the United Kingdom.

It does not matter whether or not the person is in fact encouraged to commit murder. This offence may be appropriate in cases where a person is trying to arrange a 'contract killing' (see *R* v *Adamthwaite* (1994) 15 Cr App R (S) 241 where the person 'encouraged' was an undercover police officer). For this reason this offence may be preferred in cases where the defendant has 'conspired' with *one* other person and that person is an undercover police officer.

1.5.8 Domestic Homicide Reviews

In addition to the individual concerns arising in any homicide, there can be wider policing concerns where the death occurred in particular circumstances. One such area is that of domestic homicides. As a result there are further legal powers and procedures available in such circumstances. In summary, the Secretary of State may direct that a domestic homicide review be held:

- where the death of a person aged 16 or over has, or appears to have, resulted from violence, abuse or neglect by:
  — a person to whom they were related or with whom they were (or had been) in an intimate personal relationship; or
  — a member of the same household;
- with a view to identifying the lessons to be learnt from the death (see the Domestic Violence, Crime and Victims Act 2004, s. 9).

Among the bodies and organisations that can be directed to take part in such a review are chief officers of police for police areas in England and Wales and local authorities.

1.6 | Misuse of Drugs

1.6.1 Introduction

The misuse of controlled drugs has become such a pervasive feature of Western society that it now affects almost every aspect of community life. As such, this subject is one of the most written about, argued about and legislated about in our criminal law. The impact of the misuse of drugs on crime and community safety has become so significant that it is also one of the most frequently encountered areas of criminal law for police officers.

The majority of the law in this area is statutory and is supported by a considerable body of case law.

1.6.2 Classification

Drugs that are subject to the provisions of the Misuse of Drugs Act 1971 are listed in Parts I, II and III of sch. 2 to the Act.

The divisions are made largely on the basis of each substance's potential effects on both the person taking it and society in general.

- **Class A**—This class includes heroin, cocaine, LSD, 'Ecstasy' (MDMA) and methylamphetamine ('crystal meth'). It also includes fungus (of any kind) which contains psilocin (such as 'magic mushrooms').
- **Class B**—This class includes cannabis, codeine and ritalin (methylphenidate). A relatively recent addition to this list is methylmethcathinone (commonly known as mephedrone).
- **Class C**—This class includes ketamine, diazepam (valium) and gamma hydroxybutyrate (GHB).

If the charge alleges possession of one particular drug then that drug must be identified.

While crystal meth is a Class A drug, the leaves produced by the khat plant (sometimes chewed for a mild stimulant effect) are not controlled drugs for the purposes of the 1971 Act.

Note that, although a substance may appear in sch. 2 to the Act, there may be restrictions on the occasions where possession is treated as an offence (**see para. 1.6.5.6**).

The main practical effect of the classification of controlled drugs relates to the mode of trial, available powers and sentencing provisions. Difficulties in identifying a plant, pill or powder precisely mean that officers will frequently have to rely on criminal intelligence and/or their 'reasonable suspicions' when dealing with suspected drugs offences.

It is not necessary, when prosecuting an offence, to distinguish between the various chemical forms in which a drug exists (i.e. as a salt, ester or other form) (*R* v *Greensmith* [1983] 1 WLR 1124).

A defendant's admission may, in some cases, be relied upon to prove his/her knowledge as to what a particular substance is (see *R* v *Chatwood* [1980] 1 WLR 874).

1.6.2.1   Cannabis

The Misuse of Drugs Act 1971, s. 37 states:

'cannabis' (except in the expression 'cannabis resin') means any plant of the genus *Cannabis* or any part of any such plant (by whatever name designated) except that it does not include cannabis resin or any of the following products after separation from the rest of the plant, namely—

(a) mature stalk of any such plant,

(b) fibre produced from mature stalk of any such plant, and

(c) seed of any such plant,

'cannabis resin' means the separated resin, whether crude or purified, obtained from any plant of the genus *Cannabis*;

KEYNOTE

On 26 January 2009 cannabis was reclassified from a Class C to a Class B drug under sch. 2 to the Misuse of Drugs Act 1971. The reclassification means that cannabis, cannabis resin, cannabinol and its derivatives, any preparations or other product containing these substances and any substance which is an ester or ether either of cannabinol or of a cannabinol derivative is reclassified as a Class B drug. It should be noted that cannabis oil is also subject to control as a Class B drug. As cannabis and cannabis resin are both in the same class for the purposes of the 1971 Act there would be no duplicity if a person is charged with possessing either one or the other in the same charge (*R* v *Best* [1980] 70 Cr App R 21).

1.6.2.2   Drug Testing

Section 63B of the Police and Criminal Evidence Act 1984 enables the police to require urine or non-intimate samples to be taken from adults in police detention under certain circumstances. The purpose of such tests is to ascertain whether the person has any specified Class A drug in their body. The power to require such a sample can be activated in a number of ways (**see Evidence and Procedure, chapter 2.10**).

The Powers of Criminal Courts (Sentencing) Act 2000 makes further provision for the courts to impose drug treatment and testing orders. For a full discussion of these powers, **see Evidence and Procedure, chapter 2.10.**

1.6.3   Possession

Possession is a concept that is relevant to a number of different offences. In respect of drugs offences it is necessary to consider issues relating to physical control and knowledge of possession.

1.6.3.1   Physical Control

A good starting point in understanding 'possession' is to realise that it is a neutral concept, not implying any kind of blame or fault. This is the key feature to understand before going on to consider specific offences under *any* legislation. In order to be in possession of *anything*, the common law requires physical control of the object plus knowledge of its presence. This requirement is particularly problematic where containers of some sort (whether they be boxes, handbags, cigarette packets or whatever) are involved or where the person claims not to have realised what it was that he/she 'possessed'. In such cases, the common law makes the same requirements; you need to show that the person had physical control of the container together with a knowledge that it contained *something*. Once you have established possession, you then need to show that the substance/object/material possessed was in fact proscribed by the relevant statute.

In *R v Forsyth* [2001] EWCA Crim 2926, the defendant argued that there was a distinction between a person carrying something *in* a container and a person carrying *something inside something else* in a container! In that particular case, the defendant was found in possession of a box which contained a safe; inside the safe was a significant quantity of a controlled drug. The defendant argued that this type of possession should be differentiated from the situation where someone simply had possession of a box with drugs in it. The Court of Appeal ruled that there was no difference and the issues of proof were the same.

1.6.3.2 Knowledge of Possession

If a person has a container with him/her and that container is found to have controlled drugs in it, he/she is in possession of those drugs *provided he/she knew that there was something in the container*. That does not mean that, at this point, the person necessarily commits an offence (and he/she may still have a statutory defence); it means that he/she was in 'possession' of the drugs. This merely satisfies one element of a number of possible offences.

The Misuse of Drugs Act 1971 creates offences under certain circumstances where a person has been shown to have been in 'possession' of a controlled drug. However, the Act also provides a defence which includes a mental element on the part of the defendant. It is true that this situation in relation to possession is impracticable—like many others in our system—and it is not even consistently applied; nevertheless, until the concept of 'possession' at common law is changed to include an element of blame or fault, these rules will continue to apply and presumably statutes will continue to contain defences which, like s. 28 of the 1971 Act, are aimed at correcting any unjust results.

It is clear from the House of Lords' decisions in *Warner v Metropolitan Police Commissioner* [1969] 2 AC 256 and *R v Boyesen* [1982] AC 768, and also the Court of Appeal judgment in *R v McNamara* (1988) 87 Cr App R 246 that the basic elements required are that a person 'knows' that he/she is in possession of something which is, in fact, a prohibited or controlled object or substance.

Some of the further practical difficulties that can arise from this view of 'possession' were highlighted in *Adams v DPP* [2002] EWHC 438 (Admin). In that case a small quantity of controlled drugs was found in the defendant's home during the execution of a search warrant. There was no proof that the drugs were owned by the defendant, nor that she was specifically aware of their presence but the defendant *did* know that her home was used by various people who were highly likely to bring controlled drugs into it. She was convicted of possession. In hearing her appeal against conviction by way of case stated, the Administrative Court held that, where knowledge of possession of drugs was limited to the fact that a visitor had brought drugs into the defendant's home intending to take them, that was not sufficient evidence from which it was appropriate to infer that she had control over the drugs.

The court also held that giving consent (explicitly or impliedly) for the use of a controlled drug did not of itself constitute possession. Similarly, an inference that the defendant knew whose drugs had been found in her home did not amount to evidence of control over the drug itself—even though she may well have been able to exercise control over what actually took place in her home.

1.6.3.3 **Points to Prove**

To prove possession of a controlled drug then, you must show that a defendant both:

- *had* a controlled drug in his/her possession; and
- *knew* that he/she had something in his/her possession which was in fact a controlled drug.

....

EXAMPLE

A person is subject to a stop and search procedure and is found with a knife in his pocket. The knife has traces of brown powder on the blade. Later examination shows the powder to be heroin.

In order to prove 'possession' of the heroin you must show:

- that the defendant actually had the knife
- that the knife had a substance which was a controlled drug on it and that
- the defendant knew *of the existence of the substance* (i.e. the powder).

....

1.6.3.4 **Quality**

You would not have to show that he/she knew what the powder was. That is, you do not need to show that the defendant knew the *quality* of what he/she possessed.

If the defendant admits to knowing that the powder was there but thought it was sand, he/she is in possession of it (see *R v Marriott* [1971] 1 WLR 187).

Therefore if a defendant had a packet of cigarettes with him/her and admitted to knowing that he/she had them, he/she would be in possession of a controlled drug if one cigarette was shown to have contained cannabis. The fact that the defendant thought they contained tobacco would be irrelevant (*Searle v Randolph* [1972] Crim LR 779) (although clearly they may be able to raise the defence under s. 28: **see para. 1.6.4.2**).

1.6.3.5 **Quantity**

The *quantity* of a controlled drug, however, may be so small that the defendant could not possibly have known about it; therefore it could not be 'possessed'.

Each case will have to be decided on its merits but the House of Lords have suggested that if something is 'visible, tangible and measurable', that may be sufficient (*Boyesen*). If the amount recovered is too small to support a charge of possession, it might be used to prove earlier possession of the drug (see *R v Graham* [1970] 1 WLR 113n and *Hambleton* v *Callinan* [1968] 2 QB 427 (traces of a controlled drug in a urine sample held to be possible evidence of earlier possession of that drug)).

Quantity is not only relevant to the fact of possession; it is also relevant to the intention of the person in whose possession the drug is found. Larger quantities (particularly if they are also divided into smaller amounts) may be indicative of an intention to supply and may be assumed to be proof of that intention in some circumstances.

1.6.3.6 **Regulated Possession and Supply of Controlled Drugs**

The statutory framework governing controlled drugs does not simply ban substances and their possession outright. People working at various levels within the system need to be able to access, analyse and prescribe substances that are controlled by the 1971 Act. To that end, the framework takes account of the differing legitimate activities that may be relevant to individual people or particular circumstances. The majority of the exceptions and conditions imposed on this lawful possession and use can be found in the Misuse of Drugs Regulations 2001 (SI 2001/3998) as amended and also in the Misuse of Drugs and Misuse of Drugs (Safe Custody) (Amendment) Regulations (SI 2007/2154).

The importance of the 2001 Regulations lies in the fact that they exempt certain drugs and certain people (pharmacists, medical staff and laboratory workers etc.)—including police officers—from the main offences of possession, supply and importation.

Among the key regulations are:

- Regulation 4—which sets out those controlled drugs which will be exempted from the main offences of importation/exportation when they are contained in medicinal products.
- Regulation 5—allowing people holding a licence issued by the Secretary of State to produce, supply, offer to supply or have in their possession a controlled drug—provided that their activities (e.g. of supplying etc.) are carried out in accordance with their licence and any conditions attached to it. If the licence holder goes outside the terms of his/her licence (say by offering to supply a drug that is not covered by it) or fails to comply with any conditions attached to the licence (e.g. by keeping the drugs in a different place from that specified), he/she commits the relevant offence(s) in the ordinary way.
- Regulation 6—this allows anyone who is *lawfully* in possession of a controlled drug to give the drug back to the person from whom he/she obtained it and would cover registered heroin addicts properly returning methadone to a chemist. Regulation 6 also allows others to possess and supply certain controlled drugs under strict conditions. Regulation 6 allows police constables to have any controlled drug in their possession, or to supply such a drug to anyone who is lawfully allowed to have it (reg. 6(5)–(7)). These exemptions only apply where the constable is *acting in the course of his/her duty as such*.

Other people who are given the same protection are customs and excise officers, postal workers and people engaged in conveying the drug to someone who may lawfully possess it. This last category would include civilian support staff, exhibits officers and others who, although not police constables, are nevertheless properly engaged in conveying controlled drugs to others.

The remainder of the regulations are generally concerned with exemptions for doctors, dentists, vets and others who may need to store or supply controlled drugs; the 2001 Regulations also impose requirements on some such people in relation to record keeping and the provision of information when requested.

The Regulations make provision for medical practitioners and some nurses (extended formulary nurse prescribers) to prescribe controlled drugs under certain circumstances. Where controlled drugs are supplied lawfully by healthcare providers, other regulations (e.g. the Misuse of Drugs (Supply to Addicts) Regulations 1997 (SI 1997/1001)) may also be relevant and should be consulted.

The 2001 Regulations provide that records of activity, authority and prescription may be preserved in computerised form in accordance with specified best practice guidance. The Secretary of State or an authorised person can request that a computerised register form be produced by sending a copy of it to the appropriate person.

1.6.4 Defences

In addition to the generic defences available in criminal law, offences under the Misuse of Drugs Act 1971 may attract specific defences set out in the legislation. So far as the generic defences are concerned, there have been several (unsuccessful) attempts to claim defences such as 'medical necessity' in respect of possession, supply and production of controlled drugs (**see para. 1.4.6**).

Before considering the various offences under the Misuse of Drugs Act 1971 it is useful to address the specific statutory defences provided by ss. 5 and 28 of the Act.

1.6.4.1 Section 5 Defence to Unlawful Possession

Section 5 provides a defence to an offence of unlawful *possession*:

> (4) In any proceedings for an offence under subsection (2) above in which it is proved that the accused had a controlled drug in his possession, it shall be a defence for him to prove—
>
> (a) that, knowing or suspecting it to be a controlled drug, he took possession of it for the purpose of preventing another from committing or continuing to commit an offence in connection with that drug and that as soon as possible after taking possession of it he took all such steps as were reasonably open to him to destroy the drug or to deliver it into the custody of a person lawfully entitled to take custody of it; or
>
> (b) that, knowing or suspecting it to be a controlled drug, he took possession of it for the purpose of delivering it into the custody of a person lawfully entitled to take custody of it and that as soon as possible after taking possession of it he took all such steps as were reasonably open to him to deliver it into the custody of such a person.

KEYNOTE

This defence envisages two distinct situations. The purpose in taking possession of the controlled drug under s. 5(4)(a) must be to:

- prevent *another*
- from committing (in the future) or
- continuing to commit

an offence in connection with *that* drug.

The first situation might arise where a parent, guardian or carer finds a child in possession of something which appears to be a controlled drug. Provided that that person takes all reasonable steps to destroy the drug or to take it to someone lawfully entitled to possess it (like a general practitioner or police officer), *as soon as possible after taking possession of it*, he/she commits no offence *of unlawful possession*.

The finer technical issues of this defence were examined in *R* v *Murphy* [2002] EWCA Crim 1587. In that case the defendant found some cannabis in his father's car which was outside a prison at the time. The defendant took the drug and buried it in the hope that it would be destroyed by the forces of nature over time. The Administrative Court held that the trial judge had been right not to leave the s. 5(4)(a) defence to the jury. The defendant had to show that he had taken all steps that were reasonably open to him to destroy the drug directly and relying on the forces of nature did not provide this defence on that occasion.

The second situation (under s. 5(4)(b)) may arise where a person finds what he/she believes to be a controlled drug and he/she takes possession of it *solely for the purpose of delivering it to a person lawfully entitled to take custody of it*. The defendant must prove that this was his/her intention at the time of taking possession (*R* v *Dempsey and Dempsey* [1986] 82 Cr App R 291).

In either case above, s. 5(4) will not provide a defence to any other offence connected with the controlled drug (e.g. supplying or offering to supply).

1.6.4.2 General Defence under Section 28

However, there is a more general defence provided by s. 28 of the Act. Section 28 applies to offences of:

- unlawful production (s. 4(2))

- unlawful supply (s. 4(3))
- unlawful possession (s. 5(2))
- possession with intent to supply (s. 5(3))
- unlawful cultivation of cannabis (s. 6(2))
- offences connected with opium (s. 9).

The defences under s. 28 are *not* available in cases of conspiracy as they are not offences under the 1971 Act (*R* v *McGowan* [1990] Crim LR 399). In *R* v *Lambert* [2001] UKHL 37 it was argued that the defences under ss. 5(4) and 28 were incompatible with the European Convention on Human Rights. The House of Lords held that the defences could legitimately be read by the courts in a way that moved the *evidential* burden only onto the defendant. Such an approach, they held, was compatible with the Convention and the Human Rights Act 1998.

Section 28 states:

(2) Subject to subsection (3) below, in any proceedings for an offence to which this section applies it shall be a defence for the accused to prove that he neither knew of nor suspected nor had reason to suspect the existence of some fact alleged by the prosecution which it is necessary for the prosecution to prove if he is to be convicted of the offence charged.

(3) Where in any proceedings for an offence to which this section applies it is necessary, if the accused is to be convicted of the offence charged, for the prosecution to prove that some substance or product involved in the alleged offence was the controlled drug which the prosecution alleges it to have been, and it is proved that the substance or product in question was that controlled drug, the accused—

   (a) shall not be acquitted of the offence charged by reason only of proving that he neither knew nor suspected nor had reason to suspect that the substance or product in question was the particular controlled drug alleged; but

   (b) shall be acquitted thereof—

     (i) if he proves that he neither believed nor suspected nor had reason to suspect that the substance or product in question was a controlled drug; or

     (ii) if he proves that he believed the substance or product in question to be a controlled drug, or a controlled drug of a description, such that, if it had in fact been that controlled drug, or a controlled drug of that description, he would not at the material time have been committing any offence to which this section applies.

KEYNOTE

This defence envisages three distinct situations:

- a lack of knowledge by the defendant of some fact which is alleged by the prosecution;
- a general lack of knowledge by the defendant about the drug in question;
- a conditional belief held by the defendant about the drug in question.

These situations are discussed below.

1.6.4.3 Lack of Knowledge of Some Alleged Fact

Section 28(2) allows a defence where the defendant did not *know, suspect* or *have reason to suspect* the existence of some fact which is essential to proving the case.

....

EXAMPLE

A youth is stopped in the street by a stranger who asks him to drop off an envelope at a nearby address in exchange for £10. As the youth approaches the address he is arrested for possessing a controlled drug (which is inside the envelope), with intent to supply.

Section 28(2) would allow the youth to discharge the evidential burden by showing that he neither knew, nor suspected that the envelope contained a controlled drug, and that he neither knew nor suspected that he was supplying it to another. Both of these elements would be facts which the prosecution would have to allege in order to prove the offence.

If the youth knew the person to be a local drug dealer, or the reward for his errand was disproportionately large—say £1000—then he may not be able to discharge this evidential burden.

It has been held that the test for 'reason to suspect' is an *objective* one (*R* v *Young* [1984] 1 WLR 654). Consequently, where a 'reason to suspect' was not apparent to a defendant because he/she was too intoxicated to see it, the defence will not apply.

1.6.4.4 General Lack of Knowledge about Drug in Question

The wording of s. 28(3)(a) prevents defendants from claiming a 'defence' when what they thought was one type of controlled drug was in fact another, different controlled drug.

Section 28(3)(b) however, has two strands, one concerned with the defendant's general lack of knowledge about the drug in question and the other (see below) concerning the defendant's conditional belief.

Section 28(3)(b)(i) will allow a defendant to prove that he/she did not believe or suspect the substance in question to be a controlled drug and that he/she had no reason so to suspect.

This clearly overlaps with s. 28(2) and the youth in the above example would also be able to claim this lack of knowledge. If he believed the envelope to contain amphetamine when it turned out to contain heroin, however, this lack of knowledge would not be permitted as a defence under s. 28(3).

1.6.4.5 Conditional Belief about Drug in Question

In contrast to s. 28(3)(a), the second strand of s. 28(3)(b)(ii) allows a defendant to discharge the evidential burden by showing that he/she *did* believe the drug in question to be a particular controlled drug. It is then open to him/her to claim that, had the drug in question actually been the drug which he/she believed it to be, then he/she would not have committed any offences in relation to that drug.

EXAMPLE

A registered heroin addict may have been prescribed methadone. If she collects her prescription from a chemist but is mistakenly given pethidine instead, she may be able to discharge the evidential burden by showing that she *believed* the drug in question to be methadone *and* that, if it had been, she would not have committed an offence by possessing it.

1.6.5 Offences Involving the Misuse of Controlled Drugs

In the offences which follow, the aspects that generally make the behaviour 'unlawful' are either the lack of authority under the relevant Misuse of Drugs Regulations 2001, or the absence of the circumstances outlined in the defences under s. 28.

1.6.5.1 Production

OFFENCE: **Producing Controlled Drug—*Misuse of Drugs Act 1971, s. 4(2)***
   • Triable either way • Class A (life imprisonment and/or fine on indictment; six months' imprisonment and/or prescribed sum summarily) • Class B (14 years' imprisonment and/or fine on indictment; six months' imprisonment and/or prescribed sum summarily) • Class C (five years' imprisonment and/or fine on indictment; three months' imprisonment and/or fine summarily)

The Misuse of Drugs Act 1971, s. 4 states:

(2) Subject to section 28 of this Act, it is an offence for a person—
   (a) to produce a controlled drug in contravention of subsection (1)...; or
   (b) to be concerned in the production of such a drug in contravention of that subsection by another.

KEYNOTE

'Produce' means producing by manufacture, cultivation or any other method and 'production' has a corresponding meaning (Misuse of Drugs Act 1971, s. 37).

Converting one form of a Class A drug into another has been held to be 'producing' (*R v Russell* (1992) 94 Cr App R 351) as has harvesting, cutting and stripping a cannabis plant (*R v Harris* [1996] 1 Cr App R 369).

1.6.5.2 Supply

OFFENCE: **Supplying Controlled Drug—*Misuse of Drugs Act 1971, s. 4(3)***
   • Triable either way • Class A (life imprisonment and/or fine on indictment; six months' imprisonment and/or prescribed sum summarily) • Class B (14 years' imprisonment and/or fine on indictment; six months' imprisonment and/or prescribed sum summarily) • Class C (14 years' imprisonment and/or fine on indictment; three months' imprisonment and/or fine summarily)

The Misuse of Drugs Act 1971, s. 4 states:

(3) Subject to section 28 of this Act, it is an offence for a person—
   (a) to supply or offer to supply a controlled drug to another in contravention of subsection (1) above; or
   (b) to be concerned in the supplying of such a drug to another in contravention of that subsection; or
   (c) to be concerned in the making to another in contravention of that subsection of an offer to supply such a drug.

KEYNOTE

In *R v Maginnis* [1987] AC 303, the House of Lords held that 'supply' involves more than a mere transfer of physical control of the item from one person to another but includes a further concept, namely that of 'enabling the recipient to apply the thing handed over to purposes for which he desires or has a duty to apply it'—in other words *the person who the drug is given to must derive some benefit from it*.

'Supplying' includes distributing (s. 37(1)).

1.6.5.3   **Supplying Explained**

In *R* v *Dempsey & Dempsey* (1985) 82 Cr App R 291, a registered drug addict (A) was in law-ful possession of a drug. A asked his partner (B) to hold on to some of that drug while he went to administer the remainder of it to himself in a gents' toilet. Both A and B were arres-ted, A being subsequently charged with 'supplying' B with the drug. The Court of Appeal held that, if B had simply been given the drug for safekeeping until A's return, there would be no 'supplying' by A. If, however, she had been given the drug for her own use, then there would clearly be a 'supplying' of that drug (from A to B) and the offence would be complete.

> **KEYNOTE**
>
> The key to working out if there has been a 'supply' is to ask 'Does being given the drug benefit the person to whom the drug has been given?' If the answer is 'Yes' then the person giving the drug is 'supplying' it.
>
> In *Dempsey* (above) there is no 'supply' from A to B as when A gives the drug to B, B *does not benefit* from the action; B is simply holding on to the drug (although, of course, B would be in unlawful possession of the drug at this stage). If A had given the drug to B for B to use, there would be a 'supply' by A to B as B *is benefitting* from the action; B gets to use the drug. If B intends to give back the drug to A then B would commit the offence of possession with intent to supply.
>
> In *R* v *Maginnis* [1987] AC 303, a drug trafficker (A) temporarily left drugs with (B); B expected A to pick up the drugs the following day and was charged and convicted of possession with intent to supply. The same approach taken with *Dempsey* applies. In *Maginnis* when A gives the drugs to B, B does not benefit from it and there is no 'supply' from A to B; if B returns the drugs to A there is a 'supply' from B to A as A benefits from being given the drug (to sell or use). As B intends to return the drug to A, B is in possession with intent to supply.
>
> If the drug trafficker in *Maginnis* had given the custodian of the drug £50 as a reward for holding the drug then there would have been a 'supply' from A to B as B would benefit from holding the drug (he has been paid £50).

The issue has been further explored in a case involving a person who claimed that he had been coerced into holding controlled drugs for unnamed dealers. When found in posses-sion of the drugs, the defendant claimed the defence of duress (as to which, **see chapter 1.4**) and said that he had only been an 'involuntary custodian' of them, intending to return them at a later date. The Court of Appeal decided that it was irrelevant whether a person was a voluntary or involuntary custodian of the drugs and that an intention to return them to their depositor amounted to an 'intention to supply' (*R* v *Panton* [2001] EWCA Crim 611).

If a police informer provides a controlled drug to another in order that the other be ar-rested, there will still be a 'supplying' of the drug (*R* v *X* [1994] Crim LR 827).

Injecting Others

Injecting another with his/her own controlled drug has been held not to amount to 'sup-plying' in a case where the defendant assisted in pushing down the plunger of a syringe that the other person was already using (*R* v *Harris* [1968] 1 WLR 769). It may, however, amount to an offence of 'poisoning' under s. 23 of the Offences Against the Person Act 1861 (**see chapter 1.8**). The problem with charging the supplier of drugs for self-injection by someone who then dies as a result lies in the issues of causation. While there are some authorities which say that supply of a drug for self-injection which leads to the death of the recipient *can potentially* amount to unlawful act manslaughter, great difficulties have arisen and the general view is that the supplier is unlikely to be held liable for *causing* death in such a case (see *R* v *Dias* [2001] EWCA Crim 2986). Where the defendant actually carries out the injection as opposed to merely the supply of the drug, liability for causing the death of another in this way can be made out however—even if the drug injected is not a controlled drug (see *R* v *Andrews* [2002] EWCA Crim 3021—injection of insulin with consent; see also *R* v *Rogers* [2003] EWCA Crim 945—applying and holding a tourniquet to the arm of a drug abuser while injecting heroin can amount to the *actus reus* for manslaughter).

Dividing up controlled drugs which have been jointly purchased and then handing them out so that persons may use the drug will amount to 'supplying' (*R* v *Buckley* (1979) 69 Cr App R 371).

The offence of offering to supply a controlled drug is complete when the offer is made. It is irrelevant whether or not the defendant actually has the means to meet the offer or even intends to carry it out (see *R* v *Goodard* [1992] Crim LR 588). If the offer is made by conduct alone (i.e. without any words), it may be difficult to prove this offence. If words are used, the defence under s. 28 (**see para. 1.6.4**) does not appear to apply (see *R* v *Mitchell* [1992] Crim LR 723). If the offer is made to an undercover police officer, the offence is still committed and the defendant cannot claim that such an offer was not a 'real' offer (*R* v *Kray* (1998) 10 November, unreported).

1.6.5.4 Points to Prove

In order to prove the offence of being concerned in the supply/offer to supply a controlled drug, you must show:

- the actual supply of, or making of an offer to supply, a controlled drug;
- the participation of the defendant in that enterprise; and
- knowledge by the defendant that the enterprise involved the supply of, or making of an offer to supply, a controlled drug (*R* v *Hughes* (1985) 81 Cr App R 344).

If the object of a conspiracy (**see chapter 1.3**) is to supply a controlled drug to a co-conspirator, any subsequent charge must make that clear; stating that the defendants conspired to supply the drug to 'another' implies that the supply was to be made to someone *other than any of the conspirators* (*R* v *Jackson* [2000] 1 Cr App R 97n).

1.6.5.5 Specific Situations

The different prevailing circumstances of the 'supply' must be taken into account. Section 4A of the Misuse of Drugs Act 1971 recognises this and requires courts to treat certain conditions as 'aggravating' factors when considering the seriousness of the offence under s. 4(3) if committed by a person aged 18 or over.

The conditions are either:

1. that the offence was committed on or in the vicinity of school premises at a relevant time. 'Vicinity' is not defined and will be left to each court relying on its local knowledge. Other buildings and premises (e.g. cafes and shopping centres) can fall within this description and courts may decide that a route used to get to or from a school or a place where schoolchildren gather (even if trespassing) may be in the 'vicinity'. School premises are land used for the purposes of a school but *excluding* any land occupied solely as a dwelling *by a person employed at the school* (s. 4A(8)). A 'relevant time' is any

time when the school premises are in use by people under the age of 18 (and one hour before the start/after the end of any such time) (s. 4A(5)); or

2. that in connection with the commission of the offence the offender used a 'courier' who, at the time the offence was committed, was under the age of 18. A person uses a courier if he/she causes or permits another person (the courier):

   (a) to deliver a controlled drug to a third person, or

   (b) to deliver a 'drug related consideration' (basically any money, goods etc. obtained or intended to be used in connection with the supply of a controlled drug) to him/herself or a third person (s. 4A(6) and (7)).

1.6.5.6   Possession

OFFENCE: **Possession of Controlled Drug—*Misuse of Drugs Act 1971, s. 5(2)***
• Triable either way • Class A (seven years' imprisonment and/or fine on indictment; six months' imprisonment and/or prescribed sum summarily) • Class B (five years' imprisonment and/or fine on indictment; three months' imprisonment and/or fine summarily) • Class C (two years' imprisonment and/or fine on indictment; three months' imprisonment and/or fine summarily) • See Keynote for possession of cannabis or cannabis resin

The Misuse of Drugs Act 1971, s. 5 states:

(2) Subject to section 28 of this Act and to subsection (4) below, it is an offence for a person to have a controlled drug in his possession in contravention of subsection (1) ...

KEYNOTE

Where the controlled drug involved is a fungus containing psilocin (a class A drug) or an ester of psilocin (commonly known as magic mushrooms) possession will not be unlawful in certain circumstances. In summary, those circumstances are generally where the fungus is growing *uncultivated* and it:

• is picked by a person already in *lawful possession* of it (for example the landowner on whose land the mushrooms are growing) for the purpose of delivering it (as soon as is reasonably practicable) into the custody of a person lawfully entitled to take custody of it and it remains in that person's possession for (and in accordance with) that purpose; or

• it is picked by anyone either for the purpose of delivering it (as soon as reasonably practicable) into the custody of a person lawfully entitled to take custody of it or destroying it (as soon as is reasonably practicable) and it is held for that purpose.

Possession of cannabis can be dealt with under the Penalty Notice Disorder (PND) Scheme. PNDs cannot be issued for any other drug related offences other than possession of cannabis or cannabis derivatives. PNDs may be issued to any adult found in possession of cannabis for personal use; they are not appropriate for offenders under the age of 18.

1.6.5.7   Possession with Intent to Supply

OFFENCE: **Possession with Intent to Supply—*Misuse of Drugs Act 1971, s. 5(3)***
• Triable either way • Class A (life imprisonment and/or fine on indictment; six months' imprisonment and/or prescribed sum summarily) • Class B (14 years' imprisonment and/or fine on indictment; six months' imprisonment and/or prescribed sum summarily) • Class C (14 years' imprisonment and/or fine on indictment; three months' imprisonment and/or fine summarily)

The Misuse of Drugs Act 1971, s. 5 states:

(3) Subject to section 28 of this Act, it is an offence for a person to have a controlled drug in his possession, whether lawfully or not, with intent to supply it to another in contravention of section 4(1) of this Act.

KEYNOTE

It is important to note that the lawfulness or otherwise of the *possession* is irrelevant; what matters here is the lawfulness of the intended supply. If a vet or a police officer or some other person is in lawful possession of a controlled drug but they intend to supply it unlawfully to another, this offence will be made out.

You must show that the intention was that *the person in possession of the controlled drug* (rather than some third party) would supply it at some point in the future (*R* v *Greenfield* [1984] 78 Cr App R 179).

If more than one person has possession of the relevant controlled drug, you must show an individual intention to supply it by each person charged; it is not enough to show a joint venture whereby one or more parties simply knew of another's intent (*R* v *Downes* [1984] Crim LR 552). Given the decision of the Court of Appeal in *Kray* (see para. 1.6.5.3), possession with intent to supply a controlled drug to a person who is in fact an undercover police officer would appear to amount to an offence under this section.

All that is necessary in proving the offence under s. 5(3) is to show that the defendant had a controlled drug in his/her possession and intended to supply that substance to another. If the substance in the defendant's possession is a Class A drug and he/she intended to supply it to another person, the fact that he/she thought the drug was some other type of drug does not matter (*R* v *Leeson* [2000] 1 Cr App R 233).

While the possession by a defendant of drugs paraphernalia (e.g. clingfilm, paper, scales, contact details, etc.) will be relevant evidence to show that he/she was an active dealer in drugs generally, it does not prove the intention to supply and the trial judge will give a jury very careful directions as to the probative value of such items found in the defendant's possession (see *R* v *Haye* [2002] EWCA Crim 2476).

Where a Rastafarian was prosecuted for possessing cannabis with intent to supply others as part of their religious worship, he claimed that his rights under Articles 8 and 9 of the European Convention had been unnecessarily and disproportionately interfered with. The Court of Appeal, while reducing the sentence, held that such a prosecution had been properly brought (*R* v *Taylor* [2001] EWCA Crim 2263).

In proving an intention to supply you may be able to adduce evidence of the defendant's unexplained wealth (*R* v *Smith (Ivor)* [1995] Crim LR 940) or the presence of large sums of money with the drugs seized (see *R* v *Wright* [1994] Crim LR 55).

1.6.5.8 **Cultivation of Cannabis**

OFFENCE: **Cultivation of Cannabis—*Misuse of Drugs Act 1971, s. 6***
- Triable either way • 14 years' imprisonment and/or a fine
  on indictment • Six months' imprisonment and/or prescribed sum summarily

The Misuse of Drugs Act 1971, s. 6 states:

(1) Subject to any regulations under section 7 of this Act for the time being in force, it shall not be lawful for a person to cultivate any plant of the genus *Cannabis*.
(2) Subject to section 28 of this Act, it is an offence to cultivate any such plant in contravention of subsection (1) above.

KEYNOTE

'Cultivate' is not defined but it appears that you would have to show some element of attention (such as watering or feeding) to the plant by the defendant in order to prove this offence. This offence does not permit police officers to tend plants which have been seized as evidence in order to preserve them as exhibits for court.

In proving the offence, you need only show that the plant is of the genus *Cannabis* and that the defendant cultivated it; you need not show that the defendant knew it to be a cannabis plant (*R* v *Champ* [1981] 73 Cr App R 367).

A person may be licensed to cultivate cannabis plants by the Secretary of State (under reg. 12 of the Misuse of Drugs Regulations 2001).

1.6.5.9 Supply of Articles

OFFENCE: **Supplying Articles for Administering or Preparing Controlled Drugs—*Misuse of Drugs Act 1971, s. 9A***

- Triable summarily • Six months' imprisonment and/or fine

The Misuse of Drugs Act 1971, s. 9A states:

(1) A person who supplies or offers to supply any article which may be used or adapted to be used (whether by itself or in combination with another article or other articles) in the administration by any person of a controlled drug to himself or another, believing that the article (or the article as adapted) is to be so used in circumstances where the administration is unlawful, is guilty of an offence.

(2) ...

(3) A person who supplies or offers to supply any article which may be used to prepare a controlled drug for administration by any person to himself or another believing that the article is to be so used in circumstances where the administration is unlawful is guilty of an offence.

KEYNOTE

This offence is designed to address the provision of drug 'kits'.

'Supply' for these purposes is likely to be interpreted in the same way as for the earlier sections in the 1971 Act.

Hypodermic syringes, or parts of them, are not covered by this offence (s. 9A(2)).

The administration for which the articles are intended must be 'unlawful'. Section 9A states:

(4) For the purposes of this section, any administration of a controlled drug is unlawful except—
  (a) the administration by any person of a controlled drug to another in circumstances where the administration of the drug is not unlawful under section 4(1) of this Act, or
  (b) the administration by any person of a controlled drug to himself in circumstances where having the controlled drug in his possession is not unlawful under section 5(1) of this Act.

(5) In this section, references to administration by any person of a controlled drug to himself include a reference to his administering it to himself with the assistance of another.

1.6.5.10 Occupiers, etc.

OFFENCE: **Occupier or Manager of Premises Permitting Drug Misuse— *Misuse of Drugs Act 1971, s. 8***

- Triable either way • Class A or B (14 years' imprisonment and/or fine on indictment; six months' imprisonment and/or prescribed sum summarily) • Class C (14 years' imprisonment and/or a fine on indictment; three months' imprisonment and/or fine summarily)

The Misuse of Drugs Act 1971, s. 8 states:

A person commits an offence if, being the occupier or concerned in the management of any premises, he knowingly permits or suffers any of the following activities to take place on those premises, that is to say—
(a) producing or attempting to produce a controlled drug in contravention of section 4(1) of this Act;
(b) supplying or attempting to supply a controlled drug to another in contravention of section 4(1) of this Act, or offering to supply a controlled drug to another in contravention of section 4(1);
(c) preparing opium for smoking;
(d) smoking cannabis, cannabis resin or prepared opium.

KEYNOTE

The courts have adopted a 'common sense' approach to the interpretation of whether someone is an 'occupier' or not (see *R* v *Tao* [1977] QB 141). You will not need to prove that a defendant falls within some narrow legal meaning of an occupier. What is important in proving this offence is showing that the defendant had enough control over the premises to prevent the sort of activity listed above (see *R* v *Coid* [1998] Crim LR 199).

If a person cannot be shown to be an occupier in this sense, it may be that he/she can be shown to be involved in the planning, organising and actual use of the premises by taking part in more than just menial tasks. If so, this level of involvement may amount to 'management' of the premises (see *R* v *Josephs* (1977) 65 Cr App R 253).

'Premises' is not defined and has not been clarified at common law but the meaning has been given a wide definition in other legislation.

The permitting or suffering of these activities requires a degree of *mens rea*—*Sweet* v *Parsley* [1970] AC 132—even if that degree is little more than wilful blindness (see *R* v *Thomas* (1976) 63 Cr App R 65). For the purposes of s. 8(b)—and therefore presumably s. 8(a)—it is not necessary to show that the defendant knew exactly which drugs were being produced, supplied etc.; only that they were 'controlled drugs' (*R* v *Bett* [1999] 1 All ER 600).

However, the precise activities that are described under s. 8 will need to be proved. So, for instance, if the offence charged is one of knowingly permitting the smoking of cannabis (under subs. (d)), it must be shown that this actually took place; it is not enough that the owner/occupier had given permission for this to happen (see *R* v *Auguste* [2003] EWCA Crim 3929).

An occupier who permits the growing of cannabis plants also commits this offence (*Taylor* v *Chief Constable of Kent* [1981] 1 WLR 606).

An occupier will not commit the above offence *in relation to the smoking of cannabis or cannabis resin* if the premises are covered by a research licence from the Secretary of State (see reg. 13 of the Misuse of Drugs Regulations 2001).

1.6.5.11 Closure Notices

Section 1 of the Anti-social Behaviour Act 2003 states:

(1) This section applies to premises if a police officer not below the rank of superintendent (the authorising officer) has reasonable grounds for believing—
(a) that at any time during the relevant period the premises have been used in connection with the unlawful use, production or supply of a Class A controlled drug, and
(b) that the use of the premises is associated with the occurrence of disorder or serious nuisance to members of the public.

KEYNOTE

This provision is primarily designed to allow the police to close so-called 'crack houses'. If the above conditions are met the authorising officer may authorise the issuing of a closure notice.

The 'relevant period' referred to means the period of three months ending with the day on which the authorising officer considers whether to authorise the issue of a closure notice in respect of the premises (s. 1(10)).

'Premises' are defined as including any land or other place (whether enclosed or not) and any outbuildings which are or are used as part of the premises (s. 11).

The authorising officer may authorise the issue of a closure notice in respect of premises to which this section applies if he/she is satisfied:

(a) that the local authority for the area in which the premises are situated has been consulted;

(b) that reasonable steps have been taken to establish the identity of any person who lives on the premises or who has control of or responsibility for or an interest in the premises.

An authorisation may be given orally or in writing, but if it is given orally the authorising officer must confirm it in writing as soon as is practicable (s. 1(3)).

Note that it is immaterial whether any person has been convicted of an offence relating to the use, production or supply of a controlled drug (though clearly it will help in showing relevant grounds to support a closure notice and a closure order (see below) if someone has been convicted in connection with the use of the premises). The Secretary of State may make regulations specifying premises or descriptions of premises to which this power does not apply (s. 1(9)).

1.6.5.12 The Notice

The notice, which must be served by a police officer, must also:

- give notice that an application will be made under s. 2 for the closure of the premises
- state that access to the premises by any person (other than a person who habitually resides in the premises or the owner of the premises) is prohibited
- specify the date and time when and the place at which the application will be heard
- explain the effects of a closure order
- state that failure to comply with the notice amounts to an offence
- give information about the names of and means of contacting people and organisations in the area that provide advice about housing and legal matters.

Service of the notice will be effected by fixing a copy of the notice to:

- at least one prominent place on the premises
- each normal means of access to the premises
- any outbuildings which appear to the constable to be used with or as part of the premises; and

by giving a copy of the notice to at least one person who appears to the constable to have control of or responsibility for the premises and also to any person who lives on the premises or who has control of or responsibility for or an interest in the premises (see s. 1(6)).

For the purpose of effecting service of the notice a constable may enter any premises to which the section applies, using reasonable force if necessary (s. 1(7A)).

1.6.5.13   The Closure Order

If a closure notice has been issued under s. 1 a police officer must apply to a magistrates' court for the making of a closure order and that application must be heard by the court not later than 48 hours after the notice has been served (s. 2).

However, the court may adjourn the hearing of the application for a period of not more than 14 days to enable the occupier or another person with control of, responsibility for or an interest in the premises to show why an order should not be made (s. 2(6)).

The magistrates' court cannot use a power under other enactments relating to adjournments to adjourn any hearing of that application for more than 14 days (see *Commissioner of Police for the Metropolis* v *Hooper* [2005] EWHC 199 (Admin)).

The magistrates' court may make a closure order only if it is satisfied that:

- the premises in respect of which the closure notice was issued have been used in connection with the unlawful use, production or supply of a Class A controlled drug
- the use of the premises is associated with the occurrence of disorder or serious nuisance to members of the public, and
- the making of the order is necessary to prevent the occurrence of such disorder or serious nuisance for the period specified in the order.

(s. 2(3))

A closure order is an order that all or any part of the premises are closed to all people for such period (not exceeding three months) as the court decides (s. 2(4)). The police can apply for an order to be extended at any time before it expires but that application must be authorised by an officer not below the rank of superintendent after consultation with the local authority (see s. 5). An order cannot be extended beyond a total of six months (s. 5(5)). Further specific provisions are made by the Act in relation to the discharge of closure notices and the bringing of appeals.

1.6.5.14   Enforcement

A police officer or an authorised person may enter the premises in respect of which the order is made and/or do anything reasonably necessary to secure the premises against entry by any person and may use reasonable force to do so (see s. 3).

A police officer or authorised person may also enter the premises at any time while the order is in force for the purpose of carrying out essential maintenance of or repairs to the premises (s. 3(5)).

A police officer or authorised person seeking to enter the premises for these purposes must, if required to do so by or on behalf of the owner, occupier or other person in charge of the premises, produce evidence of his/her identity and authority before entering the premises (s. 3(4)).

1.6.5.15   Obstructing or Breaching Closure Order

OFFENCE: **Obstruction and Breaching Closure Order—*Anti-social Behaviour Act 2003, s. 4***
- Triable summarily • Six months' imprisonment and/or fine

The Anti-social Behaviour Act 2003, s. 4 states:

(1) A person commits an offence if he remains on or enters premises in contravention of a closure notice.
(2) A person commits an offence if—
    (a) he obstructs a constable or an authorised person acting under section 1(6) or 3(2),

(b) he remains on premises in respect of which a closure order has been made, or

(c) he enters the premises.

KEYNOTE

A person does not commit an offence under subs. (1) or subs. (2)(b) or (c) if he/she has a reasonable excuse for entering or being on the premises (as the case may be) (s. 4(4)).

Any person who occupies or owns any part of a building or structure in which closed premises are situated and in respect of which the closure order does not have effect may apply to the court for an order allowing access to any part of the premises.

1.6.5.16 Importation of Controlled Drugs

It is an offence under s. 3 of the Misuse of Drugs Act 1971 to import or export a controlled drug unless authorised by the regulations made under the Act. The relevant offences and their respective penalties are contained in the Customs and Excise Management Act 1979. Schedule 1 to the 1979 Act provides for the following penalties for the improper importation or exportation of controlled drugs:

- **Class A**—life imprisonment
- **Class B**—14 years' imprisonment
- **Class C**—14 years' imprisonment.

1.6.5.17 Assisting or Inducing Offence Outside United Kingdom

OFFENCE: **Assisting or Inducing Misuse of Drugs Offence Outside UK—*Misuse of Drugs Act 1971, s. 20***

- Triable either way • 14 years' imprisonment and/or a fine on indictment
- Six months' imprisonment and/or fine summarily

The Misuse of Drugs Act 1971, s. 20 states:

> A person commits an offence if in the United Kingdom he assists in or induces the commission in any place outside the United Kingdom of an offence punishable under the provisions of a corresponding law in force in that place.

KEYNOTE

In order to prove this offence, you must show that the offence outside the United Kingdom actually took place. The circumstances where this offence is likely to be committed will clearly overlap with the offences of importation/exportation.

'Assisting' has been held to include taking containers to another country in the knowledge that they would later be filled with a controlled drug and sent on to a third country (*R* v *Evans* (1977) 64 Cr App R 237). For an offence to amount to one under 'corresponding law' for these purposes, a certificate relating to the domestic law concerned with the misuse of drugs must be obtained from the government of the relevant country (s. 36).

1.6.5.18 Incitement

OFFENCE: **Incitement—*Misuse of Drugs Act 1971, s. 19***

- Triable and punishable as for substantive offence incited

The Misuse of Drugs Act 1971, s. 19 states:

> It is an offence for a person to incite another to commit an offence under any other provision of this Act.

KEYNOTE

The Act makes a specific offence of inciting another to commit an offence under its provisions. On the arguments in *DPP* v *Armstrong* [2000] Crim LR 379 (**see para. 1.3.6.2**), it would seem that a person inciting an undercover police officer may commit an offence under s. 19 even though there was no possibility of the officer actually being induced to commit the offence.

1.6.6 Enforcement

In addition to the general policing powers available for offences, the 1971 Act provides a number of specific enforcement powers.

1.6.6.1 Powers of Entry, Search and Seizure

The Misuse of Drugs Act 1971, s. 23 states:

(1) A constable or other person authorised in that behalf by a general or special order of the Secretary of State (or in Northern Ireland either of the Secretary of State or the Ministry of Home Affairs for Northern Ireland) shall, for the purposes of the execution of this Act, have power to enter the premises of a person carrying on business as a producer or supplier of any controlled drugs and to demand the production of, and to inspect, any books or documents relating to dealings in any such drugs and to inspect any stocks of any such drugs.

(2) If a constable has reasonable grounds to suspect that any person is in possession of a controlled drug in contravention of this Act or of any regulations made thereunder, the constable may—

    (a) search that person, and detain him for the purpose of searching him;

    (b) search any vehicle or vessel in which the constable suspects that the drug may be found, and for that purpose require the person in control of the vehicle or vessel to stop it;

    (c) seize and detain, for the purposes of proceedings under this Act, anything found in the course of the search which appears to the constable to be evidence of an offence under this Act.

    In this subsection 'vessel' includes a hovercraft within the meaning of the Hovercraft Act 1968; and nothing in this subsection shall prejudice any power of search or any power to seize or detain property which is exercisable by a constable apart from this subsection.

(3) If a justice of the peace (or in Scotland a justice of the peace, a magistrate or a sheriff) is satisfied by information on oath that there is reasonable ground for suspecting—

    (a) that any controlled drugs are, in contravention of this Act or of any regulations made thereunder, in the possession of a person on any premises; or

    (b) that a document directly or indirectly relating to, or connected with, a transaction or dealing which was, or an intended transaction or dealing which would if carried out be, an offence under this Act, or in the case of a transaction or dealing carried out or intended to be carried out in a place outside the United Kingdom, an offence against the provisions of a corresponding law in force in that place, is in the possession of a person on any premises,

    he may grant a warrant authorising any constable acting for the police area in which the premises are situated at any time or times within one month from the date of the warrant, to enter, if need be by force, the premises named in the warrant, and to search the premises and any persons found therein and, if there is reasonable ground for suspecting that an offence under this Act has been committed in relation to any controlled drugs found on the premises or in the possession of any such persons, or that a document so found is such a document as is mentioned in paragraph (b) above, to seize and detain those drugs or that document, as the case may be.

KEYNOTE

This is a very wide statutory provision granting authority for a broad range of enforcement measures in connection with controlled drugs.

Particular care will need to be taken when drafting the application for a warrant under s. 23. Where police officers are on premises under the authority of such a warrant it will be important to have established the precise *extent* of the warrant. If such a warrant authorises the search of *premises only*, that in itself will not give the officers authority to search *people* found on those premises unless the officer can point to some other power authorising the search (see e.g. *Chief Constable of Thames Valley* v *Hepburn* [2002] EWCA Civ 1841).

However, where the warrant authorises the search of premises *and* people, the Divisional Court has held that it is reasonable to restrict the movement of people within the premises to allow the search to be conducted properly (see *DPP* v *Meaden* [2003] EWHC 3005 (Admin)).

For the procedure involved in applying for, and executing warrants, **see General Police Duties, chapter 4.8.**

PACE Code A (**see General Police Duties**), applies to the exercise of any power to search people for controlled drugs specifically included in a warrant issued under s. 23.

The Serious Organised Crime and Police Act 2005 has not changed the duration of a warrant issued under s. 23 of the Misuse of Drugs Act 1971. A warrant issued under s. 23 of the Act lasts for a period of *one month* from the date of issue.

1.6.6.2 Obstruction

OFFENCE: **Obstruction—*Misuse of Drugs Act 1971, s. 23(4)***

> • Triable either way • Two years' imprisonment and/or a fine on indictment • Six months' imprisonment and/or fine summarily

The Misuse of Drugs Act 1971, s. 23 states:

(4) A person commits an offence if he—
  (a) intentionally obstructs a person in the exercise of his powers under this section; or
  (b) conceals from a person acting in the exercise of his powers under subsection (1) above any such books, documents, stocks or drugs as are mentioned in that subsection; or
  (c) without reasonable excuse (proof of which shall lie on him) fails to produce any such books or documents as are so mentioned where their production is demanded by a person in the exercise of his powers under that subsection.

KEYNOTE

The offence of obstructing a person in the exercise of his/her powers is only committed if the obstruction was intentional (*R* v *Forde* (1985) 81 Cr App R 19).

1.6.6.3 Travel Restriction Orders

The Criminal Justice and Police Act 2001 makes provision for courts to impose travel restrictions on offenders convicted of drug trafficking offences. Travel restriction orders prohibit the offender from leaving the United Kingdom at any time during the period beginning from his/her release from custody (other than on bail or temporary release for a fixed period) and up to the end of the order. The minimum period for such an order is two years (s. 33(3)).

Where a court

- has convicted a person of a drug trafficking offence
- and it has determined that a sentence of four years or more is appropriate

it is under a *duty* to consider whether or not a travel restriction order would be appropriate (s. 33). If the court decides not to impose an order, it must give its reasons for not doing so.

An offender may also be required to surrender his/her UK passport as part of the order.

The offences which are covered by travel restriction orders include the production and supply of controlled drugs, the importation/exportation offences described at **para. 1.6.5.16** along with inciting under the Misuse of Drugs Act 1971, s. 19.

The Secretary of State may add to this list (see s. 34(2)).

An offender may apply to the court that made a restriction order to have it revoked or suspended (s. 35) and the court must consider the strict criteria set out in s. 35 when considering any such suspension or revocation. If an order is suspended, the offender has a legal obligation to be back in the United Kingdom when the period of suspension ends (s. 35(5)(a)).

The general importance of all this to police officers is in the offence below.

OFFENCE: **Contravening a Travel Restriction Order—*Criminal Justice and Police Act 2001, s. 36***
- Triable either way • Five years' imprisonment and/or a fine on indictment
- Six months' imprisonment and/or fine summarily

The Criminal Justice and Police Act 2001, s. 36 states:

(1) A person who leaves the United Kingdom at a time when he is prohibited from leaving it by a travel restriction order is guilty of an offence ...
(2) A person who is not in the United Kingdom at the end of a period during which a prohibition imposed on him by a travel restriction order has been suspended shall be guilty of an offence ...

KEYNOTE

These offences make no specific requirement for a particular state of mind. The first offence simply requires proof of two things—that there was an order in existence in respect of the offender and that he/she left the United Kingdom during the time it was in force. There is no requirement that the person leave the United Kingdom *voluntarily* in order to be guilty (although they would have a pretty good argument if they were taken out of the jurisdiction against their will or without their knowledge).

However, travel restriction orders do not prevent the proper exercise of any prescribed power to remove a person from the United Kingdom (see s. 37—the relevant powers are set out in the Travel Restriction Order (Prescribed Removal Powers) Order 2002 (SI 2002/313)). For instance, if the Secretary of State deports someone who is under a travel restriction order, that person would not commit the above offence.

The second offence requires proof that there was a suspended order in existence in respect of the offender and that, at the end of the suspension period, the offender was not in the United Kingdom.

Failing to deliver up a travel authorisation when required by an order will be a summary offence carrying six months' imprisonment and/or a fine (s. 36(3)).

1.6.7 Intoxicating Substances

OFFENCE: **Supply of Intoxicating Substance—*Intoxicating Substances (Supply) Act 1985, s. 1***
- Triable summarily • Six months' imprisonment and/or a fine

The Intoxicating Substances (Supply) Act 1985, s. 1 states:

(1) It is an offence for a person to supply or offer to supply a substance other than a controlled drug—
    (a) to a person under the age of 18 whom he knows, or has reasonable cause to believe, to be under that age; or
    (b) to a person—
        (i) who is acting on behalf of a person under that age; and
        (ii) whom he knows, or has reasonable cause to believe, to be so acting,
if he knows or has reasonable cause to believe that the substance is, or its fumes are, likely to be inhaled by the person under the age of 18 for the purpose of causing intoxication.

KEYNOTE

This offence is aimed at curbing 'glue sniffing'. Retailers who sell solvents to people apparently under 18, or to people apparently acting on the behalf of someone under 18, would commit this offence.

The requirement as to the personal knowledge of the age and intentions of the person supplied makes this a difficult offence to prove.

It is a defence for a person charged with this offence to show that at the time he/she made the supply or offer he/she was both:

- under the age of 18 and
- acting otherwise than in the course or furtherance of a business (s. 1(2)).

OFFENCE: **Supply of Butane Lighter Refill to Person under 18—*Cigarette Lighter Refill (Safety) Regulations 1999, reg. 2***
- Triable summarily • Six months' imprisonment and/or a fine

The Cigarette Lighter Refill (Safety) Regulations 1999 (SI 1999/1844), reg. 2 states:

No person shall supply any cigarette lighter refill canister containing butane or a substance with butane as a constituent part to any person under the age of eighteen years.

KEYNOTE

For this offence there is no requirement that the person believed or even suspected the person to be under 18. The 1999 Regulations are made under the Consumer Protection Act 1987, s. 11.

1.7 | Firearms and Gun Crime

1.7.1 Introduction

The key piece of legislation governing the possession and use of firearms is the Firearms Act 1968. The Act covers numerous activities involving firearms (such as possession) and also deals with serious offences involving the criminal use of firearms. These activities and other supplementary firearms legislation will be examined in this chapter.

Many firearms offences carry a considerable maximum sentence of imprisonment and the circumstances surrounding the commission of the offence will play a significant part in determining the length of sentence for a person found guilty of such an offence. The leading authority giving guidance in relation to sentencing for offences involving firearms is *R v Avis* [1998] 1 Cr App R 420. There it was held that there were four questions a sentencing court had to ask itself when assessing the seriousness of a firearms offence:

- what sort of weapon was involved;
- what use had been made of the weapon;
- with what intention did the defendant possess or use the firearm; and
- what was the defendant's record.

All of these issues should arguably be borne in mind when gathering and presenting evidence in firearms cases.

1.7.2 Definitions—Firearm, Ammunition and Imitation Firearm

Before examining any offences relating to firearms, it is useful to begin with some basic definitions—particularly those of firearm, ammunition and imitation firearm.

1.7.2.1 Firearms

Section 57 of the Firearms Act 1968 states:

(1) In this Act, the expression 'firearm' means a lethal barrelled weapon of any description from which any shot, bullet or other missile can be discharged, and includes—
   (a) any prohibited weapon, whether it is such a lethal weapon as aforesaid or not; and
   (b) any component part of such a lethal or prohibited weapon; and
   (c) any accessory to any such weapon designed or adapted to diminish the noise or flash caused by firing the weapon.

KEYNOTE

'Lethal barrelled weapon' is not defined under the 1968 Act.

The way in which the courts have determined whether or not something amounts to such a weapon is by asking:

- Can any shot, bullet or other missile be discharged from the weapon, or
- Could the weapon be adapted so that any shot, bullet or other missile can be discharged?
- If so, is the weapon a 'lethal barrelled' weapon?

(See *Grace* v *DPP* [1989] COD 374.)

A weapon is a lethal barrelled weapon if it is capable of causing injury, irrespective of the intentions of its maker (*Read* v *Donovan* [1947] KB 326). In determining whether a firearm is in fact a lethal barrelled weapon from which missiles can be discharged a court need not consider any specific evidence of someone who has seen the effects of it being fired. Therefore, where magistrates had heard evidence from a gun shop assistant that an air rifle was in working order, they were entitled to conclude that it fell within the definition even though no evidence was given as to the actual effects of the gun being fired (*Castle* v *DPP* (1998) *The Times*, 3 April).

Air pistols (*R* v *Thorpe* [1987] 1 WLR 383) and imitation revolvers (*Cafferata* v *Wilson* [1936] 3 All ER 149) have all been held to be lethal barrelled weapons. A signalling pistol which fired explosive magnesium and phosphorous flares which was capable of killing at short range has been held to be lethal (*Read* v *Donovan*, above). That is not to say, however, that they will always be so and each case must be determined in the light of the evidence available.

Component parts are not defined in the Act but CPS Charging Standards state that the expression may include items such as triggers or barrels.

While silencers and flash eliminators are clearly accessories, a silencer or a flash eliminator *on its own* is not a firearm. However, if a defendant is found in possession of a silencer which has been manufactured for a weapon *that is also in the defendant's possession*, that will be enough to bring the silencer or flash eliminator under s. 57(1). If the silencer is made for a different weapon, it may still come under the s. 57 definition but the prosecution will have to show that it could be used with the defendant's weapon and that he/she had it for that purpose (*R* v *Buckfield* [1998] Crim LR 673). Section 57(1) does not include telescopic sights.

1.7.2.2 Deactivation of Firearms

A weapon ceases to be a firearm if it is deactivated in line with the provisions of the Firearms (Amendment) Act 1988, s. 8 which states:

For the purposes of the principal Act and this Act it shall be presumed, unless the contrary is shown, that a firearm has been rendered incapable of discharging any shot, bullet or other missile, and has consequently ceased to be a firearm within the meaning of those Acts, if—

(a) it bears a mark which has been approved by the Secretary of State for denoting that fact and which has been made either by one of the two companies mentioned in section 58(1) of the principal Act or by such other person as may be approved by the Secretary of State for the purposes of this section; and

(b) that company or person has certified in writing that work has been carried out on the firearm in a manner approved by the Secretary of State for rendering it incapable of discharging any shot, bullet or other missile.

1.7.2.3 Ammunition

Ammunition is defined by s. 57 of the Firearms Act 1968 which states:

> (2) In this Act, the expression 'ammunition' means any ammunition for any firearm and includes grenades, bombs and other like missiles, whether capable of use with a firearm or not, and also includes prohibited ammunition.

1.7.2.4 Imitation Firearm

Some, though not all, offences which regulate the use of firearms will also apply to *imitation* firearms. Whether they do so can be found either in the specific wording of the offence, or by virtue of the Firearms Act 1982.

There are two types of imitation firearms:

- general imitations—those which have the appearance of firearms (which are covered by s. 57 of the Firearms Act 1968); and
- imitations of section 1 firearms—those which both have the appearance of a *section 1 firearm* and which *can be readily converted* into such a firearm (which are covered by ss. 1 and 2 of the Firearms Act 1982).

The House of Lords has held that the definition in s. 57 requires the defendant to be carrying a 'thing' which is separate and distinct from him/herself and therefore capable of being possessed (*R* v *Bentham* [2005] UKHL 18). Holding your fingers under your coat and pretending that this is a firearm—as happened in *Bentham*—will not therefore amount to an imitation firearm for the relevant offences. Their lordships held that an unsevered hand or finger was part of oneself and therefore could not be 'possessed' in the way envisaged by the Act. The 'imitation' must have the appearance of a firearm and it is not necessary for any object to have been constructed, adapted or altered so as to resemble a firearm (*R* v *Williams* [2006] EWCA Crim 1650). In *K* v *DPP* [2006] EWHC 2183 (Admin) it was held that in some circumstances a realistic toy gun, in this case a plastic ball bearing gun, could become an imitation firearm. Note that this category does not include anything which resembles a prohibited weapon that is designed or adapted to discharge noxious liquid etc.

Whether or not something has the appearance of being a firearm will be a question of fact for the jury/magistrate(s) to decide in each case.

1.7.3 Categories of Firearms and Related Offences

The law regulating firearms classifies weapons into several categories, each of which is specifically defined. These definitions have closely associated offences dealing with activities such as their possession, acquisition and sale. Alongside these offences are exemptions which allow those activities to be lawful.

1.7.4 Prohibited Weapon

A prohibited weapon is defined under the Firearms Act 1968, s. 5. The definition not only covers the more powerful or potentially destructive firearms—and their ammunition—(such as automatic weapons and specialist ammunition) but also, since the Firearms (Amendment) Act 1997, covers small firearms which were formerly covered by other parts of the 1968 Act.

The test as to whether a weapon is a 'prohibited' weapon is a purely objective one and is not affected by the intentions of the defendant. Therefore, where a firearm was capable of successively discharging two or more missiles without repeated pressure on the trigger, that weapon was 'prohibited' irrespective of the intentions of the firearms dealer who was in possession of it (*R* v *Law* [1999] Crim LR 837).

Whereas a firearms certificate is usually needed in order to possess, buy or acquire firearms and ammunition, the authority of the Secretary of State is needed if the firearm or ammunition is a 'prohibited weapon'.

1.7.4.1 List of Prohibited Weapons and Ammunition

The full list of prohibited weapons and ammunition is contained in s. 5(1) and (1A) of the Firearms Act 1968 (see *Blackstone's Criminal Practice 2010*, para. B12.47). This list often (but not always) relates to weapons used in a military context and includes:

- automatic weapons
- most self-loading or pump-action weapons
- any firearm which either has a barrel less than 30 cm in length or is less than 60 cm in length overall, other than an air weapon, a muzzle-loading gun or a firearm designed as signalling apparatus
- most smooth bore revolvers
- any weapon, of whatever description, designed or adapted for the discharge of any noxious liquid, gas or other thing

- any air rifle, air gun or air pistol which uses, or is designed or adapted for use with, a self-contained gas cartridge system
- military weapons and ammunition including grenades and mortars.

KEYNOTE

In relation to weapons designed or adapted for the discharge of any noxious liquid, gas or other thing, taking an empty Fairy Liquid washing-up bottle and filling it with hydrochloric acid does not amount to adapting it, neither is such a thing a 'weapon' for the purposes of s. 5 (*R* v *Formosa*, *R* v *Upton* [1991] 2 QB 1). This is because to do so does not change the nature of the washing-up bottle itself—the bottle has not been adapted or altered and is therefore not a weapon 'designed or adapted' for the discharge of any noxious liquid etc. The same logic applies to a water pistol filled with ammonia (*R* v *Titus* [1971] Crim LR 279).

An electric 'stun gun' has been held to be a prohibited weapon as it discharges an electric current (*Flack* v *Baldry* [1988] 1 WLR 393) and it continues to be such even if it is not working (*Brown* v *DPP* (1992) *The Times*, 27 March).

1.7.4.2 Possessing or Distributing Prohibited Weapons or Ammunition

OFFENCE: **Possessing or Distributing Prohibited Weapons or Ammunition—** *Firearms Act 1968, s. 5*

- Triable either way ● Ten years' imprisonment and/or a fine on indictment
- Six months' imprisonment and/or a fine summarily

The Firearms Act 1968, s. 5 states:

(1) A person commits an offence if, without the authority of the Secretary of State or the Scottish Ministers, he has in his possession, or purchases, or acquires, or manufactures, sells or transfers [a prohibited weapon or ammunition] ...

KEYNOTE

This offence is one of strict liability.

A person may still be in possession of a prohibited weapon even when it is in parts and the accused is in possession of those parts (*R* v *Pannell* (1982) 76 Cr App R 53), or where the weapon is missing an essential part such as the trigger (*R* v *Clarke* [1986] 1 WLR 209).

1.7.4.3 Possession

As an offence contrary to s. 5 of the 1968 Act is a strict liability offence, it is irrelevant whether or not a person knew he/she was in possession of a firearm or ammunition (*R* v *Deyemi* [2008] EWCA Crim 2060). In *Sullivan* v *Earl of Caithness* [1976] QB 966, it was held that a person can remain in possession of a firearm even if someone else has custody of it.

There is no need to prove that the accused knew the nature of the thing he/she possessed in order to prove the offence. If an accused is carrying a rucksack and the rucksack contains ammunition for a section 1 firearm, the accused is in 'possession' of the ammunition irrespective of his/her knowledge or ignorance of its presence in the rucksack (see *R* v *Waller* [1991] Crim LR 381 and *R* v *Cremin* [2007] EWCA Crim 666).

1.7.4.4 Exemptions

There are two sets of exemptions in respect of s. 5 prohibited weapons. They are:

- European exemptions—exemptions to conform with the European Weapons Directive.
- Special exemptions.

European Weapons Directive

The effect of the European Weapons Directive (91/477/EEC) is to create exemptions in relation to the possession of, or some transactions in, specified firearms and ammunition by people who have the relevant certificates or who are recognised as collectors under the law of another country.

To this end, s. 5A of the Firearms Act 1968 provides for a number of occasions where the authority of the Secretary of State will not be required to possess or deal with certain weapons under certain conditions.

The main areas covered by s. 5A are:

- authorised collectors and firearms dealers possessing or being involved in transactions of weapons and ammunition;
- authorised people being involved in transactions of particular ammunition used for lawful shooting and slaughtering of animals, the management of an estate or the protection of other animals and humans.

Section 57(4A) of the Firearms Act 1968 makes other provisions in relation to the European directive as an authority for certain uses of firearms.

Special exemptions

The list of special exemptions to the offences involving firearms under s. 5(1)(aba) focuses largely on people in jobs where they will need to come into contact with firearms mainly in connection with animals or leisure activities.

The exemptions include:

- **Slaughterers**—A slaughterer, if entitled under s. 10 of the 1968 Act, may possess a slaughtering instrument. In addition, persons authorised by certificate to possess, buy, acquire, sell or transfer slaughtering instruments are exempt from the provisions of s. 5 (s. 2 of the Firearms (Amendment) Act 1997). This is the most common exemption.
- **Humane killing of animals**—This exemption allows a person authorised by certificate to possess, buy, acquire or transfer a firearm solely for use in connection with the humane killing of animals (s. 3 of the Firearms (Amendment) Act 1997). When determining whether a firearm falls within the meaning of a 'humane killer', the definition of a 'slaughtering instrument' under s. 57(4) may be referred to (*R v Paul (Benjamin)* (1998) 95(32) LSG 30).
- **Shot pistols for vermin**—This exemption allows a person authorised by certificate to possess, buy, acquire or transfer a 'shot pistol' solely for the shooting of vermin (s. 4(1) of the Firearms (Amendment) Act 1997). A 'shot pistol' is a smooth-bored gun chambered for .410 cartridges or 9mm rim-fire cartridges (s. 4(2)).
- **Treatment of animals**—This exemption allows a person authorised by certificate to possess, buy, acquire or transfer a firearm for use in connection with the treatment of animals or for the purpose of tranquillising any animal (s. 8 of the Firearms (Amendment) Act 1997). This exemption also applies to offences involving firearms under s. 5(1)(b) and (c).
- **Races at athletic meetings**—A person may possess a firearm at an athletic meeting for the purpose of starting races at that meeting (s. 5(a) of the Firearms (Amendment) Act

1997). Similarly, a person authorised by certificate to possess, buy or acquire a firearm solely for the purposes of starting such races may possess, buy, acquire, sell or transfer a firearm for such a purpose (s. 5(b)).

- **Trophies of war**—A person authorised by certificate to do so may possess a firearm which was acquired as a trophy before 1 January 1946 (s. 6 of the Firearms (Amendment) Act 1997).
- **Firearms of historic interest**—Some firearms are felt to be of particular historical, aesthetic or technical interest. Section 7(4) of the Firearms (Amendment) Act 1997 makes detailed provision for the exemption of such firearms, exemptions which exist in addition to the general exemptions under s. 58 of the Firearms Act 1968 (**see para. 1.7.8**). These provisions are set out in the Firearms (Amendment) Act 1997 (Firearms of Historic Interest) Order 1997 (SI 1997/1537) and the Firearms (Amendment) Act 1997 (Transitional Provisions and Savings) Regulations 1997 (SI 1997/1538).
- **Air weapons**—In relation to air weapons with self-contained gas cartridges, owned before 20 January 2004, the owner, if he/she applied for a firearms certificate before 1 April 2004, may retain his/her weapons.

1.7.5 Section 1 Firearm

There is a group of firearms which, although not a category defined in the 1968 Act, are subject to a number of offences including s. 1 (see below). Firearms which fall into this group are often referred to as 'section 1 firearms' and include all firearms except shotguns (**see para. 1.7.4.3**) and conventional air weapons. However, shotguns which have been 'sawn off' (i.e. had their barrels shortened) are section 1 firearms, as are air weapons declared to be 'specially dangerous'.

Section 1 ammunition includes any ammunition for a firearm except:

- cartridges containing five or more shot, none of which is bigger than 0.36 inches in diameter;
- ammunition for an airgun, air rifle or air pistol; and
- blank cartridges not more than one inch in diameter (s. 1(4)).

1.7.5.1 Conversion

Some weapons which began their life as section 1 firearms or prohibited weapons will remain so even after their conversion to a shotgun, air weapon or other type of firearm (see s. 7 of the Firearms (Amendment) Act 1988).

1.7.5.2 Possessing etc. Firearm or Ammunition without Certificate

OFFENCE: **Possessing etc. Firearm or Ammunition without Certificate—**
Firearms Act, 1968 s. 1
- Triable either way • Five years' imprisonment and/or a fine on indictment
- Six months' imprisonment and/or a fine summarily

The Firearms Act 1968, s. 1 states:

(1) Subject to any exemption under this Act, it is an offence for a person—
    (a) to have in his possession, or to purchase or acquire, a firearm to which this section applies without holding a firearm certificate in force at the time, or otherwise than as authorised by such a certificate;
    (b) to have in his possession, or to purchase or acquire, any ammunition to which this section applies without holding a firearm certificate in force at the time, or otherwise than as authorised by such a certificate, or in quantities in excess of those so authorised.

KEYNOTE

This offence relates to those firearms described above as section 1 firearms.

If the firearm involved is a sawn-off shotgun, the offence becomes 'aggravated' (under s. 4(4)) and attracts a maximum penalty of seven years' imprisonment.

The Firearms Act 1982 applies to this section and so the 'general definition' of an imitation firearm *does not* apply. For this offence the definition of an imitation firearm is one 'that has the appearance of a section 1 firearm and which can be readily converted into such a firearm' (which is covered by ss. 1 and 2 of the Firearms Act 1982).

The certificate referred to is issued by the chief officer of police under s. 26A. Such certificates may carry significant restrictions on the types of firearms which the holder is allowed, together with the circumstances under which he/she may have them (see s. 44(1) of the Firearms (Amendment) Act 1997).

The purpose of the legislation regulating the licensing of firearms is to provide certainty and consistency in the effective control of such weapons. Therefore the issue of whether a certificate covers a particular category of weapon is a matter of law for the judge to decide and cannot be affected by the intentions or misunderstanding of the defendant (*R* v *Paul* (1998) 95(32) LSG 30).

A person may hold a European firearms pass or similar document, in which case he/she will be governed by the provision of ss. 32A to 32C of the Firearms Act 1968.

If a person has such a certificate which allows the possession etc. of the firearm in question and under the particular circumstances encountered, no offence is committed.

Acquire will include hiring, accepting as a gift and borrowing, and 'acquisition' is to be construed accordingly (s. 57(4) of the Firearms Act 1968).

The Violent Crime Reduction Act 2006 has created a summary offence that restricts the purchase and sale of cap-type primers (primers are components of ammunition designed for use in metallic ammunition for a firearm which contain a chemical compound that detonates on impact) to persons who hold a relevant firearms certificate or who otherwise have lawful authority for having them (s. 35).

1.7.5.3   Shortening Section 1 Firearm

OFFENCE: **Shortening Barrel of Other Smooth-bore Section 1 Firearm to Less than 24 Inches—*Firearms (Amendment) Act 1988 s. 6(1)***

- Triable either way • Five years' imprisonment and/or a fine on indictment
- Six months' imprisonment and/or a fine summarily

The Firearms (Amendment) Act 1988, s. 6 states:

(1) Subject to subsection (2) below, it is an offence to shorten to a length less than 24 inches the barrel of any smooth-bore gun to which section 1 of the principal Act applies other than one which has a barrel with a bore exceeding 2 inches in diameter;...

1.7.6 Shotguns

A shotgun is defined under s. 1(3)(a) of the Firearms Act 1968. Section 1 (amended by Firearms (Amendment) Act 1988 s. 2) states:

(3) ...

    (a) a shotgun within the meaning of this Act, that is to say a smooth-bore gun (not being an airgun) which—

        (i) has a barrel not less than 24 inches in length and does not have any barrel with a bore exceeding 2 inches in diameter;

        (ii) either has no magazine or has a non-detachable magazine incapable of holding more than two cartridges; and

        (iii) is not a revolver gun...

(3A) A gun which has been adapted to have such a magazine as is mentioned in subsection (3)(a)(ii) above shall not be regarded as falling within that provision unless the magazine bears a mark approved by the Secretary of State for denoting that fact and that mark has been made, and the adaptation has been certified in writing as having been carried out in a manner approved by him, either by one of the two companies mentioned in section 58(1) of this Act or by such other person as may be approved by him for that purpose.

1.7.6.1 Shotgun Offences

OFFENCE: **Possessing Shotgun without Certificate—*Firearms Act 1968, s. 2(1)***

- Triable either way • Five years' imprisonment and/or a fine on indictment
- Six months' imprisonment and/or a fine summarily

The Firearms Act 1968, s. 2 states:

(1) Subject to any exemption under this Act, it is an offence for a person to have in his possession, or to purchase or acquire, a shotgun without holding a certificate under this Act authorising him to possess shot guns.

OFFENCE: **Failing to Comply with Conditions of Shot gun Certificate—*Firearms Act 1968, s. 2(2)***

- Triable summarily • Six months' imprisonment and/or a fine

The Firearms Act 1968, s. 2 states:

(2) It is an offence for a person to fail to comply with a condition subject to which a shot gun certificate is held by him.

The conditions and forms used in relation to the grant of shotgun certificates are contained in the Firearms Rules 1998 (SI 1998/1941) and the Firearms (Amendment) Rules 2005 (SI 2005/3344).

1.7.6.2 Shortening a Shotgun Barrel

OFFENCE: **Shortening Barrel of Shotgun to Less than 24 Inches—*Firearms Act 1968, s. 4(1)***

- Triable either way • Five years' imprisonment and/or a fine on indictment
- Six months' imprisonment and/or a fine summarily

The Firearms Act 1968, s. 4 states:

(1) Subject to this section, it is an offence to shorten the barrel of a shot gun to a length less than 24 inches.

1.7.7 Air Weapons

Air weapons are defined under s. 1(3)(b) of the Firearms Act 1968. In summary these are air rifles, air guns or air pistols which do not fall within s. 5(1) and which are not of a type declared to be specially dangerous. Any air rifle, air gun or air pistol that uses or is designed or adapted for use with a self-contained gas cartridge system *does* fall within the definition of a prohibited weapon at s. 5(1).

Some air weapons are deemed to be specially dangerous and therefore subject to stricter control than conventional air weapons. Those which are subject to this stricter control are those declared to be so by the Secretary of State. Listed in r. 2 of the Firearms (Dangerous Air Weapons) Rules 1969, as amended, they include:

(1) [any] air rifle, air gun or air pistol—
  (a) which is capable of discharging a missile so that the missile has, on being discharged from the muzzle of the weapon, kinetic energy in excess, in the case of an air pistol, of 6ft lb or, in the case of an air weapon other than an air pistol, of 12ft lb, or
  (b) which is disguised as another object.

Note that this does not include a weapon falling within para. (1)(a) above and which is designed for use only when submerged in water (r. 2(2)).

Section 32 of the Violent Crime Reduction Act 2006 imposed a 'face to face' requirement on trade transactions by persons selling air weapons.

1.7.7.1 Air Weapon Offences

OFFENCE: **Sales of Air Weapons by Way of Trade or Business to be Face to Face—*Violent Crime Reduction Act 2006, s. 32***

- Triable summarily • 51 weeks' imprisonment and/or a fine

The Violent Crime Reduction Act 2006, s. 32 states:

(1) This section applies where a person sells an air weapon by way of trade or business to an individual in Great Britain who is not registered as a firearms dealer.
(2) A person is guilty of an offence if, for the purposes of the sale, he transfers possession of the air weapon to the buyer otherwise than at a time when both—
  (a) the buyer, and
  (b) either the seller or a representative of his,
  are present in person.

KEYNOTE

A representative of the seller is a reference to a person who is:

- employed by the seller in his/her business as a registered firearms dealer;
- a registered firearms dealer who has been authorised by the seller to act on his/her behalf in relation to the sale; or
- a person who is employed by a person falling within s. 32(3)(b) in his/her business as a registered firearms dealer.

This allows an air weapon to be sent from one registered firearms dealer to another to make the final transfer in person to the buyer. It also enables someone to buy an air weapon from a dealer in a distant part of the country without one or other party to the transaction having to make a long journey, while still preserving the safeguards of a face-to-face handover.

OFFENCE: **Firing an Air Weapon Beyond Premises—*Firearms Act 1968, s. 21A***

- Triable summarily • Fine

The Firearms Act 1968, s. 21A states:

(1) A person commits an offence if—
  (a) he has with him an air weapon on any premises; and
  (b) he uses it for firing a missile beyond those premises.

(2) In proceedings against a person for an offence under this section it shall be a defence for him to show that the only premises into or across which the missile was fired were premises the occupier of which had consented to the firing of the missile (whether specifically or by way of a general consent).

KEYNOTE

This offence makes it an offence for a person of *any* age to fire an air weapon beyond the boundary of premises. Note that a defence is provided to cover the situation where the person shooting has the consent of the occupier of the land over or into which he/she shoots.

1.7.8 General Exemptions

The general exemptions, which apply to the provisions of ss. 1 to 5 of the Firearms Act 1968 are mainly concerned with the various occupations of people whom you might expect to be in contact with firearms in one form or another. They include:

Police permit holders

Under s. 7(1) of the 1968 Act, the chief officer of police may grant a permit authorising the possession of firearms or ammunition under the conditions specified in the permit.

Clubs, athletics and sporting purposes

Section 11 of the 1968 Act provides exemptions for a person:

- borrowing the firearm/ammunition from a certificate holder *for sporting purposes only* (s. 11(1));
- possessing a firearm at an athletic meeting for the purposes of starting races (s. 11(2));
- in charge of a miniature rifle range buying, acquiring or possessing miniature rifles and ammunition, and using them at such a rifle range (s. 11(4));
- who is a member of an approved rifle club, miniature rifle club or pistol club to possess a firearm or ammunition *when engaged as a club member in target practice* (s. 15(1) of the Firearms (Amendment) Act 1988);
- borrowing a shotgun from the occupier of private premises and using it on those premises *in the occupier's presence* (s. 11(5) of the 1968 Act);
- using a shotgun at a time and place approved by the chief officer of police for shooting at artificial targets (s. 11(6)).

Borrowed rifle on private premises

Section 16 of the Firearms (Amendment) Act 1988 allows a person to borrow a rifle from the occupier of private premises, provided the person is on those premises and in the presence of the occupier (or his/her servant), as long as the occupier holds a certificate and the borrowing of the rifle complies with that certificate. The person borrowing the rifle may buy or acquire ammunition for it in accordance with the certificate's conditions.

Visitors' permits

Section 17 of the Firearms (Amendment) Act 1988 provides for the issuing of a visitors' permit by a chief officer of police and for the possession of firearms and ammunition by the holder of such a permit.

Visitors' permits will not be issued to anyone without a European firearms pass. It is a summary offence (punishable with six months' imprisonment) to make a false statement in order to get a visitors' permit, and it is a similar offence to fail to comply with any conditions within such a permit (see s. 17(10)).

Antiques as ornaments or curiosities

Section 58(2) of the 1968 Act allows for the sale, buying, transfer, acquisition or possession of antique firearms *as curiosities or ornaments*. Whether a firearm is such an antique will be a question of fact to be determined by the court in each case. Mere belief in the fact that a firearm is an antique will not be enough (*R v Howells* [1977] QB 614).

Authorised firearms dealers

Section 8(1) of the 1968 Act provides for registered firearms dealers (or their employees) to possess, acquire or buy firearms or ammunition in the ordinary course of their business without a certificate. If the possession etc. is not in the ordinary course of their business, the exemption will not apply.

KEYNOTE

In addition to the above, other occupations of people exempt include: auctioneers, carriers and warehouse staff; licensed slaughterers; theatrical performers; ships, aircraft or aerodrome equipment; Crown servants; proof houses; and holders of a museums licence.

1.7.9 Criminal Use of Firearms

Further to the offences relating to possession etc. of firearms there is a series of offences intrinsically linked to criminal behaviour. The aggravating factor of the presence of a firearm in the commission of such offences is evidenced by the fact that the majority carry a life imprisonment sentence—those that do not still carry ten years' imprisonment.

1.7.9.1 Possession with Intent to Endanger Life

OFFENCE: **Possession with Intent to Endanger Life—*Firearms Act 1968, s. 16***

- Triable on indictment • Life imprisonment and/or a fine

The Firearms Act 1968, s. 16 states:

> It is an offence for a person to have in his possession any firearm or ammunition with intent by means thereof to endanger life or to enable another person by means thereof to endanger life, whether any injury has been caused or not.

KEYNOTE

This offence *cannot be committed by possessing an imitation firearm.*

The offence involves 'possession' so there is no need for the firearm to be produced or shown to another.

To prove this offence you will have to show an intention by the defendant to behave in a way that he/she knows will in fact endanger the life of another (*R v Brown & Ciarla* [1995] Crim LR 327). The life endangered must be the life of 'another', not the defendant's (*R v Norton* [1977] Crim LR 478) so that possession with intent to commit suicide would not be covered by the offence. The person whose life

---

is endangered may be outside the United Kingdom (*R* v *El-Hakkaoui* [1975] 1 WLR 396). Note that the intention *is not* to enable the defendant or another to kill.

That intent does not have to be an immediate one and it may be conditional (e.g. an intent to shoot someone if they do not do as they are asked) (*R* v *Bentham* [1973] QB 357).

The firearm must provide the means by which life is endangered; it is not enough to have a firearm at the time when life is endangered by some other means (e.g. by dangerous driving).

There may be occasions when self-defence can be raised in answer to a charge under s. 16 of the 1968 Act but these circumstances will be very unusual (see *R* v *Georgiades* [1989] 1 WLR 759). This defence could apply where the defendant is carrying a weapon for his own defence anticipating an imminent attack (*R* v *Salih* [2007] EWCA Crim 2750).

1.7.9.2 Possession with Intent to Cause Fear of Violence

OFFENCE: **Possession with Intent to Cause Fear of Violence—*Firearms Act 1968, s. 16A***

> • Triable on indictment • Ten years' imprisonment and/or a fine

The Firearms Act 1968, s. 16A (added by Firearms (Amendment) Act 1994, s. 1) states:

It is an offence for a person to have in his possession any firearm or imitation firearm with intent—
(a) by means thereof to cause, or
(b) to enable another person by means thereof to cause,
any person to believe that unlawful violence will be used against him or another person.

KEYNOTE

Section 16A is committed by possession, accompanied by an intention to cause fear of violence at or immediately before the defendant's actions which are designed to cause such fear (*R* v *Goluchowski* [2006] EWCA Crim 1972). There is no need for a firearm/imitation firearm to be produced or shown to anyone, though it must provide the 'means' of the threat. Possession of a firearm/imitation firearm while making a general threat to someone who does not know of its presence is unlikely to fall within this section.

This offence includes imitation firearms in the general sense (see para. 1.7.2.4).

1.7.9.3 Using Firearm to Resist Arrest

OFFENCE: **Using Firearm to Resist Arrest—*Firearms Act 1968, s. 17(1)***

> • Triable on indictment • Life imprisonment and/or a fine

The Firearms Act 1968, s. 17 states:

(1) It is an offence for a person to make or attempt to make any use whatsoever of a firearm or imitation firearm with intent to resist or prevent the lawful arrest or detention of himself or another person.

KEYNOTE

This offence relates to *using* a firearm to resist arrest—it is closely connected to the offence of *having* a firearm with intent to resist arrest (s. 18(1) of the Act—see para. 1.7.9.4).

The 'firearm' to which s. 17 refers is that defined at para. 1.7.2.1, *except* component parts and silencers/flash diminishers (s. 17(4)). For that reason, whilst the offence includes imitation firearms in the general sense (see para. 1.7.2.4) it does not include imitation component parts, etc.

This offence requires proof, not of possession, but of evidence that the defendant made some *actual use* of the firearm and did so intending to resist/prevent the arrest of him/herself or someone else. Any arrest which the defendant intended to prevent/resist must have been 'lawful'.

1.7.9.4 Having Firearm with Intent to Commit Indictable Offence or Resist Arrest

OFFENCE: **Having Firearm with Intent to Commit an Indictable Offence or Resist Arrest—*Firearms Act 1968, s. 18(1)***

- Triable on indictment • Life imprisonment and/or a fine

The Firearms Act 1968, s. 18 states:

(1) It is an offence for a person to have with him a firearm or imitation firearm with intent to commit an indictable offence, or to resist arrest or prevent the arrest of another, in either case while he has the firearm or imitation firearm with him.

KEYNOTE

This offence, which overlaps with that under s. 17(1) (see para. 1.7.9.3), requires the defendant to 'have with him' a firearm. This is a more restrictive expression than 'possession' and requires that the firearm is 'readily accessible' to the defendant. In *R v Pawlicki* [1992] 1 WLR 827, the Court of Appeal decided that defendants in an auction room had firearms 'with them' which were in a car 50 yards away. Where a defendant left a firearm in his house which was a few miles from the scene of the relevant criminal offence, the Court of Appeal held that this was not enough to meet the requirement of 'having with him'—*R v Bradish* [2004] EWCA Crim 1340. Despite this narrower meaning, the defendant does not have to be shown to have been 'carrying' the firearm (*R v Kelt* [1977] 1 WLR 1365).

Intention

In proving the intent for this offence, s. 18 states:

(2) In proceedings for an offence under this section proof that the accused had a firearm or imitation firearm with him and intended to commit an offence, or to resist or prevent arrest, is evidence that he intended to have it with him while doing so.

It is not necessary to show that the defendant intended to *use* the firearm to commit the indictable offence or to prevent/resist the arrest (*R v Duhaney* [1998] 2 Cr App R 25).

The mental element is, however, an essential part of this offence. Therefore, if the defendant only formed the intent as a result of duress (as to which see chapter 1.4), this ingredient will not have been established—*R v Fisher* [2004] EWCA Crim 1190.

Section 18 does not appear to require that any arrest be 'lawful' and it may be that Parliament intended for this offence to be broader in that respect than the offence under s. 17.

This offence includes imitation firearms in the general sense (see para. 1.7.2.4).

The power of entry and search under s. 47 of the 1968 Act applies to this offence (see para. 1.7.13).

1.7.9.5 Possessing Firearm while Committing a Schedule 1 Offence

OFFENCE: **Possessing Firearm while Committing or Being Arrested for sch. 1 Offence—*Firearms Act 1968, s. 17(2)***

- Triable on indictment • Life imprisonment and/or a fine

The Firearms Act 1968, s. 17 states:

(2) If a person, at the time of his committing or being arrested for an offence specified in schedule 1 to this Act, has in his possession a firearm or imitation firearm, he shall be guilty of an offence under this subsection unless he shows that he had it in his possession for a lawful object.

KEYNOTE

This offence may be committed in two ways; either by being in possession of the weapon *at the time of committing* the sch. 1 offence or by being in possession of it *at the time of being arrested* for such an offence. Clearly in the second case, there may be some time between actually committing the sch. 1 offence and being arrested for it. Nevertheless, if the defendant is in possession of the firearm at the time of his/her arrest, the offence is committed (unless he/she can show that it was for a lawful purpose).

There is no need for the defendant to be subsequently *convicted* of the sch. 1 offence, nor even to prove the elements of it; all that is needed is to show that the defendant, at the time of his/her arrest for a sch. 1 offence, had a firearm/imitation firearm in his/her possession (*R* v *Nelson* [2000] 3 WLR 300).

It is for the defendant to prove that the firearm was in his/her possession for a lawful purpose.

This offence includes imitation firearms in the general sense (see para. 1.7.2.4).

Schedule 1 Offences

The *main* offences listed in sch. 1 are:

- Damage—s. 1 of the Criminal Damage Act 1971.
- Assaults and woundings—ss. 20 and 47 of the Offences Against the Person Act 1861, assault on police (s. 89 of the Police Act 1996) and civilian custody officers (s. 90(1) of the Criminal Justice Act 1991 and s. 13(1) of the Criminal Justice and Public Order Act 1994).
- Rape and other sexual/abduction offences—the following offences under the Sexual Offences Act 2003: s. 1 (rape), s. 2 (assault by penetration), s. 4 (causing a person to engage in sexual activity without consent), where the activity caused involved penetration within subs. (4)(a) to (d) of that section, s. 5 and s. 6 (rape and assault of a child under 13), s. 8 (causing or inciting a child under 13 to engage in sexual activity), where an activity involving penetration within subs. (2)(a) to (d) of that section was caused, s. 30 and s. 31 (sexual activity with/causing or inciting a person with a mental disorder impeding choice), where the touching involved or activity caused penetration within subs. (3)(a) to (d) of that section. Also offences under part I of the Child Abduction Act 1984.
- Theft, robbery, burglary, blackmail and taking a conveyance—Theft Act 1968. (**D.A.R.T.**)

Although covering several types of assault, sch. 1 does not extend to wounding/causing grievous bodily harm with intent (s. 18 of the Offences Against the Person Act 1861). Schedule 1 also covers the aiding, abetting or attempting to commit such offences.

1.7.9.6   Using Someone to Mind a Weapon

OFFENCE: **Using Someone to Mind a Weapon—*Violent Crime Reduction Act 2006, s. 28(1)***

- Triable on indictment • Ten years' imprisonment and/or a fine (firearms, etc.)
- Four years' imprisonment and/or a fine (offensive weapons, etc.)

The Violent Crime Reduction Act 2006, s. 28 states:

(1) A person is guilty of an offence if—
(a) he uses another to look after, hide or transport a dangerous weapon for him; and

(b) he does so under arrangements or in circumstances that facilitate, or are intended to facilitate, the weapon's being available to him for an unlawful purpose.

(2) For the purposes of this section the cases in which a dangerous weapon is to be regarded as available to a person for an unlawful purpose include any case where—

(a) the weapon is available for him to take possession of it at a time and place; and

(b) his possession of the weapon at that time and place would constitute, or be likely to involve or to lead to, the commission by him of an offence.

KEYNOTE

The offence was introduced by the 2006 Act to close a perceived loophole in the law where people have escaped prosecution by entrusting their weapon to another person, in particular to a child. Using children in this way may risk injury to them and in the longer term draw them into gun and knife crime as a result of their early association with weapons. Using a minor to mind a firearm is an aggravating factor attracting harsher sentences (s. 29(3)(a)).

A 'dangerous weapon' means a firearm *other than* an air weapon or a component part of, or accessory to, an air weapon; or a weapon to which s. 141 or 141A of the Criminal Justice Act 1988 applies (specified offensive weapons, knives and bladed weapons—**see General Police Duties, para. 4.14**) (s. 28(3)).

1.7.10 Further Firearms Offences

Alongside offences associated with the criminal use of firearms are several offences dealing with an offender 'having with him' a firearm in a public place and whilst trespassing.

1.7.10.1 Having Firearm or Imitation Firearm in Public Place

OFFENCE: **Having Firearm/Imitation Firearm in Public Place—*Firearms Act 1968, s. 19***

- Triable either way • Seven years' imprisonment and/or a fine on indictment
- Twelve months' imprisonment and/or a fine summarily

The Firearms Act 1968, s. 19 states:

A person commits an offence if, without lawful authority or reasonable excuse (the proof whereof lies on him), he has with him in a public place—

(a) a loaded shot gun,

(b) an air weapon (whether loaded or not),

(c) any other firearm (whether loaded or not) together with ammunition suitable for use in that firearm, or

(d) an imitation firearm.

KEYNOTE

A 'public place' includes any highway and any other premises or place to which, at the material time, the public have or are permitted to have access whether on payment or otherwise (s. 57(4) of the Act).

If the weapon is a shotgun it must be loaded. 'Loaded' here means if there is ammunition in the chamber or barrel (or in any magazine or other device) whereby the ammunition can be fed into the chamber or barrel by the manual or automatic operation of some part of the weapon (see s. 57(6)(b)). If the weapon is an imitation firearm (**see para. 1.7.2.4**) or an air weapon the offence is committed by the defendant having it with him/her. In the case of other firearms the offence is committed by the defendant having the firearm with him/her together with ammunition suitable for use in it.

For the meaning of 'has with him', see para. 1.7.9.4.

This offence is one of strict liability. Therefore, if you can show that the defendant (X) knew he had something with him and that the 'something' was a loaded shotgun, an air weapon, an imitation firearm, or another firearm with ammunition, the offence is complete (*R* v *Vann* [1996] Crim LR 52). It is for the defendant to show lawful authority or reasonable excuse; possession of a valid certificate does not of itself provide lawful authority for having the firearm/ammunition in a public place (*Ross* v *Collins* [1982] Crim LR 368).

1.7.10.2 Trespassing with Firearms

OFFENCE: **Trespassing with Firearm in Building—*Firearms Act 1968, s. 20(1)***

- Triable either way (unless imitation firearm or air weapon) • Seven years' imprisonment and/or a fine on indictment • Six months' imprisonment and/or a fine summarily

The Firearms Act 1968, s. 20 states:

(1) A person commits an offence if, while he has a firearm or imitation firearm with him, he enters or is in any building or part of a building as a trespasser and without reasonable excuse (the proof whereof lies on him).

KEYNOTE

This offence can be committed either by entering a building/part of a building or simply by *being* in such a place, in each case as a trespasser while having the firearm. As there is no need for the defendant to have 'entered' the building as a trespasser in every case, the offence might be committed after the occupier has withdrawn any permission for the defendant to be there.

For the interpretation of 'has with him', see para. 1.7.9.4.

It will be for the defendant to prove that he/she had reasonable excuse and the standard of that proof will be judged against the balance of probabilities.

If the relevant firearm is an imitation or an air weapon, the offence is triable summarily.

This offence includes imitation firearms in the general sense (see para. 1.7.2.4). If the relevant firearm is an imitation or an air weapon, the offence is triable summarily.

The power of entry and search under s. 47 of the 1968 Act applies to this offence (see para. 1.7.13).

OFFENCE: **Trespassing with Firearm on Land—*Firearms Act 1968, s. 20(2)***

- Triable summarily • Three months' imprisonment and/or a fine

The Firearms Act 1968, s. 20 states:

(2) A person commits an offence if, while he has a firearm or imitation firearm with him, he enters or is on any land as a trespasser and without reasonable excuse (the proof whereof lies on him).

KEYNOTE

The elements of this offence are generally the same as those for the s. 20(1) offence above.

As with the s. 20(1) offence, there is no requirement that the defendant had the firearm/imitation firearm with him/her when entering onto the land.

'Land' for these purposes will include land covered by water (s. 20(3)).

This offence includes imitation forearms in the general sense (see para 1.7.2.4).
The power of entry and search under s. 47 of the 1968 Act applies to this offence (see para. 1.7.13).

1.7.11 Possession or Acquisition of Firearms by Convicted Persons

Section 21 of the Firearms Act 1968 places restrictions on convicted persons in respect of their possession of firearms and/or ammunition.

Section 21 generally provides that any person who has been sentenced to:

- custody for *life*, or
- to preventive detention, imprisonment, corrective training, youth custody or detention in a young offender institution for *three years or more*

must not, *at any time*, have a firearm or ammunition in his/her possession, i.e. a life-time ban.

Section 21 goes on to provide that any person who has been sentenced to imprisonment, youth custody, detention in a young offender institution or a secure training order for *three months or more, but less than three years*, must not have a firearm or ammunition in his/her possession at any time before the end of a five-year period beginning on the date of his/her release.

Date of release means, for a sentence partly served and partly suspended, the date on which the offender completes the part to be served and, in the case of a person subject to a secure training order, the date on which he/she is released from detention (under the various relevant statutes) or the date halfway through the total specified by the court making the order, whichever is the latest (s. 21(2A)).

A person holding a licence under the Children and Young Persons Act 1933 or a person subject to a recognisance to keep the peace or be of good behaviour with a condition relating to the possession of firearms, must not, *at any time during the licence or the recognisance*, have a firearm or ammunition in his/her possession (s. 21(3)).

Where sentences or court orders are mentioned, their Scottish equivalents will also apply and a person prohibited in Northern Ireland from possessing a firearm/ammunition will also be prohibited in Great Britain (s. 21(3A)).

Section 21 *does not apply to imitation firearms* as there is no express reference to them in the section and because the reference in the Firearms Act 1982 does not apply.

1.7.11.1 Supplying Firearm to Person Prohibited by Section 21

OFFENCE: **Selling or Transferring Firearm to Person Prohibited by s. 21—** *Firearms Act 1968, s. 21(5)*

- Triable either way • Five years' imprisonment and/or a fine on indictment
- Six months' imprisonment and/or a fine summarily

The Firearms Act 1968, s. 21 states:

(5) It is an offence for a person to sell or transfer a firearm or ammunition to, or to repair, test or prove a firearm or ammunition for, a person whom he knows or has reasonable ground for believing to be prohibited by this section from having a firearm or ammunition in his possession.

KEYNOTE

Given that all people are presumed to know the law once it is published, it would seem that the knowledge or belief by the defendant would apply to the *convictions* of the other person, not the fact that possession by that person was an offence.

What you must show is knowledge by the defendant or at least *reasonable ground for believing*; this latter requirement is stronger than mere cause to *suspect*.

1.7.12 Other Restrictions on Possession or Acquisition

Sections 22 to 24 of the Firearms Act 1968 creates a number of summary offences restricting the involvement of people of various ages in their dealings with certain types of firearm and ammunition.

In summary the age restrictions are as follows:

- a person under 18:
  - ✦ must not purchase or hire an air weapon or ammunition for an air weapon (s. 22(1)(a));
  - ✦ must not have with him/her an air weapon or ammunition for an air weapon (s. 22(4)). An exception to this is where the person is under the supervision of another who is at least 21 years old. However, if the person under 18 fires the weapon beyond the relevant premises, he/she will commit an offence under s. 21A (**see para. 1.7.7.1**) and the person supervising him/her will be guilty of an offence under s. 23(1). Generally it is not an offence under this section for a person aged 14 or over to have with him/her an air weapon or ammunition on private premises with the consent of the occupier (s. 23(3));
  - ✦ it is an offence to sell or let on hire an air weapon or ammunition for an air weapon to a person under the age of 18 (s. 24(1)(a)), or to make a gift/part with possession of an air weapon or ammunition for an air weapon to such a person (unless under the permitted circumstances above) (s. 24(4));
  - ✦ it is an offence to sell an imitation firearm to a person under the age of 18 (s. 24A(2)), or for a person under 18 to purchase one (s. 24A(1)). It is a defence to show that the vendor believed that the purchaser was 18 or over and had reasonable grounds for that belief (s. 24A(3));
- a person under 17:
  - ✦ must not purchase or hire any firearm or ammunition (s. 22(1)(b)); or
  - ✦ it is an offence to sell or let on hire to a person under 17 any firearm or ammunition (s. 24(1)(b));
- a person under 15:
  - ✦ must not have with him/her an assembled shotgun unless supervised by a person aged at least 21 or while the shotgun is securely covered so it cannot be fired (s. 22(3)); and
  - ✦ it is an offence to make a gift of a shotgun/ammunition to such a person (s. 24(3));
- a person under 14:
  - ✦ must not have in his/her possession a section 1 firearm or ammunition (s. 22(2)); and
  - ✦ it is an offence to make a gift/part with possession of such a firearm/ammunition to such a person (s. 24(2)) (subject to some exceptions relating to sports and shooting clubs—see s. 11 of the Firearms Act 1968 and s. 15 of the Firearms (Amendment) Act 1988).

There is a further provision creating an offence for a person under 18 who is the holder of a certificate using a firearm for a purpose not authorised by the European Weapons Directive (s. 22(1A)).

KEYNOTE

For the full extent of these restrictions and their exemptions, reference should be made to the 1968 and 1988 Acts. Note that s. 24(5) of the Firearms Act 1968 provides that it is a defence to prove that the person charged with an offence believed that other person to be of or over the age mentioned and had reasonable grounds for the belief.

It is a summary offence (punishable by one month's imprisonment and/or a fine) to be in possession of *any* loaded firearm when drunk (s. 12 of the Licensing Act 1872). There is no requirement that the person be in a public place.

1.7.13 Police Powers

The Firearms Act 1968, s. 47 states:

(1) A constable may require any person whom he has reasonable cause to suspect—
   (a) of having a firearm, with or without ammunition, with him in a public place; or
   (b) to be committing or about to commit, elsewhere than in a public place, an offence relevant for the purposes of this section,
   to hand over the firearm or any ammunition for examination by the constable.

KEYNOTE

An 'offence relevant to this section' appears to be:

- an offence of having a firearm with intent to commit an indictable offence or resist arrest (contrary to s. 18(1)); or
- an offence of trespassing with a firearm (contrary to s. 20).

It is a summary offence to fail to hand over a firearm when required under this section (s. 47(2)).

In order to exercise this power, a police officer may search the person and may detain him/her for that purpose (s. 47(3)). The officer may also enter *any place* (s. 47(5)).

If the officer has reasonable cause to suspect that:

- there is a firearm in a vehicle in a public place, or
- a vehicle is being/about to be used in connection with the commission of an 'offence relevant to this section' (see above)

he/she may search the vehicle and, for that purpose, may require the person driving or in control of the vehicle to stop it (s. 47(4)).

The provisions of the PACE Codes of Practice, Code A, will apply to the exercise of these powers of stop and search (see General Police Duties, appendix 4.1).

1.7.13.1 Power to Demand Documentation

The Firearms Act 1968, s. 48 states:

(1) A constable may demand, from any person whom he believes to be in possession of a firearm or ammunition to which section 1 of this Act applies, or of a shot gun, the production of his firearm certificate or, as the case may be, his shot gun certificate.

KEYNOTE

The demand for the relevant documentation may be made where the police officer 'believes' that a person is in possession of a section 1 firearm or ammunition or a shotgun. There is no requirement that the officer's belief be reasonable.

Where the person fails to:

- produce the relevant certificate or
- show that he/she is not entitled to be issued with such a certificate or
- show that he/she is in possession of the firearm exclusively in connection with recognised purposes (collecting/historical/cultural) under the law of another EU Member State

the officer may demand the production of the relevant valid documentation issued in another Member State under any corresponding provisions (s. 48(1A)).

Failing to produce any of the required documents *and* to let the officer read it, or failing to show an entitlement to possess the firearm or ammunition initiates the power of seizure under s. 48(2). It also gives the officer the power to demand the person's name and address.

If the person refuses to give his/her name or address or gives a false name and address, he/she commits a summary offence (s. 48(3)).

A person from another Member State who is in possession of a firearm and who fails to comply with a demand under s. 48(1A) also commits a separate summary offence (s. 48(4)).

1.7.14 Imitation Firearm Offences

OFFENCE: Converting Imitation Firearm—*Firearms Act 1968, s. 4(3)*

- Triable either way • Five years' imprisonment and/or a fine on indictment
- Six months' imprisonment and/or a fine summarily

The Firearms Act 1968, s. 4 states:

(3) It is an offence for a person other than a registered firearms dealer to convert into a firearm anything which, though having the appearance of being a firearm, is so constructed as to be incapable of discharging any missile through its barrel.

KEYNOTE

This offence involves the conversion of anything which has the appearance of a firearm so that it can be fired. Registered firearms dealers are excluded from the offence. Once the conversion has taken place, the nature of the imitation firearm will have changed, in which case the person will also commit the relevant possession offences unless he/she has appropriate authorisation.

Sections 36 to 41 of the Violent Crime Reduction Act 2006 introduced measures to deal with the misuse of firearms. These sections created the three specific summary offences detailed below.

Section 36 makes it an offence to manufacture, import or sell *realistic imitation firearms* as defined in s. 38.

Section 39 makes it an offence to manufacture, modify or import an imitation firearm that does not conform to specifications set out in regulations to be made by the Secretary of State.

Section 40 inserted a new s. 24A into the 1968 Act and makes it an offence to sell an imitation firearm to a person under 18. It also makes it an offence for a person under 18 to purchase an imitation firearm.

KEYNOTE

For the purposes of the 2006 Act, an 'imitation firearm' is defined as that used in the Firearms Act 1968, i.e. in the 'general sense' (see para. 1.7.2.4). A 'realistic imitation firearm' is effectively a 'sub-category' of an imitation firearm in the general sense. A 'realistic imitation firearm' is defined as an imitation firearm which has an appearance that is so realistic as to make it indistinguishable, for all practical purposes, from a real firearm and is neither a deactivated firearm nor itself an antique (s. 38(1)).

An imitation firearm will be regarded as distinguishable if its size, shape or principal colour is unrealistic for a real firearm (s. 38(3)). The Violent Crime Reduction Act 2006 (Realistic Imitation Firearms) Regulations 2007 (SI 2007/2606) provide defences for an offence under s. 36, and make provision in connection with the definition of 'realistic imitation firearm' in s. 38, specifying the sizes and colours which are to be regarded as unrealistic for a real firearm.

1.7.15 Restrictions on Transfer of Firearms

The Firearms (Amendment) Act 1997 created a number of offences concerned with the transfer, lending, hiring etc. of firearms and ammunition.

In brief, a person 'transferring' (that is, selling, letting on hire, lending or giving) a section 1 firearm or ammunition to another must:

- produce a certificate or permit entitling him/her to do so (s. 32(2)(a)),
- he/she must comply with all the conditions of that certificate or permit (s. 32(2)(b)), and
- the transferor must personally hand the firearm or ammunition over to the receiver (s. 32(2)(c)).

The 1997 Act also requires that any person who is the holder of a certificate or permit who is involved in such a transfer (which includes lending a shotgun for a period of more than 72 hours) shall within seven days of the transfer give notice to the chief officer of police who granted the certificate or permit (s. 33(2)).

Notice is also required of certificate or permit holders where a firearm is lost, deactivated or destroyed or where ammunition is lost, or where firearms are sold outside Great Britain (see ss. 34 and 35).

OFFENCE: **Failing to Comply with Requirements—*Firearms (Amendment) Act 1997, ss. 32 to 35***

- Section 1 firearm/ammunition: triable either way • Five years' imprisonment and/or a fine on indictment; six months' imprisonment and/or a fine summarily • Shotguns: triable summarily • Six months' imprisonment and/or a fine

OFFENCE: **Trade Transactions by Person not Registered as Firearms Dealer—*Firearms Act 1968, s. 3(1)***

- Triable either way • Five years' imprisonment and/or a fine on indictment
- Six months' imprisonment and/or a fine summarily

The Firearms Act 1968, s. 3 states:

(1) A person commits an offence if, by way of trade or business, he—

    (a) manufactures, sells, transfers, repairs, tests or proves any firearm or ammunition to which section 1 of this Act applies, or a shot gun;

    (b) exposes for sale or transfer, or has in his possession for sale, transfer, repair, test or proof any such firearm or ammunition, or a shot gun, or

    (c) sells or transfers an air weapon, exposes such a weapon for sale or transfer or has such a weapon in his possession for sale or transfer,

without being registered under this Act as a firearms dealer.

KEYNOTE

A registered firearms dealer is a person who, by way of trade or business, manufactures, sells, transfers, repairs, tests or proves firearms or ammunition to which s. 1 of this Act applies, or shotguns, or sells or transfers air weapons.

If the person undertakes the repair, proofing etc. of a section 1 firearm or ammunition or a shotgun otherwise than as a trade or business, he/she commits an offence (carrying the same punishment as the s. 3(1) offence above) under s. 3(3) unless he/she can point to some authorisation under the Act allowing him/her to do so.

Section 3 goes on to create further either way offences of selling or transferring a firearm or ammunition to someone other than a registered firearms dealer or someone otherwise authorised under the Act to buy or acquire them and of falsifying certificates with a view to acquiring firearms. These offences also carry the same punishment as the s. 3(1) offence above.

Registration is under s. 33 of the 1968 Act.

'Transferring' is also defined under s. 57(4) and includes letting on hire, giving, lending and parting with possession.

Section 9(2) of the 1968 Act exempts auctioneers from the restrictions on selling and possessing for the purposes of sale of firearms and ammunition where the auctioneer has a permit from the chief officer of police. There are further defences provided by s. 9 (for carriers and warehouse staff) and also under s. 8 (transfer to people authorised to possess firearms without a certificate).

1.8 | Non-Fatal Offences Against the Person

1.8.1 Introduction

Non-fatal offences against others cover a wide range of behaviour from a raised fist to a calculated wounding. The importance of this subject lies not only in the number of occasions when officers will need to refer to it, but also because it deals with violence and the fear of violent crime—areas in which victims are particularly traumatised. As courts are being urged to focus on the effects of a defendant's conduct upon their victim, the scope for bringing a charge of assault is widening.

1.8.2 Key Issues

While there are several distinct categories of offence that can be committed against other people, there are some features that are important for both understanding the law and the practical application of it. These key issues are set out below.

1.8.2.1 Assault and Battery

Assault and battery are, strictly speaking, two separate things. What people generally think of as being an 'assault' (e.g. a punch on the nose) is a 'battery', that is, the infliction of unlawful force on someone else. While it would cover a punch on the nose, an 'assault' in its proper legal sense has a much wider meaning and includes any act whereby the defendant 'intentionally—or recklessly—causes another person to apprehend immediate and unlawful personal violence' (*Fagan* v *Metropolitan Police Commissioner* [1969] 1 QB 439).

1.8.2.2 Assault or Battery?

Although these terms—assault and battery—have distinct legal meanings they are often referred to as simply 'assaults' or 'common assault'. It is, however, important to separate the two expressions when charging or laying an information against a defendant as to include both may be bad for duplicity (*DPP* v *Taylor* [1992] QB 645).

The term battery, or the application of 'force', creates a misleading impression as a very small degree of physical contact will be enough. That force can be applied directly or indirectly. For example, where a defendant punched a woman causing her to drop and injure a child she was holding, he was convicted of assaulting that child (*Haystead* v *Chief Constable of Derbyshire* [2000] 3 All ER 890). The *actus reus* needed to prove an assault is an act which caused the victim to apprehend the immediate infliction of unlawful force, although 'apprehension' does not mean 'fear' and there is no need to show that the victim was actually in fear. The force or violence apprehended by the victim does not have to be a 'certainty'. Causing a fear of some possible violence can be enough (see *R* v *Ireland* [1998] AC 147) provided that the violence feared is about to happen in the immediate future (see *R* v *Constanza* [1997] 2 Cr App R 492).

There is some academic debate as to whether battery and assault are still common law offences or whether they are now statutory offences. What is clear is that s. 39 of the Criminal Justice Act 1988 stipulates that they must be tried summarily and sets out the maximum penalty that may be imposed (**see para. 1.8.3**).

While some offences can be committed by an act or an *omission* (e.g. manslaughter (**see chapter 1.5**)) for a charge of assault to succeed there must be an *act* (*Fagan*).

It also is important to remember that the state of mind of the *victim* in an assault is relevant to the *actus reus*. The victim must apprehend the immediate use of unlawful force. For these reasons, if a defendant threatened someone with an imitation pistol, he/she could still be charged with assault provided the victim *believed* that the pistol was real—the defendant had caused an apprehension of possible immediate force being used (*Logdon* v *DPP* [1976] Crim LR 121).

Words can amount to an assault provided they are accompanied by the required *mens rea*. This was made clear by the decision in *R* v *Ireland* [1998] AC 147 where it was held that telephone calls to a victim, followed by silences, could amount to an assault. In *Ireland*, the House of Lords accepted that '*a thing said is also a thing done*' and rejected the view that words can never amount to an assault. *Ireland* involved the making of threatening telephone calls which led the victims to fear that unlawful force would be used against them. The House of Lords accepted that, in such cases, even *silence* could fulfil the requirements for the *actus reus* of assault if it brought about the desired consequences (e.g. fear of the immediate use of unlawful force).

Where the words threatening immediate unlawful force come in the form of letters, the Court of Appeal has held that an assault may have been committed (see *Constanza* above).

1.8.2.3 Conditional Threats

As well as constituting an assault, words can also *negate* an assault if they make a conditional threat, e.g., where you attend an incident and one person says to another '*If these officers weren't here I'd chin you!*' (*Tuberville* v *Savage* (1669) 1 Mod R3). In this type of case the defendant is making a *hypothetical* threat and is really saying 'if it weren't for the existence of certain circumstances, I would assault you'. This should be contrasted with occasions where the defendant makes an immediate threat conditional upon some real circumstance, e.g. '*If you don't cross the road, I'll break your neck*'. Such threats have been held, in a civil case, to amount to an assault (*Read* v *Coker* (1853) 13 CB 850).

1.8.2.4 What is 'Immediate'?

Although the force threatened must be immediate, that immediacy is—like most legal interpretation—somewhat elastic. Courts have accepted that, where a person makes a threat from outside a victim's house to the victim who is inside, an assault is still committed even though there will be some time lapse before the defendant can carry out the threat.

In *Ireland* the House of Lords suggested that a threat to cause violence 'in a minute or two' might be enough to qualify as an assault. The victim must be shown to have feared the use of *force*; it will not be enough to show that a person threatened by words—or silence—feared more calls or letters. The fear of force is the key to assault.

1.8.2.5   **Intentionally or Recklessly**

The *mens rea* needed to prove common assault is either:

- an intention to cause apprehension of immediate unlawful violence, or
- subjective recklessness (i.e. foresight) as to that consequence.

When considering the *mens rea of* any assault, it is important to separate the assault or battery from *any further consequences caused by* that assault or battery. The *mens rea* needed for the assault/battery is set out above. If a defendant's behaviour causes another to fear immediate and unlawful personal violence, he/she commits an 'assault' provided it can be shown that, at the time, the defendant *intended* to cause that fear or was *subjectively reckless* as to whether such a fear would result from his/her actions.

So what happens where the defendant's actions cause more than just fear; they cause more serious injury? This appears to depend on the extent of the injury and the wording of the offence charged. Among the more serious offences under the Offences Against the Person Act 1861 are causing 'actual bodily harm' (s. 47) and 'wounding' or inflicting/causing 'grievous bodily harm' (ss. 18 and 20). The *mens rea* required for an offence under s. 47, causing actual bodily harm, is the same as that required for the basic offence of assault (*R* v *Savage* [1992] 1 AC 699). This is because s. 47 makes no specific requirement for any greater degree of *mens rea* by the defendant and, in effect, the offence of causing actual bodily harm becomes simply an assault or battery with a more serious outcome. From the defendant's point of view this is really pot luck because there is no requirement for him/her to have intended or even foreseen the actual bodily harm. In the case of woundings and grievous bodily harm, the situation is different because ss. 18 and 20 use the word 'maliciously'. This element introduces the element of intention or subjective recklessness *in relation to the injuries suffered by the victim* (*Savage* above), thereby adding a further requirement to the *mens rea.*

....

EXAMPLE

Two people in a pub are arguing. One person, the defendant, threatens to throw a pint of beer over the other, the victim. At this point the defendant has caused the victim to fear that immediate unlawful personal violence will be used against him—an 'assault'. In order to prove an offence of assault under the Criminal Justice Act 1988, you must show that, at the time of the threat, the defendant either intended to cause the fear of violence or was subjectively reckless in that regard. If such an intention or recklessness cannot be shown, there is no offence of assault.

After the threat, a third person pushes past the defendant, accidentally knocking him into the victim and spilling the beer over him. At this point there has been no 'assault' by the defendant because there has been no *actus reus* (voluntary conduct) by him, irrespective of his intentions.

The defendant continues to argue and then raises his glass and throws the contents over the victim. Clearly there has now been a voluntary application of unlawful force—a 'battery'—which the defendant intended to apply and he commits an offence under the Criminal Justice Act 1988. In the act of throwing the beer, however, the defendant's hand slips and he in fact hits the victim in the face with his beer glass causing a broken tooth. At this point the defendant's actions have gone beyond those intended by him and his victim has suffered injuries which the defendant had neither intended nor considered. Nevertheless, at the time of the assault (and battery) the defendant had the required *mens rea* for the assault/battery and therefore is liable for any actual bodily harm suffered by the victim as a result. Therefore the defendant commits the offence of assault occasioning actual bodily harm under s. 47 of the Offences Against the Person Act 1861, even though he neither intended nor considered the injuries to his victim.

Having a small amount of beer left in the glass, the defendant flicks the 'dregs' from the glass at the victim. The defendant loses his grip on the glass and it flies from his hand, hitting the victim in the eye and breaking on impact. The victim suffers a deep wound to the eye. Although the defendant is still liable for any actual bodily harm, he can only be liable for the more serious offences of wounding and causing/inflicting *grievous* bodily harm if it can be shown that he acted 'maliciously'. Malice for these purposes means that he must have intended to cause the harm or realised that there was a risk of at least *some harm* being suffered by the victim. If he did realise that the victim was at risk of being harmed by his actions, the defendant may be liable for an offence under s. 20 of the Offences Against the Person Act 1861. If it can be shown that he intended to bring about *serious* harm, the defendant may be liable for the offence under s. 18 of the 1861 Act.

If the victim goes on to die from the injury, the defendant would be guilty of murder, or manslaughter by unlawful or dangerous act, depending on the level of *mens rea*.

Given the requirements for *mens rea*, together with the respective penalties, it is not surprising that charges of 'actual bodily harm' might be preferred over charges of malicious wounding or inflicting grievous bodily harm.

....

1.8.2.6 ## Consent

A key element in proving an assault is the *unlawfulness* of the force used or threatened. Although the courts have accepted consent as a feature which negatives any offence, they have been reluctant to accept this feature in a number of notable cases.

Consent to Sado-masochistic Injuries

These cases have developed as a question of public policy and were summarised in the House of Lords in the so-called 'spanner trial' (*R* v *Brown* [1994] 1 AC 212).

That case involved members of a sado-masochist group who inflicted varying degrees of injuries on one another for their own gratification. Charged with many offences against the person, the group claimed that they had consented to the injuries and therefore no assault or battery had taken place. Their lordships followed an earlier policy that *all assaults which result in more than transient harm will be unlawful unless there is good reason for allowing the plea of 'consent'*. Good reason will be determined in the light of a number of considerations:

- the practical consequences of the behaviour
- the dangerousness of the behaviour
- the vulnerability of the 'consenting' person.

Further difficulties in clarifying what will amount to 'true' or effective consent were added by the decision of the Court of Appeal in *R* v *Wilson* [1997] QB 47. In that case the court accepted that a husband might lawfully brand his initials on his wife's buttocks with a hot knife provided she consented (as she appeared to have done). The reasoning behind the judgment seems to be based on the fact that the branding was similar to a form of tattooing (see below), but also on the policy grounds that consensual activity between husband and wife is not a matter for criminal investigation. This causes several problems, not least of which is the fact that sado-masochistic 'branding' was denounced by the House of Lords in *Brown* above. Therefore, if a situation arose where a husband and wife took part in mutual branding in the privacy of their home, their criminal liability would arguably depend on whether they caused the harm for purposes of sado-masochistic pleasure or out of some affectionate wish to be permanently adorned with the mark of their loved one. It is also unclear how far the policy aspect of the decision in *Wilson* would extend and whether or not it would encompass unmarried or homosexual couples.

Sado-masochistic injury may justifiably be made the subject of criminal law on grounds of the 'protection of health'. It was for this reason that the European Court of Human Rights held that there had been no violation of the defendants' right to private life (under Article 8) in the *Brown* case above.

Legitimate Consent to Risk of Injury

Clearly there are times when a person may consent to even serious harm such as during properly conducted sporting events (see *Attorney-General's Reference (No. 6 of 1980)* [1981] QB 715), tattooing and medical operations. Where the activity falls outside those parameters, such as an off-the-ball incident in a football match (*R v Lloyd* (1989) 11 Cr App R (S) 36) or an unauthorised prize fight, the plea of consent will not apply. However, the Court of Appeal has stated that the criminal prosecution of those who inflict injury on another in the course of a sporting event is reserved for those situations where the conduct was sufficiently grave to be properly categorised as criminal—*R v Barnes* [2004] EWCA Crim 3246. In that case the defendant appealed against his conviction for inflicting grievous bodily harm after he caused a serious leg injury by way of a tackle during a football match. The tackle took place after the victim had kicked the ball into the goal but, while accepting that the tackle was hard, the defendant maintained that it had been a fair challenge and that the injury caused was accidental. The court held that where injuries were sustained in the course of contact sports, public policy limited the availability of the defence of consent to situations where there had been implicit consent to what had occurred. Whether conduct reached the required threshold to be treated as 'criminal' would depend on all the circumstances. The fact that the actions of the defendant had been within the rules and practice of the game would be a firm indication that what had occurred was not criminal, although in highly competitive sports even conduct *outside the rules* could be expected to occur in the heat of the moment, and such conduct still might not reach the threshold level required for it to be criminal. The court held that the threshold level was an objective one to be determined by the type of sport, the level at which it was played, the nature of the 'act', the degree of force used, the extent of the risk of injury and the state of mind of the defendant.

Other more straightforward policy considerations would include the implied consent by people getting on to crowded tube trains or moving around at a packed concert venue. In these cases it will be a matter of fact to decide whether the behaviour complained of went beyond what was acceptable in those particular circumstances.

What of the situation where the consent of the victim has been obtained by fraud? In *R v Richardson* [1999] QB 444 a dentist (Diane Richardson), who had been suspended by the General Dental Council, continued practising dentistry. The suspension came to light and charges of assault were brought. Although initially convicted, the Court of Appeal quashed the conviction on the basis that fraud will only negate consent if it relates to the identity of the person or to the nature and quality of the act. Richardson did not lie about her identity (identity here does not relate to qualifications) nor about the nature and quality of the act (the dentistry carried out). While her behaviour was reprehensible, it did not amount to an offence. This does not mean that a person without appropriate qualifications sneaking into a surgery and putting on a white coat and calling themselves 'Doctor' followed by their true name could avoid liability. While there is plainly no fraud as to identity, any treatment carried out would certainly be caught by a fraud in respect of the nature and quality of the act. Consent would also be negated if a genuine doctor indecently touched his patients on the basis that this was part of a routine medical examination when its true purpose was for sexual gratification (see *R* v *Tabassum* [2000] 2 Cr App R 328).

1.8.2.7 Lawful Chastisement

For many years the common and statute law allowed for those acting in *loco parentis* (meaning in place of the parent) of a child to be able to use reasonable force in controlling the behaviour of that child. What was 'reasonable' varied widely and became increasingly difficult to define let alone justify given the breadth and depth of social attitudes and conventions within England and Wales. Legislation has assisted to define the boundaries of lawful chastisement as a defence to assault offences.

The School Standards and Framework Act 1998 outlaws corporal punishment in *all* British schools, although staff may use reasonable force in restraining violent or disruptive pupils. The Divisional Court has held that this legislation removes entirely the defence of lawful chastisement from any teacher when they are acting as such (*Williamson* v *Secretary of State for Education and Employment* [2001] EWHC Admin 960, later affirmed by the House of Lords [2005] UKHL 15). The legislation gave effect to a clear parliamentary intention to abolish corporal punishment in *all* schools, *including independent schools*, and did not infringe the human rights of any of the claimants.

Section 58 of the Children Act 2004 removes the defence of lawful chastisement for parents or adults acting *in loco parentis* where the accused person is charged with assault occasioning actual bodily harm (s. 47 of the Offences Against the Person Act 1861), wounding or causing grievous bodily harm (s. 18 or 20 of the Offences Against the Person Act 1861) or child cruelty (s. 1 of the Children and Young Persons Act 1933) to persons less than 16 years of age. However, the lawful chastisement defence remains available for parents and adults acting *in loco parentis* charged with common assault under s. 39 of the Criminal Justice Act 1988. CPS charging standards state that if an injury to a child amounts to no more than reddening of the skin, and the injury is transient and trifling, a charge of common assault may be laid against the defendant for whom the lawful chastisement defence remains available. Whether the actions of the defendant are 'reasonable' will be important; physical punishment where a child is hit (causing injury reddening to the skin) with an implement such as a cane or a belt may well be considered 'unreasonable'. It is important to note that the law does not rule out physical chastisement by a parent etc. but that chastisement should only constitute 'mild smacking' rather than cause injuries subject to assault charges. At the present time the Government has ruled out a complete ban on smacking.

1.8.3 Offences

Having considered the key common elements in this area, the specific offences are set out below.

1.8.3.1 Common Assault and Battery

OFFENCE: **Common Assault/Battery—*Criminal Justice Act 1988, s. 39***
- Triable summarily • Six months' imprisonment

OFFENCE: **Racially or Religiously Aggravated—*Crime and Disorder Act 1998, s. 29(1)(c)***
- Triable either way • Two years' imprisonment and/or a fine on indictment
- Six months' imprisonment and/or a fine summarily

KEYNOTE

The racially or religiously aggravated offence can be tried on indictment without having to be included alongside another indictable offence as is the case with common assaults generally (see s. 40 of the Criminal Justice Act 1988).

The Divisional Court has held that the words 'white man's arse licker' and 'brown Englishman' when used to accompany an assault on an Asian victim did not necessarily make the assault 'racially aggravated' and that the prosecution had not done enough to show that the assailants' behaviour fell under the definition set out in s. 28 of the 1998 Act (*DPP* v *Pal* [2000] Crim LR 756).

For a full explanation of the meaning of 'racially or religiously aggravated', see General Police Duties, chapter 4.9.

Under the racially and religiously aggravated public order offences the courts have held that police officers are entitled to the same protection under the legislation as anyone else (see *R* v *Jacobs* [2001] 2 Cr App R (S) 38) and the same principle ought to apply to physical assault.

CPS Charging Standards state that a charge under s. 39 of the Act will be appropriate where injuries amount to no more than the following:

- grazes
- scratches
- abrasions
- minor bruising
- swelling
- reddening of the skin
- superficial cuts
- a 'black eye'

The injury sustained by the victim should always be considered first, and in most cases the degree of injury will determine whether the appropriate charge is an assault under s. 39 of the Act or a more serious assault under s. 47 of the Offences Against the Person Act 1861. There will be borderline cases, such as where an undisplaced broken nose has resulted. Generally, where injuries amount to no more than those described above, common assault will be the appropriate charge.

1.8.3.2 Assault with Intent to Resist Arrest

OFFENCE: **Assault with Intent to Resist Arrest—*Offences Against the Person Act 1861, s. 38***

- Triable either way • Two years' imprisonment

The Offences Against the Person Act 1861, s. 38 states:

> Whosoever ... shall assault any person with intent to resist or prevent the lawful apprehension or detainer of himself or of any other person for any offence, shall be guilty of a misdemeanour ...

KEYNOTE

It must be shown that the defendant intended to resist or prevent a lawful arrest. It must also be shown that the arrest was lawful (*R* v *Self* [1992] 3 All ER 476; *R* v *Lee* [2001] 1 Cr App R 293). Provided they were acting within their powers, this offence can apply to arrests made, not only by police officers, but also by store detectives, Benefits Agency staff and custody assistants.

Once the lawfulness of the arrest is established, the state of mind necessary for the above offence is that required for a common assault coupled with an intention to resist/prevent that arrest. It is irrelevant whether or not the person being arrested had actually committed an offence. These principles were set out by the Court of Appeal in a case where the defendant mistakenly believed that the arresting officers had no lawful power to do so. The court held that such a mistaken belief does not provide a defendant with the defence of 'mistake'. Similarly, a belief in one's own innocence, however genuine or honestly held, cannot afford a defence to a charge under s. 38 (above).

1.8.3.3 Assaults on Police

There is an offence which deals specifically with assaults on police officers and those assisting them.

OFFENCE: **Assault Police—*Police Act 1996, s. 89***
- Triable summarily • Six months' imprisonment and/or a fine

The Police Act 1996, s. 89 states:

(1) Any person who assaults a constable in the execution of his duty, or a person assisting a constable in the execution of his duty, shall be guilty of an offence...

KEYNOTE

It is critical to this offence that the officer was acting in the execution of his/her duty when assaulted. Given the almost infinite variety of situations that police officers may find themselves in, it is difficult to define the precise boundaries of the execution of their duty. There have been many instances of officers being assaulted after entering premises as technical 'trespassers' or not following statutory or common law requirements when stopping and questioning people. If it is not proved that the constable was in the execution of his/her duty then part of the *actus reus* will be missing. However, a court may infer from all the circumstances that an officer was in fact acting in the execution of his/her duty (*Plowden* v *DPP* [1991] Crim LR 850).

Where the assault is made in reaction to some form of physical act by the officer, it must be shown that the officer's act was not in itself unlawful. A good example comes from *R (On the Application of Hawkes)* v *DPP* [2005] EWHC 3046 (Admin).

In this case, the defendant was convicted of assaulting a police officer in the execution of his duty after the police had gone to her home address to arrest her son. The defendant followed her son into the police vehicle and refused to get out. She was given a warning and was verbally abusive, and only got out of the car when a second one arrived. She started to walk towards her house at which point a police officer took hold of her arms. The defendant bit the police officer on the arm and was prosecuted on the basis that the police officer had arrested her for a breach of the peace and that the assault had occurred in the execution of that duty. Allowing her appeal, the Divisional Court held that the defendant had exhibited nothing more than an aggressive manner and that, while her conduct may have given rise to an imminent threat of violence, there was no evidence to suggest that it involved any violence justifying the conclusion that she had actually committed a breach of the peace in the presence of the police officer. In the circumstances, her arrest had been unlawful and the conviction for assaulting a police officer in the execution of his duty could not stand.

Although the common law complaint of breach of the peace still exists where appropriate, the question of the lawfulness of any arrest will become even more important to this offence in light of s. 24 of the Police and Criminal Evidence Act 1984. Other than the powers of arrest and detention, police officers have no general power to take hold of people in order to question them or keep them at a particular place while background enquiries are made about them. Therefore, if an officer does hold someone by the arm in order to question them without arresting them, there may well be a 'battery' by that officer (*Collins* v *Wilcock* [1984] 1 WLR 1172). The courts have accepted, however, that there may be occasions where a police officer is justified in taking hold of a person to attract their attention or to calm them down (*Mepstead* v *DPP* (1996) 160 JP 475).

However, where a prisoner is arrested and brought before a custody officer, that officer is entitled to assume that the arrest has been lawful. Therefore, if the prisoner goes on to assault the custody officer, that assault will nevertheless be an offence under s. 89(1) even if the original arrest turns out to have been unlawful (*DPP* v *L* [1999] Crim LR 752).

There is no need to show that the defendant knew—or suspected—that the person was in fact a police officer or that he/she was acting in the lawful execution of his/her duty (*Blackburn* v *Bowering* [1994] 1 WLR 1324). However, if the defendant claims to have been acting in self-defence under the mistaken and honestly held belief that he/she was being attacked, there may not be sufficient *mens rea* for a charge of assault.

These offences are simply a form of common assault upon someone carrying out a lawful function. There is a further offence which deals with behaviour not amounting to an actual assault. A similar offence exists in respect of assaulting designated or accredited persons (s. 46(1) of the Police Reform Act 2002).

1.8.3.4 Obstructing a Police Officer

OFFENCE: **Obstruct Police—*Police Act 1996, s. 89***
- Triable summarily • One month's imprisonment and/or a fine

The Police Act 1996, s. 89 states:

(2) Any person who resists or wilfully obstructs a constable in the execution of his duty, or a person assisting a constable in the execution of his duty, shall be guilty of an offence...

KEYNOTE

Resistance suggests some form of physical opposition; obstruction does not and may take many forms, for instance, warning other drivers of a speed check operation (*Betts* v *Stevens* [1910] 1KB 1)—note that the persons warned about the speed check must be actually committing or about to commit the speeding offence, providing misleading information (*Ledger* v *DPP* [1991] Crim LR 439), deliberately drinking alcohol before providing a breath specimen (*Ingleton* v *Dibble* [1972] 1 QB 480), or 'tipping off' people who were about to commit an offence (*Green* v *Moore* [1982] QB 1044). Obstruction has been interpreted as making it more difficult for a constable to carry out his/her duty (*Hinchcliffe* v *Sheldon* [1955] 1 WLR 1207). Refusing to answer an officer's questions is not obstruction (*Rice* v *Connolly* [1966] 2 QB 414)—unless perhaps the defendant was under some duty to provide information. Any obstruction must be *wilful*, that is the defendant must intend to do it. The obstruction will not be 'wilful' if the defendant was simply trying to help the police, even if that help turned out to be more of a hindrance (*Willmot* v *Atack* [1977] QB 498).

Obstruction can be caused by omission but only where the defendant was already under some duty towards the police or the officer. There is also a common law offence of refusing to go to the aid of a constable when asked to do so in order to prevent or diminish a breach of the peace (*R* v *Waugh* (1986) *The Times*, 1 October).

A similar offence exists in respect of obstructing designated or accredited persons (s. 46(2) of the Police Reform Act 2002).

1.8.4 Assaults on Providers of Emergency Services

The Emergency Workers (Obstruction) Act 2006 is designed to offer protection to persons outside the police (to members of the Fire Brigade and staff of the NHS, for example) who face an increasing and unacceptable amount of violence simply by carrying out their functions.

1.8.4.1 Obstructing or Hindering Emergency Workers

OFFENCE: **Obstructing or Hindering Certain Emergency Workers Responding to Emergency Circumstances—*Emergency Workers (Obstruction) Act 2006, s. 1***

- Triable summarily • Fine

The Emergency Workers (Obstruction) Act 2006, s. 1 states:

(1) A person who without reasonable excuse obstructs or hinders another while that other person is, in a capacity mentioned in subsection (2) below, responding to emergency circumstances, commits an offence.

(2) The capacity referred to in subsection (1) above is—
   (a) that of a person employed by a fire and rescue authority in England and Wales;
   (b) in relation to England and Wales, that of a person (other than a person falling within paragraph (a)) whose duties as an employee or as a servant of the Crown involve—
      (i) extinguishing fires; or
      (ii) protecting life and property in the event of a fire;
   (c) that of a person employed by a relevant NHS body in the provision of ambulance services (including air ambulance services), or of a person providing such services pursuant to arrangements made by, or at the request of, a relevant NHS body;
   (d) that of a person providing services for the transport of organs, blood, equipment or personnel pursuant to arrangements made by, or at the request of, a relevant NHS body;
   (e) that of a member of Her Majesty's Coastguard;
   (f) that of a member of the crew of a vessel operated by—
      (i) the Royal National Lifeboat Institution, or
      (ii) any other person or organisation operating a vessel for the purpose of providing a rescue service,
   or a person who musters the crew of such a vessel or attends to its launch or recovery.

KEYNOTE

It should be noted that these offences not only cover a wide variety of occupations within the emergency services but also cover those individuals as they respond to 'emergency circumstances' by:

- going anywhere for the purpose of dealing with emergency circumstances occurring there; or
- dealing with emergency circumstances or preparing to do so.

(s. 1(3)(a) and (b) of the Act)

Section 1(4) of the Act defines an 'emergency' circumstance as a present or imminent circumstance likely to cause:

(i) serious injury to or the serious injury (including mental illness) of a person;
(ii) serious harm to the environment (including the life and health of plants and animals);
(iii) serious harm to any building or other property; or
(iv) a worsening of any such injury, illness or harm;

or which is likely to cause the death of a person.

'Relevant NHS body' means (in relation to England and Wales) an NHS foundation trust, NHS trust, Special Health Authority, Primary Care Trust or Local Health Board. In relation to Northern Ireland the same phrase means a Health and Social Services trust or a Health and Social Services Board.

1.8.4.2 Obstructing or Hindering Persons Assisting Emergency Workers

OFFENCE: **Obstructing or Hindering Persons Assisting Emergency Workers— *Emergency Workers (Obstruction) Act 2006, s. 2***
- Triable summarily • Fine

The Emergency Workers (Obstruction) Act 2006, s. 2 states:

(1) A person who without reasonable excuse obstructs or hinders another in the circumstances described in subsection (2) below commits an offence.

(2) Those circumstances are where the person being obstructed or hindered is assisting another while that person is, in a capacity mentioned in section 1(2) of this Act, responding to emergency circumstances.

KEYNOTE

Section 3(1) states that a person may be convicted of an offence under ss. 1 and 2 of the Act notwithstanding that the act is effected by means other than physical means or is effected by action directed only at any vehicle, vessel, apparatus, equipment or other thing or any animal used or to be used by a person referred to in that section.

For the purposes of ss. 1 and 2 of the Act, circumstances to which a person is responding are to be taken to be emergency circumstances if the person believes and has reasonable grounds for believing they are or may be emergency circumstances (s. 3(2)).

1.8.5 Threats to Kill

OFFENCE: **Making a Threat to Kill—*Offences Against the Person Act 1861, s. 16***
- Triable either way • Ten years' imprisonment on indictment
- Six months' imprisonment and/or a fine summarily

The Offences Against the Person Act 1861, s. 16 (amended by Criminal Law Act 1977; s. 65, sch. 12) states:

A person who without lawful excuse makes to another a threat, intending that that other would fear it would be carried out, to kill that other or a third person shall be guilty of an offence . . .

KEYNOTE

The proviso that the threat must be made 'without lawful excuse' means that a person acting in self-defence or in the course of his/her duty in protecting life (e.g. an armed police officer) would not commit this offence (provided that his/her behaviour was 'lawful').

You must show that the threat was made (or implied (*R* v *Solanke* [1969] 3 All ER 1383)) with the intention that the person receiving it would fear that it would be carried out. It is the *intention* of the person who makes the threat which is important in this offence. It does not matter whether the person to whom the threat is made *does* fear that the threat would be carried out. The threat may be to kill another person at some time in the future or it may be an immediate threat, but the threatened action must be directly linked with the defendant. Simply passing on a threat on behalf of a third person without the necessary intent would be insufficient for this offence.

1.8.6 Offences Involving Significant or Lasting Injury

If an assailant causes any significant or lasting injury then one of the following offences may apply.

These offences—and the injuries they cause—can be committed in many different ways, with or without weapons or implements. In relation to injuries brought about by driving motor vehicles, although there is a specific offence of dangerous driving (**see Road Policing, para. 3.2.3**) the Court of Appeal has held that there is nothing wrong in principle in charging a driver with causing grievous bodily harm as well as dangerous driving in appropriate circumstances (*R v Bain* [2005] EWCA Crim 7). It follows that bringing about other forms of significant or lasting injury with a motor vehicle could be dealt with under the offences in this part of the chapter. However, in *Bain* it was held that where a driver was charged with both offences (causing grievous bodily harm and dangerous driving), a court could not impose consecutive terms of imprisonment for both offences arising out of the same incident.

1.8.6.1 Assault Occasioning Actual Bodily Harm

OFFENCE: **Assault Occasioning Actual Bodily Harm—*Offences Against the Person Act 1861, s. 47***
- Triable either way • Five years' imprisonment on indictment • Six months' imprisonment and/or a fine summarily

OFFENCE: **Racially or Religiously Aggravated—*Crime and Disorder Act 1998, s. 29(1)(b)***
- Triable either way • Seven years' imprisonment and/or a fine on indictment
- Six months' imprisonment and/or a fine summarily

The Offences Against the Person Act 1861, s. 47 states:

> Whosoever shall be convicted ... of any assault occasioning actual bodily harm shall be liable ... to be kept in penal servitude ...

KEYNOTE

It must be shown that 'actual bodily harm' was a consequence, directly or indirectly, of the defendant's actions. Such harm can include shock (*R v Miller* [1954] 2 QB 282) and mental 'injury' (*R v Chan-Fook* [1994] 1 WLR 689).

So what is 'actual bodily harm'? In *DPP v Smith* [1961] AC 290, it was noted that the expression needed 'no explanation' and, in *Chan-Fook*, the court advised that the phrase consisted of 'three words of the English language which require no elaboration and in the ordinary course should not receive any. While the phrase 'bodily harm' has its ordinary meaning, it has been said to include any hurt calculated to interfere with the health or comfort of the victim: such hurt need not be permanent, but must be more than transient and trifling (*R v Miller*, above).

The Administrative Court has accepted that a momentary loss of consciousness caused by a kick but without any physical injury can be 'actual harm' because it involved an injurious impairment of the victim's sensory abilities which did not fall within the 'trifling' category described in *Donovan* above (see *T* v *DPP* [2003] EWHC 266 (Admin)).

The state of mind required is the same as that for an assault or battery.

In an interesting decision the Divisional Court accepted that the cutting of a person's hair against their will could amount to actual bodily harm (*DPP* v *Smith (Ross Michael)* [2006] EWHC 94 (Admin)). In *Smith* the defendant cut off his ex-partner's ponytail, deliberately and without her permission. The court held that, even though medically and scientifically speaking, the hair above the surface of the scalp is no more than dead tissue, it remains part of the body and is attached to it. While it is so attached, it falls within the meaning of 'bodily' in the phrase 'actual bodily harm' as it is concerned with the body of the individual victim. Therefore the same would be true of fingernails.

Further examples of what will amount to 'actual bodily harm' can be found in the CPS Charging Standards and include:

- Loss or breaking of teeth
- Temporary loss of sensory functions, which may include loss of consciousness (*T* v *DPP* [2003] EWHC 266 (Admin))
- Extensive or multiple bruising
- Displaced broken nose
- Minor fractures
- Minor, but not merely superficial, cuts of a sort probably requiring medical treatment (e.g. stitches)
- Psychiatric injury that is more than merely emotions such as fear, distress or panic.

Where psychiatric injury is relied upon as the basis for an allegation of assault occasioning actual bodily harm, and the matter is not admitted by the defence, then expert evidence must be called by the prosecution (*R* v *Chan-Fook* [1994] 1 WLR 689).

1.8.6.2 Wounding or Inflicting Grievous Bodily Harm

OFFENCE: **Wounding or Inflicting Grievous Bodily Harm—*Offences Against the Person Act 1861, s. 20***

- Triable either way • Five years' imprisonment on indictment
- Six months' imprisonment and/or a fine summarily

OFFENCE: **Racially or Religiously Aggravated—*Crime and Disorder Act 1998, s. 29(1)(a)***

- Triable either way • Seven years' imprisonment and/or a fine on indictment
- Six months' imprisonment and/or a fine summarily

The Offences Against the Person Act 1861, s. 20 states:

Whosoever shall unlawfully and maliciously wound or inflict any grievous bodily harm upon any other person, either with or without any weapon or instrument, shall be guilty of a misdemeanour . . .

KEYNOTE

Wounding means the breaking of the continuity of the whole of the outer skin, or the inner skin within the cheek or lip. A cut which goes right through all the layers of a person's skin, whether caused externally (e.g. a knife wound) or internally (e.g. a punch causing a tooth to puncture the cheek), will amount to a wound. It does not include the rupturing of internal blood vessels.

The definition of wounding may encompass injuries that are relatively minor in nature, for example a small cut or laceration. An assault resulting in such minor injuries should more appropriately be charged contrary to s. 47 of the Act. An assault contrary to s. 20 should be reserved for the type of wounds considered to be serious (thus equating the offence with the infliction of grievous, or serious, bodily harm).

The House of Lords in *R* v *Ireland* [1998] AC 147 has made it clear that no 'assault' is needed for this offence and that harm could be 'inflicted' indirectly (in this case by menacing telephone calls inflicting psychiatric harm). Therefore there is now little if any difference between inflicting harm and 'causing' harm. It should be enough to show that the defendant's behaviour brought about the resulting harm to the victim.

There have also been many judicial attempts at defining grievous bodily harm. In *R* v *Saunders* [1985] Crim LR 230 it was held that the expression meant 'serious or really serious harm'. This harm will now include psychiatric harm (*Ireland*). Examples of what will amount to 'grievous bodily harm' can be found in the CPS Charging Standards and include:

- injury resulting in some permanent disability or visible disfigurement
- broken or displaced limbs or bones
- injuries requiring blood transfusion or lengthy treatment.

Following the well-publicised case of Mohammed Dica in 2003, there was an acceptance that the deliberate infection of another with the HIV virus could amount to grievous bodily harm—although there were still significant difficulties with regard to 'consent' if the infection had taken place as a result of consensual sexual activity. This issue was explored further by the Court of Appeal in *R* v *Konzani* [2005] EWCA Crim 706. In that case the defendant appealed against convictions for inflicting grievous bodily harm on three women contrary to s. 20 above. The defendant had unprotected consensual sexual intercourse with the women, but without having disclosed that he was HIV positive. The women subsequently contracted the HIV virus. In hearing the appeals, the court held that there was a critical distinction between taking a risk as to the various potentially adverse (and possibly problematic) consequences of unprotected consensual intercourse, and the giving of informed consent *to the risk of infection with a fatal disease*. Before consent to the risk of contracting HIV could provide a defence, that consent had to be an *informed* consent in this latter sense (see *R* v *Dica* [2004] EWCA Crim 1103). Therefore, simply having an honestly held belief that the other person was consenting would only help if that consent would itself have provided a defence to the passing of the infection.

This approach was confirmed in *R* v *B* [2006] EWCA Crim 2945, where the Court of Appeal stated that, while a defendant's condition (being HIV positive) was immaterial in relation to the consent issue in an offence of rape, the defendant would have no defence to the harm created by the sexual activity merely by virtue of that consent, as the consent related to the sexual activity and not to the disease.

'Maliciously'—although the word maliciously suggests some form of evil premeditation, 'malice' here amounts to *subjective recklessness*. It means that the defendant must realise that there is a risk of *some harm* being caused to the victim. The defendant does not need to foresee the degree of harm which is eventually caused, only that his/her behaviour may bring about some harm to the victim.

1.8.6.3 Wounding or Causing Grievous Bodily Harm with Intent

OFFENCE: **Wounding or Causing Grievous Bodily Harm with Intent—*Offences Against the Person Act 1861, s. 18***

- Triable on indictment only • Life imprisonment

The Offences Against the Person Act 1861, s. 18 states:

> Whosoever shall unlawfully and maliciously by any means whatsoever wound or cause any grievous bodily harm to any person with intent to do some grievous bodily harm to any person, or with intent to resist or prevent the lawful apprehension or detainer of any person, shall be guilty of felony ...

KEYNOTE

Although there are similarities with the offence under s. 20 (see above), you must show the appropriate *intent* (e.g. to do grievous bodily harm to *anyone* or to resist/prevent the lawful apprehension/detention of *anyone*). Factors that may indicate such a specific intent include:

- a repeated or planned attack
- deliberate selection of a weapon or adaptation of an article to cause injury, such as breaking a glass before an attack
- making prior threats
- using an offensive weapon against, or kicking a victim's head.

Where the intent was to cause grievous bodily harm, the issue of 'malice' will not arise. However, where the intent was to resist or prevent the lawful arrest of someone, the element of maliciousness as set out above (**see para. 1.8.6.2**) will need to be proved. The word 'cause', together with the expression 'by any means whatsoever', seems to give this offence a wider meaning than s. 20. However, the increasingly broad interpretation of the s. 20 offence means that there is little difference in the *actus reus* needed for either offence.

The provisions of ss. 28 and 29 of the Crime and Disorder Act 1998 in relation to racially or religiously aggravated assaults do not apply to this offence. However, the courts must still take notice of any element of racial or religious aggravation when determining sentence (s. 145 of the Criminal Justice Act 2003—increase in sentences for racial or religious aggravation).

1.9 | Miscellaneous Offences Against the Person

1.9.1 Introduction

In addition to the relatively common offences examined in the previous chapter, there are further offences against the person that, while not as prevalent, are nevertheless important.

1.9.2 Torture

OFFENCE: **Torture—*Criminal Justice Act 1988, s. 134***

- Triable on indictment • Life imprisonment

The Criminal Justice Act 1988, s. 134 states:

(1) A public official or person acting in an official capacity, whatever his nationality, commits the offence of torture if in the United Kingdom or elsewhere he intentionally inflicts severe pain or suffering on another in the performance or purported performance of his official duties.

(2) A person not falling within subsection (1) above commits the offence of torture, whatever his nationality, if—

    (a) in the United Kingdom or elsewhere he intentionally inflicts severe pain or suffering on another at the instigation or with the consent or acquiescence—

        (i) of a public official; or

        (ii) of a person acting in an official capacity; and

    (b) the official or other person is performing or purporting to perform his official duties when he instigates the commission of the offence or consents to or acquiesces in it.

(3) It is immaterial whether the pain or suffering is physical or mental or whether is caused by an act or an omission.

KEYNOTE

The consent of the Attorney-General (or Solicitor-General) is needed before bringing a prosecution under s. 134. This offence could be committed by a police officer in the course of his/her duties, and may have significant implications for Custody Officers.

Although the offence has a statutory defence of 'lawful authority, justification or excuse' (see below), Article 3 of the European Convention on Human Rights contains an absolute prohibition on torture. Irrespective of the prevailing circumstances, there can be no derogation from an individual's absolute right under Article 3 to freedom from torture, inhuman or degrading treatment or punishment.

These three features have been identified as having the following broad characteristics:

- Torture—deliberate treatment leading to serious or cruel suffering.
- Inhuman treatment—treatment resulting in intense suffering, both physical and mental.

- Degrading treatment—treatment giving rise to fear and anguish in the victim, causing feelings of inferiority and humiliation.

(See *Ireland* v *United Kingdom* (1974–80) 2 EHRR 25.)

It has been held by the European Commission of Human Rights that causing mental anguish without any physical assault could be a violation of Article 3 (*see Denmark* v *Greece* (1969) 12 YB Eur Conv HR special Vol.).

Article 3 does not only prohibit the deliberate application of pain and suffering, but also a range of other behaviour. Oppressive interrogation techniques such as sleep deprivation, exposure to continuous loud noise and forcing suspects to adopt uncomfortable postures for prolonged lengths of time have been held to fall within the second and third categories of inhuman and degrading treatment (*Ireland* v *United Kingdom*).

In each case, it must be shown that the prohibited behaviour went beyond the 'minimum level of severity'. In determining whether the behaviour did go beyond that level, and under which particular category that behaviour falls, the courts will take into account factors such as the age, sex, state of health and general life experience of the victim. 'Severe pain or suffering' can be mental as well as physical and can be caused by omission.

1.9.2.1 Defence

The Criminal Justice Act 1988, s. 134 states:

(4) It shall be a defence for a person charged with an offence under this section in respect of any conduct of his to prove that he had lawful authority, justification or excuse for that conduct.

1.9.3 Poisoning

OFFENCE: **Poisoning—*Offences Against the Person Act 1861, s. 23***
- Triable on indictment • Ten years' imprisonment

The Offences Against the Person Act 1861, s. 23 states:

Whosoever shall unlawfully and maliciously administer to or cause to be administered to or taken by any other person any poison or other destructive or noxious thing, so as thereby to endanger the life of such person, or so as thereby to inflict upon such person any grievous bodily harm, shall be guilty of [an offence]...

KEYNOTE

Other than the requirement for 'malice', this offence is mainly concerned with the consequences caused to the victim and not the defendant's intentions.

'Causing to be administered' would cover indirect poisoning or even inducing someone to poison themselves. 'Administering' is a very broad term which has been held to include the spraying of gas into another's face (*R* v *Gillard* (1988) 87 Cr App R 189). As such this would appear to include the use of CS spray by police officers but the 'administering' would also have to be shown to be both unlawful and malicious.

Whether a substance is poisonous, destructive or noxious will depend on both its quality and quantity. Some substances may become poisonous or noxious only in large amounts whereas others may be so *per se*.

This offence would certainly cover the administering of a controlled drug to another or inducing another to take a controlled drug.

There is a requirement to prove a consequence with this offence, namely the endangering of a person's life or the infliction of grievous bodily harm.

1.9.3.1 Poisoning with Intent

OFFENCE: **Poisoning with Intent—*Offences Against the Person Act 1861, s. 24***
- Triable on indictment • Five years' imprisonment

The Offences Against the Person Act 1861, s. 24 states:

> Whosoever shall unlawfully and maliciously administer to or cause to be administered to or taken by any other person any poison or other destructive or noxious thing, with intent to injure, aggrieve, or annoy any such person, shall be guilty of a misdemeanour...

KEYNOTE

Unlike the previous offence under s. 23, there is no requirement as to the actual consequences of a defendant's actions under s. 24 and this offence is concerned with the defendant's intentions.

There is a further, more extreme offence of using noxious substances to cause harm or intimidation under the Anti-terrorism, Crime and Security Act 2001, s. 113. This offence, which carries 14 years' imprisonment on indictment, occurs where a person takes any action which:

- involves the use of a noxious substance or other noxious thing;
- has or is likely to have an effect set out below; and
- is designed to influence the government or to intimidate the public or a section of the public.

The effects are:

- causing serious violence against a person, or serious damage to property, anywhere in the world;
- endangering human life or creating a serious risk to the health or safety of the public or a section of the public; or
- inducing in members of the public the fear that the action is likely to endanger their lives or create a serious risk to their health or safety.

Concerns over terrorist activity have greatly increased the relevance of this piece of legislation to policing.

1.9.4 False Imprisonment

OFFENCE: **False Imprisonment—*Common Law***
- Triable on indictment • Unlimited maximum penalty

It is an offence at common law falsely to imprison another person.

KEYNOTE

This offence is the first in an ascending order of aggravated offences against the person and is more usually dealt with under civil law or as kidnapping/abduction (see below).

These offences are particularly relevant to the offence of committing a criminal offence with intent to commit a relevant sexual offence (as to which **see chapter 1.10**).

The elements required for this offence are the unlawful and intentional/reckless restraint of a person's freedom of movement (*R* v *Rahman* (1985) 81 Cr App R 349). Locking someone in a vehicle or keeping them in a particular place for however short a time may amount to false imprisonment if done unlawfully. An unlawful arrest may amount to such an offence and it is not uncommon for such an allegation to be levelled at police officers against whom a public complaint has been made. On the other hand, a *lawful* arrest will provide a defence to the offence as will reasonable defence of property. In respect of the latter, a person would have a defence to a charge of false imprisonment if he/she detained a person in the genuine belief that a person was a burglar—even if this genuine belief were unreasonable (*R* v *Shwan Faraj* [2007] EWCA Crim 1033). In *Shwan Faraj*, the court stated that there was no reason why a householder should not be entitled to detain someone in his house whom he genuinely believed to be a burglar; he would be acting in defence of his property in doing so. However, a householder would have to honestly believe he needed to detain the suspect and would have to do so in a way that was reasonable.

The state of mind required to prove this offence is intention or recklessness (*R* v *Rahman* (1985) 81 Cr App R 348). Recklessness here means 'subjective' recklessness (*R* v *James* (1997) *The Times*, 2 October).

1.9.5 Kidnapping

OFFENCE: **Kidnapping—*Common Law***
- Triable on indictment • Unlimited maximum penalty

It is an offence at common law to take or carry away another person without the consent of that person and without lawful excuse.

KEYNOTE

The required elements of this offence are the unlawful taking or carrying away of one person by another by force or fraud (*R* v *D* [1984] AC 778). These requirements go beyond those of mere restraint needed for false imprisonment. Parents may be acting without lawful excuse, for instance, if they are acting in breach of a court order in respect of their children (**see chapter 1.12**). The 'taking or carrying away' need not involve great distances—a short distance (just a few yards/metres) will suffice (*R* v *Wellard* [1978] 3 All ER 161).

The taking or carrying away of the victim must be without the consent of the victim. If the victim consents to an initial taking but later withdraws that consent, the offence would be complete. If the consent is obtained by fraud, the defendant cannot rely on that consent and the offence—or attempted offence—will be made out (see *R* v *Cort* [2003] EWCA Crim 2149). In *R* v *Hendy-Freegard* [2007] EWCA Crim 1236 the defendant was a confidence trickster who pretended to be an undercover agent working for MI5 or Scotland Yard. He would tell his victims that he was investigating the activities of the IRA and that his investigations had revealed that they were in danger. This allowed him to take control of their lives for a number of years and in doing so to direct them to move about the country from location to location. The defendant was eventually arrested and convicted of kidnapping on the basis of the Crown's case that the offence of kidnapping had occurred as his victims had made journeys around the country which they had been induced to make as a result of the defendant's false story. The defendant successfully appealed against the kidnapping conviction, with the court stating that causing a person to move from place to place *when unaccompanied by the defendant* could not itself constitute either taking or carrying away or deprivation of liberty, which were necessary elements of the offence.

If the victim is a child, the consent will probably be that of the parents but the more appropriate charge in such a case may be one under the Child Abduction Act 1984 (**see chapter 1.12**).

The state of mind required for this offence is the same as that for false imprisonment, indeed the only thing separating the two offences seems to be *actus reus* (*R* v *Hutchins* [1988] Crim LR 379).

1.9.6 Hostage Taking

OFFENCE: **Hostage Taking—*Taking of Hostages Act 1982, s. 1***
- Triable on indictment • Life imprisonment

The Taking of Hostages Act 1982, s. 1 states:

(1) A person, whatever his nationality, who, in the United Kingdom or elsewhere—
  (a) detains any other person ('the hostage'), and
  (b) in order to compel a State, international governmental organisation, or person to do or abstain from doing any act, threatens to kill, injure or continue to detain the hostage, commits an offence.

KEYNOTE

The consent of the Attorney-General (or Solicitor-General) is needed before bringing a prosecution for this offence. To be guilty, a defendant must detain a person *and* threaten to kill, injure or continue to detain them with the intentions outlined under s. 1(1)(b). It is therefore an offence of 'specific' intent (**see chapter 1.1**).

1.10 Sexual Offences

1.10.1 Introduction

Sexual offences represent a particularly important area of criminal law for two main reasons: the sensitivity required in their investigation and prosecution and their potential effect on the victim. For those reasons, together with the growth in the range of legal provisions dealing with sexual offences, they are addressed in this separate chapter.

It is important to note that there is overlap between many of the offences, for example a mentally disordered person could be raped under s. 1 (because of his/her lack of ability to give true consent) or subjected to sexual activity contrary to s. 30 (due to an inability to refuse). In all circumstances it is essential that the most appropriate option is chosen.

1.10.1.1 Human Rights Considerations

It is clear that sexual activities are aspects of a person's 'private life' as protected by Article 8 of the Convention (see *Dudgeon* v *United Kingdom* (1981) 4 EHRR 149 and *ADT* v *United Kingdom* [2000] Crim LR 1009). This concept applies to homosexual and heterosexual relationships (*X* v *United Kingdom* (1997) 24 EHRR 143).

Any attempt by the criminal law to place restrictions on the consensual sexual activities of individuals has to be considered very carefully in light of the Human Rights Act 1998.

The Sexual Offences Act 2003 and its compatibility with the European Convention on Human Rights were considered in *R* v *G & Secretary of State for the Home Department* [2006] EWCA Crim 821. The Court of Appeal held that the imposition of strict liability in relation to the offence under s. 5 of the Act (rape of a child under 13) did not infringe Article 6.2 of the Convention (presumption of innocence).

1.10.1.2 Anonymity

Under the Sexual Offences (Amendment) Act 1992, victims of most sexual offences (including rape, incest, and indecency with children) are entitled to anonymity throughout their lifetime. This means that there are restrictions on the way in which trials and cases may be reported and the courts have powers to enforce these provisions. Further protection preventing victims from cross-examination by their alleged attackers is provided by the Youth Justice and Criminal Evidence Act 1999. The 1999 Act also imposes restrictions on the introduction of evidence in most of the sexual offences covered in this chapter.

1.10.2 The Sexual Offences Act 2003

The Sexual Offences Act creates a whole series of sexual offences and sets out the elements that will be needed in proving the relevant offences and also introduces some further practical measures such as the presumptions about consent that will be made by a court under certain circumstances. In many of the mainstream offences it creates, the Act uses the approach of describing actions of a hypothetical offender 'A' towards the victim 'B'.

The Act has some recurring themes and terms; in order to understand—and prove—many of the offences set out in the Act, it is necessary to understand some of the themes and terms first.

1.10.2.1 The Definition of 'Sexual'

This is an important concept in the statutory framework. Some activities carried out in order to gain sexual gratification are difficult to classify—and certainly to prove—as 'sexual' in the ordinary meaning of the word. Fetishes in particular, e.g.—for things such as feet and shoes—have caused difficulties in this regard.

What a Reasonable Person would Consider

Section 78 provides that penetration, touching or any other activity will be sexual if a reasonable person would consider that:

(a) whatever its circumstances or any person's purpose in relation to it, it is sexual by its very nature or,
(b) because of its nature it *may* be sexual and because of its circumstances or the purpose of any person in relation to it, it is sexual.

Therefore, activity under (a) covers things that a reasonable person would always consider to be sexual (for example, masturbation), while activity under (b) covers things that may or may not be considered sexual by a reasonable person depending on the circumstances or the intentions of the person carrying it out (or both). For instance, a doctor inserting a finger into a vagina might be sexual under certain circumstances, but if done for a purely medical purpose in a hospital, it would not be.

If the activity would not appear to a reasonable person to be sexual, then it will not meet either criterion and, irrespective of any sexual gratification the person might derive from it, the activity will not be 'sexual'. Therefore weird or exotic fetishes that no ordinary person would regard as being sexual or potentially sexual will not be covered. This pretty well follows the common law developments in this area (see e.g. *R v Court* [1989] AC 28 and *R v Tabassum* [2000] 2 Cr App R 328).

1.10.2.2 The Definition of 'Touching'

This activity is relevant to a number of specific offences. Section 79(8) states that touching includes touching:

- with any part of the body
- with anything else
- through anything

and in particular, touching amounting to penetration.

'Touching' for the purposes of an offence under s. 3 (**see para. 1.10.4.2**) includes the touching of a victim's clothing. This is clear from the Court of Appeal's decision in *R v H* [2005] EWCA Crim 732. There it was held that it was not Parliament's intention to preclude the touching of a victim's clothing from amounting to a sexual 'assault'. Where touching was not automatically by its nature 'sexual' the test under s. 78(b) applies (**see para. 1.10.2.1**). In a case where that section applies it will be appropriate for a trial judge to ask the jury to determine whether touching was 'sexual' by answering two questions. First, would the jury, as 12 reasonable people, consider that the touching could be sexual and, if so, whether in all the circumstances of the case, they would consider that the purpose of the touching *had in fact been* sexual.

1.10.3 Rape

OFFENCE: **Rape—*Sexual Offences Act 2003, s.1***
- Triable on indictment • Life imprisonment

The Sexual Offences Act 2003, s. 1 states:

(1) A person (A) commits an offence if—
    (a) he intentionally penetrates the vagina, anus or mouth of another person (B) with his penis,
    (b) B does not consent to the penetration, and
    (c) A does not reasonably believe that B consents

KEYNOTE

Rape is an offence that can *only* be committed via the use of the penis. It can be committed if the defendant penetrates the vagina, anus or mouth of the victim with the penis.

Consent is a key aspect of rape. In proving rape you must show that the victim did not in fact consent at the time and that the defendant did not reasonably believe that he/she consented. The wording is supported by the further provision that whether or not the defendant's belief is reasonable will be determined having regard to all the circumstances (s. 1(2)). Both this, and the aspects of the criminal conduct required to prove rape are considered in greater detail below.

Sections 75 and 76 apply to this offence (see paras 1.10.3.3 and 1.10.3.4).

If the victim is a child under 13, you simply have to prove intentional penetration and the child's age. No issue of 'consent' arises and a specific offence under s. 5 is committed.

Section 103(2)(b) of the Criminal Justice Act 2003 provides that a defendant's propensity to commit offences of the kind with which he/she is charged may (without prejudice to any other way of doing so) be established by evidence that he/she has been convicted of an offence of 'the same category'. An offence under s. 1, if committed in relation to a person under the age of 16, or under s. 5 (including aiding, abetting, counselling, procuring, inciting or attempting the commission of such an offence) falls within the relevant sexual offences category. A number of other sexual offences that follow in this chapter are also covered and will fall within the relevant sexual offences category (see the Criminal Justice Act 2003 (Categories of Offences) Order 2004 (SI 2004/3346)). For a further discussion of this highly controversial legislation see Evidence and Procedure.

1.10.3.1 Criminal Conduct

To prove rape you must show that the defendant penetrated the vagina, mouth or anus of the victim. It should be noted that penetration is a continuing act from entry to withdrawal (s. 79(2)). The 'continuing' nature of this act is of practical importance when considering the issue of consent and the statutory presumptions (see below). While it is not necessary to prove ejaculation, clearly the presence of semen or sperm is important in proving the elements of a sexual offence, as is other scientific evidence recovered from the victim, the offender and the scene etc. References to a part of the body (for example, penis, vagina) will include references to a body part which has been surgically constructed, particularly if it is through gender reassignment (s. 79(3)).

1.10.3.2 Consent

The issue of consent is a question of fact and is critical to proving the offence of rape. It is also potentially the most difficult aspect of the offence to prove and that is why the legislation has included some specific sections raising presumptions and conclusions in certain circumstances. Whereas an act of intercourse or physical intimacy may be proved or corroborated by forensic evidence, the true wishes of the victim at the time of the offence are much more difficult to prove beyond a reasonable doubt. Any consent given must be 'true' consent, not simply a *submission* induced by fear or fraud. Some people however are not capable of giving the required consent—these are generally addressed in further sections of this chapter.

The starting point in examining consent is s. 74 which states that a person consents if he or she agrees by choice and has the freedom and capacity to make that choice. Therefore, if the person does not have any real choice in the matter, or their choice is not a genuine exercise of their free will, then they have not 'consented'.

In *R v B* [2006] EWCA Crim 2945, the Court of Appeal stated that whether an individual had a sexual disease or condition, such as being HIV positive, was not an issue as far as consent was concerned. The case related to a man who was alleged to have raped a woman after they had met outside a nightclub in the early hours of the morning. When arrested, the man informed the custody officer that he was HIV positive, a fact he had not disclosed to the victim prior to sexual intercourse. At the original trial, the judge directed that this non-disclosure was relevant to the issue of consent. On appeal the court stated that this was not the case and that the consent issue for a jury to consider was whether or not the victim consented to sexual intercourse, not whether she consented to sexual intercourse with a person suffering from a sexually transmitted disease.

The next key considerations in relation to consent are the important provisions set out at ss. 75 and 76. These are presumptions about consent and can be divided into *evidential* presumptions and *conclusive* presumptions.

1.10.3.3 Section 75—Evidential Presumptions and Consent

The Sexual Offences Act 2003, s. 75 states:

(1) If in proceedings for an offence to which this section applies it is proved—
   (a) that the defendant did the relevant act,
   (b) that any of the circumstances specified in subsection (2) existed, and
   (c) that the defendant knew that those circumstances existed,
   the complainant is to be taken not to have consented to the relevant act unless sufficient evidence is adduced to raise an issue as to whether he consented, and the defendant is to be taken not to have reasonably believed that the complainant consented unless sufficient evidence is adduced to raise an issue as to whether he reasonably believed it.

KEYNOTE

This means that, if the prosecution can show that the defendant carried out the relevant act in relation to certain specified sexual offences (for example, penetration in rape) and that any of the circumstances below existed and the defendant knew they existed, it will be presumed that the victim did not consent. Then the defendant will have to satisfy the court, by reference to evidence, that this presumption should not be made.

The circumstances are that:

(a) *any person* was, at the time of the relevant act (or immediately before it began), using violence against *the complainant* or causing *the complainant* to fear that immediate violence would be used against him/her;

(b) *any person* was, at the time of the relevant act or immediately before it began, causing *the complainant* to fear that violence was being used, or that immediate violence would be used, against *another person*;

(c) *the complainant* was, and the defendant was not, unlawfully detained at the time of the relevant act;

(d) *the complainant* was asleep or otherwise unconscious at the time of the relevant act;

(e) because of *the complainant's* physical disability, *the complainant* would not have been able at the time of the relevant act to communicate to the defendant whether the complainant consented;

(f) *any person* had administered to or caused to be taken by the complainant, without the complainant's consent, a substance which, having regard to when it was administered or taken, was capable of causing or enabling the complainant to be stupefied or overpowered at the time of the relevant act.

It can be seen that these conditions cover a range of circumstances, including the use or threat of violence by any person (not just the defendant) against the victim of the sexual offence and circumstances where the victim was asleep or had been drugged.

The 'relevant act' for each offence covered by s. 75 will generally be obvious but is set out specifically at s. 77.

1.10.3.4 Conclusive Presumptions about Consent

Section 76 of the Sexual Offences Act 2003 states that, if it is proved in some sexual offences (listed in s. 77) that the defendant did the relevant act and that he/she:

(a) intentionally deceived the complainant as to the nature or purpose of the relevant act or

(b) intentionally induced the complainant to consent to the relevant act by impersonating a person known personally to the complainant,

there will be a *conclusive* presumption both that the victim did not consent and also that the defendant did not believe he/she consented.

These provisions deal with the problems where the defendant either misrepresents the nature or purpose of what he/she is doing (for example, pretending that inserting a finger into the victim's vagina is for medical reasons) or impersonates the victim's partner. Section 76 requires that a misunderstanding was created by the defendant and that it was done deliberately. Once it is proved, beyond a reasonable doubt, that these circumstances existed then it is conclusive and the defendant cannot argue against them. An example of a deception as to the purpose of the act comes from the case *R v Devonald* [2008] EWCA Crim 527. In this case, the defendant (a male) posed as a young woman and induced the complainant to masturbate in front of a web cam. The complainant only did so because he thought that he was masturbating for the sexual gratification of a young woman. The court held that the complainant had been deceived as to the purpose of the masturbation.

It is important to emphasise the fact that s. 76 deals with situations where the defendant either:

• deceives the victim regarding the nature and purpose of the act or
• deceives the victim regarding the identity of the person who is carrying out the act.

If the deception does not relate to either of these aims then s. 76 has no application. For example, in *R* v *Harvinder Jheeta* [2007] EWCA Crim 1699, the defendant deceived the complainant into having sex more frequently than she would have done otherwise. In these circumstances the conclusive presumptions under the Sexual Offences Act 2003 had no relevance as the complainant had not been deceived as to the nature or purpose of the sexual intercourse.

As with s. 75, the 'relevant act' for each offence covered by s. 76 will generally be obvious but is set out specifically at s. 77.

Even if freely given, consent may still be withdrawn at any time. Once the 'passive' party to sexual penetration withdraws consent, any continued activity (for example, penetration in rape—*R* v *Cooper* [1994] Crim LR 531) can amount to a sexual offence provided all the other ingredients are present.

1.10.4 Sexual Assault

There are several specific offences dealing with types of sexual assault: these are discussed below.

1.10.4.1 Assault by Penetration

OFFENCE: **Assault by Penetration—*Sexual Offences Act 2003, s. 2***

- Triable on indictment • Life imprisonment

The Sexual Offences Act 2003, s. 2 states:

(1) A person (A) commits an offence if—
  (a) he intentionally penetrates the vagina or anus of another person (B) with a part of his body or anything else,
  (b) the penetration is sexual,
  (c) B does not consent to the penetration, and
  (d) A does not reasonably believe that B consents.

KEYNOTE

As with all the offences in the Sexual Offences Act 2003 except rape, this offence can be committed by a male or a female against a male or female.

This offence involves penetration by any part of the body or anything else whatsoever. It is therefore a very broad offence covering insertion into the vagina or anus (though not the mouth) of *anything*, provided that the penetration is 'sexual'. Penetration must be intentional, made without the consent of the victim and you must show that the defendant did not reasonably believe that the victim did consent. Whether a belief is reasonable is to be determined having regard to all the circumstances, including any steps the defendant has taken to ascertain whether the victim consents (s. 2(2)).

The introduction of the series of sexual offences under the 2003 Act has raised some questions as to the extent to which they mirror or replace similar offences under the former regime. The Court of Appeal has held that, so far as the above offence is concerned, its introduction attracting a potential sentence of life imprisonment means that it must be dealt with at a higher level than the previous generic offence of indecent assault. The ingredient of penetration has always been regarded by the law as being particularly serious and the starting point in s. 2 offences for sentencing ought to be in the region of four years (*Attorney-General's Reference (No. 104 of 2004)* [2004] EWCA Crim 2672).

Sections 75 and 76 apply to this offence.

If the victim is a child under 13, you simply have to prove intentional, sexual penetration and the child's age. No issue of 'consent' arises and a specific offence under s. 6 is committed.

1.10.4.2 Sexual Assault by Touching

OFFENCE: **Sexual Touching—*Sexual Offences Act 2003, s. 3***

   • Triable either way • If victim is child under 13—fourteen years' imprisonment; otherwise ten years' imprisonment on indictment • Six months' imprisonment summarily

The Sexual Offences Act 2003, s. 3 states:

(1) A person (A) commits an offence if—
  (a) he intentionally touches another person (B),
  (b) the touching is sexual,
  (c) B does not consent to the touching, and
  (d) A does not reasonably believe that B consents.

KEYNOTE

The part of the body touched does not have to be a sexual organ or orifice. Touching for the purposes of the above offence includes touching a person's clothing. Therefore, where a man approached a woman and asked '*Do you fancy a shag?*', grabbing at a pocket on her tracksuit bottoms as she tried to walk away, he was properly convicted of the s. 3 offence (*R* v *H* [2005] EWCA Crim 732).

As with the offence under s. 2, you need to prove that the conduct was intentional (rather than accidental), that it was sexual, that the victim did not consent and that the defendant did not reasonably believe that the victim consented.

Whether a belief is reasonable is to be determined having regard to all the circumstances, including any steps the defendant has taken to ascertain whether the victim consents (s. 3(2)).

Sections 75 and 76 apply to this offence.

If the victim is a child under 13, you simply have to prove intentional, sexual touching and the child's age. No issue of 'consent' arises and a specific offence under s. 7 is committed.

1.10.4.3 Causing Sexual Activity without Consent

OFFENCE: **Causing a Person to Engage in Sexual Activity without Consent—*Sexual Offences Act 2003, s. 4***

   • If involves penetration: of the victim's anus or vagina, of victim's mouth with penis, of any other person's anus or vagina with a part of victim's body or by victim, or of any person's mouth by victim's penis—triable on indictment; life imprisonment

   • Otherwise triable either way; ten years' imprisonment on indictment; six months' imprisonment summarily

The Sexual Offences Act 2003, s. 4 states:

(1) A person (A) commits an offence if—
  (a) he intentionally causes another person (B) to engage in an activity,
  (b) the activity is sexual,
  (c) B does not consent to engaging in the activity, and
  (d) A does not reasonably believe that B consents.

KEYNOTE

The offence can involve a number of permutations—for example a woman making a man penetrate her, a man forcing someone else to masturbate him or a woman making another woman masturbate a third person. Apart from the defendant and the victim, there may be others involved who also consent. Clearly they may be liable for aiding and abetting under the right circumstances. If the permutations involve penetration, the chances are it will carry life imprisonment. You need to prove that the conduct was intentional, that the 'activity' engaged in was sexual, that the *victim* (rather than any other participant) did not consent and that the defendant did not reasonably believe that the victim consented.

Whether a belief is reasonable is to be determined having regard to all the circumstances, including any steps the defendant has taken to ascertain whether the victim consents (s. 4(2)).

Sections 75 and 76 apply to this offence.

There is a specific offence of causing or *inciting* a child under 13 to engage in sexual activity (s. 8). It is important to remember that an individual can commit an offence of incitement even if the activity he/she is encouraging, etc. does not take place. In *R* v *Walker* [2006] EWCA Crim 1907, the Court of Appeal held that s. 8 of the Act created two offences: (i) intentionally causing, and (ii) intentionally inciting a child under 13 to engage in sexual activity. The offence was centred on the concept of incitement and the acts had to be intentional or deliberate, but it was not a necessary ingredient for incitement of sexual activity that the defendant had intended the sexual activity to take place.

1.10.5 Child Sex Offences

The Sexual Offences Act 2003 creates several specific offences relating to sexual activity involving or directed towards children. These are set out below. In considering each offence it is important to remember the relevant ages, both of offenders and victims. In addition, the Act makes special exceptions to some offences of aiding, abetting or counselling some offences involving children (**see para. 1.10.5.4** for such an example).

The full list of offences is set out in s. 73(2); basically it covers specific offences against children under 13 and offences involving sexual activity with a child under 16.

1.10.5.1 Sexual Activity with a Child

OFFENCE: **Sexual Activity with a Child**—*Sexual Offences Act 2003, s. 9*
- If involves penetration: of victim's anus or vagina by a part of defendant's body or anything else, of victim's mouth with defendant's penis, of defendant's anus or vagina by a part of victim's body or of defendant's mouth by victim's penis—triable on indictment; 14 years' imprisonment • Otherwise triable either way; 14 years' imprisonment on indictment; six months' imprisonment summarily

The Sexual Offences Act 2003, s. 9 states:

(1) A person aged 18 or over (A) commits an offence if—
   (a) he intentionally touches another person (B),
   (b) the touching is sexual, and
   (c) either—
      (i) B is under 16 and A does not reasonably believe that B is 16 or over, or
      (ii) B is under 13.

KEYNOTE

The person committing this offence must be at least 18. If the defendant is under 18, he or she commits a specific offence, punishable by 5 years' imprisonment (if tried on indictment) under s. 13. Similarly, if the person committing the offence is in a position of trust in relation to the victim, he/she commits a specific offence under s. 16.

You must show that the defendant intentionally touched the victim sexually and either that the victim was under 13 (in which case the offence is complete) or that the victim was under 16 and that the defendant did not reasonably believe he/she was 16 or over. In either case consent is irrelevant.

There is a further specific offence (s. 10) of a person aged 18 or over intentionally causing or inciting another to engage in the type of sexual activity set out above. The sexual activity caused or envisaged may be with the defendant or with a third person. In the case of incitement there is no need for the sexual activity itself to take place. If the person committing the offence is in a position of trust in relation to the victim, he/she commits a specific offence under s. 17 (see para. 1.10.5.5).

1.10.5.2 Sexual Activity in Presence of a Child

OFFENCE: **Engaging in Sexual Activity in the Presence of a Child**—*Sexual Offences Act 2003, s. 11*

- Triable either way • Ten years' imprisonment on indictment • Six months' imprisonment summarily

The Sexual Offences Act 2003, s. 11 states:

(1) A person aged 18 or over (A) commits an offence if—
  (a) he intentionally engages in an activity,
  (b) the activity is sexual,
  (c) for the purpose of obtaining sexual gratification, he engages in it—
    (i) when another person (B) is present or is in a place from which A can be observed, and
    (ii) knowing or believing that B is aware, or intending that B should be aware, that he is engaging in it, and
  (d) either—
    (i) B is under 16 and A does not reasonably believe that B is 16 or over, or
    (ii) B is under 13.

KEYNOTE

The person committing this offence must be at least 18. If the defendant is under 18, he/she commits a specific offence, punishable by 5 years' imprisonment (if tried on indictment) under s. 13. Similarly, if the person committing the offence is in a position of trust in relation to the victim, he/she commits a specific offence under s. 18.

The activity in which the offender is engaged must be 'sexual' and intentional and must be in order to obtain sexual gratification (for the defendant). The display of sexual images or sexual activity might, in certain circumstances, be appropriate, for example, for medical or educational reasons, hence the requirement that the offence depended on the corrupt purpose of 'sexual gratification'. However, the offence under s. 12 of the Act does not require that such gratification has to be taken immediately; i.e. the section does not require that the offence can only be committed if the purposed sexual gratification and the viewed sexual act, or display of images, were simultaneous, contemporaneous or synchronised. For example, the defendant may cause a child to watch a sexual act to put the child in a frame of mind for future sexual abuse, as well as where the defendant does so to obtain enjoyment from seeing the child watch the sexual act (*R* v *Abdullahi* [2006] EWCA Crim 2060). The approach to 'sexual gratification' taken in *Abdullahi* appears equally applicable to other offences where this phrase appears (the offence under s. 11 of the Act, for example).

You must show that a person under 16 is present or is in a place from which the defendant can be observed *and* that the defendant knew, believed or intended that the child was aware that he/she was engaging in that activity. Therefore, it is not necessary to show that the child was in fact aware of the activity in every case (although that would clearly help in terms of proving the defendant's state of mind). Because of the wording in s. 79(7), 'observation' includes direct observation or by looking at any image.

In relation to the child you must show also that either the child was under 13 (in which case the offence is complete) or that he/she was under 16 and that the defendant did not reasonably believe him/her to be 16 or over.

This offence is aimed at, for example, people masturbating in front of children or performing sexual acts with others where they know they can be seen (or they want to be seen) by children directly or via a camera/video phone etc.

1.10.5.3 Causing a Child to Watch a Sex Act

OFFENCE: **Causing a Child to Watch a Sexual Act—*Sexual Offences Act 2003, s. 12***
- Triable either way • Ten years' imprisonment on indictment • Six months' imprisonment summarily

The Sexual Offences Act 2003, s. 12 states:

(1) A person aged 18 or over (A) commits an offence if—
   (a) for the purpose of obtaining sexual gratification, he intentionally causes another person (B) to watch a third person engaging in an activity, or to look at an image of any person engaging in an activity,
   (b) the activity is sexual, and
   (c) either—
      (i) B is under 16 and A does not reasonably believe that B is 16 or over, or
      (ii) B is under 13.

KEYNOTE

The person committing this offence must be at least 18. If the defendant is under 18, he/she commits a specific offence, punishable by 5 years' imprisonment (if tried on indictment) under s. 13. Similarly, if the person committing the offence is in a position of trust in relation to the victim, he/she commits a specific offence under s. 19.

While the related offence under s. 11 is concerned with the engaging in sexual activity which the person knows, believes or intends to be observed by a child, the above offence is concerned with intentionally causing a child to watch a third person engaging in such activity *or* to look at an image of a person *engaging in such activity*. 'Image' includes a moving or still image and includes an image produced by any means and, where the context permits, a three-dimensional image (s. 79(4)); it also includes images of an imaginary person (s. 79(5)).

As with the s. 11 offence, you must show that the defendant acted for the purposes of obtaining sexual gratification. For issues in relation to the term 'sexual gratification' see the explanation given in **para. 1.10.5.2**. Similarly, you must also show that either the child was under 13 (in which case the offence is complete) or that he/she was under 16 and that the defendant did not reasonably believe him/her to be 16 or over.

1.10.5.4   **Arranging Intended Child Sex Offences**

OFFENCE: **Arranging or Facilitating Commission of Child Sex Offences—**
Sexual Offences Act 2003, s. 14

• Triable either way • 14 years' imprisonment on indictment • Six months'
imprisonment summarily

The Sexual Offences Act 2003, s. 14 states:

(1) A person commits an offence if—
  (a) he intentionally arranges or facilitates something that he intends to do, intends another
    person to do, or believes that another person will do, in any part of the world, and
  (b) doing it will involve the commission of an offence under any of sections 9 to 13.

KEYNOTE

This offence addresses the activities of those who arrange or facilitate child sex offences. The relevant
offences are those set out in ss. 9–13 of the Act set out in the earlier paragraphs of this chapter.

The offence applies to activities by which the defendant intends to commit one of those relevant child
sex offences him/herself, or by which the defendant intends or believes another person will do so, in either
case in any part of the world. The offence is complete whether or not the sexual activity actually takes
place. Examples of the offence would include a defendant approaching a third person to procure a child to
take part in sexual activity with him or where the defendant makes travel arrangements for another in the
belief that the other person will commit a relevant child sex offence.

This part of the Act specifically excludes the actions of those who are protecting the child in question.
The exception will apply to a person acting for the child's protection who arranges or facilitates something
that he/she believes another person will do, but that he/she does not intend to do or intend another person
to do. Acting for the child's protection must fall within one of the following:

• protecting the child from sexually transmitted infection,
• protecting the physical safety of the child,
• preventing the child from becoming pregnant, or
• promoting the child's emotional well-being by the giving of advice,

and not for obtaining sexual gratification or for causing or encouraging the activity constituting the relevant
child sex offence or the child's participation in it. This statutory exception (contained in s. 14(2) and (3)) covers activities such as health workers supplying condoms to people under 16 who are intent on having sex in
any event and need protection from infection; it also potentially extends to covert investigative operations.

OFFENCE: **Meeting a Child Following Sexual Grooming—***Sexual Offences
Act 2003, s. 15*

• Triable either way • Ten years' imprisonment on indictment • Six months'
imprisonment summarily

The Sexual Offences Act 2003, s. 15 states:

(1) A person aged 18 or over (A) commits an offence if—
  (a) A has met or communicated with another person (B) on at least two occasions and sub-
    sequently—
    (i) A intentionally meets B,
    (ii) A travels with the intention of meeting B in any part of the world or arranges to meet
       B in any part of the world, or
    (iii) B travels with the intention of meeting A in any part of the world,

(b) A intends to do anything to or in respect of B, during or after the meeting mentioned in paragraph (a)(i) to (iii) and in any part of the world, which if done will involve the commission by A of a relevant offence,

(c) B is under 16, and

(d) A does not reasonably believe that B is 16 or over.

KEYNOTE

This offence was created to deal with the increase in child grooming, largely as a result of contact being made via the Internet. The initial action of the defendant involves either a meeting or a communication with the victim (who must be under 16) on at least two previous occasions. Such meetings or communications can be innocuous, such as family occasions or during the course of youth activities, sports fixtures and so on. The communications can include text messaging or interactions in Internet 'chat rooms'. Such contact can have taken place in any part of the world.

Once these earlier meetings or communications have taken place, the offence is triggered by:

- an intentional meeting with the victim;
- a defendant travelling with the intention of meeting the victim;
- the victim travelling to meet the defendant in any part of the world.

The activity at s. 15(1)(a)(iii) was introduced as a consequence of the Criminal Justice and Immigration Act 2008 and widens the grooming offence so that an offence will be committed by an adult where a child under 16 travels to meet the adult or the adult arranges to meet the child.

At the time of any of the above activities, the defendant must intend to do anything to or in respect of the victim, during or even after the meeting, that would amount to a relevant offence. A relevant offence here is generally any offence under part I of the Act (all the offences covered in this chapter). Note that the intended offence does not have to take place.

You must show that the victim was under 16 and that the defendant did not reasonably believe that he/she was 16 or over.

1.10.5.5 Abuse of Position of Trust

OFFENCE: **Abuse of Position of Trust—*Sexual Offences Act 2003, ss. 16–19***

It is a function of Local Safeguarding Children Boards (LSCBs) to develop policies and procedures for safeguarding and promoting the welfare of children, including policies and procedures in relation to the investigation of allegations concerning persons who work with children, including teachers and educational support staff.

'Position of Trust'

The Sexual Offences Act 2003, s. 21 states:

(1) For the purposes of sections 16 to 19, a person (A) is in a position of trust in relation to another person (B) if—
   (a) any of the following subsections applies, or
   (b) any condition specified in an order made by the Secretary of State is met.

(2) This subsection applies if A looks after persons under 18 who are detained in an institution by virtue of a court order or under an enactment, and B is so detained in that institution.

(3) This subsection applies if A looks after persons under 18 who are resident in a home or other place in which—

(a) accommodation and maintenance are provided by an authority under section 23(2) of the Children Act 1989 (c. 41) . . . , or

(b) accommodation is provided by a voluntary organisation under section 59(1) of that Act . . . ,

and B is resident, and is so provided with accommodation and maintenance or accommodation, in that place.

(4) This subsection applies if A looks after persons under 18 who are accommodated and cared for in one of the following institutions—

(a) a hospital,

(b) an independent clinic,

(c) a care home,

(d) a community home, voluntary home or children's home, or

(e) a home provided under section 82(5) of the Children Act 1989,

and B is accommodated and cared for in that institution.

(5) This subsection applies if A looks after persons under 18 who are receiving education at an educational institution and B is receiving, and A is not receiving, education at that institution.

(6) . . .

(7) This subsection applies if A is engaged in the provision of services under, or pursuant, to anything done under—

(a) sections 8 to 10 of the Employment and Training Act 1973 (c. 50), or

(b) section 68, 70(1)(b) or 74 of the Education and Skills Act 2008,

and, in that capacity, looks after B on an individual basis.

(8) This subsection applies if A regularly has unsupervised contact with B (whether face to face or by any other means)—

(a) in the exercise of functions of a local authority under section 20 or 21 of the Children Act 1989 (c. 41),

(b) . . .

(9) This subsection applies if A, as a person who is to report to the court under section 7 of the Children Act 1989 . . . on matters relating to the welfare of B, regularly has unsupervised contact with B (whether face to face or by any other means).

(10) This subsection applies if A is a personal adviser appointed for B under—

(a) section 23B(2) of, or paragraph 19C of Schedule 2 to, the Children Act 1989,

(b) . . .

and, in that capacity, looks after B on an individual basis.

(11) This subsection applies if—

(a) B is subject to a care order, a supervision order or an education supervision order, and

(b) in the exercise of functions conferred by virtue of the order on an authorised person or the authority designated by the order, A looks after B on an individual basis.

(12) This subsection applies if A—

(a) is an officer of the Service or Welsh family proceedings officer (within the meaning given by section 35 of the Children Act 2004) appointed for B under section 41(1) of the Children Act 1989,

(b) is appointed a children's guardian of B under rule 6 or rule 18 of the Adoption Rules 1984 (S.I. 1984/265), or

(c) is appointed to be the guardian ad litem of B under rule 9.5 of the Family Proceedings Rules 1991 (S.I. 1991/1247) . . .

and, in that capacity, regularly has unsupervised contact with B (whether face to face or by any other means).

(13) This subsection applies if—

(a) B is subject to requirements imposed by or under an enactment on his release from detention for a criminal offence, or is subject to requirements imposed by a court order made in criminal proceedings, and

(b) A looks after B on an individual basis in pursuance of the requirements.

KEYNOTE

The key to this list lies in establishing whether the defendant looked after people under 18 in the contexts described or his/her relationship with the victim fell into one of the other categories at subss. (7)–(13). Further clarification for the interpretation of these definitions is set out in s. 22.

The importance of the categories in subss. (2)–(5) is that the evidential presumptions described below will apply.

A position of trust may also exist under conditions specified by statutory instrument made by the Home Secretary (s. 21(1)(b)).

In summary, positions of trust include the wide range of settings in which a child is being lawfully detained or accommodated, including situations such as foster care, residential care and education. Those who look after children on an individual basis such as Connexions Personal Advisors and people with unsupervised contact appointed under the relevant parts of the Children Act 1989 will be covered.

There are specific procedures in place for dealing with allegations of abuse made against teachers and educational support staff. These are overseen by the relevant Local Safeguarding Children Boards.

Essentially the above provisions make it a specific offence for a person aged 18 or over in a position of trust to engage in sexual activity which is prohibited by the general child sex offences considered earlier in this chapter (ss. 9–12) in relation to a child, namely:

- sexual activity with a child;
- causing or inciting a child to engage in sexual activity;
- sexual activity in the presence of a child;
- causing a child to watch a sexual act.

There are however some key differences. For instance, in such cases involving an abuse of a position of trust, the 'child' victim can be 16 or 17 years old. Another difference is that the maximum sentence is generally lower in the corresponding offences by a person in a position of trust. In addition, except in cases where the victim is under 13, it must be shown that the defendant did not reasonably believe that the victim was 18 or over. Once it is proved that the victim was under 18 an evidential burden passes to the defendant. This means that, unless the defendant can point to some evidence to raise an arguable case to the contrary, it will be presumed that he or she did not reasonably believe that the victim was 18 or over.

There are further provisions relating to presumptions of knowledge by the defendant. Generally, if the position of trust held by the defendant falls within the first four categories set out in subss. (2)–(5) (basically where the defendant looks after children at an institution and the victim is at that institution), there will be a further evidential burden on the defendant. In such cases, it will be presumed that a defendant knew (or could reasonably have been expected to know) of the circumstances that gave rise to the position of trust. In other words, where the defendant works in an institution where the victim is, it will be presumed that the defendant knew (or could reasonably have been expected to know) that there was a position of trust between him/her and the victim unless he/she can point to some evidence to the contrary.

There is an exception to the offences under ss. 16–19 where a lawful sexual relationship existed between the defendant and the victim before the position of trust arose (s. 24) and where the defendant and the victim were lawfully married to each other at the time (s. 23). The omissions from the above statutory extract relate to Northern Ireland: for the full wording of the requirements and presumptions reference should be made to the statutory text.

1.10.5.6   **Sex Offences with Family Members**

OFFENCE: **Sexual Activity with Child Family Member**—*Sexual Offences Act* 2003,
ss. **25** *and* **26**

- Where defendant is 18 or over at the time of the offence and if involves penetration: of victim's anus or vagina by a part of defendant's body or anything else, of
victim's mouth with defendant's penis, of defendant's anus or vagina by a part of
victim's body or of defendant's mouth by victim's penis—triable on indictment:
14 years' imprisonment • Otherwise triable either way; 14 years' imprisonment
on indictment; six months' imprisonment and/or fine summarily • Or, where
defendant is under 18 at the time of the offence; five years' imprisonment on indictment; six months' imprisonment and/or fine summarily

The Sexual Offences Act 2003, s. 25 states:

(1) A person (A) commits an offence if—
   (a) he intentionally touches another person (B),
   (b) the touching is sexual,
   (c) the relation of A to B is within section 27,
   (d) A knows or could reasonably be expected to know that his relation to B is of a description
       falling within that section, and
   (e) either—
       (i) B is under 18 and A does not reasonably believe that B is 18 or over, or
       (ii) B is under 13.

KEYNOTE

Where the defendant intentionally incites another person (the victim) to touch him/her or to allow him/
herself to be touched by the defendant, there is a specific—and to all practical purposes identically
worded—offence under s. 26.

For the relevant definitions of touching and sexual see the earlier paragraphs in this chapter.

There are two further elements that must be proved in relation to these offences. The first is the existence
of the relevant family relationship between the defendant and the victim, the second is the age of the victim.

Note that, where the relevant family relationship is proved, it will be presumed that the defendant knew
or could reasonably have been expected to know that he or she was related to the victim in that way.
Similarly where it is proved that the victim was under 18, there will be a presumption that the defendant
did not reasonably believe that the victim was 18 or over. In respect of both the relationship and the age
of the defendant under these circumstances, the defendant will have an evidential burden to discharge in
that regard (see s. 25(2) and (3)).

The relevant family relationships are set out in s. 27. These cover all the close family relationships that
you would expect, along with adoptive relationships. In summary the relationships are where:

- the defendant or the victim is the other's parent, grandparent, brother, sister, half-brother, half-sister,
aunt or uncle or
- the defendant is or has been the victim's foster parent.

Additional categories are where the defendant and victim live or have lived in the same household, or the
defendant is or has been regularly involved in caring for, training, supervising or being in sole charge of
the victim and:

- one of them is or has been the other's step-parent,
- they are cousins,

- one of them is or has been the other's stepbrother or stepsister, or
- they have the same parent or foster parent.

For a full definition of the various familial relationships and their application to the specific offences, reference should be made to the statutory text.

There are exceptions for situations where the defendant and the victim are lawfully married at the time or where (under certain circumstances) the sexual relationship pre-dates the family one—for example, where two divorcees each have a child of 17 who are engaged in a sexual relationship before their respective parents marry and move all four of them into the same household.

1.10.5.7 Other Offences with Family Members

The Sexual Offences Act goes on to clarify and extend a number of other sexual offences involving adult family members (see ss. 64–65). These replace the former offences of incest and generally create either way offences punishable by up to two years' imprisonment. They can be committed by both parties where one relative (who is 16 or over) intentionally penetrates the vagina or anus of another relative (aged 18 or over) with anything, or penetrates their mouth with his penis and in each case the relative knows (or could reasonably be expected to know) that he/she is related to the other in the way described. The relatives are parent, grandparent, child, grandchild, brother, sister, half-brother, half-sister, aunt, uncle, nephew or niece. The Criminal Justice and Immigration Act 2008 amended ss. 64 and 65 of the Sexual Offences Act 2003 so that the offences of sex with an adult relative are committed where an adoptive parent has consensual sex with his/her adopted child when he/she is aged 18 or over. The adopted person does not commit this offence unless he/she is aged 18 or over.

1.10.5.8 Child Prostitution, Pornography and Payment for Sex

OFFENCE: **Paying for Sexual Services of a Child—*Sexual Offences Act 2003, s. 47***
- If victim is child under 13; triable on indictment; life imprisonment • Where victim is under 16 at the time of the offence and if involves penetration of victim's anus or vagina by a part of defendant's body or anything else, of victim's mouth with defendant's penis, of defendant's anus or vagina by a part of victim's body or by victim with anything else—triable on indictment; 14 years' imprisonment
- Otherwise triable either way; seven years' imprisonment on indictment; six months' imprisonment and/or fine summarily

The Sexual Offences Act 2003, s. 47 states:

(1) A person (A) commits an offence if—
    (a) he intentionally obtains for himself the sexual services of another person (B),
    (b) before obtaining those services, he has made or promised payment for those services to B or a third person, or knows that another person has made or promised such a payment.

KEYNOTE

In proving this offence you must show that the defendant intentionally obtained the sexual services of a child for him/herself; you must also show that, before doing so, he/she made or promised payment either to the child or another person, or that he/she knew that someone else had made or promised such payment.

If the child is under 13, the offence is complete at this point. If the child is under 18, you must prove that the defendant did not reasonably believe that the child was 18 or over (s. 47(1)(c)).

Payment means any financial advantage, including the discharge of an obligation to pay or the provision of goods or services (including sexual services) gratuitously or at a discount (s. 47(2)). This is a very wide definition and would include situations where the child victim or some other person is given drugs or other goods/services at a cheaper rate in exchange for sexual services from the child.

OFFENCE: **Causing, Inciting, Controlling, Arranging or Facilitating Child Prostitution or Pornography—*Sexual Offences Act 2003, ss. 48–50***
• Triable either way • 14 years' imprisonment on indictment • Six months' imprisonment and/or fine summarily

The Sexual Offences Act 2003, s. 48 states:

(1) A person (A) commits an offence if—
   (a) he intentionally causes or incites another person (B) to become a prostitute, or to be involved in pornography, in any part of the world...

The Sexual Offences Act 2003, s. 49 states:

(1) A person (A) commits an offence if—
   (a) he intentionally controls any of the activities of another person (B) relating to B's prostitution or involvement in pornography in any part of the world...

The Sexual Offences Act 2003, s. 50 states:

(1) A person (A) commits an offence if—
   (a) he intentionally arranges or facilitates the prostitution or involvement in pornography in any part of the world of another person (B)...

KEYNOTE

These offences are aimed at those who seek to recruit children for prostitution or to take part in pornography, or otherwise control these activities and arrangements anywhere in the world.

If the child is under 13, the offences are complete once the relevant conduct of the defendant has been proved and any belief he/she may have had as to the child's age is irrelevant to guilt. If the child is under 18, you must prove that the defendant did not reasonably believe that the child was 18 or over (see subs. (1)(b) of each).

A person is involved in pornography if an indecent image of that person is recorded and pornography and similar expressions are to be interpreted accordingly (s. 51(1)). This will cover every type of recording of images including camera phones, video footage and computer scanned images.

Prostitute means a person (A) who, *on at least one occasion and whether or not compelled to do so*, offers or provides sexual services to another person in return for payment or a promise of payment to A or a third person (s. 51(2)). Therefore the mere offering of the provision of services is covered and there is no need to show that the 'prostitute' (victim) was compelled to act in this way.

Payment means any financial advantage, including the discharge of an obligation to pay or the provision of goods or services (including sexual services) gratuitously or at a discount (s. 51(3)).

Therefore these offences would be committed if the child is recruited on a one-off basis, as well as on those occasions where the child is habitually involved. Note that, unlike the general offence of controlling prostitution (see para. 1.10.11.2) there is no need to show that the causing or inciting was done for gain. The expressions used in the sections are deliberately wide and will, in places, overlap. Controlling the activities of the child would include, for example, setting the relevant price or specifying which room or equipment is to be used. Arranging will include taking an active part in the transport or travel arrangements or organising relevant facilities (such as hotel rooms etc.).

1.10.5.9 Indecent Photographs

OFFENCE: **Indecent Photographs—*Protection of Children Act 1978, s. 1***

• Triable either way • Ten years' imprisonment on indictment • Six months' imprisonment and/or a fine summarily

The Protection of Children Act 1978, ss. 1, 1A and 1B state:

1 Indecent photographs of children

(1) Subject to sections 1A and 1B, it is an offence for a person—
  (a) to take, or permit to be taken or to make, any indecent photograph or pseudo-photograph of a child...; or
  (b) to distribute or show such indecent photographs or pseudo-photographs; or
  (c) to have in his possession such indecent photographs or pseudo-photographs, with a view to their being distributed or shown by himself or others; or
  (d) to publish or cause to be published any advertisement likely to be understood as conveying that the advertiser distributes or shows such indecent photographs or pseudo-photographs, or intends to do so.

(2) For purposes of this Act, a person is to be regarded as distributing an indecent photograph or pseudo-photograph if he parts with possession of it to, or exposes or offers it for acquisition by, another person.

(3) ...

(4) Where a person is charged with an offence under subsection (1)(b) or (c), it shall be a defence for him to prove—
  (a) that he had a legitimate reason for distributing or showing the photographs or pseudo-photographs or (as the case may be) having them in his possession; or
  (b) that he had not himself seen the photographs or pseudo-photographs and did not know, nor had any cause to suspect, them to be indecent.

(5) References in the Children and Young Persons Act 1933 (except in sections 15 and 99) to the offences mentioned in Schedule 1 to that Act shall include an offence under subsection (1)(a) above.

1A Marriage and other relationships

(1) This section applies where, in proceedings for an offence under section 1(1)(a) of taking or making an indecent photograph of a child, or for an offence under section 1(1)(b) or (c) relating to an indecent photograph of a child, the defendant proves that the photograph was of the child aged 16 or over, and that at the time of the offence charged the child and he—
  (a) were married, or civil partners of each other or
  (b) lived together as partners in an enduring family relationship.

(2) Subsections (5) and (6) also apply where, in proceedings for an offence under section 1(1)(b) or (c) relating to an indecent photograph of a child, the defendant proves that the photograph was of the child aged 16 or over, and that at the time when he obtained it the child and he—
  (a) were married, or civil partners of each other or
  (b) lived together as partners in an enduring family relationship.

(3) This section applies whether the photograph showed the child alone or with the defendant, but not if it showed any other person.

(4) In the case of an offence under section 1(1)(a), if sufficient evidence is adduced to raise an issue as to whether the child consented to the photograph being taken or made, or as to whether the defendant reasonably believed that the child so consented, the defendant is not guilty of the offence unless it is proved that the child did not so consent and that the defendant did not reasonably believe that the child so consented.

(5) In the case of an offence under section 1(1)(b), the defendant is not guilty of the offence unless it is proved that the showing or distributing was to a person other than the child.

1B Exception for criminal proceedings, investigations etc.

(1) In proceedings for an offence under section 1(1)(a) of making an indecent photograph or pseudo-photograph of a child, the defendant is not guilty of the offence if he proves that—
   (a) it was necessary for him to make the photograph or pseudo-photograph for the purposes of the prevention, detection or investigation of crime, or for the purposes of criminal proceedings, in any part of the world,
   (b) at the time of the offence charged he was a member of the Security Service or the Secret Intelligence Service, and it was necessary for him to make the photograph or pseudo-photograph for the exercise of any of the functions of that Service, or
   (c) at the time of the offence charged he was a member of GCHQ, and it was necessary for him to make the photograph or pseudo-photograph for the exercise of any of the functions of GCHQ.

What is a photograph?

Section 7 of the Protection of Children Act 1978 (as amended by the Criminal Justice and Immigration Act 2008) provides a definition of a photograph for the purposes of the Act and states:

(1) The following subsections apply for the interpretation of this Act.
(2) References to an indecent photograph include an indecent film, a copy of an indecent film, and an indecent photograph comprised in a film.
(3) Photographs (including those comprised in a film) shall, if they show children and are indecent, be treated for all purposes of this Act as indecent photographs of children and so as respects of pseudo-photographs.
(4) References to a photograph include—
   (a) the negative as well as the positive version; and
   (b) data stored on a computer disc or by other electronic means which is capable of conversion into a photograph.
(4A) References to a photograph also include—
   (a) a tracing or other image, whether made by electronic or other means (of whatever nature)—
      (i) which is not itself a photograph or pseudo-photograph, but
      (ii) which is derived from the whole or part of a photograph or pseudo-photograph (or a combination of either or both); and
   (b) data stored on a computer disc or by other electronic means which is capable of conversion into an image within paragraph (a);
   and subsection (8) applies in relation to such an image as it applies in relation to a pseudo-photograph.
(5) 'Film' includes any form of video-recording.
(6) 'Child', subject to subsection (8), means a person under the age of 18.
(7) 'Pseudo-photograph' means an image, whether made by computer graphics or otherwise howsoever, which appears to be a photograph.
(8) If the impression conveyed by a pseudo-photograph is that the person shown is a child, the pseudo-photograph shall be treated for all purposes of this Act as showing a child and so shall a pseudo-photograph where the predominant impression conveyed is that the person shown is a child notwithstanding that some of the physical characteristics shown are those of an adult.
(9) References to an indecent pseudo-photograph include—
   (a) a copy of an indecent pseudo-photograph; and
   (b) data stored on a computer disc or by other electronic means which is capable of conversion into an indecent pseudo-photograph.

OFFENCE: **Indecent Photographs—*Criminal Justice Act 1988, s. 160***

- Triable either way • Five years' imprisonment on indictment • Six months' imprisonment and/or a fine

The Criminal Justice Act 1988, ss. 160 and 160A state:

160 Possession of indecent photograph of child

(1) Subject to section 160A, it is an offence for a person to have any indecent photograph or pseudo-photograph of a child in his possession.

(2) Where a person is charged with an offence under subsection (1) above, it shall be a defence for him to prove—

   (a) that he had a legitimate reason for having the photograph or pseudo-photograph in his possession; or

   (b) that he had not himself seen the photograph or pseudo-photograph and did not know, nor had any cause to suspect, it to be indecent; or

   (c) that the photograph or pseudo-photograph was sent to him without any prior request made by him or on his behalf and that he did not keep it for an unreasonable time.

160A Marriage and other relationships

(1) This section applies where, in proceedings for an offence under section 160 relating to an indecent photograph of a child, the defendant proves that the photograph was of the child aged 16 or over, and that at the time of the offence charged the child and he—

   (a) were married, or civil partners of each other or

   (b) lived together as partners in an enduring family relationship.

(2) This section also applies where, in proceedings for an offence under section 160 relating to an indecent photograph of a child, the defendant proves that the photograph was of the child aged 16 or over, and that at the time when he obtained it the child and he—

   (a) were married, or civil partners of each other or

   (b) lived together as partners in an enduring family relationship.

(3) This section applies whether the photograph showed the child alone or with the defendant, but not if it showed any other person.

(4) If sufficient evidence is adduced to raise an issue as to whether the child consented to the photograph being in the defendant's possession, or as to whether the defendant reasonably believed that the child so consented, the defendant is not guilty of the offence unless it is proved that the child did not so consent and that the defendant did not reasonably believe that the child so consented.

KEYNOTE

Once the defendant realises, *or should realise*, that material is indecent, any distribution, showing or retention of the material with a view to its being distributed will result in a *prima facie* offence being made out under the 1978 Act if the person depicted turns out to be a child (*R v Land* [1999] QB 65). This is because s. 160(4) provides no defence of mistake as to a child's age.

A person will be a 'child' for the purposes of both Acts above if it appears from the evidence as a whole that he/she was, at the material time, under the age of 18 (Protection of Children Act 1978, s. 2(3) and Criminal Justice Act 1988, s. 160(4)).

However, if the impression conveyed by a pseudo-photograph is that the person shown is a child or where the predominant impression is that the person is a child, that pseudo-photograph will be treated for these purposes as a photograph of a child, notwithstanding that some of the physical characteristics shown are those of an adult (s. 7(8) of the 1978 Act).

'Pseudo-photographs' include computer images and the above offences will cover the situation where part of the photograph is made up of an adult form. The widespread use of the Internet to facilitate offences relating to indecent photographs has led to a great deal of case law on the subject, much of which involves technical issues surrounding the way such images are downloaded, stored and viewed. What follows is a summary of several key decisions by the courts on these issues:

- Downloading images from the Internet will amount to 'making' a photograph for the purposes of s. 1(1)(a) of the 1978 Act (*R* v *Bowden* [2000] 2 WLR 1083).
- 'Making' pseudo-photographs includes voluntary browsing through indecent images of children on and from the Internet. Once an image is downloaded, the length of time it remains on the screen is irrelevant (*R* v *Smith and Jayson* [2002] EWCA Crim 683).
- In the same case the Court of Appeal held that a person receiving an unsolicited e-mail attachment containing an indecent image of a child would not commit the offence under s. 1(1)(a) by opening it if he/she was unaware that it contained or was likely to contain an indecent image. This was because s. 1(1)(a) does not create an absolute offence.
- Copying onto a hard drive and storing 'pop-ups' containing indecent images of children amounts to possessing those images (*R* v *Harrison* [2007] EWCA Crim 2976).
- If images have been deleted from a computer so that their retrieval is impossible and, at the material time, a person cannot gain access to them and the images are beyond a person's control, that person cannot be in possession of them (*R* v *Porter* [2006] EWCA Crim 560).
- Evidence indicating an interest in paedophile material generally along with evidence to show how a computer had been used to access paedophile news groups, chat lines and websites can be relevant to show that it was more likely than not that a file containing an indecent image of a child had been created deliberately (*R* v *Mould* [2001] 2 Cr App R(S) 8).
- An image consisting of two parts of two different photographs taped together (the naked body of a woman taped to the head of a child) is not a 'pseudo-photograph'. If such an image were to be photocopied it could be (*Goodland* v *DPP* [2000] 1 WLR 1427).
- Where a defendant had knowledge that images were likely to be accessed by others, any images would be downloaded 'with a view to distribute' (*R* v *Dooley* [2005] EWCA Crim 3093).

The statutory defence under s. 160(2)(b) of the 1988 Act above is broader than it seems at first. Although the wording requires that the defendant (1) has not seen the material and (2) did not know or have *any* cause to suspect it was indecent, the defendant will be acquitted of the offence under s. 160 if he/she proves that (1) he/she had not seen the material and (2) did not know (and had no cause to suspect) that it was *an indecent photograph of a child*. This was confirmed by the Court of Appeal in *R* v *Collier* [2004] EWCA Crim 1411 and arose from an argument where the material relating to children had been among other adult material that the defendant *did* know was indecent—he just did not know that it was an indecent photograph *of a child*.

A legitimate purpose for possessing such material might be where someone has the material as an exhibits officer or as a training aid for police officers or social workers.

The consent of the DPP is needed before prosecuting an offence under the Protection of Children Act 1978.

Distributing will include lending or offering to another. Clearly cases falling within the above legislation will vary significantly and there needs to be some distinction between the seriousness of different types of material. The Court of Appeal has set out five broad levels of seriousness and these are of use, not only in helping police officers and investigators understand how the offences will be dealt with by the criminal courts, but also in explaining this to victims and witnesses. The levels are:

(1) images depicting erotic posing with no sexual activity;

(2) sexual activity between children, or solo masturbation by a child;

(3) non-penetrative sexual activity between adults and children;

(4) penetrative sexual activity between children and adults, and;

(5) sadism or bestiality.

(*R* v *Oliver* [2002] EWCA Crim 2766).

The Court of Appeal also recognised that much of this material involves abuse of the child featuring in it and held that, so far as an offender's involvement was concerned, the seriousness of an offence increased with his/her proximity to, and responsibility for, the original abuse. In considering all these factors, courts will distinguish between pseudo-photographs which had involved no abuse or exploitation of children, and photographic images that involved real children. The Court of Appeal indicated that imprisonment would normally follow where the material had been shown or distributed to others or where the offender had been in possession of a large amount of level 2 material or a small amount of material of level 3 or above.

Note that although the offences include video recordings, possession of exposed but undeveloped film (i.e. film in the form in which it is taken out of a camera) does not appear to be covered. The offence at s. 1(1)(b) and (c) of the 1978 Act can only be proved if the defendant showed/distributed the photograph etc. or intended to show or distribute the photograph etc. *to someone else.* This is clear from the decisions in *R* v *Fellows* [1997] 1 Cr App R 244 and *R* v *T* [1999] 163 JP 349. If no such intention can be proved, or if the defendant only had the photographs etc. for his/her own use, the appropriate charge would be under the 1988 Act.

Sections 1 and 2 of the Criminal Evidence (Amendment) Act 1997 apply to an offence under s. 1 of the Protection of Children Act 1978 (and to conspiracies, attempts or incitements in the circumstances set out in the 1997 Act) (see Evidence and Procedure, para. 2.11.7.1).

1.10.5.10 Defences to Indecent Photographs of Marriage and Other Relationships

There is a specific defence to offences under s. 1(1) (a), (b) and (c) of the Protection of Children Act 1978 (making, distributing or possessing with a view to distributing). This defence arises where the defendant can prove that the photograph was of a child aged 16 or over, the photograph only showed the defendant and the child, and that, at the time of the offence, they were married, in a civil partnership or lived together as partners in an enduring family relationship (s. 1A). This is a very narrow defence, restricted to photographs (as opposed to pseudo-photographs, which are not covered) in the restricted circumstances set out. If the defendant cannot show these elements, the defence will not apply. If the defendant *can* show these elements, then the following further conditions of the defence will apply:

- In the case of an offence under s. 1(1)(a) (taking or permitting to be taken etc.), the defendant will have an evidential burden of showing that the child consented or that the defendant reasonably believed that the child consented to the making of the photograph (s. 1A(4)).
- In the case of an offence under s. 1(1)(b) (distributing or showing), you must prove that the distributing or showing was to a person other than the child in the photograph (s. 1A(5)).
- In the case of an offence under s. 1(1)(c) (possession with a view to distribution or showing etc.), the defendant will have an evidential burden of demonstrating that the image was to be shown/distributed to no person other than the child and that the child consented to the defendant's possession of the photograph (s. 1A(6)).

Similar provisions are made in relation to the offence under s. 160 of the Criminal Justice Act 1988 (possession)—see s. 160A.

1.10.5.11 Exception of Indecent Photographs for Criminal Proceedings and Investigations

There is a limited defence in relation to the making of an indecent photograph or pseudo-photograph under s. 1(1)(a) of the Protection of Children Act 1978 where the defendant proves that:

- it was *necessary* for him/her to make the photograph or pseudo-photograph for the purposes of the prevention, detection or investigation of crime or for criminal proceedings in any part of the world, or
- at the time he/she was a member of the Security Service, Secret Intelligence Service or GCHQ (Government Communications Headquarters) and it was necessary for the exercise of any of the functions of that Service/GCHQ (s. 1B).

In order to assist police officers and prosecutors the Association of Chief Police Officers (ACPO) and the Crown Prosecution Service (CPS) have published a Memorandum of Understanding. This Memorandum sets out the factors that will be taken into account in deciding whether the intention of someone accused of an offence under s. 1(1)(a) attracted criminal liability when 'making' a photograph etc. As the Memorandum points out:

> This reverse burden is intended to allow those people who need to be able to identify and act to deal with such images to do so. It also presents a significant obstacle to would-be abusers and those who exploit the potential of technology to gain access to paedophilic material for unprofessional (or personal) reasons.

The purpose of the Memorandum is therefore twofold: to reassure those whose duties properly involve the prevention, detection or investigation of this type of crime and also as a warning to others who might claim this defence having taken it upon themselves to investigate such offences. In summary the following criteria will be considered:

- How soon after its discovery the image was reported and to whom.
- The circumstances in which it was discovered.
- The way in which the image was stored and dealt with, and whether it was copied.
- Whether the person's actions were reasonable, proportionate and necessary.

1.10.6 Possession of Prohibited Images of Children

OFFENCE: **Possession of Prohibited Images of Children—*Coroners and Justice Act 2009, s. 62***
- Triable either way • Three years' imprisonment on indictment and/or fine • Six months' imprisonment and/or a fine

The Coroners and Justice Act 2009, s. 62 states:

(1) It is an offence for a person to be in possession of a prohibited image of a child.
(2) A prohibited image is an image which—
    (a) is pornographic,
    (b) falls within subsection (6), and
    (c) is grossly offensive, disgusting or otherwise of an obscene character.

KEYNOTE

An image is 'pornographic' if it is of such a nature that it must reasonably be assumed to have been produced solely or principally for the purpose of sexual arousal.

An image falls within subsection (6) if it is an image which focuses solely or principally on a child's genitals or anal region, or portrays any of the acts mentioned below. Those acts are:

- the performance by a person of an act of intercourse or oral sex with or in the presence of a child;
- an act of masturbation by, of, involving or in the presence of a child;
- an act which involves penetration of the vagina or anus of a child with a part of a person's body or with anything else;
- an act of penetration, in the presence of a child, of the vagina or anus of a person with a part of a person's body or with anything else;
- the performance by a child of an act of intercourse or oral sex with an animal (whether dead or alive or imaginary);
- the performance by a person of an act of intercourse or oral sex with an animal (whether dead or alive or imaginary) in the presence of a child.

Penetration is a continuing act from entry to withdrawal.

Section 62(4) of the offence states that where (as found in a person's possession) an individual image forms part of a series of images, the question of whether it is pornographic must be determined by reference both to the image itself and the context in which it appears in the series of images. Where an image is integral to a narrative (for example a mainstream or documentary film) which when it is taken as a whole could not reasonably be assumed to be pornographic, the image itself may not be pornographic, even though if considered in isolation the contrary conclusion might have been reached (s.62(5)). This is related to the exclusion from the scope of the offence of certain excluded images under s. 63 of the Act.

Proceedings for an offence under subsection (1) may not be instituted in England and Wales, except by or with the consent of the Director of Public Prosecutions.

Meaning of 'image' and 'child'

Section 65 states that an 'image' includes a moving or still image (produced by any means) such as a photograph or film, or data (stored by any means) which is capable of conversion into a movable or still image such as data stored electronically (as on a computer disk), which is capable of conversion into an image. This covers material available on computers, mobile phones or any other electronic device. It should be noted that the term 'image' *does not* include an indecent photograph, or indecent pseudo-photograph, of a child as these are subject to other controls (see s. 160 of the Criminal Justice Act 1988 above).

A 'child' means a person under the age of 18 (s. 65(5)). Where an image shows a person the image is to be treated as an image of a child if the impression conveyed by the image is that the person shown is a child, or the predominant impression conveyed is that the person shown is a child despite the fact that some of the physical characteristics shown are not those of a child (s. 65(6)).

References to an image of a person include references to an image of an imaginary person. References to an image of a child include references to an image of an imaginary child.

1.10.6.1 Defence

The Coroners and Justice Act 2009, s. 64 states:

(1) Where a person is charged with an offence under section 62(1), it is a defence for the person to prove any of the following matters—

(a) that the person had a legitimate reason for being in possession of the image concerned;
(b) that the person had not seen the image concerned and did not know, nor had any cause to suspect, it to be a prohibited image of a child;
(c) that the person—
    (i) was sent the image concerned without any prior request having been made by or on behalf of the person, and
    (ii) did not keep it for an unreasonable time.

KEYNOTE

This section sets out a series of defences to the section 62 offence of possession of prohibited images of children. These defences are the same as those for the offence of possession of indecent images of children under section 160(2) of the Criminal Justice Act 1988.

1.10.7   Possession of Extreme Pornographic Images

This offence is set out under ss. 63–67 of the Criminal Justice and Immigration Act 2008. The introduction of the offence is not intended to extend the law to cover additional material beyond what is illegal to publish under the Obscene Publications Act 1959. Indeed this offence covers a more limited range of material than the Obscene Publications Act. It creates a possession offence in respect of a sub-text of extreme pornographic material which is defined in s. 63 of the Act.

OFFENCE: **Possession of Extreme Pornographic Images—*Criminal Justice and Immigration Act 2008, s. 63***
- Triable either way • Three years' imprisonment on indictment and/or a fine (where the images contain life-threatening acts or serious injury) • Two years' imprisonment on indictment and/or a fine (where the images contain acts of necrophilia or bestiality)
- Six months' imprisonment and/or a fine summarily

The Criminal Justice and Immigration Act 2008, s. 63 states:

(1) It is an offence for a person to be in possession of an extreme pornographic image.

KEYNOTE

Proceedings cannot be instituted without the consent of the DPP.

There are three elements to the offence. An image must come within the terms of all three elements before it will fall foul of the offence. Those elements are:

- that the image is pornographic;
- that the image is grossly offensive, disgusting, or otherwise of an obscene character, and
- that the image portrays in an explicit and realistic way, one of the following extreme acts:
  - ✦ an act which threatens a person's life (this could include depictions of hanging, suffocation or sexual assault involving a threat with a weapon);
  - ✦ an act which results in or is likely to result in serious injury to a person's anus, breasts or genitals (this could include the insertion of sharp objects or the mutilation of the breasts or genitals);
  - ✦ an act involving sexual interference with a human corpse (necrophilia);
  - ✦ a person performing an act of intercourse or oral sex with an animal (whether dead or alive) (bestiality);

- and a reasonable person looking at the image would think that the people and animals portrayed were real.

The key to assessing s. 63 accurately is to apply all three elements to an example under consideration. To focus on just one element in isolation inevitably leads to false conclusions about what is caught. The three elements, when taken together, should ensure that the offence only covers material which it is an offence to publish under the Obscene Publications Act 1959.

An 'extreme pornographic image' is an image which is both pornographic and an extreme image. An image is 'pornographic' if it is of such a nature that it must reasonably be assumed to have been produced solely or principally for the purpose of sexual arousal. Section 63(4) and (5) provides that where an image is integral to a narrative (for example a mainstream or documentary film) which taken as a whole could not reasonably be assumed to be pornographic, the image itself may be taken not to be pornographic even though if considered in isolation the contrary conclusion would have been reached.

An 'image' means either still images (such as photographs) or moving images (such as those in a film). The term also incorporates any type of data, including that stored electronically (as on a computer disk), which is capable of conversion into an image. This covers material available on computers, mobile phones or any other electronic device. The scope of the definition of image is also affected by the requirement that the persons or animals portrayed in an image must appear to be real. This requirement has the effect of excluding animated characters, sketches, paintings and the like (s. 63(8)). References to parts of the body include body parts that have been surgically constructed (s. 63(9)).

Section 64 of the Act provides an exclusion from the scope of the offence under s. 63 for classified films (films that have been classified by the British Board of Film Classification).

1.10.7.1 General Defences

Several general defences to the offence of possession of extreme pornographic images are set out in s. 65 of the Act. They are:

- that the person had a legitimate reason for being in possession of the image; this will cover those who can demonstrate that their legitimate business means that they have a reason for possessing the image;
- that the person had not seen the image and therefore neither knew, nor had cause to suspect, that the images held were extreme pornographic images; this will cover those who are in possession of offending images but are unaware of the nature of the images; and
- that the person had not asked for the image—it having been sent without request—and that he/she had not kept it for an unreasonable period of time; this will cover those who are sent unsolicited material and who act quickly to delete it or otherwise get rid of it.

1.10.7.2 Defence: Participation in Consensual Acts

Section 66 of the Act provides an additional defence for those who participate in the creation of extreme pornographic images. The defence is limited and will not cover images relating to bestiality and necrophilia images that depict a real corpse.

To use the defence, a defendant must prove (on the balance of probabilities) that he/she directly participated in the act or acts portrayed in the image and that the act(s) did not involve the infliction of non-consensual harm on any person. Where the image depicts necrophilia the defendant must also prove that the human corpse portrayed was not in fact a corpse. Non-consensual harm is harm which is of such a nature that, in law, a person cannot consent to it being inflicted on him or herself, or harm to which a person can consent but did not in fact consent.

1.10.8   Sexual Offences Against People with a Mental Disorder

The Sexual Offences Act 2003 is centred largely upon the fact that certain mental disorders deprive the sufferer of the ability to refuse involvement in sexual activity. This is different from, and wider than, a lack of consent at the time and focuses on the victim's inability to refuse.

1.10.8.1   Definition of 'Mental Disorder'

The relevant definition of a 'mental disorder' is that of s. 1(2) of the Mental Health Act 1983 which defines mental disorder as meaning any disorder or disability of the mind.

1.10.8.2   Sexual Activity with Mentally Disordered Person

OFFENCE: **Sexual Activity with a Person with a Mental Disorder—*Sexual Offences Act 2003, s. 30***
- If involves penetration of victim's anus or vagina, of victim's mouth with defendant's penis, or of defendant's mouth by victim's penis—triable on indictment; life imprisonment • Otherwise triable either way; 14 years' imprisonment on indictment; six months' imprisonment and/or fine summarily

The Sexual Offences Act 2003, s. 30 states:

(1) A person (A) commits an offence if—
   (a) he intentionally touches another person (B),
   (b) the touching is sexual,
   (c) B is unable to refuse because of or for a reason related to a mental disorder, and
   (d) A knows or could reasonably be expected to know that B has a mental disorder and that because of it or for a reason related to it B is likely to be unable to refuse.

KEYNOTE

This is very similar to the general offence of sexual touching under s. 3.

In order to prove the above offence you must show, not only that the sexual touching was intentional, but also that the victim was *unable to refuse* and that this inability was because of, or for a reason related to a mental disorder. The Act goes on to provide that a person is unable to refuse if:

- they lack the capacity to choose whether to agree to the touching (whether because they lack sufficient understanding of the nature or reasonably foreseeable consequences of what is being done, or for any other reason), or
- they are unable to communicate such a choice to the defendant. s. 30(2).

Once you have established these elements, you must also show that the defendant knew or could reasonably have been expected to know both that the victim had a mental disorder *and* that because of it (or for a reason related to it) he or she was likely to be unable to refuse. In *Hulme* v *DPP* [2006] EWHC 1347 (Admin), the Divisional Court examined a decision reached by a magistrates' court in relation to a complainant who was a cerebral palsy sufferer with a low IQ (aged 27). The magistrates' court had decided that the complainant was unable to refuse to be touched sexually; the Divisional Court agreed and the conviction against the defendant (who was 73) was upheld.

If the defendant obtains the victim's agreement to sexual touching by means of any inducement (offered or given), or a threat or deception for that purpose, the defendant commits a specific (and similarly punishable) offence under s. 34. An example of such an offence would be where the defendant promises to give the victim some reward in exchange for allowing sexual touching or where he or she deceives the victim into believing that the touching is necessary for some other purpose. If the defendant uses an inducement, threat or deception to *cause* the victim to engage in or agree to engage in sexual activity, there is a further specific offence (similarly punishable) under s. 35.

In these specific cases of inducements, threats or deception there is still the need to prove that the defendant knew (or could reasonably have been expected to know) of the victim's mental disorder but *no need to prove that the victim was unable to refuse*.

Causing or inciting a person with a mental disorder impeding choice to engage in sexual activity with another person generally (i.e. without threats, inducements or deception) is a separate offence, punishable in the same way, under s. 31. As that is an 'incomplete' or unfinished offence (as to which **see chapter 1.3**) it is not necessary to prove that the sexual activity took place.

1.10.8.3 Sexual Activity in Presence of Mentally Disordered Person

OFFENCE: **Sexual Activity in Presence of a Person with a Mental Disorder—** *Sexual Offences Act 2003, s. 32*

• Triable either way • Ten years' imprisonment on Indictment • Six months' imprisonment and/or fine summarily

The Sexual Offences Act 2003, s. 32 states:

(1) A person (A) commits an offence if—
  (a) he intentionally engages in an activity,
  (b) the activity is sexual,
  (c) for the purpose of obtaining sexual gratification, he engages in it—
    (i) when another person (B) is present or is in a place from which A can be observed, and
    (ii) knowing or believing that B is aware, or intending that B should be aware, that he is engaging in it,
  (d) B is unable to refuse because of or for a reason related to a mental disorder, and
  (e) A knows or could reasonably be expected to know that B has a mental disorder and that because of it or for a reason related to it B is likely to be unable to refuse.

KEYNOTE

This is very similar to the corresponding offence relating to children under s. 11 (as to which **see para. 1.10.5.2**).

As with the previous offence, you will need to show that the defendant intentionally engaged in sexual activity; you will also have to show that he or she did so:

• when a person (who was unable to refuse because of, or for a reason related to, a mental disorder) was present or in a place from which the defendant could be observed, and
• that the defendant knew/believed/intended that the mentally disordered person was aware that he or she was engaging in that activity

for the purposes of sexual gratification.

For the requirements in proving the victim's inability to refuse see the previous offence under s. 30.

Because of the wording of s. 79(7) 'observation' includes direct observation or by looking at any image. For the specific offence of causing a person with a mental disorder impeding choice to watch a sexual act or an image of such an act see below.

If the victim agrees to be present or in the place referred to in s. 32(1)(c)(i) above because of any inducement (offered or given), or a threat or deception practised by the defendant for that purpose, the defendant commits a specific (and similarly punishable) offence under s. 36. An example of such an offence would be where the defendant pays the mentally disordered person to stay in a particular place while the activity occurs. In these specific cases of inducements, threats or deception there is still the need to prove that the defendant knew (or could reasonably have been expected to know) of the victim's mental disorder but *no need to prove that the victim was unable to refuse.*

1.10.8.4 Causing Person with Mental Disorder to Watch Sexual Act

OFFENCE: **Causing a Person with a Mental Disorder to Watch a Sexual Act—** *Sexual Offences Act 2003, s. 33*

• Triable either way • Ten years' imprisonment on indictment • Six months' imprisonment summarily

The Sexual Offences Act 2003, s. 33 states:

(1) A person (A) commits an offence if—
  (a) for the purpose of obtaining sexual gratification, he intentionally causes another person (B) to watch a third person engaging in an activity, or to look at an image of any person engaging in an activity,
  (b) the activity is sexual, and
  (c) B is unable to refuse because of or for a reason related to a mental disorder, and
  (d) A knows or could reasonably be expected to know that B has a mental disorder and that because of it or for a reason related to it B is likely to be unable to refuse.

KEYNOTE

For the key elements to prove in relation to this offence see the earlier offences above.

While the related offence under s. 32 is concerned with engaging in sexual activity which the person knows, believes or intends to be observed by a person with a mental disorder impeding their choice, the above offence is concerned with intentionally causing such a person to watch a third person engaging in such activity *or* to look at an image of a person engaging in such activity. 'Image' includes a moving or still image and includes an image produced by any means and, where the context permits, a three-dimensional image (s. 79(4); it also includes images of an imaginary person (s. 79(5)).

If the victim agrees to watch or look because of any inducement (offered or given), or a threat or deception practised by the defendant for that purpose, the defendant commits a specific (and similarly punishable) offence under s. 37. An example of such an offence would be where the defendant (with the appropriate motive) deceives the mentally disordered person into watching a film which is actually a live video feed of sexual activity. In these specific cases of inducements, threats or deception there is still the need to prove that the defendant knew (or could reasonably have been expected to know) of the victim's mental disorder but *no need to prove that the victim was unable to refuse.*

1.10.8.5 Care Workers

There are specific sexual offences that apply to people who are involved in the care of the mentally disordered victim. These offences follow similar wording to those general offences set out above (namely engaging in, causing or inciting sexual activity, sexual activity in the presence of a mentally disordered person etc.). In proving these offences (which appear in ss. 38–41 of the Act) you must show that the person was in a relationship of care as defined at s. 42. These are generally people whose employment has brought them into regular face-to-face contact with the victim in care homes, voluntary homes or hospitals. The offences are similar to those involving a position of trust. In these offences there is no need to prove that the victim was unable to refuse to take part in the activity but you must show that the defendant knew or could reasonably have been expected to know that the victim has a mental disorder. Given that the defendant will be a care worker with direct personal knowledge of the victim's circumstances, there is a presumption against the defendant that he or she had (or could reasonably have been expected to have) such knowledge and the defendant will have to discharge an evidential burden in that regard if he/she is using this issue as part of his/her defence.

1.10.9 Sexual Displays and Voyeurism

While many of the sexual offences dealt with in this chapter concern the sexual activity itself, or the encouragement of it, there are several offences that involve sexual 'displays' of some description and of voyeurism; there is also a specific offence of sexual activity in public lavatories. All of these are addressed below.

1.10.9.1 Indecent Exposure

Although it is often trivialised, the behaviour of those who indecently expose themselves in public is both distressing and often symptomatic of a psychological disorder which can manifest itself in other, far more destructive ways.

OFFENCE: **Outraging Public Decency—*Common Law***

- Triable either way • Unlimited powers of sentence on indictment • Six months' imprisonment and/or fine summarily

It is an offence at common law to commit an act of a lewd, obscene or disgusting nature and outrage public decency.

KEYNOTE

This offence is committed by the deliberate commission of an act that is, *per se*, lewd, obscene or disgusting (*R* v *Rowley* [1991] 4 All ER 649). If an act is not lewd, obscene etc. then the motives or intentions of the defendant cannot make it so. Therefore, where the defendant's acts involved leaving messages that were not in themselves obscene in public toilets, his motives (to induce young boys to engage in gross indecency with him) did not bring his actions under this offence (*Rowley* above). In *Rowley* the court cited a speech by Lord Simon in *Knuller (Publishing, Printing and Promotions) Ltd* v *DPP* [1973] AC 435. Lord Simon had said that 'outraging public decency' goes considerably beyond offending the sensibilities of, or even shocking, reasonable people and that the recognised minimum standards of decency were likely to vary from time to time.

The offence can be committed by exposing the penis or engaging in simulated sexual acts (*R* v *Mayling* [1963] 2 QB 717) but it may also be committed in other ways and is not restricted to offences committed by men.

The act must be committed where it might be seen by the public generally and it must be shown that more than one person could have seen the act take place (*R* v *Walker* [1996] 1 Cr App R 111).

It is not necessary to prove that someone was *in fact* annoyed or insulted (*R* v *May* (1989) 91 Cr App R 157).

OFFENCE: **Exposure—*Sexual Offences Act 2003, s. 66***
• Triable either way • Two years' imprisonment on indictment • Six months' imprisonment summarily

The Sexual Offences Act 2003, s. 66 states:

(1) A person commits an offence if—
    (a) he intentionally exposes his genitals, and
    (b) he intends that someone will see them and be caused alarm or distress.

KEYNOTE

This offence requires only the intentional exposure of the genitals with the dual intention of their being seen by someone else and that this other person will be caused alarm or distress.

There is no need to show that the defendant acted for sexual gratification and simply exposing the genitals out of loutish behaviour will suffice if the other ingredients are present.

The offence is not restricted to public places and there is no need to show that anyone saw the genitals or was alarmed or distressed. This offence is gender-neutral, which means that women can be guilty of exposure. It also means that a man or boy can be a victim as well as a woman or a girl. The offence only applies to the genitals, not the buttocks, so the act of 'mooning' will not be covered. A woman who exposes her breasts will not be guilty of an offence under s. 66.

1.10.9.2 Voyeurism

OFFENCE: **Voyeurism—*Sexual Offences Act 2003, s. 67***
• Triable either way • Two years' imprisonment on indictment • Six months' imprisonment summarily

The Sexual Offences Act 2003, s. 67 states:

(1) A person commits an offence if—
    (a) for the purpose of obtaining sexual gratification, he observes another person doing a private act, and
    (b) he knows that the other person does not consent to being observed for his sexual gratification.
(2) A person commits an offence if—
    (a) he operates equipment with the intention of enabling another person to observe, for the purpose of obtaining sexual gratification, a third person (B) doing a private act, and
    (b) he knows that B does not consent to his operating equipment with that intention.
(3) A person commits an offence if—
    (a) he records another person (B) doing a private act,
    (b) he does so with the intention that he or a third person will, for the purpose of obtaining sexual gratification, look at an image of B doing the act, and
    (c) he knows that B does not consent to his recording the act with that intention.

KEYNOTE

Unlike the previous offence of exposure, these offences require proof of the defendant's motive of sexual gratification.

A person is doing a private act if they are in a place which, in the circumstances, would reasonably be expected to provide privacy, and:

- their genitals, buttocks or breasts are exposed or covered only with underwear
- they are using a lavatory, or
- they are doing a sexual act that is not of a kind ordinarily done in public (s. 68).

The word 'breasts' does not extend to the exposed male chest (*R* v *Bassett* [2008] EWCA Crim 1174).

The three offences described above require proof that the victim does not consent to the observing, recording or operating of the relevant equipment *for the purpose of the defendant's or another's sexual gratification* (i.e. they might have consented to being observed, recorded etc. for other reasons). The first offence involves a defendant observing another doing a private act (which will include looking at an image—s. 79(5)) with the relevant motive of gaining sexual gratification. The second offence deals with people operating equipment such as hoteliers or landlords using webcams to enable others to view live footage of the residents or tenants, in each case for the sexual gratification of those others. There is no need to show that the defendant intended to gain sexual gratification themselves.

The third offence deals with the recording of the private act with the intention that the person doing the recording or another will look at the image and thereby obtain sexual gratification. It does not matter that those who eventually look at the recording know that the victim did not consent, though all elements of the offence would be corroborated by the accompanying material (e.g. the descriptions of the pages on an internet website). A practical example of this offence can be seen in *R* v *Turner* [2006] EWCA Crim 63 where the defendant—the manager of a gym—had recorded images of women showering and using the sun beds. The court regarded this as an abuse of the defendant's position of trust which took him 'over the custodial threshold' and he was sentenced (following an appeal) to nine months' imprisonment.

Finally, there is also a specific offence under s. 67(4) of installing equipment or adapting structures (e.g. drilling peepholes) with the intention of committing the first offence themselves or enabling others to do so. Structures will include tents, vehicles or vessels or other temporary or movable structures.

The restricted wording of s. 67(4) appears not to cover the situation where the defendant installs equipment to *record* the private act (under s. 67(2)) rather than observing it live.

It can be seen that these offences do not extend to activities such as, for example, covertly filming up women's skirts as they go about the public act of shopping and travelling to work.

1.10.9.3 Sexual Activity in a Public Lavatory

OFFENCE: **Sexual Activity in a Public Lavatory—*Sexual Offences Act 2003, s. 71***

- Triable summarily ● Six months' imprisonment and/or a fine

The Sexual Offences Act 2003, s. 71 states:

(1) A person commits an offence if—
  (a) he is in a lavatory to which the public or a section of the public has or is permitted to have access, whether on payment or otherwise,
  (b) he intentionally engages in an activity, and,
  (c) the activity is sexual.

> **KEYNOTE**
>
> This offence will apply to any lavatory to which the public or a section of it has access. For the purposes of this offence only, an activity is sexual if a reasonable person would, in all the circumstances but regardless of any person's purpose, consider it to be sexual. This is a narrower definition than the more general one of 'sexual' used in other sections of the Act (see s. 78).

1.10.10 Preparatory Offences

In addition to the many substantive offences covered by this chapter, there are specific provisions to prevent the consequences set out in those offences from happening.

1.10.10.1 Any Offence with Intent to Commit Sexual Offence

OFFENCE: **Committing Criminal Offence with Intent to Commit a Sexual Offence**—*Sexual Offences Act 2003, s. 62*
- Where the offence committed is kidnapping or false imprisonment—triable on indictment only; life imprisonment • Otherwise triable either way; ten years' imprisonment on indictment; six months' imprisonment and/or a fine summarily

The Sexual Offences Act 2003, s. 62 states:

(1) A person commits an offence under this section if he commits any offence with the intention of committing a relevant sexual offence.

> **KEYNOTE**
>
> Relevant sexual offence means an offence under part I of the Act (virtually all regularly occurring sexual offences) including aiding, abetting, counselling or procuring such an offence (s. 62(2)). It *does not extend* to other sexual offences such as those under the Protection of Children Act 1978.
>
> This offence is designed to deal with the commission of any criminal offence where the defendant's intention is to commit a relevant sexual offence. In addition to the more obvious offences of kidnapping and false imprisonment, this would appear to cover a vast array of possible circumstances where the defendant's ulterior motive in committing the first offence is to carry out the relevant sexual offence. As there is no express requirement for there to be any immediate link in time between the two offences, the wording appears to cover any situation from the theft of drugs or equipment to be used in the course of the sexual offence and going equipped for burglary, to the taking of a vehicle or even dangerous driving with the intention in each case of committing the further relevant sexual offence.

1.10.10.2 Trespass with Intent to Commit Sexual Offence

OFFENCE: **Trespass with Intent to Commit a Relevant Sexual Offence**—*Sexual Offences Act 2003, s. 63*
- Triable either way • Ten years' imprisonment on indictment • Six months' imprisonment and/or a fine summarily

The Sexual Offences Act 2003, s. 63 states:

(1) A person commits an offence if—
   (a) he is a trespasser on any premises,
   (b) he intends to commit a relevant sexual offence on the premises, and
   (c) he knows that, or is reckless as to whether, he is a trespasser.

KEYNOTE

A person is a trespasser if they are on the premises without the owner or occupier's consent, whether express or implied. Generally, the defendant ought to know whether he/she is trespassing or not and recklessness will be enough in that regard.

Premises here will include a structure or part of a structure (including a tent, vehicle or vessel or other temporary or movable structure)—s. 63(2)—which is wider than the term 'building' used in the Theft Act offence of burglary.

Relevant sexual offence has the same meaning as in the s. 62 offence (see para. 1.10.9.1).

This offence is one of intention rather than consequence and so there is no need to prove that the substantive sexual offence took place.

Note that the defendant must intend to commit the relevant offence *on the premises*.

1.10.10.3 Administering Substance with Intent

OFFENCE: **Administering Substance with Intent—*Sexual Offences Act 2003, s. 61***

- Triable either way • Ten years' imprisonment on indictment • Six months' imprisonment and/or a fine summarily

The Sexual Offences Act 2003, s. 61 states:

(1) A person commits an offence if he intentionally administers a substance to, or causes a substance to be taken by, another person (B)—
   (a) knowing that B does not consent, and
   (b) with the intention of stupefying or overpowering B, so as to enable any person to engage in a sexual activity that involves B.

KEYNOTE

This offence is aimed at the use of the so-called date rape drugs but is far wider than that. For instance it would cover the spiking of a victim's soft drinks with alcohol if done with the relevant intent.

'Administering or causing to be taken' covers a broader range of conduct than the parallel offences of poisoning.

The key elements are the defendant's intentionally administering the substance (*any* substance), in the knowledge that the victim does not consent and with the intention of overpowering or stupefying the victim in order that *any person* can engage in sexual activity involving the victim.

As this is an offence of intent rather than consequence there is no need for the victim to be stupefied or overpowered or for the sexual activity to take place.

So far as proof of the relevant elements is concerned **see para. 1.10.3.3.**

1.10.11 Offences Outside the United Kingdom

Section 72(1) of the Sexual Offences Act 2003 (as amended by the Criminal Justice and Immigration Act 2008) makes it an offence for a UK national to commit an act outside the United Kingdom which would constitute a relevant sexual offence if done in England and Wales. The amended section removes the previous requirement that the act committed must have been illegal in the country where it took place, in respect of the prosecution of UK nationals.

1.10.12 Offences Relating to Prostitution

There are many offences connected with prostitution. Some of these offences specifically involve children and these are addressed elsewhere in this chapter.

While some European Union Member States have 'zones of toleration' where some forms of prostitution are permitted within controlled limits, the laws regulating prostitution and soliciting in England and Wales are quite clear and do not allow for such zones as presently drafted.

1.10.12.1 Definition of a Prostitute

The Sexual Offences Act 2003 defines prostitution and provides that a prostitute is a person (A) who:

- on at least one occasion and
- whether or not compelled to do so,
- offers or provides sexual services to another person
- in return for payment or a promise of payment to A or a third person

(s. 51(2)).

This definition applies to both men and women.

1.10.12.2 Offence of Causing, Inciting or Controlling Prostitution

OFFENCE: **Causing, Inciting or Controlling Prostitution for Gain—*Sexual Offences Act 2003, ss. 52 and 53***
- Triable either way • Seven years' imprisonment on indictment • Six months' imprisonment and/or fine summarily

The Sexual Offences Act 2003, s. 52 states:

(1) A person commits an offence if—
  (a) he intentionally causes or incites another person to become a prostitute in any part of the world, and
  (b) he does so for or in the expectation of gain for himself or a third person.

The Sexual Offences Act 2003, s. 53 states:

(1) A person commits an offence if—
  (a) he intentionally controls any of the activities of another person relating to that person's prostitution in any part of the world, and
  (b) he does so for or in the expectation of gain for himself or a third person.

KEYNOTE

Where the victim of these offences is under 18, the specific offence under s. 48 should be considered (**see para. 1.10.5.8**).

The first offence above is concerned with intentional causing or inciting—in the case of the latter, this is an incomplete offence (**see chapter 1.3**).

The second offence above addresses those who intentionally control the activities of prostitutes (pimps).

In each case, unlike the offence involving persons under 18, you must show that the defendant acted for, or in the expectation of, gain—either for him/herself or another. Gain means any financial advantage, including the discharge of an obligation to pay or the provision of goods or services (including sexual services) gratuitously or at a discount or the goodwill of any person which is or appears likely, in time, to bring financial advantage (s. 54). This is a wide definition covering the actions of someone who hopes to build up a relationship with, say, a drug dealer who will eventually give the defendant cheaper drugs as a result of his/her activities. Although you do not need to show that money, goods or financial advantage actually passed to the defendant, you must show that he/she wanted or at least expected that someone would benefit from the conduct.

1.10.12.3 Paying for Sexual Services of a Prostitute Subjected to Force

OFFENCE: **Paying for Sexual Services of a Prostitute Subjected to Force**—*Sexual Offences Act 2003, s. 53A*

- Triable summarily
- Fine

The Sexual Offences Act 2003, s. 53A (as amended by the Policing and Crime Act 2009) states:

(1) A person (A) commits an offence if—
   (a) A makes or promises payment for the sexual services of a prostitute (B),
   (b) a third person (C) has engaged in exploitative conduct of a kind likely to induce or encourage B to provide the sexual services for which A has made or promised payment, and
   (c) C engaged in that conduct for or in the expectation of gain for C or another person (apart from A or B).
(2) The following are irrelevant—
   (a) where in the world the sexual services are to be provided and whether those services are provided,
   (b) whether A is, or ought to be, aware that C has engaged in exploitative conduct.
(3) C engages in exploitative conduct if—
   (a) C uses force, threats (whether or not relating to violence) or any other form of coercion, or
   (b) C practises any form of deception.

KEYNOTE

The Policing and Crime Act 2009 inserted a new s. 53A into the Sexual Offences Act 2003. The new section creates an offence which is committed if someone pays or promises payment for the sexual services of a prostitute who has been subject to exploitative conduct of a kind likely to induce or encourage the provision of sexual services for which the payer has made or promised payment. The person responsible for the exploitative conduct must have been acting for or in the expectation of gain for him/herself or another person, other than the payer or the prostitute.

It does not matter where in the world the sexual services are to be provided. An offence is committed regardless of whether the person paying or promising payment for sexual services knows or ought to know or be aware that the prostitute has been subject to exploitative conduct. In other words the offence is one of *strict liability* and *no mental element* is required in respect of the offender's knowledge that the prostitute was forced, threatened, coerced or deceived.

1.10.12.4 Brothels

There are several summary offences aimed at landlords, tenants and occupiers of premises used as brothels (see ss. 34–36 of the Sexual Offences Act 1956). The Sexual Offences Act 2003 extended the relevant offences so that they covered brothels used by male prostitutes and created the following offence:

OFFENCE: **Keeping a Brothel Used for Prostitution—*Sexual Offences Act 1956, s. 33A***

- Triable either way. • Seven years' imprisonment on indictment • Six months' imprisonment and/or a fine summarily

The Sexual Offences Act 1956, s. 33A states:

(1) It is an offence for a person to keep, or to manage, or act or assist in the management of, a brothel to which people resort for practices involving prostitution (whether or not also for other practices).

KEYNOTE

A brothel is a place to which people resort for the purposes of unlawful sexual intercourse with more than one prostitute. However, it is not necessary that full sexual intercourse takes place or is even offered. A massage parlour where other acts of lewdness or indecency for sexual gratification are offered may be a brothel. While the old summary offence of keeping, managing or assisting with the management of a brothel (under s. 33) still remains, it is unlikely to be used very often in light of the above offence.

Prostitution means offering or providing sexual services, whether under compulsion or not, to another in return for payment or a promise of payment to the prostitute or a third person (see s. 51(2)).

OFFENCE: **Keeping a Disorderly House—*Common Law***

- Triable on indictment • Unlimited sentence

It is an offence at common law to keep a disorderly house.

KEYNOTE

To prove the offence of keeping a disorderly house you must show that the house is 'open' (i.e. to customers); that it is unregulated by the restraints of morality; and that it is run in a way that violates law and good order (*R* v *Tan* [1983] QB 1053).

There must be 'knowledge' on the part of the defendant that a house is being so used (*Moores* v *DPP* [1992] QB 125).

The offence also requires some persistence and will not cover a single instance, e.g. of an indecent performance.

1.10.12.5   **Soliciting**

OFFENCE: **Soliciting by Persons—*Street Offences Act 1959, s. 1***

> • Triable summarily • Fine

The Street Offences Act 1959 (as amended by the Policing and Crime Act 2009), s. 1 states:

(1) It shall be an offence for a person whether male or female persistently to loiter or solicit in a street or public place for the purpose of prostitution.

(2) ...

(3) For the purposes of this section:

  (a) conduct is persistent if it takes place on two or more occasions in any period of three months;

  (b) any reference to a person loitering or soliciting for the purposes of prostitution is a reference to a person loitering or soliciting for the purposes of offering services as a prostitute

---

KEYNOTE

This section amends the offence of loitering or soliciting for the purposes of prostitution, as set out in s. 1 of the Street Offences Act 1959. Under s. 1 of the 1959 Act it was an offence for a 'common prostitute' (whether male or female) to loiter or solicit in a street or public place for the purpose of prostitution. The term 'common prostitute" has been removed from s. 1 of the 1959 Act. The word 'persistently' has been inserted so that the offence is committed only if the person acts persistently. Persistent conduct is conduct which takes place on two or more occasions in any three month period.

This offence is committed *only by those offering services as a prostitute*, not by those receiving such services (those receiving services may however be committing 'soliciting' offences as below).

Insterad of a fine, the court may make a rehabilitative order against a person convicted of the soliciting by persons offence (s. 2A of the Street Offences Act 1959, as amended).

A 'street' includes any bridge, road, lane, footway, subway, square, court, alley or passage, whether a thoroughfare or not, which is for the time being open to the public; and the doorways and entrances of premises abutting on a street and any ground adjoining and open to a street. 'Public place' is not defined.

OFFENCE: **Soliciting by 'Kerb-crawling'—*Sexual Offences Act* 2003, *s. 51A,***

> • Triable summarily • Fine

The Sexual Offences Act 2003, s. 51A, (as amended) states:

(1) It is an offence for a person in a street or public place to solicit another (B) for the purpose of obtaining B's sexual services as a prostitute.

(2) The reference to a person in a street or public place includes a person in a vehicle in a street or public place.

KEYNOTE

This offence is applicable to both sexes.

Section 53A of the Sexual Offences Act 2003 creates a single offence of soliciting which replaces the previous offences under ss. 1 and 2 of the Sexual Offences Act 1985. These two sections dealt with offences of kerb-crawling in a street or public place (s. 1) and persistent soliciting in a street or public place (s. 2) for the purposes of prostitution. Both activities under the former legislation required an element of persistency in relation to the person kerb-crawling or soliciting in order for an offence to have been committed or, in the case of kerb-crawling, for the soliciting to be shown to be likely to cause nuisance or annoyance to the

---

person solicited or nuisance to others in the neighbourhood. *These requirements have been removed by the new offence.* Kerb-crawling or soliciting is now punishable on the first occasion the activity takes place. In the case of kerb-crawling, the requirement for the soliciting to be shown to be likely to cause nuisance or annoyance to others has also been removed.

The term 'street' is as per the definition given in the Keynote above. 'Public place' is not defined.

1.10.12.6 Placing Adverts for Prostitutes Near Public Phones

OFFENCE: **Placing an Advertisement—*Criminal Justice and Police Act 2001, s. 46***

- Triable summarily • Six months' imprisonment and/or fine

The Criminal Justice and Police Act 2001, s. 46 states:

(1) A person commits an offence if—
   (a) he places on, or in the immediate vicinity of a public telephone, an advertisement relating to prostitution, and
   (b) he does so with the intention that the advertisement should come to the attention of any other person or persons.

KEYNOTE

Advertising the services of a prostitute by leaving stickers or cards in telephone kiosks has been held not to amount to 'soliciting' (*Weisz* v *Monahan* [1962] 1 WLR 262). Although the publisher of the stickers could be charged with the wider offence of controlling prostitutes, if appropriate, this has not been particularly helpful in relation to the people who are found placing the advert themselves. The above offence now addresses this conduct.

In proving this offence you must show that, in placing the advertisement, the defendant intended that it should come to the attention of someone else. This does not seem to be a particularly onerous requirement and will be helped by evidence of the degree of care that was taken in placing the card, sticker etc., together with its actual position. The advertisement must be for the services of a prostitute—male or female—or for premises at which such services are offered (s. 46(2)). Whether or not an advertisement 'relates to prostitution' is a question of fact. Where a reasonable person would consider that the particular advertisement was 'related to prostitution' there is a presumption that it meets the requirements of this section (s. 46(3)). This presumption is, however, rebuttable.

'Public telephone' here means any telephone which is

- located in a public place *and*
- made available for use by the public or a section of the public

and includes any kiosk, booth, acoustic hood, shelter or other structure housing or attached to the telephone (s. 46(5)).

Given this wide definition, the offence will cover the placing of advertisements on or within the immediate vicinity of, not just the telephone itself, but also the kiosk, booth, etc. Therefore, although the magistrate(s) will decide whether an act fell within the immediate vicinity as a question of fact, the offence is capable of being committed by placing advertisements on pavements or shop windows immediately adjacent to a public telephone kiosk.

Section 46(5) gives a very specific definition of 'public place' for the purposes of this offence, namely:

- any place to which the public have or are permitted to have access (on payment or otherwise), *other than*
- a place to which children under 16 years of age are not permitted to have access (by law or otherwise), or
- premises used wholly or mainly as residential premises.

This means that public areas where children under 16 are not allowed, either because they are prevented by law (e.g. licensing laws) or for some other reason (e.g. where a landowner is holding a public event and has barred children from attending), will not be caught by this legislation.

1.10.12.7 Trafficking for Sexual Offences

OFFENCE: **Trafficking Into, Within or Out of the UK for Sexual Exploitation—** *Sexual Offences Act 2003, ss. 57–59*

- Triable either way • 14 years' imprisonment on indictment • Six months' imprisonment and/or a fine summarily

The Sexual Offences Act 2003, s. 57 states:

(1) A person commits an offence if he intentionally arranges or facilitates the arrival, or the entry into, the United Kingdom of another person (B) and either—
   (a) he intends to do anything to or in respect of B, after B's arrival but in any part of the world, which if done will involve the commission of a relevant offence, or
   (b) he believes that another person is likely to do something to or in respect of B, after B's arrival but in any part of the world, which if done will involve the commission of a relevant offence.

The Sexual Offences Act 2003, s. 58 states:

(1) A person commits an offence if he intentionally arranges or facilitates travel within the United Kingdom by another person (B) and either—
   (a) he intends to do anything to or in respect of B, during or after the journey and in any part of the world, which if done will involve the commission of a relevant offence, or
   (b) he believes that another person is likely to do something to or in respect of B, during or after the journey and in any part of the world, which if done will involve the commission of a relevant offence.

The Sexual Offences Act 2003, s. 59 states:

(1) A person commits an offence if he intentionally arranges or facilitates the departure from the United Kingdom of another person (B) and either—
   (a) he intends to do anything to or in respect of B, after B's departure but in any part of the world, which if done will involve the commission of a relevant offence, or
   (b) he believes that another person is likely to do something to or in respect of B, after B's departure but in any part of the world, which if done will involve the commission of a relevant offence.

KEYNOTE

These three offences address the trafficking of people for sexual exploitation. Worded almost identically, the three sections deal with the intentional arranging or facilitation of the person's arrival in, travel within, or departure from the United Kingdom. In each case you must show the defendant's intention to do something to or in respect of the victim which would involve the commission of a relevant offence *or* the defendant's belief that someone else is likely to do so. The relevant offence, intended or believed likely by the defendant, can take place in any part of the world provided it is after the victim's arrival, during or after their journey or after their departure respectively.

A relevant offence is any offence under part I of the Sexual Offences Act 2003 (virtually all regularly occurring sexual offences) and an offence under s. 1(1)(a) of the Protection of Children Act 1978 (taking, permitting to be taken or making indecent photographs of a child—**see para. 1.10.5.9**); it also includes anything done outside England and Wales which is not an offence in that country but would be if done in England and Wales where the offender is a British citizen, a British overseas territories citizen, a British National (Overseas), a British Overseas citizen, a person who is a British subject under the British Nationality Act 1981 or a British protected person within the meaning given by s. 50(1) of that Act (s. 60).

The wording of the offences means that bringing victims into the United Kingdom temporarily on their way to another destination will be caught.

Note that it is the intention or belief of the defendant that is the central feature—the fact that the relevant sexual offence never actually took place will not prevent this offence being committed. Similarly, if the intention or belief is not present, there is no offence under these provisions. This protects transport companies and their staff who are often unwittingly used in these offences. Nevertheless, the wording of the offences is wide enough to deal with any intentional involvement in planning, organising or carrying out arrangements in furtherance of trafficking where the relevant state of mind or knowledge (**see** **chapter 1.1**) is present.

1.11 Control of Sex Offenders

1.11.1 Introduction

In addition to the creation of specific criminal offences regulating and punishing certain types of sexual or sexually motivated behaviour, Parliament has also provided a framework for the control and monitoring of sex offenders. This framework is covered in the following paragraphs.

1.11.2 Statutory Regulation of Sex Offenders

Statutory regulation of the behaviour of sex offenders has increased significantly over recent years.

Part 2 of the Sexual Offences Act 2003 sets out the notification requirements for sex offenders and introduces sexual offences prevention orders, along with other measures for reducing the opportunities for sex offenders to continue to present a threat to victims anywhere in the world.

What follows is a summary of the main practical provisions but reference should be made to the statutory text for complete coverage.

1.11.3 Offenders Covered by Notification Requirements

A person is subject to the notification requirements for the period set out in s. 82 (the notification period) if:

- he is convicted of an offence listed in Schedule 3—this covers most of the commonly occurring sex offences set out elsewhere in chapter 10 (for example, the offences of rape or assault by penetration);
- he is found not guilty of such an offence by reason of insanity;
- he is found to be under a disability and to have done the act charged against him in respect of such an offence; or
- he/she is cautioned in respect of such an offence, not only in England and Wales but for an offence in Northern Ireland as well (s. 80).

In a decision relating to the former legislation, the Court of Appeal has confirmed that conditional discharges count as 'convictions' and therefore a person receiving such a punishment was subject to the notification requirements (*R* v *Longworth* [2004] EWCA Crim 2145). The reasoning behind this decision is likely to be applied to the notification requirements under the Sexual Offences Act 2003 set out below (although the Court of Appeal expressly declined to speculate on this point). The reasoning behind the finding that conditional discharges were 'convictions' in *Longworth* was because s. 14(1) of the Powers of Criminal Courts (Sentencing) Act 2000 provides that a discharge is to be regarded as a conviction 'for the purposes of the proceedings in which the order was made' and the Court of Appeal held that the notification requirements (under the old legislation) fell within the scope of those purposes.

Where the above findings, convictions or cautions are made, the court or the police may issue a certificate that will be evidence of that fact (see s. 92) and the Secretary of State may make regulations setting out the form of certificate to be used.

A person subject to the notification requirements is referred to in the legislation as a 'relevant offender'.

Clearly many sex offenders were already subject to the previous notification requirements under part 1 of the Sex Offenders Act 1997. Some of these people continue to be subject to the notification requirements. For the full details as to these offenders see s. 81.

Some relevant offenders will have attracted that status (and the relevant notification requirements below) by reason of a conviction etc. for one of the sexual offences abolished by the Sexual Offences Act 2003 (buggery or gross indecency between men under ss. 12 or 13 of the Sexual Offences Act 1956). Schedule 4 to the 2003 Act and Home Office Circular 19/2004 deal with the procedure whereby such offenders may apply to the Secretary of State for removal of their notification requirements.

A challenge to the compatibility of the notification requirements with the European Convention on Human Rights was unsuccessful in *Forbes* v *Secretary of State for the Home Department* [2005] EWHC 1597 (QB). That case arose from the very specific excise offence of importing obscene material involving children, but courts can be expected to follow the general principles applied in that case.

1.11.3.1 The Notification Period

Section 82 sets out the notification period. This is as follows:

Description of relevant offender	Notification period
A person who, in respect of the offence, is or has been sentenced to imprisonment for a term of 30 months or more	An indefinite period beginning with the relevant date
A person who, in respect of the offence or finding, is or has been admitted to a hospital subject to a restriction order	An indefinite period beginning with that date
A person who, in respect of the offence, is or has been sentenced to imprisonment for a term of more than 6 months but less than 30 months	10 years beginning with that date
A person who, in respect of the offence, is or has been sentenced to imprisonment for a term of 6 months or less	7 years beginning with that date
A person who, in respect of the offence or finding, is or has been admitted to a hospital without being subject to a restriction order	7 years beginning with that date
A person within section 80(1)(d) (cautioned)	2 years beginning with that date
A person in whose case an order for conditional discharge is made in respect of the offence	The period of conditional discharge
A person of any other description	5 years beginning with the relevant date

Where a person is under 18 on the relevant date, references to a period of 10 years, 7 years, 5 years or 2 years are substituted by a reference to half that period (s. 82(2)).

Meaning of Cautioned

Cautioned means cautioned by a police officer after the person concerned has admitted the offence, or reprimanded or warned within the meaning given by s. 65 of the Crime and Disorder Act 1998 (**see Evidence and Procedure**)—s. 133.

The wording of s. 134 means that conviction includes a conditional discharge (though not an absolute discharge). The Act makes specific provisions for offenders who are sentenced for more than one offence and for those who, having been initially found to be under a disability, are later tried for the offence.

1.11.3.2   Initial Notification

A relevant offender must notify the police of certain information within a specified time period from the 'relevant date'. Generally the relevant date will be the date of conviction, finding, caution or, in the case of people covered by the Sex Offenders Act 1997, the appropriate date under that Act.

Relevant offenders must, within the period of three days beginning with the relevant date (or, if later, the commencement of part 2 of the Act), notify to the police the information set out in s. 83(5)—(see s. 83(1)). There are some exceptions made in relation to offenders covered by the earlier legislation and those who have already complied with s. 83(1) at the date of being dealt with by the court.

The information required under s. 83(5) is the relevant offender's:

- date of birth
- national insurance number
- name on the relevant date *and* on the date on which notification is given. If he/she used one or more other names on those dates, each of those names
- home address on the relevant date *and* on the date on which notification is given

and the address of any other premises in the United Kingdom at which, at the time the notification is given, he/she regularly resides or stays.

In calculating the time under s. 83(1) account is not generally taken of time spent in custody by order of a court, detention in a hospital or while out of the United Kingdom (see s. 83(6)).

Home address means the address of the relevant offender's sole or main residence in the United Kingdom, or where he/she has no such residence, the address or location of a place in the United Kingdom where he/she can regularly be found and, if there is more than one such place, such one of those places as the person may select (s. 83(7)). This means that, if offenders are of no fixed abode, they can give details of any shelter or other place where they are regularly to be found.

1.11.3.3   Notification Requirements: Changes

Within the period of three days beginning with:

- his/her using a name which has not been notified to the police under the relevant legislative provisions
- any change of home address
- his/her having resided or stayed, for a 'qualifying period' (seven days *or* two or more periods in any 12 months which together amount to seven days), at any premises in

the United Kingdom the address of which has not been notified to the police under the relevant legislative provision, or

- his/her release from custody pursuant to an order of a court or from imprisonment, service detention or detention in a hospital,

a relevant offender must notify to the police that name, the new home address, the address of those premises or (as the case may be) the fact that he/she has been released, and (in addition) the information set out in s. 83(5)—(see s. 84(1)).

Any notification under the above requirement can be given in advance of the change, provided the actual change takes place within a given 'margin' of time either side of the notified date. For that reason the relevant offender must also specify the date when the event is expected to occur (s. 84(2)). As long as the change notified in advance takes place no earlier than two days before the date notified or no more than three days after, the offender does not need to notify the police of the actual date when it took place. However, if the change takes place outside this margin, the offender must notify the change as required by s. 84(1)—e.g. within three days of the actual change. Similarly, if the change takes place three days or more after the date notified in advance, the offender must also tell the police within six days that the change he/she gave advance notice of did not occur as specified (see s. 84(3) and (4)).

As with the initial notification requirements, account is not generally taken of time spent in custody by order of a court, detention in a hospital or while out of the United Kingdom (see s. 84(5)).

Section 142 of the Criminal Justice and Immigration Act 2008 allows the Home Secretary to amend, through secondary legislation, the notification requirements placed on those convicted or cautioned of relevant sexual offences or otherwise subject to the sex offender notification requirements. The Act also allows the Secretary of State to add to the information that sex offenders subject to the notification requirements must notify the police. If the Secretary of State does add to the information required to be notified by a sex offender and there is a change in those details, the offender must notify the police within three days of the change. As occurs with the current information which must be notified, the sex offender can notify the police of an expected change in the prescribed details before the change occurs. The Secretary of State may also provide in regulations that an offender who does not have a sole or main residence in the United Kingdom must notify his/her details to the police more frequently.

1.11.3.4 Notification Requirements: Periodic Notification

A relevant offender must also re-notify the police of the details in s. 83(5) above within one year of either the initial notification or the notification of the changes unless he/she has already notified them within that period (under s. 84) as a result of changing circumstances (s. 85). In summary this means that, if a relevant offender does not change his/her name or address, or stay away from home for seven days or more, he/she will have to re-notify the police of the relevant details within a year of the initial notification and every year afterwards. Under s. 85(3), if offenders are detained or are abroad when their periodic notification becomes due, they have until three days after their release/return to the United Kingdom to re-notify.

1.11.3.5 Notification Requirements: Travel Outside the United Kingdom

The Secretary of State has the power to make regulations setting out the notification requirements for relevant offenders who travel outside the United Kingdom (s. 86). The current regulations are the Sexual Offences Act 2003 (Travel Notification Requirements) Regulations 2004 (S1 2004/1220).

1.11.3.6 Method of Notification and Related Matters

A relevant offender complies with the obligations to notify the police set out above by attending at such police station in his local police area as the Secretary of State may by regulations prescribe—see the Sexual Offences Act 2003 (Prescribed Police Stations) Regulations 2010 (SI 2010/207) for a list of specific police stations identified for this purpose—(or, if there is more than one, at any of them), and giving an oral notification to any police officer, or to any person authorised for the purpose by the officer in charge of the station (s. 87(1)). 'Local police area' means:

- the police area in which the offender's home address is situated or,
- if he/she does not have a home address, the police area in which the home address last notified is situated or,
- if he/she does not have a home address or in the absence of any such notification, the police area in which the court which last dealt with the offender for a relevant matter is situated (see s. 88).

If the notification relates to staying away from home for seven days or more, or to an advance change of address, the offender may give the notification at a police station in the police area of the other address (s. 87(2)).

When the offender gives a notification to the police (other than in relation to travel outside the United Kingdom), the police can fingerprint and/or photograph the offender (s. 87(4)) for the purpose of verifying the identity of the relevant offender. 'Photograph' includes any process by means of which an image may be produced and therefore would include methods such as iris scans (see s. 88(2)).

1.11.3.7 Notification Orders

In addition to the above, a chief officer of police may apply to a magistrates' court for an order against a person who has been convicted, cautioned or had another relevant finding recorded against him/her for a relevant offence outside the United Kingdom (see s. 97). Basically a relevant offence here means an offence abroad which, had it been committed here, would also have been a sch. 3 offence. This provision closed a loophole in the earlier sex offenders registration and monitoring scheme and applies where the relevant offender lives in the chief officer's police area or where the chief officer believes that he/she is intending to come to that police area. This means that a chief officer can apply to a magistrates' court for a notification order against a foreign national who has been convicted abroad and who is intending to come to the chief officer's police area. Notification orders will, broadly speaking, make the offender subject to the notification requirements, however there are specific differences in relation to the calculation of the relevant periods (see s. 97(3) and (4) and s. 98).

1.11.3.8 Interim Notification Orders

In addition, the police may apply for an interim notification order while the application for a full notification order is determined (s. 100). Such an interim order may be necessary because the relevant paperwork is likely to delay the hearing for the main order. Once an interim notification order is granted, the relevant offender becomes subject to the notification requirements above and the notification period starts from the date of service of the order (s. 100(5) and (6)).

An offender has a right of appeal against both interim or full notification orders to the Crown Court (s. 101).

1.11.3.9 Young Offenders: Parental Directions

Section 89 of the Sexual Offences Act 2003 makes provisions for young offenders and allows the courts to direct a person with parental responsibility for the offender to comply with their notification requirements instead—until either the young offender reaches 18 or an earlier date specified by the court. Under a parental direction the parent must ensure that the young offender attends at the police station with him/her, when a notification is being given (s. 89(2)(b)).

A chief officer may (by complaint to any magistrates' court whose commission area includes any part of his/her police area) apply for a parental direction in respect of any relevant offender who is under 18 and who resides in that police area, or who the chief officer believes is in or is intending to come to his/her police area (see s. 89(4) and (5)). A court may alter or discharge a parental direction order on application by the offender, parent or relevant chief officer (s. 90). A variation or alteration might be needed where, for example, the offender's parents divorce or where they cannot exercise enough control over the offender to ensure compliance with the notification requirements.

1.11.3.10 Failure to Notify

OFFENCE: **Failing to Comply with Notification Requirements—*Sexual Offences Act 2003, s. 91***

- Triable either way • Five years' imprisonment on indictment • Six months' and/or fine summarily

The Sexual Offences Act 2003, s. 91 states:

(1) A person commits an offence if he—
 (a) fails, without reasonable excuse, to comply with section 83(1), 84(1), 84(4)(b), 85(1), 87(5A) or (5B) or 89(2)(b) or any requirement imposed by regulations made under section 86(1); or
 (b) notifies to the police, in purported compliance with section 83(1), 84(1) or 85(1) or any requirement imposed by regulations made under section 86(1), any information which he knows to be false.

KEYNOTE

Reasonable excuse will be a question of fact in all the circumstances for the court to decide. In relation to a parental direction, it is more likely that the person will have such an excuse, particularly if they have done all they can to ensure that the young offender comes with them to the police station.

This is a continuing offence, in that the offender continues to commit it for each and every day that he/she fails to give notification as required (s. 91(3)). Although the offender can only be prosecuted once for the same continuing failure, if he/she is convicted for the above offence and then fails again to comply, he/she commits another offence.

1.11.3.11 Supply of Information for Verification

Section 94 provides that a specified person or body may supply information to the Secretary of State (or a person supplying a relevant function to the Secretary of State) for the purposes of the prevention, detection, investigation or prosecution of offences under part 2 of the Act, for use in verifying that information. The information is that which was notified to the police under ss. 83, 84 or 85 (see above) or the equivalent earlier legislation (s. 2(1)–(3) of the Sex Offenders Act 1997). Those people and bodies are:

- a chief officer of police
- the National Policing Improvement Agency (NPIA)
- the Director General of the Serious Organised Crime Agency.

Verification and Use

Verifying the information here means checking its accuracy by comparing it with information held by the Secretary of State or bodies responsible for functions such as social security, child support, employment or training, the Identity and Passport Service or the Driver and Vehicle Licensing Agency (DVLA). Checking accuracy includes compiling a report, though this part of the Act does not authorise anything that would amount to a breach of the Data Protection Act 1998. The recipient of the report must be one of the people/bodies set out above and they may use the information only for the purposes of the prevention, detection, investigation or prosecution of an offence under part 2 but can retain it whether or not it is in fact used for that purpose (see s. 95).

1.11.3.12 Power of Entry—Risk Assessment of Sex offenders

Section 96B of the Sexual Offences Act 2003 (inserted by s. 58 of the Violent Crime Reduction Act 2006) provides a power of entry and search to risk assess sex offenders subject to the notification requirements.

The power enables the police to gather all the information they need about a relevant offender for the purposes of assessing the risks he/she poses, even if he/she is in apparent compliance with the notification requirements and there are insufficient grounds to believe he/she has committed a new substantive offence.

Under the section, the police are allowed to seek a warrant from a magistrates' court to enter and search, by force if necessary, the last notified address of a registered sex offender (or a place where there are grounds to believe the offender resides or can be regularly found) where there have been two failed attempts to enter a specified premises, for the purpose of assessing the risks he/she poses.

The application must be made by a senior police officer, not below the rank of superintendent. The senior police officer should attend court in person to apply for the warrant.

A warrant will only be issued by a magistrate if he/she is satisfied that the following conditions have been met:

- that the offender is a relevant offender (i.e. an offender subject to the notification requirements)
- that the offender is not: remanded or committed to custody by order of a court; serving a sentence of imprisonment or a term of service detention; detained in hospital; or outside the United Kingdom
- that the address of each set of premises to which the warrant relates is either the home address which was last notified in accordance with part 2 of the Sexual Offences Act 2003,

or there are reasonable grounds to believe that the registered sex offender resides there or may regularly be found there
- that it is necessary for the constable to enter and search the premises for the purpose of assessing the risk posed by the offender
- that on at least two occasions, a constable has sought entry to the premises in order to search them for that purpose and has been unable to obtain entry for that purpose.

The warrant may also authorise entry to and search of premises on more than one occasion if, on the application, the magistrate is satisfied that it is necessary to authorise multiple entries for the purpose of risk assessment. When a warrant authorises multiple entries, the number of entries authorised may be unlimited or limited to a maximum.

If more than one address is to be searched, the constable will need to attempt (and fail) to enter each address for which the warrant is sought.

In circumstances where a constable has been allowed into the premises to search for the purposes of risk assessment, but not allowed into parts of the premises (e.g. a particular room), this will count as being 'unable to obtain entry' for the purposes of risk assessment.

As a warrant does not grant a power of seizure, where evidence of a crime is found during the course of a search under such a warrant, constables can use their general power of seizure under s. 19 of the Police and Criminal Evidence Act 1984.

1.11.4 Orders to Control Sex Offenders

In addition to the notification requirements for relevant offenders, there are other powers available in the appropriate circumstances to restrain or prevent sex offending. The Sexual Offences Act 2003 creates a series of different orders which, although civil in nature, are of significant value to the police in preventing and controlling the activities of sex offenders and people who have presented a risk of sexual harm to children. The first of these orders is the Sexual Offences Prevention Order (SOPO).

1.11.4.1 Sexual Offences Prevention Orders

SOPOs are civil law measures to prevent offending and protect the public. They have replaced the old sex offender orders and restraining orders (although someone who is still subject to those older orders remains under the relevant obligations contained in them).

A court can make a SOPO in a number of circumstances where it is satisfied that it is necessary to do so for the purpose of protecting the public (or any particular member(s) of the public) from serious sexual harm from the defendant. In summary, the SOPO can be made where:

- the court deals with (rather than simply 'convicts') a person for a sch. 3 offence
- the court decides that a defendant is not guilty of an offence listed in sch. 3 or sch. 5 (these include offences of murder and manslaughter, causing the death of a child or vulnerable adult, violence, fear or intimidation as well as sexual offences and firearms offences; they also include those offences relating to 'dangerous offenders' created by the Criminal Justice Act 2003) by reason of insanity, or that he/she is under a disability and has done the act charged against him/her in respect of such an offence, or
- a chief officer applies for one in respect of a 'qualifying offender' (see below) and certain conditions are met. (See s. 104.)

1.11.4.2 Police Application for SOPO

As described above, the police can apply for a SOPO in respect of certain people in certain circumstances. Section 104(5) provides that a chief officer may, by complaint to a magistrates' court, apply for an order under this section in respect of a person who resides in his/her police area or who the chief officer believes is in, or is intending to come to, his/her police area if it appears to the chief officer that:

- the person is a qualifying offender (basically this means he/she has been convicted of, cautioned for or found not guilty by reason of insanity or to have been under a disability, in respect of an offence under sch. 3 or 5 here or by a foreign court for an equivalent offence), *and*
- the person has, since the appropriate date (e.g. date of first conviction or caution) acted in such a way as to give reasonable cause to believe that it is *necessary* (rather than just desirable or a 'good idea') for such an order to be made.

The court will have to decide whether the order is necessary to protect the public or any particular member(s) of the public in the United Kingdom from serious physical or psychological harm, caused by the defendant committing one or more offences listed in sch. 3 (s. 106(3)). In doing so, the court will consider the acts of the defendant since the relevant date. Therefore the availability of good quality intelligence as to the defendant's conduct within the relevant period will be critical.

As this procedure is a civil one, the standard of proof required in proving the elements above is on a balance of probabilities.

1.11.4.3 The Order

The Sexual Offences Act 2003, s. 107 states:

(1) A sexual offences prevention order—
  (a) prohibits the defendant from doing anything described in the order, and
  (b) has effect for a fixed period (not less than 5 years) specified in the order or until further order.
(2) The only prohibitions that may be included in the order are those necessary for the purpose of protecting the public or any particular members of the public from serious sexual harm from the defendant.

KEYNOTE

A SOPO can cover any activity by the offender at all, whether or not that activity amounts to a criminal offence or a civil wrong, provided it is shown to be necessary for the purposes of protecting the public (or any particular member of the public) from serious sexual harm from the defendant. This phrase is defined under s. 106 and is discussed in the previous paragraph.

  The order will last for at least five years but can be for an indefinite period, provided that period is specified in the order. Further orders can be made after the original expires but there can only be one SOPO in respect of the same offender at any one time (see s. 107(6)).

Effect on Notification Requirements

If an offender is not subject to the notification requirements discussed in previous paragraphs, he/she will become subject to them for the duration of a SOPO (s. 107(4)). In such circumstances the relevant date is the date of service of the order (s. 107(5)).

This means that, in relation to the initial notification requirements under s. 83(1), for example, the relevant offender will have three days *from service of the order* within which to comply with his or her obligations.

Where the offender is already subject to the notification requirements and those requirements will cease during the period of the SOPO, he/she will still have to comply with those notification requirements for the duration of the order (s. 107(3)). Conversely, if the notification requirements last *longer* than any SOPO made since conviction, finding or caution, then the SOPO does not have any effect on them and they continue as originally imposed by the court.

1.11.4.4 Changes to a SOPO

Where a SOPO has been made, an application to vary, renew or discharge the order can be made, either by the defendant or:

- the chief officer of police for the area in which the defendant resides, or
- a chief officer of police who believes that the defendant is in, or is intending to come to, his/her police area, or
- where the order was made on an application under s. 104(5), the chief officer of police who made the application (s. 108).

It may become necessary for a SOPO to be varied or renewed. For instance, the original order may be limited to a certain geographical area and the defendant intends to move, or it is discovered that he/she is travelling more widely and frequently than originally believed. An order may be renewed, or varied so as to impose additional prohibitions on the defendant, only if it is necessary to do so for the purpose of protecting the public or any particular members of the public from serious sexual harm from the defendant (and any renewed or varied order may contain only such prohibitions as are necessary for this purpose)—s. 108(5).

A court must not discharge a SOPO before the end of five years beginning with the day on which it was made, without the consent of the defendant and, if it was made on the application of a chief officer of police, that chief officer. If it was not made on application by a chief officer, then the chief officer for the area where the defendant resides must also consent before such a variation can be made (s. 108(6)).

1.11.4.5 Interim Orders

The police can apply for an interim SOPO where an application has been made for a full order. Here the test that will be applied by the court is whether it is 'just' to do so—a wider consideration than 'necessary'. The purpose of interim orders is to allow restrictions to be placed on a defendant's conduct and movements before the full order is determined. An interim order will be for a fixed specified period (without a minimum length) during which time the defendant will be subject to the notification requirements (see above) and the relevant date will be the date of service of the interim order. The interim order will cease to have effect once a decision has been made about the full order (see generally s. 109).

There is a system by which the defendant can appeal against the making of a SOPO (including an interim order)—this is set out in s. 110. There is no equivalent section allowing the police to appeal against a decision, though in appropriate cases, a fresh application or an application for the decision to be judicially reviewed by the Administrative Court might be made (**see Evidence and Procedure**).

1.11.4.6 Breach of an Order

OFFENCE: **Breach of Sexual Offences Prevention Order—*Sexual Offences Act 2003, s. 113***

- Triable either way • Five years' imprisonment on indictment • Six months' imprisonment and/or fine summarily

The Sexual Offences Act 2003, s. 113 states:

(1) A person commits an offence if, without reasonable excuse, he does anything which he is prohibited from doing by—

(a) a sexual offences prevention order;

(b) an interim sexual offences prevention order;

(c) an order under section 5A of the Sex Offenders Act 1997 (restraining orders);

(d) an order under section 2, 2A or 20 of the Crime and Disorder Act 1998 (sex offender orders and interim orders made in England and Wales and in Scotland);

(e) an order under Article 6 or 6A of the Criminal Justice (Northern Ireland) Order 1998 (S.I. 1998/2839 (N.I. 20)) (sex offender orders and interim orders made in Northern Ireland).

KEYNOTE

This offence applies to a breach, without reasonable excuse, of a SOPO—including an interim order—and also of an order under the former legislation as set out above.

Where a person is convicted of an offence under this section, it is not open to the court to make, in respect of the offence, an order for conditional discharge (s. 113(3)).

Whether or not the defendant had a reasonable excuse will be a matter of fact for the court to decide in light of all the circumstances. Examples might include where the defendant accidentally encountered a person named in the order as being someone he should not approach or have contact with, or where he is a passenger in a vehicle that is driven, without his knowledge, into a particular area where the order states he should not go.

1.11.5 Foreign Travel Orders

The Sexual Offences Act 2003, s. 114 states:

(1) A chief officer of police may by complaint to a magistrates' court apply for an order under this section (a 'foreign travel order') in respect of a person ('the defendant') who resides in his police area or who the chief officer believes is in or is intending to come to his police area if it appears to the chief officer that—

(a) the defendant is a qualifying offender, and

(b) the defendant has since the appropriate date acted in such a way as to give reasonable cause to believe that it is necessary for such an order to be made.

(2) An application under subsection (1) may be made to any magistrates' court whose commission area includes any part of the applicant's police area.

(3) On the application, the court may make a foreign travel order if it is satisfied that—

(a) the defendant is a qualifying offender, and

(b) the defendant's behaviour since the appropriate date makes it necessary to make such an order, for the purpose of protecting children generally or any child from serious sexual harm from the defendant outside the United Kingdom.

KEYNOTE

The foreign travel order is a measure provided under civil law to prevent qualifying offenders from travelling abroad.

'Qualifying offenders' are generally people who have been convicted of or cautioned for (or found not guilty by reason of insanity or to have been under disability when doing an act amounting to) an offence specified by s. 116(2). These offences are—in England and Wales—listed at paras 13 to 15 of sch. 3 (involving indecent photographs etc. of children under 18), para. 31 (trespass with intent to commit a sexual offence if the intended victim was a person under 18) and any offence within any other paragraph of the schedule, if the victim of the offence was under 18 at the time of the offence. A person will also be a qualifying offender for the purposes of s. 114 if he/she has been convicted etc. of an equivalent offence under the law in force in a country outside the United Kingdom (see s. 116(3)).

Before making the order the court must be satisfied that it is *necessary* (rather than simply desirable or appropriate) in order to protect children generally, or any child, from serious sexual harm from the defendant outside the United Kingdom. This means protecting people under 18 generally (or any particular person under 18) from serious physical or psychological harm caused by the defendant doing, outside the United Kingdom, anything which would constitute an offence listed in sch. 3 if done in any part of the United Kingdom (s. 115(2)). In other words the orders are designed to tackle so-called sex tourism and to protect children under 18 from qualifying offenders travelling from the United Kingdom.

The police can apply for a foreign travel order at the same time as applying for a SOPO or on its own.

A foreign travel order has effect for a fixed period of not more than five years, specified in the order (s. 117(1)). The order prohibits the defendant from doing whichever of the following is specified in the order:

(a) travelling to any country outside the United Kingdom *named or described in the order*,
(b) travelling to any country outside the United Kingdom *other than* a country named or described in the order, or
(c) travelling to *any* country outside the United Kingdom. (s. 117(2)).

However, the *only* prohibitions that may be included in the order are those necessary for the purpose of protecting children generally (or any child) from serious sexual harm from the defendant outside the United Kingdom (s. 117(3)).

Most qualifying offenders who are made subject to these orders will also be subject to the relevant notification requirements. If for some reason the defendant is not a 'relevant offender' at the time the order is in force, he/she will have to comply with the notification requirements of regulations made under s. 86(1).

The defendant or the chief officer who made the application (or a chief officer for the area in which the defendant resides or who reasonably believes that the defendant is in, or is intending to come to, his/her police area) may apply for the order to be varied, renewed or discharged (see s. 118). The relevant court *must* hear the person making the application and, after doing so, can impose additional prohibitions on the defendant (but only if it is necessary to do so for the purpose of protecting children generally or any child from serious sexual harm from the defendant outside the United Kingdom)—s. 118(4)). A defendant can appeal to the Crown Court against a foreign travel order or a decision made in connection with its renewal, variation or discharge (s. 119).

1.11.5.1 Breach of Foreign Travel Order

OFFENCE: **Breach of Foreign Travel Order—*Sexual Offences Act 2003, s. 122***

• Triable either way • Five years' imprisonment on indictment • Six months' imprisonment and/or fine summarily

The Sexual Offences Act 2003, s. 122 states:

(1) A person commits an offence if, without reasonable excuse, he does anything which he is prohibited from doing by a foreign travel order.

KEYNOTE

Where a person is convicted of an offence under this section, it is not open to the court to make, in respect of the offence, an order for conditional discharge (s. 122(3)).

1.11.6 Risk of Sexual Harm Order

The Sexual Offences Act 2003, s. 123 states:

(1) A chief officer of police may by complaint to a magistrates' court apply for an order under this section (a 'risk of sexual harm order') in respect of a person aged 18 or over ('the defendant') who resides in his police area or who the chief officer believes is in, or is intending to come to, his police area if it appears to the chief officer that—
   (a) the defendant has on at least two occasions, whether before or after the commencement of this Part, done an act within subsection (3), and
   (b) as a result of those acts, there is reasonable cause to believe that it is necessary for such an order to be made.

KEYNOTE

Before a chief officer can apply to the magistrates' court for an RSHO, it must appear to him/her that the defendant has on at least two occasions done an act within s. 123(3) and that, as a result of those acts, there is reasonable cause to believe that it is *necessary* for such an order to be made.

The acts under s. 123(3) are:

- engaging in sexual activity involving a child or in the presence of a child
- causing or inciting a child to watch a person engaging in sexual activity or to look at a moving or still image that is sexual (which will include cartoons and virtual images—s. 124(4))
- giving a child anything that relates to sexual activity or contains a reference to such activity
- communicating with a child, where any part of the communication is sexual.

A child for these purposes is a person under 16 and 'sexual activity' means an activity that a reasonable person would, in all the circumstances but regardless of any person's purpose, consider to be sexual (see s. 124). A communication or image is sexual if any *part of it* relates to sexual activity, or a reasonable person would, in all the circumstances but regardless of any person's purpose, consider that any part of the communication is sexual (see s. 124).

The court can only make an RSHO if it is satisfied that the defendant committed such an act on at least two occasions and that the order is *necessary* to protect children generally or any specific child from harm *from the defendant* (s. 123(4)). 'Protecting children generally or any child from harm from the defendant' means protecting them from physical or psychological harm, caused by the defendant doing acts within s. 123(3) to s. 124(2).

Therefore an RSHO can be made in respect of a person who has no previous convictions or whose reported activity was not sufficiently evidenced to bring a prosecution. Clearly this would be appropriate in a case such as that of Ian Huntley where an individual came to the notice of the police on several unconnected occasions but where the relevant parties were unwilling to provide statements of complaint or the evidence was doubtful.

An RSHO has effect for a fixed period (not less than two years) specified in the order or until further order and prevents the defendant from doing anything described in the order (s. 123(5)).

The court may, if it considers it just to do so, make an interim RSHO for a fixed period before the determination of the main application but any interim order will cease once that main application has been determined (s. 126).

Sections 125 and 126 create a system for variation, renewal and discharge of, and appeals against RSHOs in a similar way to that applying to other orders discussed earlier in this chapter.

1.11.6.1 Breach of RSHO

OFFENCE: **Breach of RSHO or Interim RSHO—*Sexual Offences Act 2003, s. 128***
- Triable either way • Five years' imprisonment on indictment • Six months' imprisonment and/or fine summarily

The Sexual Offences Act 2003, s. 128 states:

(1) A person commits an offence if, without reasonable excuse, he does anything which he is prohibited from doing by—
(a) a risk of sexual harm order; or
(b) an interim risk of sexual harm order.

KEYNOTE

Where a person is convicted of an offence under this section, it is not open to the court to make, in respect of the offence, an order for conditional discharge (s. 128(3)).

If a person is convicted of or cautioned for an offence under s. 128 (or found not guilty by reason of insanity or to have been under a disability), then he/she becomes subject to the relevant notification requirements until the relevant order ceases to have effect (s. 129). If the defendant is already subject to the notification requirements, he/she will remain subject to them at least until the RSHO ceases and, if his/her original notification period was longer than the RSHO, until the end of that longer period.

The 'relevant date' here will be the date on which the defendant was convicted of the above offence (s. 129(4)).

1.12 | Child Protection

1.12.1 Introduction

The application of the law and the use of measures to protect children and other vulnerable groups are amongst some of the most contentious issues that any police officer may be involved in. This is echoed in the amount of media interest in such matters, often as a result of tragic circumstances surrounding the death of a child or the publication of a report or inquiry related to the subject. One such report, the Bichard Inquiry Report (June 2004), provides the background for the Safeguarding Vulnerable Groups Act 2006. Since 20 January 2009, referrals that would have been dealt with under the Education Act 2002 ('List 99'), the Protection of Children Act 1999 (the PoCA List) and the Protection of Vulnerable Adults (PoVA List) are referred to the Independent Safeguarding Authority established under the Safeguarding Vulnerable Groups Act 2006. The Independent Barring Board will maintain two lists that will combine the three previous lists. This **means that** the previous lists (along with the court-imposed disqualification order regime) will no longer exist. A summary of the central provisions of the Safeguarding Vulnerable Groups Act 2006 can be found below. This chapter also deals with other child-related offences and corresponding legislation such as child abduction (Child Abduction Act 1984) and 'Police Protection' (Children Act 1989).

1.12.2 Safeguarding Vulnerable Groups Act 2006

The Safeguarding Vulnerable Groups Act 2006 was passed as a result of the Bichard Inquiry arising from the Soham murders in 2002, when schoolgirls Jessica Chapman and Holly Wells were murdered by Ian Huntley (their school caretaker). The Inquiry questioned the way in which employers recruit people to work with vulnerable groups and particularly the way background checks are carried out. Recommendation 19 of the Inquiry Report says:

> new arrangements should be introduced requiring those who wish to work with children, or vulnerable adults, to be registered. The register would confirm that there is no known reason why an individual should not work with those clients.

The Act was passed in response to this recommendation and provides a legislative framework for a vetting and barring scheme for people who work with children (in the Act a 'child' is a person who has not attained the age of 18) and vulnerable adults. The purpose of the scheme is to minimise the risk of harm posed to children and vulnerable adults by those that might seek to harm them through their work (paid or unpaid). It seeks to do this by barring unsuitable individuals not just on the basis of referrals but also at the earliest opportunity as part of a centralised vetting process that all those working closely with children and/or vulnerable adults will need to go through. The whole tenet of the Act is that it will be preventative rather than reactive and rather than just providing a snapshot of an individual on the day the check is made, it will be able to react to new information about a person. This will allow an individual to be barred as soon as information justifying this is at hand. What follows is an overview of the Act's features.

1.12.2.1 Independent Safeguarding Authority

Section 1 of the Act provides for the creation of the Independent Safeguarding Authority. This is an entirely independent organisation that will assess the information to hand about an individual. It will decide whether a person should be barred, taking this decision out of the hands of civil servants.

1.12.2.2 Regulated Activity

Regulated activity will apply to most individuals working with children. It is broadly defined and covers what might be called 'frontline' activity where individuals have direct contact with children and vulnerable adults. Regulated activities will include:

- Any activity which involves contact with children or vulnerable adults and is of a specified nature on an intensive, frequent or overnight basis, e.g teaching, training, care, supervision, advice, treatment or transport.
- Any activity which allows contact with children or vulnerable adults and is in a specified place on an intensive or frequent basis, e.g. schools or care homes.
- Fostering (public or private) and childcare.
- Certain defined positions of responsibility, e.g. school governor, director of social services or trustees of certain charities.

Regulated activity applies where the activity is intensive, frequent or takes place on three or more days in a 30-day period.

Duties and responsibilities under regulated activity will include the following:

- To undertake a regulated activity, a person must have been vetted by the scheme.
- It will be an offence for a barred person to undertake regulated activity for any length of time.
- Any employer taking on a person in a regulated activity will commit a criminal offence if they fail to check the status of an applicant, employee or volunteer.
- It will also be an offence for employers/providers to permit a barred person, or a person who has not yet had a vetting and barring check, to work for any length of time (no matter how infrequent) in a regulated activity.
- It will be an offence for a barred person to undertake a regulated activity in a domestic circumstance.
- It will be an offence for a barred person to engage in or seek or offer to engage in a regulated activity for any length of time.

1.12.2.3 Controlled Activity

Generally speaking, controlled activity is activity that gives some opportunity for contact with children or vulnerable adults and does not fall within the category of regulated activity. Controlled activities will include:

- Intensive or frequent support in general health, NHS or further education, e.g. cleaners, caretakers, shop workers, catering staff or receptionists.
- Those working for specified organisations with frequent access to sensitive records about children and vulnerable adults, e.g. working for a local authority.
- Support work in adult social care settings, e.g. those with access to social care records.

Duties and responsibilities under controlled activity include the following:

- An employer taking on a person in a controlled activity will commit a criminal offence if they fail to check the status of an applicant, employee or volunteer.

Providing sufficient safeguards are put in place, the provider can permit a barred person to work in controlled activity.

An Overview of Rights and Responsibilities

	Duty on Individual Bar applies?	Duty on Employers Individual must be checked?	Duty on Employers Engagement of barred person?
Regulated Activities Employment and Volunteer settings	✓	✓	✗
Regulated Activities Domestic Employment settings	✓	✗	✗
Controlled Activities Employers	✗	✓	✓ (with safeguards)

1.12.2.4 The Barred Lists

There will be two barred lists: the children's barred list and the adults' barred list. The children's barred list is a list of people barred from working with children and will replace 'List 99', the PoCA List and disqualification orders (Criminal Justice and Court Services Act 2000). The adults' barred list is a list of people barred from working with adults and replaces the PoVA List.

There will be three barring routes which will lead to inclusion on either list:

- Automatic bar—where the bar will be immediate with no right to make representations on caution or conviction for the most serious offences against children and/or vulnerable adults.
- Automatic bar—where the bar will be immediate but following which the individual can make representations as to why he/she should be removed from the list. The bar will be the result of a caution or conviction for serious sexual offences against children and/or vulnerable adults. The individual will not be able to work with children and/or vulnerable adults until a decision is taken to remove him/her from the list.
- Discretionary bar—where an individual may be included on the barred list because of concerns regarding his/her behaviour or because of a perceived risk that he/she might cause harm to children and/or vulnerable adults. The Independent Safeguarding Authority, if minded to bar, will allow the individual to make representations and, having considered any such representations, decide whether the individual should be included on one or both barred lists.

1.12.2.5 Duties of Employers

Under the Act, the following organisations have a duty to refer relevant information to the IBB:

- adult/child protection teams in local authorities
- named professional bodies and supervisory authorities in the Act
- employers and service providers of regulated and controlled activities
- personnel suppliers, e.g. employment agencies.

The Act stipulates that the following organisations may refer relevant information:

- all other employers of those working with children and/or vulnerable adults and
- parents/private employers, but they should refer information to social services or the police who can investigate and refer information to the Independent Safeguarding Authority if appropriate.

Employers or service providers must refer information where they have dismissed an individual, or he/she resigned, because he/she harmed or may harm a child and/or vulnerable adult.

1.12.3 Child Abduction

There are two offences of abducting children, one which applies to people 'connected with the child' and the second which applies to abduction by others 'not connected to the child'.

1.12.3.1 Person Connected with Child

OFFENCE: **Child Abduction—Person Connected with Child—*Child Abduction Act 1984, s. 1***

- Triable either way • Seven years' imprisonment on indictment • Six months' imprisonment and/or a fine summarily

The Child Abduction Act 1984, s. 1 states:

(1) Subject to subsections (5) and (8) below, a person connected with a child under the age of 16 commits an offence if he takes or sends the child out of the United Kingdom without the appropriate consent.

'Connected with a Child'

The Child Abduction Act 1984, s. 1 states:

(2) A person is connected with the child for the purposes of this section if—
    (a) he is a parent of the child; or
    (b) in the case of a child whose parents were not married to each other at the time of his birth, there are reasonable grounds for believing that he is the father of the child; or
    (c) he is a guardian of the child; or
    (ca) he is a special guardian of the child; or
    (d) he is a person in whose favour a residence order is in force with respect to the child; or
    (e) he has custody of the child.

'Appropriate Consent'

The Child Abduction Act 1984, s. 1 states:

(3) In this section 'the appropriate consent' in relation to a child, means—
    (a) the consent of each of the following—
        (i) the child's mother;
        (ii) the child's father, if he has parental responsibility for him;
        (iii) any guardian of the child;
        (iiia) any special guardian of the child;
        (iv) any person in whose favour a residence order is in force with respect to the child;
        (v) any person who has custody of the child; or
    (b) the leave of the court granted under or by virtue of any provision of Part II of the Children Act 1989; or
    (c) if any person has custody of the child, the leave of the court which awarded custody to him.

KEYNOTE

This offence can only be committed by those people listed in s. 1(2). To be guilty they must take or send the child out of the United Kingdom. The taking or sending must be shown to have been done without the consent of *each* of those persons listed in s. 1(3)(a) above.

The consent of the DPP is needed before a charge of child abduction is brought under this section (s. 4(2)): there are also restrictions on charging kidnapping (as to which, **see chapter 1.9**) where the offence involves an offence under s. 1 above by a person connected with the child (s. 5).

1.12.3.2 Defence for Person Connected with a Child

The Child Abduction Act 1984, s. 1 states:

(4) A person does not commit an offence under this section by taking or sending a child out of the United Kingdom without obtaining the appropriate consent if—

(a) he is a person in whose favour there is a residence order in force with respect to the child, and he takes or sends the child out of the United Kingdom for a period of less than one month; or

(b) he is a special guardian of the child and he takes or sends the child out of the United Kingdom for a period of less than three months.

(4A) Subsection (4) above does not apply if the person taking or sending the child out of the United Kingdom does so in breach of an order under Part II of the Children Act 1989.

(5) A person does not commit an offence under this section by doing anything without the consent of another person whose consent is required under the foregoing provisions if—

(a) he does it in the belief that the other person—

(i) has consented; or

(ii) would consent if he was aware of all the relevant circumstances; or

(b) he has taken all reasonable steps to communicate with the other person but has been unable to communicate with him; or

(c) the other person has unreasonably refused to consent.

KEYNOTE

Note the specific defence (at s. 1(5))—if the defendant believes that the appropriate person has consented or would have consented had they known of the circumstances.

A further provision (s. 1(5A)) states that s. 1(5)(c) will not apply if the person who refused to consent is a person:

- in whose favour there is a residence order in force with respect to the child; or
- who has custody of the child; or
- who is a special guardian of the child; or
- is, by taking or sending the child out of the United Kingdom, acting in breach of a court order in the United Kingdom.

1.12.3.3 Person Not Connected with Child

OFFENCE: **Child Abduction—Person Not Connected with Child—*Child Abduction Act 1984, s. 2***

- Triable either way • Seven years' imprisonment on indictment • Six months' imprisonment and/or a fine summarily

The Child Abduction Act 1984, s. 2 states:

(1) Subject to subsection (3) below, a person other than one mentioned in subsection (2) below, commits an offence if, without lawful authority or reasonable excuse, he takes or detains a child under the age of 16—

  (a) so as to remove him from the lawful control of any person having lawful control of the child: or

  (b) so as to keep him out of the lawful control of any person entitled to lawful control of the child.

(2) The persons are—

  (a) where the father and mother of the child in question were married to each other at the time of his birth, the child's father and mother;

  (b) where the father and mother of the child in question were not married to each other at the time of his birth, the child's mother; and

  (c) any other person mentioned in section 1(2)(c) to (e) above.

KEYNOTE

This offence requires the taking or detaining of a child under 16 years. This will include keeping a child in the place where he/she is found and inducing the child to remain with the defendant or another person. The distinction between subss. (a) and (b) is important. You must show that the defendant acted without lawful authority or reasonable excuse. The consent of the victim is irrelevant. The word 'remove' for the purpose of s. 2(1)(a) means effectively a substitution of authority by a defendant for that of the person lawfully having it and physical removal from a particular place is not required (see *Foster* v *DPP* [2004] EWHC 2955 (Admin)).

Section 2(1)(a) requires the child *there and then* to be in the lawful control of someone entitled to it when they are taken or detained, whereas s. 2(1)(b) requires only that the child be kept out of the lawful control of someone entitled to it when taken or detained. Whether or not a person is under the lawful control of another is a question of fact (*R* v *Leather* [1993] Crim LR 516). Proving the absence of reasonable excuse could be difficult. Clearly a defendant could argue, particularly in the case of a very young child, that he/she was acting in the child's best interests, a claim which might be difficult to refute.

1.12.3.4 **Defence for Person Not Connected with a Child**

The Child Abduction Act 1984, s. 2 states:

(3) ... it shall be a defence for [the defendant] to prove—

  (a) where the father and mother of the child in question were not married to each other at the time of his birth—

    (i) that he is the child's father; or

    (ii) that, at the time of the alleged offence, he believed, on reasonable grounds, that he was the child's father; or

  (b) that, at the time of the alleged offence, he believed that the child had attained the age of 16.

KEYNOTE

Section 2(3)(b) provides a defence if the accused can show that he/she believed the child to be 16 or over.

1.12.4 Child Cruelty

OFFENCE: **Child Cruelty—*Children and Young Persons Act 1933, s. 1***
- Triable either way • Ten years' imprisonment on indictment • Six months' imprisonment and/or a fine summarily

The Children and Young Persons Act 1933, s. 1 states:

(1) If any person who has attained the age of 16 years and has responsibility for any child or young person under that age, wilfully assaults, ill-treats, neglects, abandons, or exposes him, or causes or procures him to be assaulted, ill-treated, neglected, abandoned, or exposed, in a manner likely to cause him unnecessary suffering or injury to health (including injury to or loss of sight, or hearing, or limb or organ of the body, and any mental derangement), that person shall be guilty of a misdemeanour ...

KEYNOTE

The defendant must be shown both to have attained the age of 16 years *and* to have had responsibility for the child or young person.

Responsibility for a child or young person can be shared and whether a person had such responsibility in each case will be a matter of both fact and law (see *Liverpool Society for the Prevention of Cruelty to Children* v *Jones* [1914] 3 KB 813). Anyone having parental responsibility or any other legal liability to maintain a child or young person will be presumed to have responsibility for him/her and that responsibility does not cease simply because the person ceases to have care of him/her. Others such as babysitters and child minders may also have 'responsibility' for the child while in their care (see generally s. 17).

The Act goes on to make other specific provisions and presumptions, particularly in relation to the issues of causation. So, for example, if a parent or other person legally liable to maintain the child or young person, or a guardian, has failed to provide adequate food, clothing, medical aid or lodging for the child or young person, he/she will be deemed to have neglected the child or young person for the above purposes (see s. 1(2)).

Similarly, a person will be presumed to have neglected the child where it is proved that the child was an infant under three years old and that he/she died as a result of suffocation (other than by disease or blockage of the airways by an object) while in bed with someone of 16 years or over who was under the influence of drink when they went to bed (see s. 1(2)(b)).

A defendant may be charged with the above offence even where the child has died (see s. 1(3)(b)) but homicide should also be considered.

The above section creates only one single offence, albeit one that can be committed in many different ways, by both positive acts and omission (see *R* v *Hayles* [1969] 1 QB 364). Although any aspect of neglect must be shown to have occurred in a manner likely to cause unnecessary suffering or injury to health, there is no need to show that any such suffering or injury actually came about.

1.12.5 Police Powers under the Children Act 1989

The police have specific statutory powers to deal with the threat of significant harm posed to children and these are set out below.

Section 46 of the Children Act 1989 states:

(1) Where a constable has reasonable cause to believe that a child would otherwise be likely to suffer significant harm, he may—
    (a) remove the child to suitable accommodation and keep him there; or

    (b) take such steps as are reasonable to ensure the the child's removal from any hospital, or other place, in which he is then being accommodated is prevented.

  (2) For the purposes of this Act, a child with respect to whom a constable has exercised his powers under this section is referred to as having been taken into police protection.

KEYNOTE

For most purposes of the 1989 Act, someone who is under 18 years old is a 'child' (s. 105).

The wording of s. 46(1) means that an officer may use the powers at s. 46(1)(a) and (b) if he/she has reasonable cause to believe that, if he/she does not use them, a child is likely to suffer significant harm. The issues arising from similar wording in relation to powers of arrest have been considered by the courts on a number of occasions. Generally, tests of reasonableness impose an element of objectivity and the courts will consider whether, in the circumstances, a reasonable and sober person might have formed a similar view to that of the officer.

'Harm' is a very broad term and is defined under s. 31(9). It covers all forms of ill treatment including sexual abuse and forms of ill treatment that are not physical. It also covers the impairment of health (physical or mental) and also physical, intellectual, emotional, social or behavioural development. The definition also extends to impairment suffered from seeing or hearing the ill-treatment *of any other person*.

When determining whether harm to a child's health or development is '*significant*', the child's development will be compared with that which could reasonably be expected of a similar child (s. 31(10)).

The power under s. 46 is split into two parts:

- a power to *remove* a child to suitable accommodation and keep him/her there, and
- a power to take reasonable steps to *prevent* the child's removal from a hospital or other place.

The longest a child can spend in police protection is 72 hours (s. 46(6)). It should be remembered that this is the *maximum* time that a child can be kept in police protection, not the norm.

As soon as is reasonably practicable after using the powers under the Act, the 'Initiating Officer' (the officer who takes the child into police protection and undertakes the initial inquiries) must do a number of things as set out above. These things generally include:

- telling the local authority within whose area the child was found what steps have been, and are proposed to be, taken and why. This aspect of communicating with the local authority is a critical part of the protective powers;
- giving details to the local authority within whose area the child is ordinarily resident of the place at which the child is being kept;
- telling the child (if he/she appears capable of understanding) of what steps have been taken and why, and what further steps may be taken;
- taking such steps as are reasonably practicable to discover the wishes and feelings of the child;
- making sure that the case is inquired into by a 'designated officer' (see below);
- taking such steps as are reasonably practicable to inform:
  - ♦ the child's parents
  - ♦ every person who is not his/her parent but who has parental responsibility for the child and
  - ♦ any other person with whom the child was living immediately before being taken into police protection,

  of the steps that the officer has taken under this section, the reasons for taking them and the further steps that may be taken with respect to the child. This element of informing the child, parent and/or relevant carers of what is happening and why is also a vital part of the protective process.

Where the child was taken into police protection by being removed to accommodation which is not provided by or on behalf of a local authority or as a refuge (under s. 51), the officer must, as soon as is reasonably practicable after taking a child into police protection, make sure that the child is moved to accommodation provided by the local authority. Every local authority must receive and provide accommodation for children in police protection where such a request is made (s. 21).

The requirement under s. 46(3)(c) to give the child information, reflects the 1989 Act's theme that children should have some influence over their own destiny.

The 'Initiating Officer' and the 'Designated Officer' must not carry out these two separate roles (Home Office Circular 17/2008). The Circular also states that a police station is not 'suitable accommodation' and children should not be brought to a police station except in exceptional circumstances, such as a lack of immediately available local authority accommodation, and then only for a short period. *On no account should a child who has been taken into police protection be taken to the cellblock area of a police station.*

Note that, when considering action under s. 46, it is possible that the child may already be the subject of an Emergency Protection Order (EPO) applied for by a local authority or authorised body under s. 44.

In considering the proper approach under these circumstances the Court of Appeal has held that:

- There is no express provision in the Act prohibiting the police from invoking s. 46 where an EPO is in place and it is not desirable to imply a restriction which prohibits a constable from removing a child under s. 46 where he/she has reasonable cause to believe that the child would otherwise be likely to suffer significant harm.
- The s. 46 power to remove a child can therefore be exercised even where an EPO is in force in respect of the child.
- Where a police officer knows that an EPO is in force, he/she should not exercise the power of removing a child under s. 46, unless there are compelling reasons to do so.
- The statutory scheme accords primacy to the EPO procedure under s. 44 because removal under that section is sanctioned by the court and involves a more elaborate, sophisticated and complete process of removal than under s. 46.
- Consequently, the removal of children should usually be effected pursuant to an EPO, and s. 46 should only be invoked where it is not reasonably practicable to execute an EPO.
- In deciding whether it is practicable to execute an EPO, the police should always have regard to the paramount need to protect children from significant harm.
- Failure to follow the statutory procedure may amount to the police officer's removal of the child under s. 46 being declared unlawful.

(*Langley* v *Liverpool City Council and Chief Constable of Merseyside* [2005] EWCA Civ 1173)

1.12.5.1 Designated Officer

The reference at s. 46(3)(e) of the Act to a 'designated officer' is a reference to the appropriate officer designated for that police station for the purposes of this legislation by the relevant chief officer of police. This is a key role in ensuring the effective use of the statutory framework set up for the protection of children in these circumstances. The responsibility for ensuring that the case is inquired into by the designated officer, together with the other responsibilities under s. 46(3) and the responsibility for taking steps to inform people under s. 46(4), clearly rest with the police officer exercising the power under s. 46.

Practically, the designated officer must inquire fully and thoroughly into the case; he/she must also do what is reasonable in all the circumstances for the purpose of safeguarding or promoting the child's welfare (having regard in particular to the length of the period during which the child will be so protected) (s. 46(9)(b)).

Where a child has been taken into police protection, the designated officer shall allow:

- the child's parents
- any person who is not a parent of the child but who has parental responsibility for him
- any person with whom the child was living immediately before he/she was taken into police protection
- any person in whose favour a contact order is in force with respect to the child
- any person who is allowed to have contact with the child by virtue of an order under s. 34; and
- any person acting on behalf of any of those persons,

to have such contact (if any) with the child as, in the opinion of the designated officer, is both reasonable and in the child's best interests (s. 46(10)).

The designated officer may apply for an 'emergency protection order' under s. 44 (s. 46(7)). Such an order allows the court to order the removal of the child to certain types of accommodation and to prevent the child's removal from any other place (including a hospital) where he/she was being accommodated immediately before the making of the order (s. 44(4)). An emergency protection order gives the applicant 'parental responsibility' for the child while it is in force. It also allows the court to make certain directions in relation to contact with the child and a medical or psychiatric assessment of them. Section 44A allows the court to make an order excluding certain people from a dwelling house where the child lives and to attach a power of arrest accordingly.

While the designated officer can apply for an emergency protection order without the local authority's knowledge or agreement (see s. 46(8)), there should be no reason why, given proper multi-agency co-operation and a well-planned child protection strategy, this situation would come about. For further guidance on multi-agency working in the area of child protection, see *Working Together to Safeguard Children* (TSO 2006).

On completing his/her inquiry into the case, the designated officer must release the child from police protection *unless he/she considers that there is still reasonable cause for believing that the child would be likely to suffer significant harm if released* (s. 46(5)).

While a child is in police protection, neither the officer concerned nor the designated officer will have parental responsibility for him/her (s. 46(9)(a)).

When a local authority is informed that a child is in police protection, they have a duty to make 'such enquiries as they consider necessary to enable them to decide whether they should take any action to safeguard' the child (s. 47(1)(b)). A court may issue a warrant for a constable to assist a relevant person to enter premises in order to enforce an emergency protection order.

1.12.5.2 Contravention of Protection Order or Police Protection

OFFENCE: **Acting in Contravention of Protection Order or Power Exercised under s. 46—***Children Act 1989, s. 49*
- Triable summarily • Six months' imprisonment

The Children Act 1989, s. 49 states:

(1) A person shall be guilty of an offence if, knowingly and without lawful authority or reasonable excuse, he—
  (a) takes a child to whom this section applies away from the responsible person;
  (b) keeps such a child away from the responsible person; or
  (c) induces, assists or incites such a child to run away or stay away from the responsible person.

(2) This section applies in relation to a child who is—
   (a) in care;
   (b) the subject of an emergency protection order; or
   (c) in police protection,
   and in this section 'the responsible person' means any person who for the time being has care of him by virtue of the care order, the emergency protection order, or section 46, as the case may be.

KEYNOTE

Where a child is taken in contravention of s. 49 above, the court may issue a 'recovery order' under s. 50. Such an order, which is also available where a child is missing or has run away, requires certain people to produce the child to an authorised person (which includes a constable (s. 50(7)(b)) or to give certain information about the child's whereabouts to a constable or officer of the court (s. 50(3)). It can also authorise a constable to enter any premises and search for the child.

Under s. 102 of the 1989 Act a court may issue a warrant to enter premises in connection with certain provisions of the Act which regulate children's homes, foster homes, child-minding premises and nursing homes for children. Section 102 allows for constables to assist any person in the exercise of their powers under those provisions. It also makes allowances for a constable to be accompanied by a medical practitioner, nurse or health visitor (s. 102(3)).

1.12.5.3 **Disclosure of Information Regarding Child**

Where a child is reported missing problems can arise once he/she is discovered to be safe and well but one of the parents wants the police to disclose the whereabouts of the child. This situation arose in *S v S (Chief Constable of West Yorkshire Police Intervening)* [1999] 1 All ER 281 and the Court of Appeal provided some clarification of the issues. In that case the mother left home with her three-year-old child after a marriage breakdown. The father reported the child's absence to the police who found the child and her mother in a refuge. At the request of the mother, the police advised the father that both she and the child were safe but refused to disclose their whereabouts. The father applied 'without notice' (i.e. without telling the police) to the county court which then made an order under s. 33 of the Family Law Act 1986, requiring the police to disclose the information. The chief constable was granted leave to intervene and, following another order from the court to disclose the child's whereabouts, the chief constable appealed. The Court of Appeal held that it was only in exceptional circumstances that the police should be asked to divulge the whereabouts of a child under a s. 33 order. Their primary role in such cases should continue to be finding missing children and ensuring their safety.

However, the court went on to say that, in such cases:

- The police are *not* in a position to give 'categoric assurances' of confidentiality to those who provide information as to the whereabouts of a child. The most they could say is that, other than by removing the child, it would be *most unlikely* that they would have to disclose the information concerning the child's whereabouts.
- An order under s. 33 provides for the information to be disclosed to the court, not to the other party or his/her solicitor.
- An order under s. 33 should not normally be made in respect of the police without their being present (*ex parte*).

Note that the provision of information by police officers in relation to civil proceedings involving children is governed by regulations; specific advice should therefore be sought before disclosing any such information.

1.12.6 Harmful Publications

OFFENCE: **Harmful Publications—*Children and Young Persons (Harmful Publications) Act 1955, s. 2***

- Triable summarily • Four months' imprisonment and/or a fine

The Children and Young Persons (Harmful Publications) Act 1955, s. 2 states:

(1) A person who prints, publishes, sells or lets on hire a work to which this Act applies, or has any such work in his possession for the purpose of selling it or letting it on hire, shall be guilty of an offence...

KEYNOTE

A prosecution for this offence can only be brought with the consent of the Attorney-General (or Solicitor-General). The sort of 'works' to which the Act applies are set out in s. 1 and include books, magazines or other like works of a kind likely to fall into the hands of children or young persons which consist wholly or mainly of stories told in pictures which portray:

- the commission of crimes, or
- acts of violence or cruelty, or
- incidents of a repulsive or horrible nature,

in such a way that the work as a whole would tend to corrupt a child or young person.

Power of Search

A search warrant may be issued under s. 3 of the 1955 Act.

Defence

The Children and Young Persons (Harmful Publications) Act 1955, s. 2 states:

(1) ... in any proceedings taken under this subsection against a person in respect of selling or letting on hire a work or of having it in his possession for the purpose of selling it or letting it on hire, it shall be a defence for him to prove that he had not examined the contents of the work and had no reasonable cause to suspect that it was one to which this Act applies.

1.13.1 Introduction

Many of the offences contained in this chapter will be all too familiar to policing personnel. Their real life experiences will provide them with first-hand knowledge of the physical, emotional and financial cost to victims of offences such as theft, burglary and robbery. The prevalence, and consequent significant impact, that these offences have on society as a whole can leave no doubt as to their importance in terms of policing.

1.13.2 Theft

OFFENCE: **Theft—*Theft Act 1968, s. 1***

- Triable either way • Seven years' imprisonment on indictment • Six months' imprisonment and/or a fine summarily

The Theft Act 1968, s. 1 states:

> (1) A person is guilty of theft if he dishonestly appropriates property belonging to another with the intention of permanently depriving the other of it; and 'thief' and 'steal' shall be construed accordingly.

KEYNOTE

In order for an offence of theft to exist, each element of the definition must be proved and those elements are considered in detail below.

Note that offences of theft from businesses (classed as 'theft from a shop') involving values not exceeding £100 can be dealt with by way of fixed penalty notice (see General Police Duties, para. 4.6.3).

As described above, there are five key elements to the offence of theft. These are:

- dishonesty
- appropriation
- property
- belonging to another
- intention of permanently depriving.

1.13.2.1 Dishonestly

If a person cannot be shown to have acted 'dishonestly', he/she is not guilty of theft. The decision as to whether or not a defendant was in fact dishonest is one for the jury or magistrate(s). There is no statutory definition of this term. Instead the 1968 Act sets out a number of specific circumstances where the relevant person will *not* be treated as dishonest and one circumstance where a person *may* be dishonest.

The Theft Act 1968, s. 2 states:

(1) A person's appropriation of property belonging to another is not to be regarded as dishonest—
  (a) if he appropriates the property in the belief that he has in law the right to deprive the other of it, on behalf of himself or of a third person; or
  (b) if he appropriates the property in the belief that he would have the other's consent if the other knew of the appropriation and the circumstances of it; or
  (c) (except where the property came to him as trustee or personal representative) if he appropriates the property in the belief that the person to whom the property belongs cannot be discovered by taking reasonable steps.
(2) A person's appropriation of property belonging to another may be dishonest notwithstanding that he is willing to pay for the property.

KEYNOTE

In all three instances it is the person's *belief* that is important.

Right

● Under s. 2(1)(a) if a person in dispute with a bookmaker believes he/she has a legal contractual *right* to take something of a value equal to his/her unpaid winnings from the bookmaker's stand, that person will not be regarded as dishonest—even though gambling debts are not legally enforceable. His/her belief need not even be reasonable, only honestly held, and could be based on a 'mistake' (contrast the general defence of mistake, see chapter 1.4).

Consent

● Under s. 2(1)(b) the person appropriating the property must believe both elements, i.e. that the other person would have *consented* had he/she known of the appropriation *and the circumstances of it*. For example, a person is about to run out of time on a street parking meter and needs £2 to park for the next hour otherwise he/she will incur a £20 fine. Believing that his/her work colleague would consent in this situation, the person takes £2 belonging to the work colleague from a change jar on the work colleague's desk. Although the person need not have given his/her consent to the appropriation, the presence of such consent may be very relevant in establishing the honest existence of the defendant's belief.

Lost

● Under s. 2(1)(c), the belief has to be in relation to the likelihood of *discovering* the 'owner' by taking reasonable steps. Both the nature and value of the property, together with the attendant circumstances, will be relevant. The chances of finding the owner of a valuable, monogrammed engagement ring found after a theatre performance would be considerably greater than those of discovering the owner of a can of beer found outside Twickenham stadium following a Six Nations match between Wales and England. Again, it is the defendant's *belief* at the time of the appropriation that is important here, not that the defendant went on to take reasonable steps to discover the person to whom the property belongs.

Under s. 2(2), if a person appropriates another's property, leaving money or details of where he/she can be contacted to make restitution will not *of itself* negate dishonesty (see *Boggeln* v *Williams* [1978] 1 WLR 873). The wording of s. 2(2) gives latitude to a court where the defendant was willing to pay for the property. The subsection says that such an appropriation *may* be dishonest, not that it *will always* be dishonest.

1.13.2.2 Dishonesty: The Ruling in *Ghosh*

Section 2 will not cater for every circumstance and indeed ss. 2 to 6 only affect the interpretation of the basic elements of theft as set out in s. 1 unless the Act says otherwise

(s. 1(3)). Since the case of *R* v *Ghosh* [1982] QB 1053 there has been a requirement for juries to be given some form of direction where the issue of dishonesty is raised and s. 2 is of no assistance. As well as clarifying that the defendant's dishonesty is a matter for a jury to decide, the Court of Appeal in *Ghosh* also identified two aspects which the jury should consider when so deciding. If s. 2 is not applicable or helpful then a jury must decide:

- whether, according to the ordinary standards of reasonable and honest people, what was done was 'dishonest'; *and*, if it was
- whether 'the defendant himself must have realised that what was done was dishonest' *by those standards*.

This test against the standards of reasonable and honest people means that a defendant who has a purely *subjective* belief that he/she is doing what is morally right (e.g. an anti-vivisectionist taking animals from a laboratory) can still be 'dishonest'. The *Ghosh* test is probably the source of the questions so loved by some interviewing officers: 'But what would an *honest* person have done?' or 'What would have been the *honest* thing to do?'

1.13.2.3 Appropriates

The Theft Act 1968, s. 3 states:

(1) Any assumption by a person of the rights of an owner amounts to an appropriation, and this includes, where he has come by the property (innocently or not) without stealing it, any later assumption of a right to it by keeping or dealing with it as owner.

KEYNOTE

It is important to note that there can be an 'appropriation' without any criminal liability and appropriation itself does not amount to an offence; it describes one of the elements of the criminal conduct that must exist before a charge of theft can be made out. An appropriation requires no mental state on the part of the appropriator. It is an objective act.

Where an appropriation takes place and is accompanied by the required dishonesty and intention to deprive permanently, there will be a theft.

Appropriation under s. 3(1) envisages a *physical* act—*Biggs* v *R* (2003) 12 December, unreported.

When and where the particular act amounting to an appropriation took place is therefore of critical importance when bringing a charge of theft; it is also vital when establishing other offences such as robbery, aggravated burglary and handling stolen goods.

Appropriation and Consent: *R* v *Gomez*

The decision of the House of Lords in *R* v *Gomez* [1993] AC 442 significantly developed the meaning of 'appropriation'. Following an earlier case (*Lawrence* v *Metropolitan Police Commissioner* [1972] AC 626), Lord Keith disagreed with the argument (made in *Gomez*) that an act expressly or impliedly authorised by the owner of the property in question can never amount to an 'appropriation' and pointed out that the decision in *Lawrence* was a direct contradiction of that proposition. The House of Lords upheld the convictions for theft in *Gomez* and accepted that there are occasions where property can be 'appropriated' for the purposes of the Theft Act 1968, *even though the owner has given his/her consent or authority*.

A number of issues come from this decision:

- *Taking or depriving.* First, it is not necessary that the property be 'taken' in order for there to be an appropriation, neither need the owner be 'deprived' of the property. Similarly, there is no need for the defendant to 'gain' anything by an appropriation which can also be caused by damaging or destroying property (*R* v *Graham* [1997] 1 Cr App R 395). Note that while damaging property amounts to

---

'appropriation', all the other elements of the offence of theft (such as 'dishonesty') are required before the full offence of theft is committed.

- *Consent*. Secondly, it is irrelevant to the issue of appropriation whether or not the owner consented to that appropriation. This is well illustrated in *Lawrence*, the decision followed by the House of Lords in *Gomez*. In *Lawrence* a tourist gave his wallet full of unfamiliar English currency to a taxi driver for the latter to remove the correct fare. The driver in fact helped himself to ('appropriated') far more than the amount owed. It has held that the fact that the wallet and its contents were handed over freely (with consent) by the owner did not prevent the taxi driver's actions from amounting to an 'appropriation' of it. The Court of Appeal appears—at least on one occasion—to have interpreted *Gomez* as deciding that consent *obtained by fraud* is irrelevant to the issue of appropriation (see *R* v *Mazo* [1997] 2 Cr App R 518). However, there is no such restriction placed on the decision in *Gomez* and it seems safe to assume that consent given by the owner will not prevent an 'appropriation' of property for the purposes of the Theft Act 1968.

- *Interfering with goods.* A third point that is now clear from the decision in *Gomez* is that simply swapping the price labels on items displayed for sale in a shop *would* amount to an 'appropriation'. This is because to do so, irrespective of any further intention, involves an assumption of one of the owner's rights in relation to the property. If that appropriation were accompanied by the required circumstances of dishonesty and intention to deprive, then there would be a *prima facie* case of theft.

- *More than one appropriation.* A fourth point apparent from *Gomez* is that there may be an appropriation of the same property on more than one occasion. However, once property has been *stolen* (as opposed to merely appropriated), that same property cannot be stolen again by the same thief (*R* v *Atakpu* [1994] QB 69). Appropriation can also be a continuing act, that is, it can include the whole episode of entering and ransacking a house and the subsequent removal of property (*R* v *Hale* (1978) 68 Cr App R 415). Therefore identifying the exact point at which property was appropriated with the requisite intention and accompanying dishonesty can cause practical difficulties.

Summary

In *R* v *Hinks* [2001] 2 AC 24, the House of Lords was asked to rule on whether a person could 'appropriate' property belonging to another where the other person made her an absolute gift of property, retaining no proprietary interest in the property or any right to resume or recover it. In that case the defendant had befriended a middle-aged man of limited intelligence who had given her some £60,000 over a period of time. The defendant was charged with five counts of theft and, after conviction, eventually appealed to the House of Lords. Their lordships held that:

- in a prosecution for theft it was unnecessary to prove that the taking was without the owner's consent (as in *Lawrence* above);
- it was immaterial whether the act of appropriation was done with the owner's consent or authority (as in *Gomez*); and
- *Gomez* therefore gave effect to s. 3(1) by treating 'appropriation' as a neutral word covering 'any assumption by a person of the rights of an owner'.

This finding is consistent with earlier cases.

If a person, having come by property—innocently or not—without stealing it, later assumes any rights to it by keeping it or treating it as his/her own, then he/she 'appropriates' that property (s. 3(1)).

An exception to these circumstances is provided by s. 3 which states:

(2) Where property or a right or interest in property is or purports to be transferred for value to a person acting in good faith, no later assumption by him of rights which he believed himself

to be acquiring shall, by reason of any defect in the transferor's title, amount to theft of the property.

KEYNOTE

If a person buys a car in good faith and gives value for it (i.e. a reasonable price) but then discovers it has been stolen, his/her refusal to return it to the vendor will not, without more, *attract liability for theft.* Without s. 3(2) the retention of the vehicle would be caught by s. 3(1). This narrow exemption does not mean however that the innocent purchaser gets good title to the car (see *National Employers' Mutual Insurance Association Ltd* v *Jones* [1990] 1 AC 24), nor would it provide a defence if the stolen goods are a gift and the 'donee' (recipient) subsequently discovers that they had been stolen.

1.13.2.4 Property

The Theft Act 1968, s. 4 states:

(1) 'Property' includes money and all other property, real or personal, including things in action and other intangible property.

(2) A person cannot steal land, or things forming part of land and severed from it by him or by his directions, except in the following cases, that is to say—

(a) when he is a trustee or personal representative, or is authorised by power of attorney, or as liquidator of a company, or otherwise, to sell or dispose of land belonging to another, and he appropriates the land or anything forming part of it by dealing with it in breach of the confidence reposed in him; or

(b) when he is not in possession of the land and appropriates anything forming part of the land by severing it or causing it to be severed, or after it has been severed; or

(c) when, being in possession of the land under a tenancy, he appropriates the whole or part of any fixture or structure let to be used with the land.

For purposes of this subsection 'land' does not include incorporeal hereditaments; 'tenancy' means a tenancy for years or any less period and includes an agreement for such a tenancy, but a person who after the end of a tenancy remains in possession as statutory tenant or otherwise is to be treated as having possession under the tenancy, and 'let' shall be construed accordingly.

(3) A person who picks mushrooms growing wild on any land, or who picks flowers, fruit or foliage from a plant growing wild on any land, does not (although not in possession of the land) steal what he picks unless he does it for reward or for sale or other commercial purpose. For purposes of this subsection 'mushroom' includes any fungus, and 'plant' includes any shrub or tree.

(4) Wild creatures, tamed or untamed, shall be regarded as property; but a person cannot steal a wild creature not tamed nor ordinarily kept in captivity, or the carcase of any such creature, unless either it has been reduced into possession by or on behalf of another person and possession of it has not since been lost or abandoned, or another person is in course of reducing it into possession.

KEYNOTE

Specific Types of Property

Under s. 4(1) 'things in action' would include patents and trademarks and other things which can only be enforced by legal action as opposed to physical possession. Other intangible property would include software programs and perhaps credits accumulated on 'smart cards'. Confidential information—such as the contents of an examination paper—is not intangible property *per se* (see *Oxford* v *Moss* (1978) 68 Cr App R 183). However, the document itself would be property. It has been accepted by the Court of Appeal that contractual rights obtained by buying a ticket for the London Underground may amount to a 'thing in action' (see *R* v *Marshall* [1998] 2 Cr App R 282).

An area of criminal activity causing concern (and cost) is that of so-called 'identity theft', this is something of a misnomer. Adopting another person's characteristics and using their administrative data (such as national insurance number) is not theft of the information, as this information is not 'property' for these purposes, however confidential it might be.

Cheques

Cheques will be property as they are pieces of paper (albeit of very little intrinsic value). The contents of a bank or building society account, however, are also a 'thing in action' that can be stolen *provided the account is in credit or within the limits of an agreed overdraft facility* (*R* v *Kohn* (1979) 69 Cr App R 395). Therefore reducing the credit balance in one account, and transferring a like sum into your own account amounts to an 'appropriation' of property within the meaning of s. 1. This principle (set out in *Kohn*) was reaffirmed in *R* v *Williams (Roy)* [2001] 1 Cr App R 362 by the Court of Appeal.

Land

Under s. 4(2) you cannot generally steal land even though it is 'property' for the purposes of criminal damage (see chapter 1.15). An exception to this general rule is that if you are a trustee or personal representative or someone in a position of trust to dispose of land belonging to another, you can be guilty of stealing it if, in such circumstances, you dishonestly dispose of it.

If you are in possession of land under a tenancy then things forming part of that land to be used with it are 'property' capable of being stolen. Such fittings and fixtures (including fireplaces, fitted kitchens, etc.) would be particularly relevant to agricultural tenants or those occupying council property.

Section 4(3) obliquely includes mushrooms, flowers, fruit and foliage in the ambit of 'property' unless they are growing wild on any land. If they are so growing, then the person picking them must be shown to have done so for reward, sale or other commercial purpose in order to be guilty of theft. It is arguable that, if the person does not have such a *purpose at the time of the picking*, any later intention to sell the fruit, etc. may not bring it within the provisions of s. 4(3).

Animals

Section 4(4) acknowledges that all wild creatures are 'property' but goes on to qualify the occasions when they will be capable of being the subject matter of a charge of theft. Once a person has reduced it into possession (say, by trapping, capturing or shooting it), a wild animal can be 'stolen', by another, but not the person reducing it into possession. This is why poaching is not generally theft. If the animal is lost or abandoned after it has been reduced into possession or killed then it cannot be 'stolen'.

Pets and animals that are tamed or ordinarily kept in captivity are always property for the purposes of theft.

1.13.2.5 What is not Property?

Human bodies are not property (*Doodeward* v *Spence* (1908) 6 CLR 406) although a driver has been convicted of stealing a specimen of his own urine (*R* v *Welsh* [1974] RTR 478). This principle was upheld by the Court of Appeal in *R* v *Kelly* [1999] QB 621, after the conviction of two people involved in the theft of body parts from the Royal College of Surgeons. The court upheld the convictions for theft on the grounds that the process of *alteration* (amputation, dissection and preservation) which the body parts had undergone did make them 'property' for the purposes of the 1968 Act. The common law rule was that there is no property in a corpse and any change to that rule would have to be made by Parliament.

Electricity is the subject of a specific offence.

1.13.2.6 **Belonging to Another**

The Theft Act 1968, s. 5 states:

(1) Property shall be regarded as belonging to any person having possession or control of it, or having in it any proprietary right or interest (not being an equitable interest arising only from an agreement to transfer or grant an interest).

(2) Where property is subject to a trust, the persons to whom it belongs shall be regarded as including any person having a right to enforce the trust, and an intention to defeat the trust shall be regarded accordingly as an intention to deprive of the property any person having that right.

KEYNOTE

Property can be 'stolen' from any person who has possession or control or a right or interest in that property. In one case where the defendant recovered his own recently repaired car from a street outside the garage where the repairs had taken place, he was convicted of stealing the car which at the time 'belonged to' the garage proprietor who had possession and control of it (*R* v *Turner (No. 2)* [1971] 1 WLR 901). In determining whether or not a person had 'possession' of property for the purposes of s. 5(1), the period of possession can be finite (i.e. for a given number of hours, days, etc.) or infinite (*R* v *Kelly* [1998] 3 All ER 741).

It is not necessary to show who does own the property—only that it 'belongs to' someone other than the defendant.

A good example of how this principle operates can be seen in a case before the Court of Appeal where the two defendants went diving in a lake on a golf course, recovering sacks of 'lost' balls which it was believed they were going to sell. Although the defendants argued that the balls had been abandoned by their owners, the Crown had shown that they were 'property belonging to another' and therefore the convictions were safe (*R* v *Rostron*; *R* v *Collinson* [2003] EWCA Crim 2206).

Where money is given by members of the public to charity collectors it becomes the property of the relevant charitable trustees at the moment it goes into the collecting tin (*R* v *Dyke* [2001] EWCA Crim 2184). This will be important when framing the relevant charge or indictment. If in doubt as to the 'ownership' of property that is the subject of a theft, the advice of the CPS should be sought.

When a cheque is written, that will create a 'thing in action'. That thing in action belongs only to the payee. Therefore a payee of a cheque cannot 'steal' the thing in action which it creates (*R* v *Davis* (1988) 88 Cr App R 347).

In proving theft, you must show that the property belonged to another *at the time of the appropriation*. This requirement has caused some difficulty where a defendant's decision not to pay for goods has been made *after* property passed to him/her. In such cases (e.g. people refusing to pay for meals after they have eaten or deciding to drive off having filled their car with petrol), the proper charge is found under the Fraud Act 2006 (see chapter 1.14) or by charging with the offence of making off without payment. The House of Lords' ruling in *Gomez* raises some questions over such cases (see para. 1.13.2.3). As the consent of the owner is irrelevant to the issue of 'appropriation', the key element in such cases is whether the property 'belonged to another' at the time of the act of appropriation. If ownership of the property had passed to the defendant *before* he/she appropriated it (e.g. by virtue of the Sale of Goods Act 1979; see *Edwards* v *Ddin* [1976] 1 WLR 942) then this element of theft would not be made out and an alternative charge should be considered.

1.13.2.7 **Obligations Regarding Another's Property**

The Theft Act 1968, s. 5 states:

(3) Where a person receives property from or on account of another, and is under an obligation to the other to retain and deal with that property or its proceeds in a particular way, the property or proceeds shall be regarded (as against him) as belonging to the other.

KEYNOTE

'Obligation' means a legal obligation, not simply a moral one (*R* v *Hall* [1973] QB 126). Whether or not such an obligation exists is a matter of law for a trial judge to decide (*R* v *Dubar* [1994] 1 WLR 1484).

Instances under s. 5(3) most commonly involve receiving money from others to retain and use in a certain way (e.g. travel agents taking deposits; solicitors holding funds for mortgagees; or pension fund managers collecting contributions (*R* v *Clowes (No. 2)* [1994] 2 All ER 316)). The Court of Appeal has held that one effect of s. 5(3) is that property can be regarded as belonging to another even where it does not 'belong' to them on a strict interpretation of civil law (*R* v *Klineberg* [1999] 1 Cr App R 427). In that case the defendants collected money from customers in their timeshare business.

Although the customers were told that their deposits would be placed with an independent trustee, the defendants paid the sums into their company account, thereby breaching the 'obligation' under s. 5(3) to deal with the money in a particular way. Section 5(3) would also include, say, the owners of shopping centres where coins thrown into a fountain are to be donated to charity; if the owners did not deal with those coins in the way intended, the provisions of s. 5(3) may well apply.

1.13.2.8 Obligation to Restore Another's Property

The Theft Act 1968, s. 5 states:

(4) Where a person gets property by another's mistake, and is under an obligation to make restoration (in whole or in part) of the property or its proceeds or of the value thereof, then to the extent of that obligation the property or proceeds shall be regarded (as against him) as belonging to the person entitled to restoration, and an intention not to make restoration shall be regarded accordingly as an intention to deprive that person of the property or proceeds.

KEYNOTE

Where an employee is mistakenly credited with extra money in his/her bank account, the employee will be liable for stealing the extra money if he/she keeps it (see *Attorney-General's Reference (No. 1 of 1983)* [1985] QB 182 where a police officer's account was credited with money representing overtime which she had not actually worked).

Section 5(4) only applies where someone *other than the defendant* has made a mistake. It is clear that such a mistake can be a mistake as to a material fact; whether or not a mistake as to *law* would be covered is unclear.

Again, the obligation to make restoration is a *legal* one and, as with s. 5(3), an unenforceable or moral obligation will not be covered by s. 5(4). (See *R* v *Gilks* [1972] 1 WLR 1341 where a betting shop mistakenly paid out winnings against the wrong horse. As gambling debts are not legally enforceable the defendant was not under 'an obligation' to restore the money and therefore s. 5(4) did not apply.)

1.13.2.9 Intention of Permanently Depriving

If you cannot prove an intention permanently to deprive you cannot prove theft (see *R* v *Warner* (1970) 55 Cr App R 93).

If there is such an intention at the time of the appropriation, giving the property back later will not alter the fact and the charge will be made out (*R* v *McHugh* (1993) 97 Cr App R 335).

In certain circumstances s. 6 may help in determining the presence or absence of such an intention.

The Theft Act 1968, s. 6 states:

(1) A person appropriating property belonging to another without meaning the other permanently to lose the thing itself is nevertheless to be regarded as having the intention of permanently depriving the other of it if his intention is to treat the thing as his own to dispose of regardless of the other's rights; and a borrowing or lending of it may amount to so treating it if, but only if, the borrowing or lending is for a period and in circumstances making it equivalent to an outright taking or disposal.

KEYNOTE

The key feature of s. 6(1) is the intention to treat 'the thing' as one's own to dispose of regardless of the other's rights. An example of such a case would be where property is 'held to ransom' (*R* v *Coffey* [1987] Crim LR 498). The borrowing or lending of another's property is specifically caught within s. 6(1). If a person takes property from his/her employer (e.g. carpet tiles) and uses it in a way which makes restoration unlikely or impossible (e.g. by laying them in his/her living room), then s. 6(1) will apply (see *R* v *Velumyl* [1989] Crim LR 299).

Similarly, if a person borrowed a season ticket causing the owner to miss a match, s. 6(1) would help prove the required intention because the circumstances of the borrowing make it equivalent to an outright taking.

In a case involving robbery (see below), the defendants took the victim's personal stereo headphones from him and broke them in two, rendering them useless before returning them to him. The Administrative Court held that a person who took something and dealt with it for the purpose of rendering it useless in this way demonstrated the intention of treating that article as his/her own to dispose of. The court did not accept the argument that the property had to be totally exhausted before s. 6 applied (see also *R* v *Fernandes* [1996] 1 Cr App R 175) and held that the magistrates had been wrong to accept the submission of no case to answer on this point (*DPP* v *J* [2002] EWHC 291 (Admin)). Therefore, the deliberate breaking of an item of property will amount to the 'intention to permanently deprive'; however, unless this action is accompanied by the other theft elements it will be criminal damage. Note that in this case the offence dealt with was robbery so that the other elements of theft were plainly satisfied when the defendant initially took the property.

The Theft Act 1968, s. 6 states:

(2) Without prejudice to the generality of subsection (1) above, where a person, having possession or control (lawfully or not) of property belonging to another, parts with the property under a condition as to its return which he may not be able to perform, this (if done for purposes of his own and without the other's authority) amounts to treating the property as his own to dispose of regardless of the other's rights.

KEYNOTE

Section 6(2) deals with occasions such as pawning another's property. If there is a likelihood that the defendant will be unable to meet the conditions under which he/she parted with another person's property, s. 6(2) would help in proving an intention permanently to deprive.

1.13.3 Burglary

The main offence of burglary is split into two—s. 9(1)(a) and s. 9(1)(b). These are discussed below.

1.13.3.1   Section 9(1)(a)

OFFENCE: **Burglary—*Theft Act 1968, s. 9***

- Triable on indictment if 'ulterior offence' is so triable, or if committed in dwelling and violence used; otherwise triable either way • Fourteen years' imprisonment if building/part of building is dwelling • Otherwise ten years' imprisonment on indictment • Six months' imprisonment and/or a fine summarily

The Theft Act 1968, s. 9 states:

(1) A person is guilty of burglary if—

    (a) he enters any building or part of a building as a trespasser and with intent to commit any such offence as is mentioned in subsection (2) below; or . . .

(2) The offences referred to in subsection (1)(a) above are offences of stealing anything in the building or part of a building in question, of inflicting on any person therein any grievous bodily harm and of doing unlawful damage to the building or anything therein.

KEYNOTE

Enters

What action on the part of the defendant constitutes 'entry' into a building or part of a building? The Theft Act 1968 does not define the term 'entry' and so we are left to resolve the meaning of this term by reference to case law and the decisions of the courts. The common law rule was that the insertion of any part of the body, *however small*, was sufficient to be considered an 'entry'. So where D pushed in a window pane and the forepart of his finger was observed in the building that was enough (*R* v *Davis* (1823) Russ & Ry 499). This approach was narrowed considerably in *R* v *Collins* [1973] QB 100, where it was said that entry needed to be 'effective and substantial'. The ruling in *Collins* was rejected by the Court of Appeal in *R* v *Brown* [1985] Crim LR 212, where it was stated that the 'substantial' element was surplus to requirements and that entry need only be 'effective'. Whether an entry was 'effective' or not was for the jury to decide. So the decision of the court in *Brown* appears to be the current accepted approach to defining the term; entry must therefore be 'effective'.

An 'effective' entry does not mean that the defendant has to enter a building or part of a building to such a degree that the ulterior offence, which he is entering with the intention to commit (the theft, GBH or criminal damage), can be committed (*R* v *Ryan* [1996] Crim LR 320). Nor does it mean that the defendant must get his whole body into the building. In *Brown*, the defendant had his feet on the ground outside the building with the upper half inside the building as he searched for goods to steal; this was held to be an entry. In *Ryan*, the defendant, who had become trapped by his neck with only his head and right arm inside the window, was held to have 'entered' the building. In *Brown*, the Court of Appeal stated that it would be astounding if a smash-and-grab raider, who inserted his hand through a shop window to grab goods, was not considered to have 'entered' the building.

At common law, the insertion of an instrument would constitute entry as long as the instrument was inserted to enable the ulterior offence to take place, e.g. a hook inserted into premises to steal property or the muzzle of a gun pushed through a letterbox with a view to cause GBH. Insertion of an instrument merely to facilitate entry, e.g. using a coat hanger to open a window lock, *would not* be entry. Although there is no recent authority on the issue, it is likely that this line of reasoning in relation to the use of instruments in burglary is still acceptable.

Entry must be deliberate and not accidental.

Ultimately, whether the defendant has entered a building or not will be a question of fact for the jury or magistrate(s).

Trespasser

For a person to be guilty of the offence of burglary he must know that he is entering as a trespasser (i.e. he must know he is entering without a right by law or permission to do so) or be reckless as to that fact. Sometimes a defendant may have a general permission to enter a building or part of a building for a legitimate purpose; however, the true intention of the defendant when entering is not for that legitimate purpose but in order to steal or commit grievous bodily harm or to cause criminal damage. As these intentions invariably form no part of the permission to enter the building or part of it, any entry in such circumstances means that the defendant becomes a trespasser the moment he/she enters the building or part of the building. In such circumstances the exceeding of the granted permission places the defendant in a position of being a trespasser from the outset. In *R v Jones and Smith* [1976] 1 WLR 672, the defendant was convicted of burglary when he took two televisions from his father's home. He had a key to the premises and was free to come and go as he liked but when he entered his father's house (using the key) accompanied by a friend at 3am and stole the television sets, he committed burglary as it was his intention to steal—such an intent voids the general permission to enter.

1.13.3.2 **Building**

The Theft Act 1968 s. 9 states:

(4) References in subsections (1) and (2) above to a building, ... and the reference in subsection (3), above, to a building which is a dwelling, shall apply also to an inhabited vehicle or vessel, and shall apply to any such vehicle or vessel at times when the person having a habitation in it is not there as well as at times when he is.

KEYNOTE

Building

A building is generally considered to be a structure of a permanent nature (*Norfolk Constabulary v Seekings and Gould* [1986] Crim LR 167), although a substantial portable structure with most of the attributes of a building can be a 'building' for the purposes of burglary. For example, in *B & S v Leathley* [1979] Crim LR 314, a portable container measuring 25ft by 7ft by 7ft and weighing three tons, which had occupied the same position for three years, was connected to mains electricity, and which was due to remain in the same position for the foreseeable future, was considered to be a building for the purposes of burglary. An unfinished house can be a building for the purposes of burglary (*R v Manning* (1871) LR 1 CCR 338). Tents and marquees are considered to fall outside the term, even if the tent is someone's home (the Criminal Law Revision Committee intended tents to be outside the protection of burglary).

The effect of s. 9(4) is to include *inhabited* vehicles and vessels (such as house boats or motor homes) within the term. A canal boat that is not inhabited is not a building as whilst it may be capable of habitation, it is not being lived in.

Part of a Building

A person may commit burglary when, although he is in one part of a building with legitimate access, he enters another part of it as a trespasser.

- A tenant of a block of flats has a pass-key that provides access to a communal foyer of the block of flats. He uses the pass-key to enter the foyer (*entering a building and plainly not a trespasser at this stage*) Instead of entering his own flat he forces entry to a neighbour's flat by breaking down the neighbour's door that can be accessed via the communal foyer (*moving from one part of a building to another in the process and certainly a trespasser at this stage*).

Part of a building does not mean that there has to be a physical separation of one room from another. In *R v Walkington* [1979] 2 All ER 716, the defendant walked behind a moveable counter in a shop with the intention to steal and was found guilty of burglary as this was held to be 'part of a building'. A 'No Entry' sign or a rope could mark off one part of a building from another.

1.13.3.3 Intentions at the Time of Entry

The intentions must be as follows:

- Stealing—this means an intention to commit theft under s. 1. It will not include abstracting electricity because abstracting under s. 13 is not stealing (*Low* v *Blease* [1975] Crim LR 513), neither will it include taking a conveyance (as there is no intention to permanently deprive). The property which the defendant intends to steal must be in a building or part of a building.
- Inflicting grievous bodily harm—if grievous bodily harm is inflicted (**see chapter 1.8**), then the second offence under s. 9(1)(b) below would apply. In proving an intention to commit grievous bodily harm under s. 9(1)(a), it is not necessary to prove that an assault was actually committed (*Metropolitan Police Commissioner* v *Wilson* [1984] AC 242). The offence in question in respect of a burglary under s. 9(1)(a) is of grievous bodily harm contrary to s. 18 of the Offences Against the Person Act 1861.
- Causing unlawful damage—this includes damage, not only to the building but to anything in it (**see chapter 1.15**).

1.13.3.4 Conditional Intent

Provided the required intention can be proved, it is immaterial whether or not there is anything 'worth stealing' within the building (*R v Walkington* [1979] 1 WLR 1169). The same will be true if the person whom the defendant intends to cause serious harm is not in the building or part of the building at the time (see also criminal attempts, **chapter 1.3**).

1.13.3.5 Section 9(1)(b)

OFFENCE: **Burglary—*Theft Act 1968, s. 9***

The Theft Act 1968, s. 9 states:

(1) A person is guilty of burglary if—
  . . .
  (b) having entered any building or part of a building as a trespasser he steals or attempts to steal anything in the building or that part of it or inflicts or attempts to inflict on any person therein any grievous bodily harm.

KEYNOTE

The second type of burglary involves a defendant's behaviour *after* entering a building or part of a building as a trespasser.

The defendant must have entered the building or part of a building as a trespasser; it is not enough that he/she subsequently became a trespasser by exceeding a condition of entry (e.g. hiding in the public area of a shop during open hours until the shop closes). However, where a person has entered a particular building (such as a shop or a pub) lawfully and without trespassing, if he/she later moves to *another part* of the building as a trespasser, this element of the offence will be made out.

EXAMPLE

D enters a public house near closing time with a friend who buys him a drink from the bar. D's entry onto that part of the premises has been authorised by the implied licence extended to members of the adult public by the publican and therefore D is not a trespasser. D then goes into the lavatories to use them as such. At this point he has entered another part of a building but again his entry is made under the implied licence to customers wishing to use the lavatories. While inside the lavatory area, D decides to hide until closing time in order to avoid buying his friend a drink. At this point, although D's intention in hiding may be considered a little mean-spirited, he has none of the required intentions for the purposes of s. 9(1)(a).

Once the publican has shut the pub for the night, D leaves the lavatory and walks into the bar area. Now D has entered *a part of a building as a trespasser* because the licence extended to members of the public by the publican certainly does not cover wandering around in the bar after it has been closed. Having no particular intention at this point, however, D has still not committed an offence of burglary.

On seeing the gaming machines in the public bar, D decides to break into them and steal the money inside. At this point, although he has *two* of the required intentions for s. 9(1)(a) (an intention to steal and an intention to cause unlawful damage), those intentions were formed *after* his entry. Therefore, D has not committed burglary under s. 9(1)(a). Because he has not stolen/attempted to steal or inflicted/attempted to inflict grievous bodily harm on any person therein, D has not committed burglary under s. 9(1)(b) either.

D then breaks open a gaming machine. At this point he commits burglary under s. 9(1)(b). This is because, having entered a part of a building (the public bar area) as a trespasser (because the pub is closed and D knows that to be the case), he *attempts to steal*. If he simply damaged the machine without an intention of stealing the contents, D would not commit this offence because causing unlawful damage is only relevant to the offence under s. 9(1)(a).

Unlike s. 9(1)(a), there are only two further elements to the offence under s. 9(1)(b)—the subsequent theft/attempted theft of anything in the building or part of it, and the subsequent inflicting/attempted inflicting of grievous bodily harm to any person therein. The offence in question in respect of a burglary under s. 9(1)(b) is of grievous bodily harm contrary to s. 18 or s. 20 of the Offences Against the Person Act 1861.

It has been suggested that if, having entered a building or part of a building as a trespasser, the defendant commits an offence of criminal damage then this will be an offence under s. 9(1)(b) of the Act as to damage or destroy something is also to steal it. *This is not the case.* If a person enters in such circumstances and causes criminal damage, there is little argument that such an activity would satisfy part of the offence of theft, i.e. appropriating property belonging to another with the intention of permanently depriving the other of it—but where is the 'dishonesty'? In addition, this would clearly be an unwarranted extension of the burglary offence under s. 9(1)(b)of the Theft Act 1968. If Parliament wanted such activity to be caught by the legislation, they would have included the offence of criminal damage within the definition of burglary under s. 9(1)(b).

1.13.4 Aggravated Burglary

OFFENCE: **Aggravated Burglary—*Theft Act 1968, s. 10***
- Triable on indictment • Life imprisonment

The Theft Act 1968, s. 10 states:

(1) A person is guilty of aggravated burglary if he commits any burglary and at the time has with him any firearm or imitation firearm, any weapon of offence, or any explosive;...

KEYNOTE

An aggravated burglary is committed when a person commits an offence of burglary (either a s. 9(1)(a) or a s. 9(1)(b)) and at the time he has with him his **WIFE**.

W —Weapon of offence

I —Imitation firearm

F —Firearm

E —Explosive

Two points in the definition merit further discussion: (i) *at the time* and (ii) *has with him*.

At the time

These words require consideration of the type of burglary the defendant is charged with. The moment at which a burglary under s. 9(1)(a) is committed is at the point of entry, therefore it is essential that the defendant has the WIFE with him/her when entering a building or part of a building with the intention of committing one of the trigger offences under s. 9(1)(a). If that is the case, the defendant commits aggravated burglary. The moment at which a burglary under s. 9(1)(b) is committed is when the defendant steals, inflicts grievous bodily harm on any person or attempts to do either. If the defendant has the WIFE with him/her when committing or attempting to commit either offence, an aggravated burglary is committed.

....

EXAMPLE

A person (X) enters the kitchen of a house as a trespasser intending to steal the contents. At the point of entry X does not have any WIFE item with him, so at this point in time X has committed a s. 9(1)(a) burglary. While X is in the kitchen the occupier of the house enters the kitchen and disturbs him. X picks up a carving knife and threatens the occupier with it. This is not an aggravated burglary as X has not committed or attempted to commit theft or to inflict GBH. The occupier rushes towards X who stabs the occupier, inflicting GBH in the process. This is a s. 9(1)(b) burglary and at the time of its commission X has a WIFE item with him; as a result this becomes an aggravated burglary.

....

Has with him

'Has with him' is more restrictive than the term 'possession'. It will require the defendant to have some degree of *immediate control* of the item (*R v Pawlicki* [1992] 1 WLR 827) and will normally be the same as 'carrying' (*R v Klass* [1998] 1 Cr App R 453) although the defendant need not actually have the WIFE item *on his/her person* to be in *immediate control* of it. It is also essential that the individual has knowledge of the presence of the WIFE item. So if a burglary is committed by a single offender who knows he/she has a bayonet in his coat pocket when the offence is committed the issue of aggravated burglary is clear. However, what of the situation where two offenders commit such a burglary? Liability depends on knowledge.

....

EXAMPLE

X and Y decide to commit a burglary together. X is concerned about being disturbed during the burglary and decides to take a flick-knife along with him when the burglary takes place; he does not tell Y about the flick-knife. When X and Y enter the building they intend to burgle, both commit a s. 9(1)(a) burglary. As X has a flick-knife with him at the time, X commits an aggravated burglary. However, Y does not commit the aggravated offence because he has no knowledge of the existence of the WIFE item. If X had told Y about the flick-knife then Y would have the required knowledge and would be deemed to have it with him so both would be guilty under s. 10 (*R* v *Jones* [1979] CLY 411).

....

Therefore, if the defendant has no knowledge of the WIFE item he/she does not commit the aggravated offence. If several people are charged with the offence of aggravated burglary, it must be shown that one of the defendants who actually entered the building or part of a building had the weapon with him/her (*R* v *Klass* [1998] 1 Cr App R 453).

It is important to note that the aggravated offence is committed due to the presence of the WIFE when the s. 9(1)(a) or s. 9(1)(b) burglary is carried out. It is irrelevant that the defendant had the item with him/her for some other purpose unconnected with the burglary offence. The thought process underpinning this point is that if a burglar has the WIFE item with him/her during the course of a domestic burglary and is confronted by the householder, there would be a strong temptation to make use of it regardless of why the burglar had the WIFE with him/her in the first place.

Instant Arming

Ordinary items can, instantaneously, change into weapons of offence; it is the intention of the person to use an item in a particular way that allows this to take place. A good illustration of this concept is the case of *R* v *Kelly* (1992) 97 Cr App R 245. The defendant entered a building using a screwdriver to facilitate entry. When he was confronted he prodded the person confronting him in the stomach with the screwdriver. At that moment the screwdriver instantly became a weapon of offence and the defendant was later convicted of aggravated burglary.

1.13.4.1 Firearm/Weapon of Offence/Explosive

The Theft Act 1968, s. 10 goes on to state:

(1) ... and for this purpose—

    (a) 'firearm' includes an airgun or pistol, and 'imitation firearm' means anything which has the appearance of being a firearm, whether capable of being discharged or not, and

    (b) 'weapon of offence' means any article made or adapted for use for causing injury to or incapacitating a person, or intended by the person having it with him for such use; and

    (c) 'explosive' means any article manufactured for the purpose of producing a practical effect by explosion, or intended by the person having it with him for that purpose.

Weapon of Offence

This is a wider definition than that under the Prevention of Crime Act 1953. It includes:

- Items *made* for causing injury, e.g. a bayonet or a flick-knife (as above).
- Items *adapted* for causing injury, e.g. a screwdriver that has been sharpened at the tip.
- Items *intended* for causing injury, e.g. an ordinary cutlery knife. The cutlery knife is certainly inoffensive in everyday use but if the defendant *intends* to use it to injure, it will fall into this category.
- Items *made, adapted or intended* to incapacitate a person, e.g. handcuffs, rope, CS spray and chloroform.

The defendant must not only know of the presence of the weapon but also that it is a weapon of offence.

Imitation Firearm

This includes anything which has the appearance of being a firearm, whether capable of being discharged or not (but note that this will not include the defendant's fingers pointed at someone under a coat to resemble a firearm (*R* v *Bentham* [2005] UKHL 18)).

Firearm

This does not relate to the definition under the Firearms Act 1968. Indeed, the term is not defined other than to include airguns and air pistols.

Explosive

This would cover explosives such as TNT and items such as grenades—both manufactured to produce a practical effect by explosion. It also covers an item intended by the person having it with him/her for such a purpose, potentially bringing home-made devices or substances into the equation. The issue in relation to fireworks has yet to be firmly resolved by the courts, although they may well be excluded from the definition as fireworks are, by and large, manufactured to produce a pyrotechnic rather than practical effect by explosion and have been described as 'things that are made for amusement' (*Bliss* v *Lilley* (1862) 32 LJMC 3)).

1.13.5 Taking a Conveyance without Consent

OFFENCE: **Taking a Conveyance without the Owner's Consent—*Theft Act 1968, s. 12***

- Triable summarily • Six months' imprisonment and/or a fine

The Theft Act 1968, s. 12 states:

(1) Subject to subsections (5) and (6) below, a person shall be guilty of an offence if, without having the consent of the owner or other lawful authority, he takes any conveyance for his own or another's use or, knowing that any conveyance has been taken without such authority, drives it or allows himself to be carried in or on it.

KEYNOTE

Taking a conveyance without consent (usually referred to as TWOC) is a summary only offence and as such there can be no 'attempt' (Criminal Attempts Act 1981, s. 1(1) and (4)).

As a summary offence, s. 12(1) proceedings are ordinarily subject to the time limit of six months from the day when the offence was committed (see s. 127 of the Magistrates' Courts Act 1980). However, this restriction has caused significant problems in cases where the analysis of forensic evidence has been needed. As a result, the Vehicles (Crime) Act 2001 has extended the time limit for s. 12(1) offences. Proceedings for any such offences may be brought at any time within six months from the time when sufficient evidence to justify the proceedings came to the knowledge of any person responsible for deciding whether to commence any such prosecution. However, this is subject to the proviso that such proceedings shall not be commenced after the end of the period of three years beginning with the day on which the offence was committed.

Once a conveyance has been 'taken' it cannot be 'taken' again by the same person before it has been recovered (*DPP* v *Spriggs* [1994] RTR 1). This accords with the position in relation to repeated theft of the same property by the same thief. However, where the original taker abandons the conveyance, it may be

---

'taken' again by a further defendant and the original taker may be responsible for further offences arising out of its use before it is recovered.

The person taking the conveyance must do so intentionally, i.e. not simply by moving it accidentally (*Blayney* v *Knight* (1975) 60 Cr App R 269).

1.13.5.1 Consent of the Owner

As with other offences requiring the absence of consent, any 'consent' given must be true consent if the defendant is to avoid liability.

This area of the law has been subject to some rather unusual decision-making in the courts, one of which relates to consent. Consent, even if obtained by a deception, is still a valid consent. *This will be the case unless the deception is one where identity is an issue.*

....

EXAMPLE

John Smith (who does not possess a driving licence) is walking along the street when he finds a driving licence in the name of Paul Grey. Smith takes the driving licence and visits a car hire company and asks to hire a car for a day. The assistant at the reception of the car hire company asks Smith for a driving licence and Smith produces the licence he found in the street (the one in the name of Paul Grey). The assistant photocopies the licence and asks for the fee of £100.00 which Smith pays. The assistant hands over a set of car keys and Smith drives away in the car (intending to return it later that day).

....

The above scenario *would not* represent an offence of TWOC; this is because the assistant has handed over a set of keys to Smith and consented to Smith taking the car. The deception here relates to the possession of the driving licence, *not to the name on the driving licence*. The assistant would have handed over the keys to the car if the name on the driving licence was 'Bugs Bunny'—identity is not an issue (see *Whittaker* v *Campbell* [1984] QB 318).

Where consent is obtained by misrepresentation as to the purpose or destination of the journey, that misrepresentation has been held not to negate the consent given. Once again, identity is not an issue when such consent is given (*R* v *Peart* [1970] 2 QB 672).

Going beyond the express or implied permission of the owner may negate consent (*R* v *Phipps* (1970) 54 Cr App R 300). This is often encountered when employees deviate substantially from an agreed route in their employer's vehicle or take the vehicle for a purpose entirely different from that permitted.

....

EXAMPLE

X delivers bread on an established and precise route in his employer's van. X decides to visit his friend who lives 50 miles away and diverts from the established route to do so.

....

This would constitute TWOC. X (the employee) has custody of the vehicle—that custody is known as control. When he substantially diverts from the delivery route he so radically alters the purpose for which he was given the vehicle that he can no longer be said to be in control of the vehicle for his employer's purposes—he 'takes' the vehicle. A minor deviation, for example if X were to visit his favourite café (150 metres off the established route) and then return to his delivery round would not amount to an offence as the vehicle is still substantially being used for the employer's purpose.

1.13.5.2 Lawful Authority

Lawful authority may come from many different sources. A police officer removing a vehicle which is obstructing traffic after an accident, council workers removing a vehicle parked in contravention of parking restrictions or an agent of a finance company repossessing a vehicle would be examples of such authority.

1.13.5.3 Takes

To prove this offence you must show that the conveyance was moved. It does not matter by how little the conveyance is moved but simply starting the engine is not enough (*R v Bogacki* [1973] QB 832) nor is hiding in a car or doing anything else in it while it is stationary. A conveyance is taken even if it is put onto another vehicle to do so (*R v Pearce* [1973] Crim LR 321, where a rubber dinghy was put on the roof rack of a car and taken away).

1.13.5.4 Conveyance

The Theft Act 1968, s. 12(7) states:

> (a) 'conveyance' means any conveyance constructed or adapted for the carriage of a person or persons whether by land, water or air, except that it does not include a conveyance constructed or adapted for use only under the control of a person not carried in or on it, and 'drive' shall be construed accordingly...

> **KEYNOTE**
>
> It can be seen that this definition includes cars, motor cycles, boats or aircraft. Pedal cycles are not covered as they are expressly excluded by virtue of s. 12(5) of the Act. The definition does not extend to hand carts or animals used as conveyances.

1.13.5.5 For His Own or Another's Use

The conveyance must be taken for the taker's or someone else's ultimate use *as a conveyance*. Pushing someone's car around the corner as a practical joke satisfies the first part ('taking') but not the second 'for his own or another's use as a conveyance' (*R v Stokes* [1983] RTR 59). This is because although the defendant may have 'taken' the conveyance he/she did not do so for someone ultimately to use it as such. If the practical joker pushed the car round the corner in order for a friend then to start it out of earshot and drive it to a further location, the offence would be committed at the time of pushing the car.

When a person got into a Land Rover that was blocking his path and released the handbrake, allowing the vehicle to coast for several metres, it was held that his actions satisfied both elements (*R v Bow* (1976) 64 Cr App R 54). This is because getting into (or onto) a conveyance and moving it necessarily amounts to *taking it for use as a conveyance*, therefore the motives of the defendant in doing so are irrelevant. In the rubber dinghy example (above) the dinghy was ultimately going to be used as a conveyance by someone in the future.

1.13.5.6 Allow to be Carried

The person who commits this offence *must know* that the conveyance has been taken without the consent of the owner or other lawful authority. If that person only 'suspects' that the conveyance has been taken, the offence is not committed. Further, the conveyance must *actually move* when the person drives it or allows him/herself to be carried in or on it (the same as the 'take' element of the offence).

1.13.6 Aggravated Vehicle-Taking

Given the frequency of offences under s. 12, together with the anti-social and dangerous consequences, the offence of aggravated vehicle-taking was introduced.

OFFENCE: **Aggravated Vehicle-taking—*Theft Act 1968, s. 12A***
- Triable either way • If the accident under s. 12A(2)(b) caused death 14 years' imprisonment, otherwise two years' imprisonment and/or a fine on indictment
- Six months' imprisonment and/or a fine summarily

The Theft Act 1968, s. 12A states:

(1) Subject to subsection (3) below, a person is guilty of aggravated taking of a vehicle if—
  (a) he commits an offence under section 12(1) above (in this section referred to as a 'basic offence') in relation to a mechanically propelled vehicle; and
  (b) it is proved that, at any time after the vehicle was unlawfully taken (whether by him or another) and before it was recovered, the vehicle was driven, or injury or damage was caused, in one or more of the circumstances set out in paragraphs (a) to (d) of subsection (2) below.
(2) The circumstances referred to in subsection (1)(b) above are—
  (a) that the vehicle was driven dangerously on a road or other public place;
  (b) that, owing to the driving of the vehicle, an accident occurred by which injury was caused to any person;
  (c) that, owing to the driving of the vehicle, an accident occurred by which damage was caused to any property, other than the vehicle;
  (d) that damage was caused to the vehicle.

KEYNOTE

Before this offence is made out there must first of all be an offence under s. 12(1)—including an offence of 'being carried'—and the conveyance involved must be a 'mechanically propelled vehicle' (**see Road Policing, chapter 3.1**).

You need only prove that *one* of the consequential factors occurred before the vehicle was recovered (*Dawes* v *DPP* [1995] 1 Cr App R 65) namely that, between the vehicle being taken and its being recovered:

- it was driven dangerously on a road/public place;
- owing to the driving of it, an accident occurred by which injury was caused to anyone or damage was caused to any other property; or
- damage was caused to it.

Damage to the vehicle does not include damage caused by breaking into it in order to commit the 'basic offence'. This is because damage caused at this point will be caused before the vehicle has been 'taken' and so at that stage, the 'basic offence' will not have been carried out.

If the person taking the car disposes of it in a way that amounts to an intention permanently to deprive the owner of it, he/she may commit an offence of theft.

'Dangerous driving' will require the same proof as the substantive offence (**see Road Policing, chapter 3.2**). There is no need to show any lack of care in the driving of the vehicle to prove s. 12A(2)(b), (c) or (d) (see *R* v *Marsh* [1997] 1 Cr App R 67). A vehicle will be 'recovered' once it has been restored to its owner or other lawful possession or custody (s. 12A(8)). This would include occasions where a vehicle has come into the possession of the police.

The word 'accident' for the purposes of the offence of aggravated vehicle taking gets its meaning from the context of that legislation. As such, s. 12A is intended to have regard to *the consequences of what occurred* and is not particularly concerned about the way in which those consequences came about. Therefore where a vehicle had been in motion and thereby caused the victim's death, the word 'accident' applied (*R* v *Branchflower* [2004] EWCA Crim 2042).

1.13.6.1 Defence to Aggravated Vehicle Taking

The Theft Act 1968, s. 12A(3) states:

A person is not guilty of an offence under this section if he proves that, as regards any such proven driving, injury or damage as is referred to in subsection (1)(b) above, either—

(a) the driving, accident or damage referred to in subsection (2) above occurred before he committed the basic offence; or

(b) he was neither in nor on nor in the immediate vicinity of the vehicle when that driving, accident or damage occurred.

KEYNOTE

Once the prosecution has proved the occurrence of one of the aggravating factors above, it is for the defendant to prove one of the specific defences set out under s. 12A(3). Such proof will have to meet the lower standard of 'balance of probabilities'.

'Immediate vicinity' is not defined but will be a question of fact for the jury/magistrate(s) to determine in each case.

1.13.7 Pedal Cycles

It is a separate summary offence (punishable with a fine) for a person, without having the consent of the owner or other lawful authority, to take a pedal cycle for his/her own or another's use, or to ride a pedal cycle knowing it to have been taken without such authority (Theft Act 1968, s. 12(5)). The defence under s. 12(6) also applies to pedal cycles.

1.13.8 Going Equipped

OFFENCE: **Going Equipped for Stealing etc.—*Theft Act 1968, s. 25***
- Triable either way • Three years' imprisonment on indictment • Six months' imprisonment and/or a fine summarily

The Theft Act 1968, s. 25 states:

(1) A person shall be guilty of an offence if, when not at his place of abode, he has with him any article for use in the course of or in connection with any burglary or theft.

KEYNOTE

The power of search under s. 1 of the Police and Criminal Evidence Act 1984 applies to this offence (**see** General Police Duties, chapter 4.7).

A person's place of abode means where he/she resides; it does not include his/her place of business (unless, presumably, they are one and the same place) (*R* v *Bundy* [1977] 2 All ER 382). If a person lives in a vehicle then that vehicle will be regarded only as their 'place of abode' if it is parked at the place where the person 'abides' or intends to 'abide' (*Bundy*). Therefore it would seem that, if a person is found in his/her vehicle away from such a site and at the time has with them articles as described under s. 25, they would commit this offence.

'Has with him' is a narrower requirement than 'possession' and, as with aggravated burglary generally means that the article must be readily accessible.

You do not need to prove that the person having the article with them intended to use it themselves and it will be enough to show that the person intended it to be used *by someone* for one of the purposes in s. 25(1) (*R* v *Ellames* [1974] 3 All ER 130). Simply being a passenger in a car where such an article is found is not enough to prove the offence (*R* v *Lester* (1955) 39 Cr App R 157). The articles must be for some future use; it is not enough to show that the defendant had articles that *had been used* in the course of, or in connection with, one of the proscribed offences.

If you can prove that the article was made, adapted or intended for burglary or theft, that fact will be evidence that the person had it with him/her for that purpose (s. 25(3))—a provision that probably seems more helpful than it really is, given that, in many cases, it is simply stating the obvious.

The offence is directed against acts preparatory to the offences of burglary (contrary to s. 9 of the Theft Act 1968), theft (contrary to s. 1 of the Theft Act 1968) and taking a conveyance (contrary to s. 12 of the Theft Act 1968).

'Article' can mean almost any object but does not include *animate* objects, e.g. a trained monkey (see *Daly* v *Cannon* [1954] 1 All ER 315).

1.13.9 Robbery

OFFENCE: **Robbery—*Theft Act 1968, s. 8***

- Triable on indictment • Life imprisonment

The Theft Act 1968, s. 8 states:

(1) A person is guilty of robbery if he steals, and immediately before or at the time of doing so, and in order to do so, he uses force on any person or puts or seeks to put any person in fear of being then and there subjected to force.

KEYNOTE

The Theft Element of the Offence

For there to be a robbery, there must be a theft; so if there is no theft, then there can be no robbery. The word 'steal' in the offence relates to the offence under s. 1 of the Theft Act 1968 and, therefore, if **any** element of theft cannot be proved the offence of robbery will not be made out. For example, in *R* v *Robinson* [1977] Crim LR 173, D, who was owed £7 by P's wife, approached P, brandishing a knife. A fight followed, during which P dropped a £5 note. D picked it up and demanded the remaining £2 owed to him. Allowing D's appeal against a conviction for robbery, the Court of Appeal held that the prosecution had to prove that D was guilty of theft, and that he would not be (under the Theft Act 1968, s. 2(1)(a)) if he believed that he had a right in law to deprive P of the money, even though he knew that he was not entitled to use the knife to get it, i.e. there was no dishonesty.

The Robbery Time Frame

Section 8(1) requires that the force must be used or the threat made 'immediately before or at the time' of the theft. There is no guidance as to what 'immediately before' means. Clearly, if the force used or threatened is *after* the offence of theft has taken place, there will be no robbery; however theft can be a continuing offence. This was decided in *R* v *Hale* (1978) 68 Cr App Rep 415, where the Court of Appeal stated that appropriation is a continuing act and whether it has finished or not is a matter for the jury to decide. From the robbery perspective, *Hale* decides that where D had assumed ownership of goods in a house, the 'time' of stealing is a continuing process. It does not end as soon as the property is picked up by the defendant and can be a continuing act so long as he is in the course of removing it from the premises. So, if D uses or threatens force to get away with the property (whilst still in the house for example), a robbery is committed. This would probably not be the case if the defendant used force outside the house as there must come a time when the appropriation ends. The issue may be resolved by asking the question, 'Was D still on the job?' (*R* v *Atakpu* [1994] QB 69).

In Order to Do So

The use or threat of force must be 'in order' to carry out the theft. Force used in any other context means the offence is not committed, for example:

- Two men have an argument outside a pub and begin fighting each other. One man punches the other in the face and the force of the blow knocks the man out. As the injured man falls to the floor, his wallet drops out of his jacket pocket and onto the pavement. His opponent decides that he will steal the wallet. *No robbery is committed in these circumstances because the force is used for a purpose other than to steal.*

The question to ask in such circumstances is 'Why has the force been used and/or threatened?' If the answer is anything other than 'To enable the defendant to commit theft' then there is no offence of robbery.

Force

The slightest use of force to accomplish a theft changes that theft into a robbery. An illustration can be found in the case of *R* v *Dawson* (1976) 64 Cr App R 170, where the defendant and two others surrounded their victim. One of the attackers 'nudged' the victim and while he was unbalanced another stole his wallet. In *Dawson*, the court declined to define 'force' any further than to say that juries would understand it readily enough. In line with general principles of *actus reus* (criminal conduct), the force used by the defendant must be used voluntarily. Therefore, the accidental use of force such as when a pickpocket, in the process of stealing a wallet from his victim on a train, is pushed into his victim by the train jolting on the railway line would not be a robbery.

On Any Person

The force used to accomplish a robbery need not be used against the owner or possessor of the property. For example, a gang of armed criminals use force against a security guard in order to overpower him and steal cash from the safe he is standing outside and guarding.

Force does not actually have to be used 'on' the *person* i.e. on the actual body of the victim. It may be used on something that the victim is carrying as in the case of *R* v *Clouden* [1987] Crim LR 65, where the Court of Appeal dismissed an appeal against a conviction for robbery when the defendant had wrenched the victim's shopping basket from her hand and ran off with it.

The Fear of Force

Where only the *threat* of force is involved the intention must be to put a person in fear for *himself*; an intention to put someone in fear for another is not enough (*R* v *Taylor* [1996] 10 Archbold News 2). This may seem at odds with the approach to the actual *use* of force in the offence of robbery (in that force *can* be used against a third party who is unconnected with the property subject to the theft). For example:

- A man enters a betting shop and approaches the cashier. Without saying a word he passes a note to the cashier that simply says, 'Look to your left'. The cashier looks to her left and sees the man's accomplice standing several feet away and pointing a knife at the back of one of the betting shop customers. The customer is oblivious to the actions of the man's accomplice. The man passes a second note to the cashier that says, 'Give me the money in the till or else he gets it!' *At this stage there is no robbery committed as the cashier cannot fear force for the betting shop customer. However, whilst there is no robbery there would be an offence of blackmail (Theft Act 1968, s. 21).* The cashier shakes her head and refuses to hand over any money. At this point, the man signals to his accomplice who pulls the customer's head backwards and drags the knife across the side of the customer's throat causing a small cut. The customer screams in terror and at this point the cashier concedes to the man's demand and hands over the till contents. *At this point in time a robbery is committed as force is actually being used (albeit on a third party).*

General Points

Any threats to use force at some time in the future (even by a matter of minutes) would constitute an offence of blackmail. Threats to use force at some place other than the location of the offence fall into the same category. This effectively excludes threats made via the telephone in all but the most improbable of situations.

1.13.10 Blackmail

OFFENCE: **Blackmail—*Theft Act 1968, s. 21***
- Triable on indictment • 14 years' imprisonment

The Theft Act 1968, s. 21 states:

(1) A person is guilty of blackmail if, with a view to gain for himself or another or with intent to cause loss to another, he makes any unwarranted demand with menaces; and for this purpose a demand with menaces is unwarranted unless the person making it does so in the belief—
  (a) that he has reasonable grounds for making the demand; and
  (b) that the use of the menaces is a proper means of reinforcing the demand.
(2) The nature of the act or omission demanded is immaterial, and it is also immaterial whether the menaces relate to action to be taken by the person making the demand.

KEYNOTE

In proving this offence you must show that a defendant acted either with a view to gain for himself/herself or another or with intent to cause loss to another. The distinction here is important. The phrase 'with a view to' has been held (albeit under a different criminal statute) by the Court of Appeal to be less than 'with intent to' (*R* v *Zaman* [2002] EWCA Crim 1862). In *Zaman*, the court accepted that a lesser degree of *mens rea* was required to prove that a defendant acted 'with a view to' something and that this phrase meant simply that the defendant had something in his/her contemplation as *something that realistically might occur*, not that he/she necessarily intended or even wanted it to happen. Clearly this is a very different test from 'intent'. In the above offence then, it appears that the state of mind needed to prove the first element is that the defendant contemplated some gain for himself/herself or for another as being realistically likely to flow from his/her actions. The alternative is an 'intent' to cause loss.

There is no requirement for dishonesty or theft and the offence is aimed at the making of the demands rather than the consequences of them.

1.13.10.1 Meaning of Gain and Loss

Section 34 of the 1968 Act states:

(2) For the purposes of this Act—
    (a) 'gain' and 'loss' are to be construed as extending only to gain or loss in money or other property, but as extending to any such gain or loss whether temporary or permanent; and—
        (i) 'gain' includes a gain by keeping what one has, as well as a gain by getting what one has not; and
        (ii) 'loss' includes a loss by not getting what one might get, as well as a loss by parting with what one has;

KEYNOTE

Keeping what you already have can amount to a 'gain'. Similarly, not getting something that you might expect to get can be a 'loss'.

....

EXAMPLE

A person makes unwarranted demands with menaces with a view to getting a sports fixture cancelled and thereby to avoid losing money that he has bet on the outcome of that fixture. Here it could be argued that the intention of keeping what the defendant already had (the money at risk on the bet) amounts to 'gain' as defined under s. 34(2). Similarly, the intention of preventing others getting what they might have got (their winnings or the club's earnings) could amount to a 'loss'.

....

1.13.10.2 Criminal Conduct

The offence of blackmail is complete when the demand with menaces is made. As a result it is extremely difficult, if not impossible, to have an offence of attempted blackmail as the defendant will either be preparing to make the demand or will have made it. It does not matter whether the demands bring about the desired consequences or not. If a demand is made by letter, the act of making it is complete when the letter is posted. The letter does not have to be received (*Treacy* v *DPP* [1971] AC 537).

The Court of Appeal has held that words or conduct which would not intimidate or influence anyone to respond to the demand would not be 'menaces'. As such, the term requires threats and conduct of such a nature and extent that a person of normal stability and courage might be influenced or made apprehensive so as to give in to the demands (see *R* v *Clear* [1968] 1 QB 670).

Menaces will therefore include threats but these must be significant *to the victim*. If a threat bears a particular significance for a victim (such as being locked in the boot of a car to someone who is claustrophobic) that will be enough, provided the defendant was aware of that fact. If a victim is particularly timid and the defendant knows it, that timidity may be taken into account when assessing whether or not the defendant's conduct was 'menacing' (*R* v *Garwood* [1987] 1 WLR 319).

1.13.10.3 Unwarranted?

If a defendant raises the issue that his/her demand was reasonable and proper, you will have to prove that he/she did not believe:

- that he/she had reasonable grounds for making the demand; and
- that the use of the particular menaces employed was not a proper means of reinforcing it.

The defendant's *belief* will be a subjective one and therefore could be entirely unreasonable. However, if the threatened action would itself be unlawful (such as a threat to rape the victim) then it is unlikely that the courts would accept any claim by a defendant that he/she believed such a demand to be 'proper' (see *R* v *Harvey* (1980) 72 Cr App R 139).

1.13.11 Abstracting Electricity

OFFENCE: **Abstracting Electricity—*Theft Act 1968, s. 13***
- Triable either way • Five years' imprisonment on indictment • Six months' imprisonment and/or a fine summarily

The Theft Act 1968, s. 13 states:

A person who dishonestly uses without due authority, or dishonestly causes to be wasted or diverted, any electricity shall [be guilty of an offence].

KEYNOTE

As electricity is not 'property' (for the purpose of theft), a specific offence was created to deal with its dishonest use or waste. For this reason electricity cannot be 'stolen' and therefore its dishonest use or wastage cannot form an element of burglary. Diverting a domestic electrical supply so as to bypass the meter or using another's telephone without authority (*Low* v *Blease* [1975] Crim LR 513) would be examples of this offence, as would unauthorised surfing on the Internet by an employee at work, provided in each case that dishonesty was present.

1.13.12 Advertising Rewards

OFFENCE: **Advertising a Reward—*Theft Act 1968, s. 23***
- Triable summarily • Fine

The Theft Act 1968, s. 23 states:

Where any public advertisement of a reward for the return of any goods which have been stolen or lost uses any words to the effect that no questions will be asked, or that the person producing the goods will be safe from apprehension or inquiry, or that any money paid for the purchase of the goods or advanced by way of loan on them will be repaid, the person advertising the reward and any person who prints or publishes the advertisement shall [commit an offence].

This offence applies to both the person advertising such a reward and the person/company who prints or publishes that advertisement. This second aspect of the offence attracts 'strict liability', in that there is no need to demonstrate any particular *mens rea* on the part of the printer/publisher (*Denham* v *Scott* (1983) 77 Cr App R 210). The important features are the fact that no questions will be asked or that the person will be given some form of 'immunity' from arrest or investigation. There is no mention of any promise of immunity from prosecution or civil claim.

1.13.13 Making Off without Payment

OFFENCE: **Making Off without Payment—*Theft Act 1978, s. 3***
   • Triable either way • Two years' imprisonment on indictment • Six months' imprisonment and/or a fine summarily

The Theft Act 1978, s. 3 states:

(1) Subject to subsection (3) below, a person who, knowing that payment on the spot for any goods supplied or service done is required or expected from him, dishonestly makes off without having paid as required or expected and with intent to avoid payment of the amount due shall be guilty of an offence.
(2) For purposes of this section 'payment on the spot' includes payment at the time of collecting goods on which work has been done or in respect of which service has been provided.
(3) Subsection (1) above shall not apply where the supply of the goods or the doing of the service is contrary to law, or where the service done is such that payment is not legally enforceable.

KEYNOTE

This offence is most frequently committed by motorists who drive off without paying for petrol, diners who run off after a meal and 'punters' who jump out of taxi cabs (see *DPP* v *Ray* [1974] AC 370; *Edwards* v *Ddin* [1976] 1 WLR 942; *R* v *Brooks* (1982) 76 Cr App R 66). Some problems can arise in cases of alleged theft where the ownership in the property has passed to the defendant before the act of appropriation; this offence offers a solution to some such cases.

This offence excludes occasions where the supply of goods or services is contrary to law or is not legally enforceable (s. 3(3)). Making off without payment after the provision of an unlawful service, or one for which payment is not legally enforceable (e.g. betting), would not then be caught by s. 3 though it might be an offence under s. 1. If there is some doubt as to whether the defendant has actually 'made off' from the spot then he/she can be charged with attempting the offence.

You must also prove an intention to *avoid* payment; simply delaying payment due or making someone wait for payment is not enough. In *R* v *Vincent* [2001] 1172 EWCA Crim 295, the Court of Appeal has recently acknowledged a 'loophole' in s. 3. Circumstances in which this loophole might operate can be illustrated as follows:

• A person checks into an hotel and runs up a substantial bill.
• The person deceives the proprietor into agreeing that the bill will be settled at some later date (as opposed to on departure).
• Having gained that agreement, the person checks out of the hotel and never makes any payment.

The court pointed out that, in such a situation, there was no longer an expectation of payment at the time when the person checked out of the hotel. This expectation had been removed by the agreement; the fact that the agreement had been obtained dishonestly did not reinstate the expectation of payment on departure. The court identified that the offence under s. 3 is a simple and straightforward one which applies to a limited set of circumstances only (and which, fortunately for the defendant, were not covered by the above facts). The limited scope of this offence would suggest that alternative charges of theft and/or fraud should be considered. If the person driving or running away from the garage, restaurant, taxi cab, etc. does so because he/she feels aggrieved at the service received or is in dispute with the supplier, then the question of fraud should be considered against the standards of ordinary, honest people (per *R* v *Ghosh* [1982] QB 1053).

1.13.14   **Retaining a Wrongful Credit**

OFFENCE: **Dishonestly Retaining a Wrongful Credit—*Theft Act 1968, s. 24A***
- Triable either way • Ten years' imprisonment on indictment • Six months' imprisonment and/or a fine summarily

The Theft Act 1968, s. 24A states:

(1) A person is guilty of an offence if—
   (a) a wrongful credit has been made to an account kept by him or in respect of which he has any right or interest;
   (b) he knows or believes that the credit is wrongful; and
   (c) he dishonestly fails to take such steps as are reasonable in the circumstances to secure that the credit is cancelled.
(2) References to a credit are to a credit of an amount of money.
(2A) A credit to an account is wrongful to the extent that it derives from—
   (a) theft;
   (b) blackmail;
   (c) fraud (contrary to section 1 of the Fraud Act 2006); or
   (d) stolen goods.
(subsections (3) and (4) repealed by the Fraud Act 2006)
   . . .
(5) In determining whether a credit to an account is wrongful, it is immaterial (in particular) whether the account is overdrawn before or after the credit is made.
(6) . . .
(7) Subsection (8) below applies for purposes of provisions of this Act relating to stolen goods (including subsection (2A) above).
(8) References to stolen goods include money which is dishonestly withdrawn from an account to which a wrongful credit has been made, but only to the extent that the money derives from the credit.
(9) 'Account' means an account kept with—
   (a) a bank;
   (b) a person carrying on a business which falls within subsection (10) below; or
   (c) an issuer of electronic money (as defined for the purposes of Part 2 of the Financial Services and Markets Act 2000).
(10) A business falls within this subsection if—
   (a) in the course of the business money received by way of deposit is lent to others; or
   (b) any other activity of the business is financed, wholly or to any material extent, out of the capital of or the interest on any money received by way of deposit.
(11) References in subsection (10) above to a deposit must be read with—
   (a) section 22 of the Financial Services and Markets Act 2000;
   (b) any relevant order under that section; and
   (c) Schedule 2 of that Act;
   but any restriction on the meaning of deposit which arises from the identity of the person making it, is to be disregarded.

(12) For the purposes of subsection (10) above—
    (a) all the activities which a person carries on by way of business shall be regarded as a single business carried on by him; and
    (b) 'money' includes money expressed in a currency other than sterling.

KEYNOTE

The introduction of this offence was prompted by the decision in *R* v *Preddy* [1996] AC 815. The Law Commission were anxious to ensure that the transferee of funds obtained dishonestly could be charged with 'handling' those funds. As there were considerable problems created by applying the existing legislation under s. 22 (**see para. 1.13.16**), these further offences were introduced.

The wrongful credit to an account can occur in two ways: it may come from the circumstances outlined under s. 1 of the Fraud Act 2006 or it may come from one of the dishonest sources set out in s. 24A(2A) above.

These offences will generally be restricted to transactions involving the crediting of accounts held with financial institutions.

There is a requirement for dishonesty (as to which, **see para. 1.13.2.2**). However, there is no requirement for any *deception*.

The effects of s. 24A(8) are that *money* derived from credit received under s. 24A of the Theft Act 1968 may amount to stolen goods. The provisions governing the status of the credit itself (i.e. not as cash but as a 'thing in action') are more complicated. If the proceeds of a theft by A are paid into his/her bank account they are stolen goods because they represent the stolen goods in the hands of the thief (s. 24(4)).

If they are then transferred into B's bank account, they cease to be stolen goods. This is because the 'thing in action' (the credit balance) created by the transfer in B's name is a different 'thing in action' from the one originally created by A (see *R* v *Preddy* [1996] AC 815). As such, the credit balance in B's name has never represented the proceeds of the theft *in the hands of the thief*. If B withdraws money from the credited account, that money then, by virtue of s. 24A(8), becomes stolen goods once more.

To quote from *Blackstone's Criminal Practice 2009*, para. B4.148:

It may seem strange that the proceeds of A's original theft can be classed as stolen goods when paid into A's own bank account, cease to be so classified when effectively 'transferred' to B's account, and yet revert to being stolen goods when dishonestly withdrawn as cash by B; but such is now the law.

This offence is also unusual in that the *actus reus* not only *can be* satisfied by an 'omission', but necessarily *involves* an omission or a failure to act.

1.13.15 Re-programming Mobile Phones

OFFENCE: **Re-programming Mobile Phones—*Mobile Telephones (Re-programming) Act 2002, s. 1***
    • Triable either way • Five years' imprisonment on indictment • Six months' imprisonment and/or a fine summarily

The Mobile Telephones (Re-programming) Act 2002, s. 1 states:

(1) A person commits an offence if—
    (a) he changes a unique device identifier,
    (b) he interferes with the operation of a unique device identifier,
    (c) he offers or agrees to change, or interfere with the operation of, a unique device identifier, or
    (d) he offers or agrees to arrange for another person to change, or interfere with the operation of, a unique device identifier.

(2) A unique device identifier is an electronic equipment identifier which is unique to a mobile wireless communications device.

(3) But a person does not commit an offence under this section if—

(a) he is the manufacturer of the device, or

(b) he does the act mentioned in subsection (1) with the written consent of the manufacturer of the device.

KEYNOTE

The unique device identifier is currently the International Mobile Equipment Identity (IMEI) number which identifies the handset of a mobile phone. It can be found on most mobile phones either behind the battery or by keying in the number *#06#. The wording of the section however allows for future development of mobile phones which may use different equipment identifiers. Changing the unique identifier is an offence, so too is adding a chip or otherwise interfering with that identifier.

It is the view of the Home Office that the international Global System for Mobiles (GSM) standards make it unnecessary for anyone other than a manufacturer or its agent to alter an IMEI number. For that reason, s. 1(3) creates a statutory defence for manufacturers or people with the *written* consent of the manufacturer.

1.13.15.1 Having or Supplying Anything to Facilitate Re-programming

OFFENCE: **Having or Supplying Anything for Re-programming Mobile Phones—*Mobile Telephones (Re-programming) Act 2002, s. 2.***

- Triable either way • Five years' imprisonment on indictment • Six months' imprisonment and/or a fine summarily

The Mobile Telephones (Re-programming) Act 2002, s. 2 states:

(1) A person commits an offence if—

(a) he has in his custody or under his control anything which may be used for the purpose of changing or interfering with the operation of a unique device identifier, and

(b) he intends to use the thing unlawfully for that purpose or to allow it to be used unlawfully for that purpose.

(2) A person commits an offence if—

(a) he supplies anything which may be used for the purpose of changing or interfering with the operation of a unique device identifier, and

(b) he knows or believes that the person to whom the thing is supplied intends to use it unlawfully for that purpose or to allow it to be used unlawfully for that purpose.

(3) A person commits an offence if—

(a) he offers to supply anything which may be used for the purpose of changing or interfering with the operation of a unique device identifier, and

(b) he knows or believes that the person to whom the thing is offered intends if it is supplied to him to use it unlawfully for that purpose or to allow it to be used unlawfully for that purpose.

KEYNOTE

Having something in your custody or under your control is wider than having it in your 'possession'.

The above offences apply to *anything* that may be used for the restricted purposes. It must be shown that, in each case, the defendant had the article, object, etc. or supplied/offered to supply it *and* that he/she had the requisite intent or knowledge at the time.

The definition of 'unique device identifier' is the same as for the s. 1 offence and a thing is used by a person unlawfully for a purpose if, in using it for that purpose, he/she commits an offence under s. 1.

1.13.16 **Handling Stolen Goods**

OFFENCE: **Handling Stolen Goods—*Theft Act 1968, s. 22***

> • Triable either way • Fourteen years' imprisonment on indictment • Six months' imprisonment and/or a fine summarily

The Theft Act 1968, s. 22 states:

(1) A person handles stolen goods if (otherwise than in the course of the stealing) knowing or believing them to be stolen goods he dishonestly receives the goods, or dishonestly undertakes or assists in their retention, removal, disposal or realisation by or for the benefit of another person, or if he arranges to do so.

KEYNOTE

Handling can only be committed *otherwise than in the course of stealing*. Given the extent of theft and the fact that it can be a continuing act, it is critical to identify at what point the theft of the relevant property ended. It is also useful, in cases of doubt, to include alternative charges.

You must show that the defendant *knew* or *believed* the goods to be stolen. Mere suspicion, however strong, will not be enough (*R* v *Griffiths* (1974) 60 Cr App R 14). Deliberate 'blindness' to the true identity of the goods would suffice but the distinction is a fine one in practice. It can be very difficult to prove knowledge or belief on the part of, say, a second-hand dealer who 'asks no questions'. Because there are practical difficulties in proving the required *mens rea,* s. 27(3) of the 1968 Act makes special provision to allow evidence of the defendant's previous convictions, or previous recent involvement with stolen goods, to be admitted.

'Goods' will include money and every other description of property except land, and includes things severed from the land by stealing (s. 34(2)(b) of the Act).

1.13.16.1 **Stolen Goods**

The Theft Act 1968, s. 24 states:

(1) The provisions of this Act relating to goods which have been stolen shall apply whether the stealing occurred in England or Wales or elsewhere, and whether it occurred before or after the commencement of this Act, provided that the stealing (if not an offence under this Act) amounted to an offence where and at the time when the goods were stolen; and references to stolen goods shall be construed accordingly.

(2) For purposes of those provisions references to stolen goods shall include, in addition to the goods originally stolen and parts of them (whether in their original state or not),—

(a) any other goods which directly or indirectly represent or have at any time represented the stolen goods in the hands of the thief as being the proceeds of any disposal or realisation of the whole or part of the goods stolen or of goods representing the stolen goods; and

(b) any other goods which directly or indirectly represent or have at any time represented the stolen goods in the hands of a handler of the stolen goods or any part of them as being the proceeds of any disposal or realisation of the whole or part of the stolen goods handled by him or of goods so representing them.

(3) But no goods shall be regarded as having continued to be stolen goods after they have been restored to the person from whom they were stolen or to other lawful possession or custody, or after that person and any other person claiming through him have otherwise ceased as regards those goods to have any right to restitution in respect of the theft.

(4) For purposes of the provisions of this Act relating to goods which have been stolen (including subsections (1) to (3) above) goods obtained in England or Wales or elsewhere either by blackmail or subject to subsection (5) below, by fraud (within the meaning of the Fraud Act 2006) shall be regarded as stolen; and 'steal', 'theft' and 'thief' shall be construed accordingly.

(5) Subsection (1) above applies in relation to goods obtained by fraud as if—

    (a) the reference to the commencement of this Act were a reference to the commencement of the Fraud Act 2006, and

    (b) the reference to an offence under this Act were a reference to an offence under section 1 of that Act.

The Theft Act 1968, s. 24A states:

(7) Subsection (8) below applies for purposes of provisions of this Act relating to stolen goods (including subsection (4) above).

(8) References to stolen goods include money which is dishonestly withdrawn from an account to which a wrongful credit has been made, but only to the extent that the money derives from the credit.

KEYNOTE

If goods are not stolen there is no handling. Whether they are so stolen is a question of fact for a jury or magistrate(s). There is no need to prove that the thief, blackmailer, etc. has been convicted of the primary offence before prosecuting the alleged handler, neither is it always necessary to *identify* who that person was.

However, care needs to be taken if a defendant is to be accused of handling goods stolen *from a specific person or place*. If that is the case then ownership of the goods will become an integral part of the prosecution case and it will be necessary to provide evidence proving that aspect of the offence (*Iqbal* v *DPP* [2004] EWHC 2567 (Admin)).

Goods obtained by fraud and blackmail are included in the definition of 'stolen goods' under s. 24(4) and s. 24(5). The references to fraud are to the general offence of fraud under s. 1 of the Fraud Act 2006. Clearly goods gained through robbery or burglary will, by definition, be 'stolen' as theft is an intrinsic element of both offences.

'Wrongful credits' are included within the meaning of stolen goods under certain circumstances and were dealt with earlier in this chapter (**see para. 1.13.14**).

1.13.16.2 Section 24 Explained

Under s. 24(1) a person can still be convicted of handling if the goods were stolen outside England and Wales but only if the goods were taken under circumstances which amounted to an offence in the other country.

Under s. 24(2), goods will be classed as stolen only if they are the property which was originally stolen or if they have at some time represented the *proceeds* of that property in the hands of the thief or a 'handler'.

Therefore if a DVD recorder is stolen, sold to an unsuspecting party who then part-exchanges it for a new one at a high street retailer, the first DVD recorder will be 'stolen' goods, the new one will not. If the first person buying the original DVD recorder *knew* or *believed* that it was stolen, the new DVD recorder will be treated as stolen goods.

Under s. 24(3), once goods have been restored to lawful possession they cease to be stolen. This situation formerly caused practical problems when police officers recovered stolen property but waited for it to be collected by a handler (see *Houghton* v *Smith* [1975] AC 476). Since the Criminal Attempts Act 1981 and the common-law rulings on 'impossibility' (**see chapter 1.3**), this has been less problematic. In such cases you may consider:

- Theft—collecting the property will be an 'appropriation'.
- Handling—an *arrangement* to come and collect stolen goods will probably have been made while they were still 'stolen'.

- Criminal attempt—the person collecting the goods has gone beyond merely preparing to handle them.

1.13.16.3 Proof that Goods were Stolen

The Theft Act 1968, s. 27 states:

(4) In any proceedings for the theft of anything in the course of transmission (whether by post or otherwise), or for handling stolen goods from such a theft, a statutory declaration made by any person that he dispatched or received or failed to receive any goods or postal packet, or that any goods or postal packet when dispatched or received by him were in a particular state or condition, shall be admissible as evidence of the facts stated in the declaration, subject to the following conditions:—
   (a) a statutory declaration shall only be admissible where and to the extent to which oral evidence to the like effect would have been admissible in the proceedings; and
   (b) a statutory declaration shall only be admissible if at least seven days before the hearing or trial a copy of it has been given to the person charged, and he has not, at least three days before the hearing or trial or within such further time as the court may in special circumstances allow, given the prosecutor written notice requiring the attendance at the hearing or trial of the person making the declaration.

KEYNOTE

The above provisions allow for specific evidence to be admitted in proving that goods 'in the course of transmission' have been stolen. These provisions allow for a statutory declaration by the person dispatching or receiving goods or postal packets as to when and where they were dispatched and when or if they arrived and, in each case, their state or condition (e.g. if they had been opened or interfered with). Such a statutory declaration will only be admissible in circumstances where an oral statement would have been admissible *and* if a copy has been served on the defendant at least seven days before the hearing and he/she has not—within three days of the hearing—served written notice on the prosecutor requiring the attendance of the person making the declaration.

This section is to be construed in accordance with s. 24 generally (s. 27(5)).

1.13.16.4 Handling

The offence of handling stolen goods is made up of many facets. Therefore to charge a defendant without specifying a particular form of handling is not bad for duplicity (*R v Nicklin* [1977] 1 WLR 403). However, the offence can be divided for practical purposes into two parts:

- *receiving/arranging to receive* stolen goods, in which case the defendant acts for his/her own benefit, and
- *assisting/acting for the benefit of another* person, in which case that assistance to another or benefit of another must be proved.

1.13.16.5 Receiving

Receiving does not require the physical reception of goods and can extend to exercising control over them. Things in action—such as bank credits from a stolen cheque—can be 'received'.

'Arranging to receive' would cover circumstances which do not go far enough to constitute an attempt—that is, actions which *are* merely preparatory to the receiving of stolen goods may satisfy the elements under s. 22 even though they would not meet the criteria under the Criminal Attempts Act 1981.

If the goods have yet to be stolen, then s. 22 would not apply and the offence of conspiracy should be considered (see *R v Park* (1987) 87 Cr App R 164).

1.13.16.6 Assisting/Acting for Another's Benefit

Assisting or acting for the benefit of another can be committed by misleading police officers during a search (see *R v Kanwar* [1982] 1 WLR 845).

Disposing of the stolen goods or assisting in their disposal or realisation usually involves physically moving them or converting them into a different form (see *R v Forsyth* [1997] 2 Cr App R 299).

If the only person 'benefiting' from the defendant's actions is the defendant himself/herself, this element of the offence will not be made out (*R v Bloxham* [1983] 1 AC 109).

Similarly, if the only 'other' person to benefit is a co-accused on the same charge, the offence will not be made out (*R v Gingell* [2000] 1 Cr App R 88).

1.13.16.7 Power to Search for Stolen Goods

The Theft Act 1968, s. 26 states:

(1) If it is made to appear by information on oath before a justice of the peace that there is reasonable cause to believe that any person has in his custody or possession or on his premises any stolen goods, the justice may grant a warrant to search for and seize the same; but no warrant to search for stolen goods shall be addressed to a person other than a constable except under the authority of an enactment expressly so providing.

(2) ...

(3) Where under this section a person is authorised to search premises for stolen goods, he may enter and search the premises accordingly, and may seize any goods he believes to be stolen goods.

(4) ...

(5) This section is to be construed in accordance with section 24 of this Act; and in subsection (2) above the references to handling stolen goods shall include any corresponding offence committed before the commencement of this Act.

KEYNOTE

Section 26 provides a general power to search for and seize stolen goods, whether identified in the search warrant or not and magistrates are entitled to act on material provided by the police that gives rise to a reasonable belief that stolen goods will be found (*R Cruickshank Ltd* v *Chief Constable of Kent Constabulary* [2002] EWCA Civ 1840).

1.13.16.8 Guilty Knowledge in Cases of Handling and Theft

Section 27 of the Theft Act 1968 allows for the admissibility of previous misconduct and states:

(3) Where a person is being proceeded against for handling stolen goods (but not for any offence other than handling stolen goods), then at any stage of the proceedings, if evidence has been given of his having or arranging to have in his possession the goods the subject of the charge, or of his undertaking or assisting in, or arranging to undertake or assist in, their retention, removal, disposal or realisation, the following evidence shall be admissible for the purpose of proving that he knew or believed the goods to be stolen goods—

(a) evidence that he has had in his possession, or has undertaken or assisted in the retention, removal, disposal or realisation of, stolen goods from any theft taking place not earlier than 12 months before the offence charged; and

(b) (provided that seven days' notice in writing has been given to him of the intention to prove the conviction) evidence that he has within the five years preceding the date of the offence charged been convicted of theft or of handling stolen goods.

KEYNOTE

This provision applies to all forms of handling (*R* v *Ball* [1983] 1 WLR 801) and can be used where handling is the only offence involved in the proceedings.

The question as to what constitutes recent possession is a matter of fact and degree dependent on the circumstances of each case. This presumption can be rebutted by the person offering a true explanation for the possession (*R* v *Schama* (1914) 84 LJ KB 396, *R* v *Garth* [1949] 1 All ER 773, *R* v *Aves* [1950] 2 All ER 330 and *R* v *Williams* [1962] Crim LR 54).

The term 'recent possession' is not defined and so is a question of fact in each case. In *R* v *Smythe* (1980) 72 Cr App R 8, the Court of Appeal held that property found in the possession of an accused, stolen two or three months earlier during some robberies and burglaries, did not amount to recent possession for the offence of handling stolen goods generally.

1.13.17 Proceeds of Crime

1.13.17.1 Proceeds of Crime Act 2002

The offences and powers under the Proceeds of Crime Act 2002 are not just within the purview of specialist financial investigation departments. While 'serious crime' is likely to play a significant part in the use of the powers the Act provides, police officers must remember that the Act is also connected with day to day criminality and therefore involves all police officers whatever rank and role they fulfil. This section will not attempt to provide a detailed analysis of the Act but will provide an overview of the three principal offences relating to 'Money Laundering' created by s. 327 (concealing criminal property), s. 328 (arrangements in relation to criminal property) and s. 329 (acquisition, use and possession of criminal property) of the Act. To begin with, there must be a brief examination of the concepts relating to 'criminal conduct' and 'criminal property'.

1.13.17.2 Criminal Conduct

The Proceeds of Crime Act 2002, s. 340 states:

(2) Criminal conduct is conduct which—
   (a) constitutes an offence in any part of the United Kingdom, or
   (b) would constitute an offence in any part of the United Kingdom if it occurred there.

KEYNOTE

Section 340(4) states that it is immaterial:

- who carried out the criminal conduct
- who benefited from it
- whether the conduct occurred before or after the passing of the Act.

So criminal conduct not only includes the behaviour of the defendant him/herself but also of any other person. Effectively this states that *any offence*, committed by *any person, anywhere* at all and at *any time* is 'criminal conduct'. This represents a significant departure from earlier law which required the prosecution to show that the criminal property existed as a consequence of a specific offence or class of offences. As a consequence of s. 340, a conviction can be obtained under the Proceeds of Crime Act even if the prosecution cannot specify the offence or offences that gave rise to the proceeds or identify the person(s) responsible for the offence(s).

1.13.17.3 Criminal Property

The Proceeds of Crime Act 2002, s. 340 states:

(3) Property is criminal property if—
    (a) it constitutes a person's benefit from criminal conduct or it represents such a benefit (in whole or in part and whether directly or indirectly) and,
    (b) the alleged offender knows or suspects that it constitutes or represents such a benefit.

KEYNOTE

Although the offences under ss. 327, 328 and 329 are often referred to as 'money laundering', it should be noted that the definition of 'property' is exceptionally wide and *does not just relate to money*. Section 340(9) of the Act defines property as *all* property *wherever* situated and includes:

- money
- all forms of property, real or personal, heritable or movable, and
- things in action and other intangible or incorporeal property.

(Incorporeal property relates to property or an asset that does not have value in material form, such as a right or a patent.)

The *mens rea* relating to criminal property and therefore to all three offences is knowing or *suspecting*. Dishonesty is not required. In *R v Da Silva* [2006] EWCA Crim 1654, it was said that:

to suspect something, you have to have a state of mind well short of knowing that the matter you suspect is true. It is an ordinary English word. . . the dictionary definition of 'suspicion' [is] an act of suspecting, the imagining of something without evidence or on slender evidence, inkling, mistrust.

The Court of Appeal upheld the conviction, concluding that the word 'suspect' meant that the defendant had to think that there was a possibility, which was more than fanciful, that the relevant facts existed. A vague feeling of unease would not suffice. The fact the suspicion alone will suffice means that proving such offences is remarkably less burdensome for the prosecution than the potential alternative to such offences, a charge of handling stolen goods where the defendant must be proved to know or believe that goods are stolen goods.

1.13.17.4 Concealing Criminal Property

OFFENCE: **Concealing Criminal Property—*Proceeds of Crime Act 2002, s. 327***
    - Triable either way • 14 years' imprisonment on indictment and/or fine • Six months' imprisonment and/or fine summarily

The Proceeds of Crime Act 2002, s. 327 states:

(1) A person commits an offence if he—
    (a) conceals criminal property;

> (b) disguises criminal property;
> (c) converts criminal property;
> (d) transfers criminal property;
> (e) removes criminal property from England and Wales and Scotland or from Northern Ireland.
> (2) But a person does not commit such an offence if—
>> (a) he makes an authorised disclosure under section 338 and (if the disclosure is made before he does the act mentioned in subsection (1)) he has the appropriate consent;
>> (b) he intended to make such a disclosure but had a reasonable excuse for not doing so;
>> (c) the act he does is done in carrying out a function he has relating to the enforcement of any provision of this Act or of any other enactment relating to criminal conduct or benefit from criminal conduct.
> (3) Concealing or disguising criminal property includes concealing or disguising its nature, source, location, disposition, movement or ownership or any rights with respect to it.

KEYNOTE

There is a noticeable overlap between the activities relating to concealing criminal property and the offence of handling stolen goods, particularly when considering the list of activities that a defendant may undertake in the commission of both offences. However, whereas handling only occurs 'otherwise than in the course of stealing' and 'by or for the benefit of another', the offence under s. 327 can potentially be committed *during the commission of an offence* and *for the benefit of the thief*. On a literal reading of s. 327, a thief who conceals, disguises or sells property that he has just stolen may thereby commit offences under that section because the definition of criminal property applies to the laundering of an offender's own proceeds of crime as well as those of someone else.

Section 327(2) creates several defences to charges under s. 327.

1.13.17.5   Arrangements in relation to Criminal Property

OFFENCE: **Arrangements in relation to Criminal Property—*Proceeds of Crime Act 2002, s. 328***

> • Triable either way   • 14 years' imprisonment on indictment and/or fine   • Six months' imprisonment and/or fine summarily

The Proceeds of Crime Act 2002, s. 328 states:

> (1) A person commits an offence if he enters into or becomes concerned in an arrangement which he knows or suspects facilitates (by whatever means) the acquisition, retention, use or control of criminal property by or on behalf of another person.

KEYNOTE

To establish an offence under this section, the prosecutor would need to prove that a person entered into or became concerned in an arrangement which he knew or suspected would make it easier for another person to acquire, retain, use or control criminal property and that the person concerned also knew or suspected that the property constituted or represented benefit from criminal conduct. This offence will often be apt for the prosecution of those who launder on behalf of others. Not only could this catch persons who work in financial or credit institutions, accountants etc, who in the course of their work facilitate money laundering by or on behalf of other persons, but also family members (husband/wife, partner etc.).

Section 328 includes the same defences against committing the offence, as are included in s. 327(2).

1.13.17.6 **Acquisition, Use and Possession of Criminal Property**

OFFENCE: **Acquisition, Use and Possession of Criminal Property—*Proceeds of Crime Act 2002, s. 329***

> • Triable either way • 14 years' imprisonment on indictment and/or fine • Six months' imprisonment and/or fine summarily

The Proceeds of Crime Act 2002, s. 329 states:

(1) A person commits an offence if he—
  (a) acquires criminal property;
  (b) uses criminal property;
  (c) has possession of criminal property.

KEYNOTE

As with the previous offences, this offence is only committed where a person knows or suspects that the property which is acquired etc constitutes or represents his own or another's benefit from criminal conduct. Again, the same defences against committing the offence apply as in s. 327.

An additional defence exists under s. 329(2)(c) which states that a person will not commit the offence if he acquired or used or had possession of the property for adequate consideration (an example of adequate consideration would be being paid a proper market price of £3000 to fix a roof). The effect of the defence in s. 329(2)(c) is that persons, such as tradesmen, who are paid for ordinary consumable goods and services in money that comes from crime are not under any obligation to question the source of the money. However, the defence is not available to a defendant who provides goods or services knowing or suspecting that those goods or services will help a person *to actually carry out criminal conduct.*

The coincidence between an offence of handling stolen goods and those described from the Proceeds of Crime Act 2002 might provide a dilemma as to which offence to charge. In such a situation, CPS guidance states that if it is possible to charge money laundering or handling stolen goods then money laundering may be more appropriate if 'either a defendant has possessed criminal proceeds in large amounts or in lesser amounts, but repeatedly and where assets are laundered for profit'. However, a money laundering charge should only be considered where proceeds are more than *de minimis* (about minimal things) in any circumstances where the defendant who is charged with the underlying offence has done more than simply consume his proceeds of crime.

1.14 Fraud

1.14.1 Introduction

The Fraud Act 2006 provides for a general offence of fraud with three ways of committing it (by false representation, by failing to disclose information, and by abuse of position) as well as creating offences of obtaining services dishonestly, and possessing, making, and supplying articles for use in fraud. It also creates offences in relation to fraudulent business activities by sole traders and companies but these are beyond the scope of this manual.

1.14.2 Fraud

OFFENCE: **Fraud—*Fraud Act 2006, s. 1***
- Triable either way • Ten years' imprisonment and/or a fine on indictment
- Twelve months' imprisonment and/or a fine summarily

The Fraud Act 2006, s. 1 states:

(1) A person is guilty of fraud if he is in breach of any of the sections listed in subsection (2) (which provide for different ways of committing the offence).
(2) The sections are—
   (a) section 2 (fraud by false representation),
   (b) section 3 (fraud by failing to disclose information), and
   (c) section 4 (fraud by abuse of position).

> **KEYNOTE**
>
> The heart of all three methods of committing the offence of fraud is in the *conduct and ulterior intent* of the defendant. The effect of this approach is that a defendant's unsuccessful 'attempt' to commit the offence of fraud may amount to the commission of the substantive offence, effectively excluding the possibility of an offence under the Criminal Attempts Act 1981.

1.14.3 Fraud by False Representation

The Fraud Act 2006, s. 2 states:

(1) A person is in breach of this section if he—
   (a) dishonestly makes a false representation, and
   (b) intends, by making the representation—
      (i) to make a gain for himself or another, or
      (ii) to cause loss to another or to expose another to the risk of loss.

(2) A representation is false if—
   (a) it is untrue or misleading, and
   (b) the person making it knows that it is, or might be, untrue or misleading.
(3) 'Representation' means any representation as to fact or law, including a representation as to the state of mind of—
   (a) the person making the representation, or
   (b) any other person.
(4) A representation may be express or implied.
(5) For the purposes of this section a representation may be regarded as made if it (or anything implying it) is submitted in any form to any system or device designed to receive, convey or respond to communications (with or without human intervention).

KEYNOTE

Dishonestly

The 'dishonestly' referred to in s. 2(1)(a) is a reference to the test of dishonesty established in *R* v *Ghosh* [1982] QB 1053 (see chapter 1.13). The same test applies to ss. 3 and 4 of the Act.

Gain and Loss

Section 2(1)(b) refers to 'gain' and 'loss' and that the person making the representation must do so with the intention of making a gain or causing a loss or risk of loss to another. *The gain or loss does not actually have to take place.*

Representation

A representation is false if it is untrue or misleading *and* the person making it knows this is or knows this might be the case. Therefore, an untrue statement made in the honest belief that it is in fact true, would not suffice. The words 'or might be' must involve a subjective belief on the part of the person making the representation.

The representation may be express or implied and can be communicated in words or conduct. There is no limitation on the way in which the representation must be expressed, so it could be written, spoken or posted on a website. A representation may also be implied by conduct. For example, a person dishonestly misusing a credit card to pay for items hands the card to a cashier without saying a word. By handing the card to the cashier he is falsely representing that he has authority to use it for that transaction. It is immaterial that the cashier accepting the card for payment is deceived by the representation as the cashier's state of mind plays no part in the commission of the offence. Where a defendant makes a false representation knowing that it is false or might be, the offence of fraud is complete. Any representation made must be one as to fact or law, so a broken promise is not in itself a false representation. However, a statement may be false if it misrepresents the current intentions or state of mind of the person making it or anyone else. For example, D visits V's house and tells V that he needs emergency work carried out on his roof. D states that he is in a position to do the work immediately but only if V pays him £1000 there and then. V gives D the money and D then leaves without carrying out the work; the truth of the matter was that D had never intended to carry out the work. Such a 'promise' by D would amount to an offence as it involved a false representation i.e. he never intended to keep the promise.

The offence is complete the moment the false representation is made The representation need never be heard nor communicated to the recipient and if carried out by post, would be complete when the letter is posted (*Treacy* v *DPP* [1971] AC 537).

Phishing

The offence would also be committed by someone who engages in 'phishing'. This is the practice of sending out e-mails in bulk, purporting to represent a well-known brand in the hope of sending victims to a bogus website that tricks them into disclosing bank account details. 'Phishing kits' have long been available on the Internet; the offence under s. 2 now covers such activity.

Machines

Under the old law, a machine could not be deceived and any activity carried out that fooled a machine or computer would not amount to deception. Section 2(5) of the Fraud Act enables the offence of fraud to apply in such cases, as necessity for human involvement in any response from the person making the false representation has been dispensed with (for example where a person enters a number into a 'Chip and PIN' machine).

1.14.4 Fraud by Failing to Disclose

The Fraud Act 2006, s. 3 states:

A person is in breach of this section if he—
  (a) dishonestly fails to disclose to another person information which he is under a legal duty to disclose, and
  (b) intends, by failing to disclose the information—
    (i) to make a gain for himself or another, or
    (ii) to cause loss to another or to expose another to a risk of loss.

KEYNOTE

Section 3 creates an offence of dishonestly failing to disclose information where there is a legal duty to do so. The term 'legal duty' has not been defined but will include duties under oral contracts as well as written contracts. The Law Commission's *Report on Fraud* dealt with the concept of legal duty and stated that duties might arise:

- from statute
- where the transaction is one of the utmost good faith
- from the express or implied terms of a contract
- from the custom of a particular trade or market, or
- from the existence of a fiduciary relationship between parties.

The legal duty to disclose information will exist if:

- the defendant's actions give the victim a cause in action for damages or
- if the law gives the victim the right to set aside any change in his or her legal position to which he or she may have consented as a result of the non-disclosure.

A fiduciary relationship is one relating to the responsibility of looking after someone else's money in a correct way. Examples of such behaviour would include a solicitor failing to share vital information with a client in the context of their work relationship, in order to carry out a fraud upon that client, or if a person intentionally failed to disclose information relating to a heart condition when making an application for life insurance.

1.14.5 Fraud by Abuse of Position

The Fraud Act 2006, s. 4 states:

(1) A person is in breach of this section if he—
   (a) occupies a position in which he is expected to safeguard, or not to act against, the financial interests of another person,
   (b) dishonestly abuses that position, and
   (c) intends, by means of the abuse of that position—
      (i) to make a gain for himself or another, or
      (ii) to cause loss to another or to expose another to a risk of loss.
(2) A person may be regarded as having abused his position even though his conduct consisted of an omission rather than an act.

KEYNOTE

The crux of this offence is the financial and dishonest abuse of a privileged position of trust. An offence under s. 4 may be committed in a variety of ways as the 'position' that the defendant occupies may be the result of an assortment of relationships. The Law Commission explained the meaning of 'position' at paragraph 7.38:

> The necessary relationship will be present between trustee and beneficiary, director and company, professional person and client, agent and principle, employee and employer, or between partners. It may arise otherwise, for example within a family, or in the context of voluntary work, or in any context where the parties are not at arm's length.

The term 'abuse' is not defined by the Act.

Liability for the offence could develop from a wide range of conduct, for example:

- An employee of a software company uses his position to clone software products with the intention of selling the products on.
- An estate agent values a house belonging to an elderly person at an artificially low price and then arranges for his brother to purchase the house.
- A person who is employed to care for a disabled person and has access to that person's bank account, abuses his position by transferring funds to invest in a high-risk business venture of his own.

The offence can also be committed by omission, for example:

- An employee fails to take up the chance of a crucial contract in order that an associate or rival company can take it up instead of and at the expense of the employer.

1.14.6 Gain and Loss

The Fraud Act 2006, s. 5 states:

(1) The references to gain and loss in sections 2 to 4 are to be read in accordance with this section.
(2) 'Gain' and 'loss'—
   (a) extend only to gain and loss in money or other property;
   (b) include any such gain or loss whether temporary or permanent;
   and 'property' means any property whether real or personal (including things in action and other intangible property).
(3) 'Gain' includes a gain by keeping what one has, as well as getting what one does not have.
(4) 'Loss' includes a loss by not getting what one might get, as well as a loss by parting with what one has.

> **KEYNOTE**
>
> It is important to note that the 'gain' and 'loss' relates only to *money and other property*. The definition of property covers all forms of property including intellectual property.

1.14.7 Possession or Control of Articles for Use in Frauds

OFFENCE: **Possession or Control of Articles for Use in Frauds—**
Fraud Act 2006, s. 6
   • Triable either way • Five years' imprisonment and/or fine on indictment • Twelve months' imprisonment and/or fine summarily

The Fraud Act 2006, s. 6 states:

(1) A person is guilty of an offence if he has in his possession or under his control any article for use in the course of or in connection with any fraud.

> **KEYNOTE**
>
> The offence under s. 6 can be committed *anywhere at all*, including the home of the defendant. The offence is not only committed when the defendant has articles in his possession but also when he has them in his control—a term that indicates that the defendant may be some distance away from the articles and yet still commit the offence. The offence under s. 6 applies to *all fraud offences* under the 2006 Act. However, much like the offence of 'going equipped' the offence is only committed in respect of *future* offences and not offences that have already taken place. The offence can be committed if possession, or control is to enable *another* to commit an offence of fraud. The definition of the term 'article' is discussed at **para. 1.14.9**.

1.14.8 Making or Supplying Articles for Use in Frauds

OFFENCE: **Making or Supplying Articles for Use in Frauds—*Fraud Act 2006, s. 7***
   • Triable either way • Ten years' imprisonment on indictment and/or fine • Twelve months' imprisonment and/or fine summarily

The Fraud Act 2006, s. 7 states:

(1) A person is guilty of an offence if he makes, adapts, supplies or offers to supply any article—
   (a) knowing that it is designed or adapted for use in the course of or in connection with fraud, or
   (b) intending it to be used to commit, or assist in the commission of, fraud.

> **KEYNOTE**
>
> The broad terms of the offence ensure that any activity in respect of the making, supplying etc. of any 'article' for use in fraud offences is an offence. Making an 'offer to supply' would not require the defendant to be in possession of the 'article' (a similar situation to offering to supply a controlled drug, **see para. 1.6.5.3**). Examples of such behaviour include:
>
> • A person makes a viewing card for a satellite TV system, enabling him to view all satellite channels for free.

- The same person then offers to sell similar cards to work colleagues although he has only made the one prototype card and does not actually have further cards to sell.
- A number of the person's work colleagues express an interest in buying the cards, so the person makes a dozen more cards and then actually supplies them to his work colleagues.

1.14.9 'Article'

The Fraud Act 2006, s. 8 states:

(1) For the purposes of—
  (a) sections 6 and 7, and
  (b) the provisions listed in subsection (2), so far as they relate to articles for use in the course of or in connection with fraud,
'article' includes any program or data held in electronic form.
(2) The provisions are—
  (a) section 1(7)(b) of the Police and Criminal Evidence Act 1984 (c 60),
  (b) ...
  (c) ...

Section 8 extends the meaning of 'article' for the purposes of ss. 6 and 7 of the Act to include any program or data held in electronic form. Examples of cases where electronic programs or data could be used in fraud are:

- a computer program that generates credit card numbers
- a computer template that can be used for producing blank utility bills
- a computer file that contains lists of other people's credit card details.

1.14.10 Obtaining Services Dishonestly

OFFENCE: **Obtaining Services Dishonestly—*Fraud Act 2006, s. 11***
  - Triable either way • Five years' imprisonment and/or fine on indictment • Twelve months' imprisonment and/or fine summarily

The Fraud Act 2006, s. 11 states:

(1) A person is guilty of an offence under this section if he obtains services for himself or another—
  (a) by a dishonest act, and
  (b) in breach of subsection (2).
(2) A person obtains services in breach of this subsection if—
  (a) they are made available on the basis that payment has been, is being or will be made for or in respect of them,
  (b) he obtains them without any payment having been made for in respect of them or without payment having been made in full, and
  (c) when he obtains them, he knows—
    (i) that they are being made available on the basis described in paragraph (a), or
    (ii) that they might be,
but intends that payment will not be made, or will not be made in full.

KEYNOTE

It is important to note that unlike the other offences created as a consequence of the Fraud Act 2006, the offence under s. 11 is not a conduct crime; it is a *result crime* and requires the *actual obtaining* of the service. However, the offence does not require a fraudulent representation or deception. A person would commit this offence if, intending to avoid payment, he slipped into a concert hall to watch a concert without paying for the privilege. The offence can be committed where the defendant intends to avoid payment or payment in full but the defendant must know that the services are made available on the basis that they are chargeable, i.e. services provided for free are not covered by the offence. The terms 'service' and 'obtaining' are not defined by the Act.

1.14.11 Falsification of Documents and Other Instruments

In addition to the offence of fraud, there are a series of closely-related offences which deal with falsification of documents or other 'instruments'.

1.14.11.1 False Accounting

OFFENCE: **False Accounting—*Theft Act 1968, s. 17***

- Triable either way • Seven years' imprisonment on indictment • Six months' imprisonment and/or a fine summarily

The Theft Act 1968, s. 17 states:

(1) Where a person dishonestly, with a view to gain for himself or another or with intent to cause loss to another,—
   (a) destroys, defaces, conceals or falsifies any account or any record or document made or required for any accounting purpose; or
   (b) in furnishing information for any purpose produces or makes use of any account, or any such record or document as aforesaid, which to his knowledge is or may be misleading, false or deceptive in a material particular;
   he shall [commit an offence].
(2) For purposes of this section a person who makes or concurs in making in an account or other document an entry which is or may be misleading, false or deceptive in a material particular, or who omits or concurs in omitting a material particular from an account or other document, is to be treated as falsifying the account or document.

KEYNOTE

This section creates two offences: destroying, defacing, etc. accounts and documents; and using false or misleading accounts or documents in furnishing information.

An offence under s. 17 can be committed by omission as well as by an act. Failing to make an entry in an accounts book, altering a till receipt or supplying an auditor with records that are incomplete may, if accompanied by the other ingredients, amount to an offence.

Unlike theft there is no requirement to prove an intention permanently to deprive but there is a need to show dishonesty (as to both points, see chapter 1.13). The requirement as to gain and loss is the same as for blackmail (see para. 1.13.10).

The misleading, false or deceptive nature of the information furnished under s. 17(1)(b) must be 'material' to the defendant's overall purpose, i.e. the ultimate gaining or causing of loss. Such an interpretation means that the defendant's furnishing of information need not relate directly to an accounting process and could be satisfied by lying about the status of a potential finance customer (see *R* v *Mallett* [1978] 1 WLR 820).

Where the documents falsified are not intrinsically 'accounting' forms, such as insurance claim forms filled out by policyholders, you must show that those forms are treated for accounting purposes by the victim (*R* v *Sundhers* [1998] Crim LR 497).

1.14.11.2 Forgery

Offences classed as 'forgery' include virtually every kind of document *except* bank notes. Coins and currency are the subject of a separate group of offences classed as counterfeiting and are dealt with later in this chapter.

Many of the offences dealt with below are divided into two categories:

- Offences where there is an *intention* by the defendant to pass the document, note or coin off as being genuine. These, more serious offences, attract higher penalties.
- Offences where there is no requirement to prove any *ulterior* intent.

1.14.11.3 Police Powers Regarding False Instruments

A warrant to search for and seize false instruments and materials may be issued under s. 7 of the 1981 Act.

1.14.11.4 False Instruments

OFFENCE: **Making a False Instrument with Intent—*Forgery and Counterfeiting Act 1981, s. 1***
- Triable either way • Ten years' imprisonment on indictment • Six months' imprisonment and/or a fine summarily

The Forgery and Counterfeiting Act 1981, s. 1 states:

A person is guilty of forgery if he makes a false instrument, with the intention that he or another shall use it to induce somebody to accept it as genuine, and by reason of so accepting it to do or not to do some act to his own or any other person's prejudice.

OFFENCE: **Using a False Instrument with Intent—*Forgery and Counterfeiting Act 1981, s. 3***
- Triable either way • Ten years' imprisonment on indictment • Six months' imprisonment and/or a fine summarily

The Forgery and Counterfeiting Act 1981, s. 3 states:

It is an offence for a person to use an instrument which is, and which he knows or believes to be, false, with the intention of inducing somebody to accept it as genuine, and by reason of so accepting it to do or not to do some act to his own or any other person's prejudice.

OFFENCE: **Copying a False Instrument with Intent—*Forgery and Counterfeiting Act 1981, s. 2***
- Triable either way • Ten years' imprisonment on indictment • Six months' imprisonment and/or a fine summarily

The Forgery and Counterfeiting Act 1981, s. 2 states:

It is an offence for a person to make a copy of an instrument which is, and which he knows or believes to be, a false instrument, with the intention that he or another shall use it to induce somebody to accept it as a copy of a genuine instrument, and by reason of so accepting it to do or not to do some act to his own or any other person's prejudice.

OFFENCE: **Using a Copy of a False Instrument with Intent**—*Forgery and Counterfeiting Act 1981, s. 4*

  • Triable either way • Ten years' imprisonment on indictment • Six months' imprisonment and/or a fine summarily

The Forgery and Counterfeiting Act 1981, s. 4 states:

> It is an offence for a person to use a copy of an instrument which is, and which he knows or believes to be, a false instrument, with the intention of inducing somebody to accept it as a copy of a genuine instrument, and by reason of so accepting it to do or not to do some act to his own or any other person's prejudice.

KEYNOTE

The essence of these offences is that they concern documents or instruments which purport to be something which they are not; that is, they 'tell a lie about themselves'.

In the defining terms used by s. 9 of the 1981 Act:

(1) An instrument is false for the purposes of this Part of this Act—
  (a) if it purports to have been made in the form in which it is made by a person who did not in fact make it in that form; or
  (b) if it purports to have been made in the form in which it is made on the authority of a person who did not in fact authorise its making in that form; or
  (c) if it purports to have been made in the terms in which it is made by a person who did not in fact make it in those terms; or
  (d) if it purports to have been made in the terms in which it is made on the authority of a person who did not in fact authorise its making in those terms; or
  (e) if it purports to have been altered in any respect by a person who did not in fact alter it in that respect; or
  (f) if it purports to have been altered in any respect on the authority of a person who did not in fact authorise the alteration in that respect; or
  (g) if it purports to have been made or altered on a date on which, or at a place at which, or otherwise in circumstances in which, it was not in fact made or altered; or
  (h) if it purports to have been made or altered by an existing person but he did not in fact exist.

KEYNOTE

The list of ways in which instruments can be false might be remembered by the following mnemonic. An instrument may be false if:

F it falsely claims to have been made in a **F**orm or in terms by, or on the authority of, another

A it falsely claims to have been **A**ltered by, or on the authority of, another

L it **L**ies about the date, place or any other circumstances in which it claims to have been made or altered

S it falsely claims to have been made or altered by **S**omeone who did not in fact

E **E**xist.

This list is exhaustive; if an instrument cannot be brought under one of these heads it will not be regarded as 'false'. However, you do not have to specify which of the heads an action comes under in a charge or indictment.

Section 9 goes on to say that:

(2) A person is to be treated for the purposes of this part of this Act as making a false instrument if he alters an instrument so as to make it false in any respect (whether or not it is false in some other respect apart from that alteration).

An 'instrument' is defined in s. 8 of the 1981 Act which states:

(1) Subject to subsection (2) below, in this Part of this Act 'instrument' means—
  (a) any document, whether of a formal or informal character;
  (b) any stamp issued or sold by a postal operator;
  (c) any Inland Revenue stamp; and
  (d) any disc, tape, sound track or other device on or in which information is recorded or stored by mechanical, electronic or other means.
(2) A currency note within the meaning of Part II of this Act is not an instrument for the purposes of this Part of this Act.
(3) A mark denoting payment of postage which a postal operator authorises to be used instead of an adhesive stamp is to be treated for the purposes of this Part of this Act as if it were a stamp issued by the postal operator concerned.
(3A) In this section, 'postal operator' has the same meaning as in the Postal Services Act 2000.
(4) In this Part of this Act 'Inland Revenue stamp' means a stamp as defined in section 27 of the Stamp Duties Management Act 1891.

KEYNOTE

The reference at s. 8(1)(d) above does not extend to electronic impulses keyed into a computer and therefore simply 'hacking' into a computer cannot amount to forgery (*R* v *Gold* [1988] AC 1063).

Note that 'document' is not defined. As discussed above, this definition does not include currency notes which are the subject of a specific offence (see counterfeiting below).

1.14.11.5 Specific Instruments

In addition to the above offences which apply to any instrument, there are several specific offences which apply to specific types of 'formal' instrument.

OFFENCE: **Having Custody or Control of Specific Instruments and Materials with Intent—*Forgery and Counterfeiting Act 1981, s. 5(1) and (3)***
  • Triable either way • Ten years' imprisonment on indictment • Six months' imprisonment and/or a fine summarily

The Forgery and Counterfeiting Act 1981, s. 5 states:

(1) It is an offence for a person to have in his custody or under his control an instrument to which this section applies which is, and which he knows or believes to be, false, with the intention that he or another shall use it to induce somebody to accept it as genuine, and by reason of so accepting it to do or not to do some act to his own or any other person's prejudice.
(2) ...
(3) It is an offence for a person to make or to have in his custody or under his control a machine or implement, or paper or any other material, which to his knowledge is or has been specially designed or adapted for the making of an instrument to which this section applies, with the intention that he or another shall make an instrument to which this section applies which is false and that he or another shall use the instrument to induce somebody to accept it as genuine, and by reason of so accepting it to do or not to do some act to his own or any other person's prejudice.

OFFENCE: **Having Custody or Control of Specific Instruments and Materials—** *Forgery and Counterfeiting Act 1981, s. 5(2) and (4)*

- Triable either way • Two years' imprisonment on indictment • Six months' imprisonment and/or a fine summarily

The Forgery and Counterfeiting Act 1981, s. 5 states:

(2) It is an offence for a person to have in his custody or under his control, without lawful authority or excuse, an instrument to which this section applies which is, and which he knows or believes to be, false.

(3) ...

(4) It is an offence for a person to make or to have in his custody or under his control any such machine, implement, paper or material, without lawful authority or excuse.

The instruments to which the above offences under s. 5 apply are:

(5) ...
- (a) money orders;
- (b) postal orders;
- (c) United Kingdom postage stamps;
- (d) Inland Revenue stamps;
- (e) share certificates;
- (f) ...
- (g) cheques and other bills of exchange;
- (h) travellers' cheques;
- (ha) bankers' drafts;
- (hb) promissory notes;
- (j) cheque cards;
- (ja) debit cards;
- (k) credit cards;
- (l) certified copies relating to an entry in a register of births, adoptions, marriages, civil partnerships or deaths and issued by the Registrar General, the Registrar General for Northern Ireland, a registration officer or a person lawfully authorised to register marriages; and
- (m) certificates relating to entries in such registers.

(6) In subsection (5)(e) above 'share certificate' means an instrument entitling or evidencing the title of a person to a share or interest—
- (a) in any public stock, annuity, fund or debt of any government or state, including a state which forms part of another state; or
- (b) in any stock, fund or debt of a body (whether corporate or unincorporated) established in the United Kingdom or elsewhere.

(7) An instrument is also an instrument to which this section applies if it is a monetary instrument specified for the purposes of this section by an order made by the Secretary of State.

...

KEYNOTE

Many of these 'instruments' are self explanatory. 'Immigration document' essentially means a card, adhesive label or other instrument given under the Immigration Acts to someone to confirm their right of entry to or residence in the United Kingdom. The expression extends to cards, labels and other instruments which carry information (including information wholly or partly stored electronically) about the leave granted to that person.

1.14.11.6 **Prejudice and Induce**

The intent of *inducing* somebody to accept an instrument with the result that he/she does something to his/her own *prejudice* must be read in the light of s. 10 of the 1981 Act which states:

(1) Subject to subsections (2) and (4) below, for the purposes of this Part of this Act an act or omission intended to be induced is to a person's prejudice if, and only if, it is one which, if it occurs—

    (a) will result—

      (i) in his temporary or permanent loss of property; or

      (ii) in his being deprived of an opportunity to earn remuneration or greater remuneration; or

      (iii) in his being deprived of an opportunity to gain a financial advantage otherwise than by way of remuneration; or

    (b) will result in somebody being given an opportunity—

      (i) to earn remuneration or greater remuneration from him; or

      (ii) to gain a financial advantage from him otherwise than by way of remuneration; or

    (c) will be the result of his having accepted a false instrument as genuine, or a copy of a false instrument as a copy of a genuine one, in connection with his performance of any duty.

(2) An act which a person has an enforceable duty to do and an omission to do an act which a person is not entitled to do shall be disregarded for the purposes of this Part of this Act.

(3) In this Part of this Act references to inducing somebody to accept a false instrument as genuine, or a copy of a false instrument as a copy of a genuine one, include references to inducing a machine to respond to the instrument or copy as if it were a genuine instrument or, as the case may be, a copy of a genuine one.

KEYNOTE

This section extends the meaning of inducing someone to accept something as genuine to *machines*. The extension is limited to offences under part I of the 1981 Act and therefore does not apply to offences contained elsewhere such as counterfeiting (as to which, see below).

1.14.12 Counterfeiting with Intent to Pass or Tender as Genuine

OFFENCE: **Making Counterfeit Note or Coin with Intent—*Forgery and Counterfeiting Act 1981, s. 14(1)***

    • Triable either way • Ten years' imprisonment on indictment • Six months' imprisonment and/or a fine summarily

The Forgery and Counterfeiting Act 1981, s. 14 states:

(1) It is an offence for a person to make a counterfeit of a currency note or of a protected coin, intending that he or another shall pass or tender it as genuine.

KEYNOTE

Although there is a requirement to prove an intent, there is no need to show that the defendant intended to induce someone to do something to his/her own prejudice.

OFFENCE: **Having Custody or Control of Counterfeit Note or Coin with Intent—** *Forgery and Counterfeiting Act 1981, s. 16(1)*
• Triable either way • Ten years' imprisonment on indictment • Six months' imprisonment and/or a fine summarily

The Forgery and Counterfeiting Act 1981, s. 16 states:

(1) It is an offence for a person to have in his custody or under his control any thing which is, and which he knows or believes to be, a counterfeit of a currency note or of a protected coin, intending either to pass or tender it as genuine or to deliver it to another with the intention that he or another shall pass or tender it as genuine.

OFFENCE: **Passing Counterfeit Notes or Coins with Intent—***Forgery and Counterfeiting Act 1981, s. 15(1)(a) and (b)*
• Triable either way • Ten years' imprisonment and/or a fine on indictment • Six months' imprisonment and/or a fine summarily

The Forgery and Counterfeiting Act 1981, s. 15 states:

(1) It is an offence for a person—
  (a) to pass or tender as genuine any thing which is, and which he knows or believes to be, a counterfeit of a currency note or of a protected coin; or
  (b) to deliver to another any thing which is, and which he knows or believes to be, such a counterfeit, intending that the person to whom it is delivered or another shall pass or tender it as genuine.

1.15 | Criminal Damage

1.15.1 Introduction

The chances of any police officer going through their career without dealing in some way with an offence of criminal damage are minuscule. The prevalence of offences of criminal damage is well documented and damage in all forms has harmful effect on the environment, the community and the economy.

1.15.2 Simple Damage

OFFENCE: **Simple damage—*Criminal Damage Act 1971, s. 1(1)***
- Triable either way • Ten years' imprisonment on indictment • Six months' imprisonment and/or a fine summarily

OFFENCE: **Racially or Religiously Aggravated—**
Crime and Disorder Act 1998, s. 30(1)
- Triable either way • Fourteen years' imprisonment and/or a fine on indictment
- Six months' imprisonment and/or a fine summarily

The Criminal Damage Act 1971, s. 1 states:

(1) A person who without lawful excuse destroys or damages any property belonging to another intending to destroy or damage any such property or being reckless as to whether any such property would be destroyed or damaged shall be guilty of an offence.

KEYNOTE

Although triable either way, if the value of the property destroyed or the damage done is less than £5,000, the offence is to be tried summarily (Magistrates' Courts Act 1980, s. 22). If the damage in such a case was caused by fire (arson) then this rule will not apply.

The fact that the substantive offence is, by virtue of the value of the damage caused, triable only summarily does not make simple damage a 'summary offence' for all other purposes. If it did, you could only be found guilty of *attempting* to commit criminal damage if the value of the intended damage was more than £5,000 (because the Criminal Attempts Act 1981 does not extend to summary offences) (see chapter 1.3). Therefore, where a defendant tried to damage a bus shelter in a way that would have cost far less than £5,000 to repair, his argument that he had only attempted what was in fact a 'summary offence' was dismissed by the Divisional Court (*R v Bristol Magistrates' Court, ex parte E* [1998] 3 All ER 798). Note that offences of damage involving values not exceeding £200 can be dealt with by way of fixed penalty notice (see General Police Duties, chapter 4.6.3).

If the offence involves only the painting or writing on, or the soiling, marking or other defacing of, any property by whatever means, the power to issue a graffiti notice may apply (as to which see para. 1.15.7).

The racially or religiously aggravated form of this offence (see below) is triable either way irrespective of the cost of the damage.

1.15.2.1 Racially or Religiously Aggravated Damage

The racially or religiously aggravated circumstances set out at s. 28(1)(a) of the Crime and Disorder Act 1998 (**see General Police Duties, chapter 4.5**) deal with situations where the defendant demonstrates hostility:

- at the time of
- or immediately before or after

committing the offence, towards the *victim* and that hostility is *based on the victim's membership or presumed membership of a racial or religious group*. The courts have shown that they are prepared to adopt a wide approach when interpreting this important legislation. This can be seen in two particular cases. In the first, the Divisional Court confirmed that the relevant hostility can be demonstrated even if the victim is no longer present—*DPP* v *Parry* [2004] EWHC 3112 (Admin). However, the need for any such hostility to be demonstrated *immediately* means that it must be shown to have taken place in the immediate context of the criminal damage offence. In *Parry* the only evidence of the racial hostility towards the victim came in the form of comments made to the officers attending the scene *some 20 minutes after* the defendant had caused the damage (by throwing nail polish at a neighbour's door). The court held that the wording of the statute meant that any hostility had to be demonstrated *immediately* before or *immediately* after the substantive offence and that the courts below had not been entitled to consider the retrospective effect of the comments made later by the defendant.

In another case where a juvenile used the words 'bloody foreigners' immediately before smashing the window of a kebab shop, the Divisional Court held that this was capable of amounting to an expression of hostility based on a person's membership or presumed membership of a racial group for the purposes of s. 28(1)(a) of the Crime and Disorder Act 1998—*DPP* v *M* [2004] EWHC 1453 (Admin). Although the statutory wording used the expression 'a racial group', the court held that a specific and inclusive definition of such a group had to be used by the defendant (e.g. the defendant did not have to single out a specific nationality) and the size of group referred to by a defendant (such as all 'foreigners') was irrelevant. However, in the case of *M* the youth court had inadvertently mixed the two tests of hostility and motivation under s. 28(1)(b) and his appeal was allowed. Therefore, when considering whether an offence was racially motivated under s. 28 of the Crime and Disorder Act 1998, hostility demonstrated to foreign nationals simply because they are 'foreign' can be just as objectionable as hostility based on some more limited racial characteristic. This was clarified by the Court of Appeal in *R* v *Rogers* [2005] EWCA Crim 2863 where the defendant had called three Spanish women 'bloody foreigners' and told them to 'go back to your own country'. The prosecution case was that the defendant had demonstrated hostility based on the women's membership of a racial group. The court's decision clarifies the position that, for an offence to be aggravated under s. 28, the defendant has first to form a view that the victim is a member of a racial group (within the definition in s. 28(4)—**see General Police Duties, para. 4.9.2.3**) and then has to say (or do) something that demonstrates hostility towards the victim based on membership of that group. However, the Court of Appeal noted that the very wide meaning of racial group under s. 28(4) gives rise to a danger of aggravated offences being charged where mere 'vulgar abuse' had included racial descriptions that did not truly indicate hostility to the race in question.

Consequently, s. 28 should not be used unless the prosecuting authority is satisfied that the facts truly suggest that the offence was aggravated (rather than simply accompanied) by racism.

To clarify such situations in relation to racially or religiously aggravated damage, s. 30(3) provides that the person to whom the property belongs or is treated as belonging, will be treated as the 'victim'.

This provision is helpful where the aggravated offence is one under s. 28(1)(a)—the 'demonstration' type of aggravation—and the property is privately owned.

Where the property is owned by a corporate body (e.g. a bus shelter or tube station) however, there will clearly be problems in proving that the defendant's hostility was based on the *victim's* membership/presumed membership of a racial or religious group. Even though property for these purposes may be treated as belonging to more than one person (**see para. 1.15.2.4**) this means that, where the damage is caused by racist graffiti in publicly-owned places or on property owned by large corporations, the most suitable charge will probably be under s. 28(1)(b) of the Act (motivation)—by far the harder to prove. Harder still would be the situation where any such graffiti is of a *religious* nature and the hostility was based on the victim's membership of a religious group.

The provisions of s. 30 of the Crime and Disorder Act 1998 only apply to the offence of 'simple' damage under s. 1(1) of the 1971 Act; they do not apply to any of the other offences in this chapter.

1.15.2.2 Destroy or Damage

Although a key feature of the 1971 Act, the terms 'destroy' or 'damage' are not defined. The courts have taken a wide view when interpreting these terms. 'Destroying' property would suggest that it has been rendered useless but there is no need to prove that 'damage' to property is in any way permanent or irreparable.

....

EXAMPLE

A group of youths in a shopping precinct walk up to a grocery display and begin juggling with some apples. They drop several apples, some of which smash on the pavement while others are soiled and bruised.

....

In the example above, the apples which were smashed were clearly 'destroyed'; those which were soiled, even though they could be washed, would probably be unfit for sale and therefore 'damaged' for the purposes of s. 1(1).

Whether an article has been damaged will be a question of fact for each court to determine on the evidence before it. Situations where courts have accepted that property has been damaged include the defacing of a pavement by an artist using only water-soluble paint (*Hardman* v *Chief Constable of Avon and Somerset* [1986] Crim LR 330). It has also been held by the Divisional Court that graffiti smeared in mud can amount to damage, even though it is easily washed off (*Roe* v *Kingerlee* [1986] Crim LR 735).

A good operational example of the courts' approach can be seen in *R* v *Fiak* [2005] EWCA Crim 2381. In that case the defendant had been arrested and placed in a police cell which he flooded by stuffing a blanket down the cell lavatory and repeatedly flushing. The defendant argued that there was no evidence that the blanket or the cell had been 'damaged'; the water had been clean and both the blanket and the cell could be used again when dry. The Court of Appeal disagreed and held that, while the effect of the defendant's actions in relation to the blanket and the cell was remediable, the reality was that the blanket could not be used until it had been dried and the flooded cell was out of action until the water had been cleared. Therefore both had sustained damage for the purposes of the Act.

It can be seen therefore that putting property temporarily out of use—even for a short time and in circumstances where it will revert to its former state of its own accord—may fall within the definition of 'damage'.

1.15.2.3 Property

Property is defined in the 1971 Act by s. 10 which states:

(1) In this Act 'property' means property of a tangible nature, whether real or personal, including money and—
  (a) including wild creatures which have been tamed or are ordinarily kept in captivity and any other wild creatures or their carcasses if, but only if, they have been reduced into possession...or are in the course of being reduced into possession; but
  (b) not including mushrooms growing wild on any land or flowers, fruit or foliage of a plant growing wild on any land.
  ...

KEYNOTE

This definition has similarities with the definition of 'property' for the purposes of theft (**see chapter 1.13**) but 'real' property (i.e. land and things attached to it) can be damaged even though it cannot be stolen. Trampling flower beds, digging up cricket pitches, chopping down trees in a private garden and even pulling up genetically-modified crops may all amount to criminal damage if accompanied by the required circumstances.

Pets or farm animals are property for the purposes of this Act. Cases of horses being mutilated would, in addition to the offence of 'cruelty' itself, amount to criminal damage. There may also be occasions—such as domestic or neighbour disputes—involving harm or cruelty to such animals where it will be more appropriate and effective to consider offences under the 1971 Act.

1.15.2.4 Belonging to Another

Section 10 states:

(2) Property shall be treated for the purposes of this Act as belonging to any person—
  (a) having the custody or control of it;
  (b) having in it any proprietary right or interest (not being an equitable interest arising only from an agreement to transfer or grant an interest); or
  (c) having a charge on it.

KEYNOTE

This extended meaning of 'belonging to another' is similar to that used in the Theft Act 1968. One result is that if a person damages his/her own property, he/she may still commit the offence of simple criminal damage if that property also 'belongs to' someone else.

1.15.2.5 Lawful excuse

Section 5 of the Criminal Damage Act 1971 provides for two occasions where a defendant may have a 'lawful excuse'. These can be remembered as 'permission' (s. 5(2)(a)) and 'protection' (s. 5(2)(b)). Both involve the belief of the defendant. The wording of s. 5 indicates that these particular defences are not the only ones available to a charge of criminal damage and other general defences (**see chapter 1.4**) may apply.

1.15.2.6 Permission

A person shall be treated as having lawful excuse under s. 5(2):

    (a) if at the time of the act or acts alleged to constitute the offence he believed that the person or persons whom he believed to be entitled to consent to the destruction of or damage to the property in question had so consented, or would have so consented to it if he or they had known of the destruction or damage and its circumstances . . .

KEYNOTE

An example of 'lawful excuse' under s. 5(2)(a) would be if you, as a police officer, were asked by a motorist to help them get into their partner's car after locking the keys inside. If, during that attempt you damaged the rubber window surround, s. 5(2)(a) would provide you with a statutory defence to any later charge of criminal damage by the owner. The key elements here would be:

- the consent of someone whom you believed to be entitled to consent to that damage, and
- the circumstances under which it was caused.

If the driver was not available and your reason for opening the door was to get a better look at some personal documents for intelligence purposes, it is unlikely that the driver or the owner would have consented, either to the damage or the circumstances in which it was caused. Therefore you could not use this particular defence.

1.15.2.7 Protection

A person shall be treated as having lawful excuse under s. 5(2):

    (b) if he destroyed or damaged or threatened to destroy or damage the property in question or, in the case of a charge of an offence under section 3 above, intended to use or cause or permit the use of something to destroy or damage it, in order to protect property belonging to himself or another or a right or interest in property which was or which he believed to be vested in himself or another, and at the time of the act or acts alleged to constitute the offence he believed—
      (i) that the property, right or interest was in immediate need of protection; and
      (ii) that the means of protection adopted or proposed to be adopted were or would be reasonable having regard to all the circumstances.

KEYNOTE

Situations where such a defence can be used involve causing damage to property in order to protect other property. This defence also applies to the offence of having articles for causing damage (**see para. 1.15.6**). Key features of this defence are the immediacy of the need to protect the property and the reasonableness of the means of protection adopted. This defence has attracted the most attention of the courts in cases involving demonstrators claiming to be acting in furtherance of their political beliefs. For instance, in a case involving 'peace campaigners' it was held that the threat presented by a possible nuclear attack in the future did not excuse the carrying of a hacksaw for cutting through the perimeter fence of an airbase (*R* v *Hill* (1989) 89 Cr App R 74).

Belief

The 1971 Act goes on to say that it is immaterial whether a 'belief' above was justified as long as it was honestly held (s. 5(3)). This test is problematic because, although it is supposed to be an *objective* one, the evidence will be based largely on what was going through a defendant's mind at the time—or sometimes what was *not* going through their mind! In *Jaggard* v *Dickinson* [1981] QB 527 the defendant had broken a window to get into a house. Being drunk at the time, she had got the wrong house but the court accepted that her belief (that it was the right house and that the owner would have consented) had been honestly held, and that it did not matter whether that belief was brought about by intoxication, stupidity, forgetfulness or inattention. That is not to say, however, that *any* honestly held belief will suffice. An example of someone claiming—though unsuccessfully—a defence under both s. 5(2)(a) and (b) can be seen in *Blake* v *DPP* [1993] Crim LR 586. There the defendant was a vicar who wished to protest against Great Britain's involvement in the Gulf War. In order to mark his disapproval, the defendant wrote a quotation from the Bible in ink on a pillar in front of the Houses of Parliament. He claimed:

- that he was carrying out God's instructions and therefore had a lawful excuse based on his belief that God was the person entitled to consent to such damage and that he had in fact consented or would have done so (s. 5(2)(a)); and
- that he had damaged the property as a reasonable means of protecting other property located in the Gulf from being damaged by warfare (s. 5(2)(b)).

Perhaps unsurprisingly the Divisional Court did not accept either proposition holding that, in the first case a belief in The Almighty's consent was not a 'lawful excuse' and, in the second, that the defendant's conduct was too remote from any immediate need to protect property in the Gulf States. The test in relation to the defendant's belief appears then to be largely subjective (i.e. what was/was not going on in his/her head at the time) but with an objective element in that the judge/magistrate(s) must decide whether, on the facts as believed by the defendant, his/her acts were capable of protecting property.

Taking a different tack, peace campaigners in *R* v *Jones (Margaret)* [2004] EWCA Crim 1981 argued that their fear of the consequences of war in Iraq—which they claimed to be illegal—prompted them to conspire to cause damage at an airbase and that such fear amounted both to duress (as to which **see para. 1.4.7**) and lawful excuse under s. 5(2)(b) above. The Court of Appeal held that a jury would be entitled to consider some of the subjective beliefs of the defendants in determining the reasonableness of their actions.

Finally, a demonstrator at the Guildhall Gallery knocked the head off a statue of Baroness Thatcher and claimed that he acted in fear for his son's future which had been placed in jeopardy by the joint actions of the US and UK governments, and for which Baroness Thatcher was partly responsible. His appeal against conviction brought under s. 5(2)(b)—with a few technicalities added on—failed (*R* v *Kelleher* [2003] EWCA Crim 2846).

The Act also states, at s. 5(4), that a right or interest in property includes any right or privilege in or over land, whether created by grant, licence or otherwise.

Section 5(5) allows for other general defences (**see chapter 1.4**) at criminal law to apply in addition to those listed under s. 5.

It is not an offence to damage your own property unless there are aggravating circumstances. Even if the intention in doing so is to carry out some further offence—such as a fraudulent insurance claim—this fact still does not make it an offence under s. 1(1) of the Criminal Damage Act 1971 (*R* v *Denton* [1981] 1 WLR 1446).

1.15.2.8 Recklessness

An offence of criminal damage under s. 1(1) can be proved by showing that the defendant was 'reckless'. The former concept of *objective* or 'Caldwell' recklessness (as set out in *Metropolitan Police Commissioner* v *Caldwell* [1982] AC 341) has now gone and the law has been restored to its former position by *R* v *G & R* [2003] UKHL 50. In that case, the House of Lords decided that 'recklessness' in the context of criminal damage did not mean something different from the previous requirement of 'malicious damage'—namely that the defendant had foreseen the risk yet gone on to take it. Their lordships held that a person acts recklessly for the purposes of s. 1(1) of the Act:

- with respect to a circumstance when he/she is aware of a risk that existed or would exist;
- with respect to a result or consequence when he/she is aware of a risk that it would occur and it is, in the circumstances known to him/her, unreasonable to take the risk.

In the *R* v *G & R* case, two children (aged 11 and 12) set fire to some newspapers in the rear yard of a shop premises while camping out. The children put the burning papers under a wheelie bin and left them, expecting the small fire to burn itself out on the concrete floor of the yard. In fact the fire spread causing around £1,000,000 of damage. Under the former law (*Caldwell*), the children were convicted on the basis that the risk of the fire would have been obvious to any reasonable bystander. However, their convictions were quashed by the House of Lords who reinstated the general subjective element described above.

1.15.3 Aggravated Damage

OFFENCE: **Aggravated damage—*Criminal Damage Act 1971, s. 1(2)***
- Triable on indictment • Life imprisonment

The Criminal Damage Act 1971, s. 1 states:

(2) A person who without lawful excuse destroys or damages any property, whether belonging to himself or another—
  (a) intending to destroy or damage any property or being reckless as to whether any property would be destroyed or damaged; and
  (b) intending by the destruction or damage to endanger the life of another or being reckless as to whether the life of another would be thereby endangered;
  shall be guilty of an offence.

KEYNOTE

The aggravating factor in this offence, and the reason why it attracts such a heavy maximum sentence, is the intention of endangering life or recklessness as to whether life is endangered. This form of 'aggravation' should not be confused with the 'racially or religiously aggravated' form of criminal damage.

The reference to 'without lawful excuse' does not refer to the statutory excuses under s. 5 which are not applicable here, but to general excuses such as self-defence or the prevention of crime.

For the relevant test of recklessness see para. 1.15.2.8.

You must also show that the defendant either intended or was reckless as to each of the following consequences:

- the damage being caused, and
- the *resultant* danger to life.

It does not matter that the *actual* damage caused by the defendant turned out to be minor. What matters is the *potential* for damage and danger created by the defendant's conduct.

Where a defendant set fire to furniture in a house which was unoccupied at the time, the court nevertheless found him guilty of this offence. The court's reasoning for doing so turned on the fact that, had a reasonable bystander been present, he/she would have seen the possible risk that the fire might cause to the lives of others in the area, even though with hindsight it was shown that there had been no likelihood of the fire spreading to neighbouring properties (*R* v *Sangha* [1988] 1 WLR 519). This decision was taken while the concept of 'objective' or *Caldwell* recklessness was still in place for criminal damage offences. As a result, it will need to be reconsidered and it will probably be necessary to show that there *was* some likelihood of life being endangered. In this case there was clearly recklessness as to the damage caused *and* recklessness as to the danger to life *presented by the damage*. In contrast, where a defendant fired a gun through a window pane he was clearly reckless as to the damage his actions would cause. However, the court felt that, even though two people were standing behind the window and that they were obviously put in some danger, it was the *missile* which endangered their lives and not the result of the damage. Therefore the court held that the defendant was not guilty of this particular offence (*R* v *Steer* [1988] AC 111). This distinction seems to be a fine one, particularly if you are the person behind the window.

If someone were to smash the windscreen of a moving car or to cause a large display window to collapse into a busy street, this would probably be enough to support a charge under s. 1(2) (see *R* v *Webster* [1995] 2 All ER 168).

1.15.4 Arson

OFFENCE: **Arson—*Criminal Damage Act 1971, s. 1(3)***

• Triable either way • Life imprisonment on indictment • Where life is not endangered six months' imprisonment and/or a fine summarily

The Criminal Damage Act 1971, s. 1 states:

(3) An offence committed under this section by destroying or damaging property by fire shall be charged as arson.

KEYNOTE

In any of the above cases of criminal damage, if the destruction or damage is caused by fire, the offence will be charged as 'arson'. Given the potential for extensive damage and danger to life that fire-raising has, the restrictions on the mode of trial for simple damage under s. 1(1) do not apply to cases of arson.

Again, in light of the potential for serious injury and death, the link between this offence and the various homicide offences (**see chapter 1.5**) often arises. An example of where criminal liability for either gross negligence or unlawful act manslaughter arose from an offence of arson can be seen in *R* v *Willoughby* [2004] EWCA Crim 3365. In that case the defendant enlisted the help of another man in burning down a public house on which the defendant owed money. Having poured petrol around the inside of the building, the defendant set fire to it, killing the other person and injuring himself in the process. The defendant was convicted of both arson and manslaughter. The Court of Appeal held that by convicting the defendant of arson, the jury had showed that they were sure that he (on his own or jointly) had deliberately spread petrol by being reckless or with the intention that the premises would be destroyed. Provided that such conduct had been the cause of the death, the jury were therefore also bound to convict the defendant of manslaughter.

Aggravated damage caused by arson is triable only on indictment and carries a maximum penalty of life imprisonment.

1.15.5 Threats to Destroy or Damage Property

OFFENCE: **Threats to destroy or damage property—**
Criminal Damage Act 1971, s. 2

- Triable either way • Ten years' imprisonment on indictment • Six months' imprisonment and/or a fine summarily

The Criminal Damage Act 1971, s. 2 states:

A person who without lawful excuse makes to another a threat, intending that that other would fear it would be carried out,—
(a) to destroy or damage any property belonging to that other or a third person; or
(b) to destroy or damage his own property in a way which he knows is likely to endanger the life of that other or a third person;
shall be guilty of an offence.

KEYNOTE

This is an offence of *intention*, that is, the key element is the defendant's intention that the person receiving the threat fears it would be carried out.

The s. 2 offence is very straightforward: there is no need to show that the other person actually feared or even believed that the threat would be carried out. There is no need to show that the defendant intended to carry it out; nor does it matter whether the threat was even capable of being carried out.

....

EXAMPLE

If a person, enraged by a neighbour's inconsiderate parking, shouts over the garden wall, '*When you've gone to bed I'm going to T-cut that heap with paint stripper!*', the offence will be complete, provided you can show that the person making the threat intended the neighbour to fear it would be carried out.

Where a group of protestors staged a protest in the pods of the London Eye and threatened to set fire to themselves, their conduct was held by the Court of Appeal to be capable of amounting to a threat to damage the property of another contrary to s. 2(a) (*R* v *Cakmak* [2002] EWCA Crim 500).

In *Cakmak* the court held that the gist of the offence under s. 2(a) was the making of a threat and that any such threat had to be considered objectively.

Whether:

- there has been such a threat to another
- the threat amounted to 'a threat to damage or destroy property'
- the defendant had the necessary state of mind at the time

are all questions of fact for the jury to decide (per *Cakmak*).

....

While not usually enough to amount to the substantive offence under s. 2 above, a person's *conduct* which represents a threat to damage property may be relevant in triggering police action. This can be seen in yet another case involving a political protest against war. In *Clements* v *DPP* [2005] EWHC 1279 (Admin) several protestors left a public highway, crossed a ditch and approached the perimeter fence of an RAF base. The defendant ignored a police warning to return to the road and the police attempted to restrain the protestors in order to prevent criminal damage to the fence. After a scuffle the defendant was subsequently convicted of assaulting a police constable in the execution of his duty (as to which **see para. 1.8.3.3**). The key issues at trial were whether the police officer had acted in the course of his duty and the extent to which the officer had reasonable grounds to believe that the defendant would cause criminal damage. The Divisional Court held that the officer had to consider the whole event in context and at the relevant time a political protest was ensuing; the defendant had deliberately left the public highway and refused to return to it; he had no legitimate reason to approach the fence; and it was plainly reasonable for the police officer to believe that he could cause criminal damage to the fence.

1.15.6 Having Articles with Intent to Destroy or Damage Property

OFFENCE: **Having Articles with Intent to Destroy or Damage Property—**
Criminal Damage Act 1971, s. 3

- Triable either way • Ten years' imprisonment on indictment • Six months' imprisonment and/or a fine summarily

The Criminal Damage Act 1971, s. 3 states:

A person who has anything in his custody or under his control intending without lawful excuse to use it or cause or permit another to use it—
(a) to destroy or damage any property belonging to some other person; or
(b) to destroy or damage his own or the user's property in a way which he knows is likely to endanger the life of some other person;
shall be guilty of an offence.

KEYNOTE

This offence covers *anything* which a defendant has '*in his custody or under his control*', a deliberately broader term than 'possession'.

As a result, this offence applies to graffiti 'artists' carrying aerosols and advertisers with adhesives for sticking illicit posters. The key element, once again, is an *intention*. This time the required intention is that the 'thing' be used to cause criminal damage to another's property or to the defendant's own property in a way which he/she knows is likely to endanger the life of another. Such articles are now 'prohibited' articles for the purposes of the power of stop and search under s. 1 of the Police and Criminal Evidence Act 1984 (**see General Police Duties, chapter 4.7**).

A conditional intent—that is, an intent to use something to cause criminal damage if the need arises—will be enough (*R* v *Buckingham* (1976) 63 Cr App R 159).

Just as it is not an offence to damage your own property in a way which endangers no one else, neither is it an offence to have something which you intend to use to cause damage under those circumstances.

EXAMPLE

If the owner of a 10 metre high conifer decides to trim the top with a chainsaw and a ladder, putting himself—but no one else—at considerable risk, he commits no offence, either by causing the damage or by having the chainsaw. If he intends to fell the tree in a way which he realises will endanger the life of his neighbours or passers by, then he may commit the offence under s. 3(b).

Police Powers

There is a statutory power to apply to a magistrate for a search warrant under s. 6.

1.15.7 Penalty and Removal Notices for Graffiti

Where an authorised officer of a local authority has reason to believe that a person has committed a relevant offence in the area of that authority, he/she may give that person a penalty notice under s. 43 of the Anti-social Behaviour Act 2003 (unless the offence amounts to a racially or religiously aggravated damage offence).

Examples of a 'relevant offence' include:

- s. 1(1) of the Criminal Damage Act 1971 which involves only the painting or writing on, or the soiling, marking or other defacing of, any property by whatever means
- s. 132(1) of the Highways Act 1980 (painting or affixing things on structures on the highway etc.)
- para. 10 of s. 54 of the Metropolitan Police Act 1839 (affixing posters etc.)
- s. 20(1) of the London County Council (General Powers) Act 1954 (defacement of streets with slogans etc.)
- s. 131(2) of the Highways Act 1980 (including that provision as applied by s. 27(6) of the Countryside Act 1968) which involves only an act of obliteration
- s. 224(3) of the Town and Country Planning Act 1990 (displaying advertisement in contravention of regulations). (s. 44).

Police community support officers and accredited employees under schs 4 and 5 to the Police Reform Act 2002 can be given the power to issue these penalty notices.

In addition, where a local authority is satisfied that a relevant surface in an area has been defaced by graffiti and the defacement is detrimental to the amenity of the area or is offensive, the authority may serve a defacement removal notice upon any person who is responsible (s. 48). A 'relevant surface' means broadly the surface of any street or of any building, structure or other object in or on any street, or the surface of any land owned, occupied or controlled by an educational institution or any building, structure etc. on any such land (see s. 48(9)). For further practical advice in relation to these powers see the guidance provided by the Secretary of State under s. 50.

OFFENCE: **Sale of Aerosol Paint to Children—*Anti-social Behaviour Act 2003, s. 54***
- Triable summarily • Fine

The Anti-social Behaviour Act 2003, s. 54 states:

(1) A person commits an offence if he sells an aerosol paint container to a person under the age of sixteen.

(2) ...

(3) ...

(4) It is a defence for a person charged with an offence under this section in respect of a sale to prove that—
  (a) he took all reasonable steps to determine the purchaser's age, and
  (b) he reasonably believed that the purchaser was not under the age of sixteen.

(5) It is a defence for a person charged with an offence under this section in respect of a sale effected by another person to prove that he (the defendant) took all reasonable steps to avoid the commission of an offence under this section.

KEYNOTE

An 'aerosol paint container' means a device which contains paint stored under pressure, and is designed to permit the release of the paint as a spray (s. 54(2)).

Once the elements in relation to the selling and the age of the buyer are proved, the offence is complete. There is no need to show that the person buying the aerosol intended to use it for causing damage (though if this can be shown, the offence under s. 3 of the Criminal Damage Act 1971 should be considered—**see para. 1.15.6**).

Note the two different elements of the defence that will be available in the relevant circumstances under subss. (4) and (5) above.

1.15.8 Contamination or Interference with Goods

OFFENCE: **Contamination or Interference with Goods—*Public Order Act 1986, s. 38(1)***

- Triable either way • Ten years' imprisonment and/or a fine on indictment • Six months' imprisonment and/or a fine summarily

The Public Order Act 1986, s. 38 states:

(1) It is an offence for a person, with the intention—
   (a) of causing public alarm or anxiety, or
   (b) of causing injury to members of the public consuming or using the goods, or
   (c) of causing economic loss to any person by reason of the goods being shunned by members of the public, or
   (d) of causing economic loss to any person by reason of steps taken to avoid any such alarm or anxiety, injury or loss,
   to contaminate or interfere with goods, or make it appear that goods have been contaminated or interfered with, or to place goods which have been contaminated or interfered with, or which appear to have been contaminated or interfered with in a place where goods of that description are consumed, used, sold or otherwise supplied.
(2) It is also an offence for a person, with any such intention as is mentioned in paragraph (a), (c) or (d) of subsection (1), to threaten that he or another will do, or to claim that he or another has done, any of the acts mentioned in that subsection.
(3) It is an offence for a person to be in possession of any of the following articles with a view to the commission of an offence under subsection (1)—
   (a) materials to be used for contaminating or interfering with goods or making it appear that goods have been contaminated or interfered with, or
   (b) goods which have been contaminated or interfered with, or which appear to have been contaminated or interfered with.
(4) ...
(5) In this section 'goods' includes substances whether natural or manufactured and whether or not incorporated in or mixed with other goods.
(6) The reference in subsection (2) to a person claiming that certain acts have been committed does not include a person who in good faith reports or warns that such acts have been, or appear to have been, committed.

KEYNOTE

Section 38 creates two offences. The first involves the contamination of, interference with or placing of goods with the intentions set out at s. 38(1)(a)–(d).

Section 38(2) involves the making of threats to do, *or* the claiming *to have done* any of the acts in s. 38(1), with any of the intentions set out at s. 38(1)(a), (c) or (d). It is difficult to see how a threat or claim made with the intention of causing injury to the public (s. 38(1)(b)) would not also amount to an intention to cause them alarm or anxiety.

Given the sensitivity of food preparation and production to some sections of the community, there may be occasions where deliberate interference with foodstuffs amounts to an offence of racially or religiously aggravated criminal damage.

Section 38(6) allows for people to communicate warnings in good faith where such acts appear to have been committed.

Where threats to contaminate goods are made there may also be grounds for charging blackmail. A good example of this offence—and the overlap with blackmail—is the case of *R* v *Witchelo* (1991) 13 Cr App R (S) 371 where the defendant, a police officer, was sentenced to 13 years' imprisonment after obtaining £32,000 from food producers to whom he had sent threatening letters.

1.16 Offences Against the Administration of Justice and Public Interest

1.16.1 Introduction

This chapter deals with a wide range of offences against the administration of justice and also the public interest. The first group of offences involve some form of interference with the machinery of justice such as perjury and witness intimidation, while others have an indirect effect on the process.

1.16.2 Perjury

OFFENCE: **Perjury in Judicial Proceeding—*Perjury Act 1911, s. 1***
- Triable on indictment • Seven years' imprisonment

The Perjury Act 1911, s. 1 states:

(1) If any person lawfully sworn as a witness or as an interpreter in a judicial proceeding wilfully makes a statement material in that proceeding, which he knows to be false or does not believe to be true, he shall be guilty of perjury...

(2) The expression 'judicial proceeding' includes a proceeding before any court, tribunal, or person having by law power to hear, receive, and examine evidence on oath.

(3) Where a statement made for the purposes of a judicial proceeding is not made before the tribunal itself, but is made on oath before a person authorised by law to administer an oath to the person who makes the statement, and to record or authenticate the statement, it shall, for the purposes of this section, be treated as having been made in a judicial proceeding.

KEYNOTE

To commit this offence a defendant must have been *lawfully sworn* (see the Evidence Act 1851, s. 16). The statement made in 'judicial proceeding' can be one given orally before the court or tribunal, or it can be given in the form of an affidavit (sworn statement). If a witness tenders a false statement used under s. 89 of the Criminal Justice Act 1967, he/she commits a separate, lesser offence (see para. 1.16.3).

'Wilful' in this case means deliberate as opposed to accidental.

A 'statement material in that proceeding' means that the content of the evidence tendered in that case must have some importance to it and not just be of passing relevance. Whether something is material to a case is a question of law for a judge to decide. Whether a motorist had taken a drink between the time of his/her having a road traffic accident and being breathalysed would be such a material issue, and to get

---

a witness to provide false evidence about that matter would be a 'statement material in that proceeding' (*R* v *Lewins* (1979) 1 Cr App R (S) 246).

To prove perjury you must also show that the defendant *knew* the statement to be false or *did not believe it to be true*.

Evidence of an opinion provided by a witness who does not genuinely hold such an opinion may also be perjury.

Perjury may be proved by using a court transcript or the evidence of others who were present at the proceeding in question (see Perjury Act 1911, s. 14).

Corroboration is required in cases of perjury (see Perjury Act 1911, s. 13). The requirement for corroboration is solely in relation to the *falsity* of the defendant's statement. There is no requirement under s. 13 for corroboration of the fact that the defendant *actually made* the alleged statement, nor that he/she knew or believed it to be untrue. However, as that corroboration can be documentary and may even come from the defendant's earlier conduct (*R* v *Threlfall* (1914) 10 Cr App R 112) this requirement does not appear to present much of a hurdle to the prosecution.

Evidence given by live TV link under the provisions of the Criminal Justice Act 1988, s. 32 is also subject to the offence of perjury.

1.16.2.1 Aiding and Abetting

OFFENCE: **Aiding and Abetting Perjury—*Perjury Act 1911, s. 7***
- If principal offence is contrary to s.1 triable on indictment • Seven years' imprisonment • Otherwise either way • Two years' imprisonment on indictment
- Six months' imprisonment and/or a fine summarily

The Perjury Act 1911, s. 7 states:

(1) Every person who aids, abets, counsels, procures, or suborns another person to commit an offence against this Act shall be liable to be proceeded against, indicted, tried and punished as if he were a principal offender.

(2) Every person who incites...another person to commit an offence against this Act shall be guilty of a misdemeanour.

KEYNOTE

'Subornation' is the same as procuring. This specific section does not appear to add anything to the general offences of aiding and abetting principal offenders (see chapter 1.2).

1.16.3 Offences Similar to Perjury

OFFENCE: **False Statements in Criminal Proceedings—*Criminal Justice Act 1967, s. 89***
- Triable either way • Two years' imprisonment and/or a fine on indictment
- Six months' imprisonment and/or a fine summarily

The Criminal Justice Act 1967, s. 89 states:

(1) If any person in a written statement tendered in evidence in criminal proceedings by virtue of section 9 of this Act, or in proceedings before a court-martial...wilfully makes a statement material in those proceedings which he knows to be false or does not believe to be true, he shall be liable...
(2) The Perjury Act 1911 shall have effect as if this section were contained in that Act.

OFFENCE: **False Statements on Oath—*Perjury Act 1911, s. 2***
- Triable either way • Seven years' imprisonment and/or a fine on indictment • Six months' imprisonment and/or a fine summarily

The Perjury Act 1911, s. 2 states:

If any person—
(1) being required or authorised by law to make any statement on oath for any purpose, and being lawfully sworn (otherwise than in a judicial proceeding) wilfully makes a statement which is material for that purpose and which he knows to be false or does not believe to be true; ...

he shall be [guilty of an offence].

KEYNOTE

The first offence covers witnesses who tender false statements in criminal proceedings. The second offence covers the making of false statements under an oath which is not sworn in connection with a judicial proceeding.

1.16.4 Perverting the Course of Justice

OFFENCE: **Perverting the Course of Justice—*Common Law***
- Triable on indictment • Life imprisonment and/or a fine

It is an offence at common law to do an act tending and intended to pervert the course of public justice.

KEYNOTE

'The course of public justice' includes the process of criminal investigation (see *R* v *Rowell* (1977) 65 Cr App R 174).

Although traditionally referred to—and charged—as 'attempting' to pervert the course of justice, it is recognised that behaviour which is *aimed* at perverting the course of public justice does just that and the substantive offence should be charged (see *R* v *Williams* (1991) 92 Cr App R 158).

One way in which this offence is commonly committed is where a prisoner uses a false identity when he/she is arrested. Although the offence of perverting the course of justice may be made out in these—or similar—circumstances in connection with a number of other substantive offences, the Court of Appeal has held that, in many cases, the addition of such a charge is unnecessary and only serves to complicate the sentencing process (*R* v *Sookoo* [2002] EWCA Crim 800). Where, as in *Sookoo*, a defendant makes an unsophisticated attempt to hide their identity and fails, the court felt that a specific separate count of perverting the course of justice should not be laid. If it was shown that there were serious aggravating features, for instance where a lot of police time and resources had been involved or innocent members of the public had been arrested as a result, a specific charge may be appropriate and could be justified.

Perverting the course of justice requires positive acts by the defendant, not merely standing by and allowing an injustice to take place, i.e. omissions. The offence will include cases where evidence is deliberately destroyed, concealed or falsified as well as cases where witnesses and jurors are intimidated.

Admitting to a crime to enable the true offender to avoid prosecution would fall under this offence (*R* v *Devito* [1975] Crim LR 175), as would abusing your authority as a police officer to excuse someone of a criminal charge (*R* v *Coxhead* [1986] RTR 411). Other examples include:

- making a false allegation of an offence (*R* v *Goodwin* (1989) 11 Cr App R (S) 194 (rape), and consider the more recent example of Metropolitian Police Commander Ali Dizaei who made a false allegation of assault and was convicted of this offence);
- giving another person's personal details when being reported for an offence (*R* v *Hurst* (1990) 12 Cr App R (S) 373);
- destroying and concealing evidence of a crime (*R* v *Kiffin* [1994] Crim LR 449).

It is important that the requisite intention is proved in every case as that intention cannot be implied, even from admitted facts (*R* v *Lalani* [1999] 1 Cr App R 481).

Where a person makes a false allegation to the police justifying a criminal investigation with the possible consequences of detention, arrest, charge or prosecution and that person intends that the allegation be taken seriously, the offence of perverting the course of justice is *prima facie* made out—whether or not the allegation is capable of identifying specific individuals. This is clear from *R* v *Cotter* [2002] EWCA Crim 1033, a case involving the boyfriend of a well-known black Olympic athlete who claimed to have been attacked as part of a racist campaign.

1.16.5 Considerations Affecting Witnesses, Jurors and Others

Great care is needed by police officers in handling witnesses. Any behaviour that is seen as interfering with witnesses (or potential witnesses) by promises of favours and rewards or by threats will be a contempt of court (see *R* v *Kellett* [1975] 3 All ER 468). However, there is no 'property' in a witness. Protecting witnesses is one thing but trying to restrict the way in which defendants and/or their legal advisers obtain evidence for their defence—e.g. by properly approaching witnesses—can also amount to a contempt of court (see *Connolly* v *Dale* [1996] 1 All ER 224).

So far as the police are concerned there are several significant areas of common and statute law to consider when considering witnesses. The main legislative provisions are set out below.

The Serious Organised Crime and Police Act 2005 sets out specific provisions relating to witness protection arrangements. In fact these arrangements stretch beyond witnesses and extend to a series of people involved in the criminal justice process, including people who are *or have been*:

- constables
- employees accredited under the Police Reform Act 2002
- jurors
- magistrates (or their equivalent outside the United Kingdom)
- holders of judicial office (whether in the United Kingdom or elsewhere)
- the DPP, criminal prosecutors and staff of the Crown Prosecution Service

(see the Serious Organised Crime and Police Act 2005, sch. 5).

Chapter 4 of the Act allows for the making of arrangements to protect these and other relevant people ordinarily resident in the United Kingdom where the 'protection provider' (usually the Chief Officer of Police or the Director General of the Serious Organised Crime Agency) considers that the person's safety is at risk by virtue of their being a witness, constable, juror etc. (s. 82(1)). A protection provider may vary or cancel any arrangements made by him/her under subs. (1) if he/she considers it appropriate to do so. Joint arrangements (e.g. between police forces) can be made where appropriate, and public authorities (other than courts and tribunals or parliament) are under a duty to take reasonable steps to assist protection providers where requested to do so (see ss. 83 and 85).

1.16.5.1 Witnesses or Jurors in Investigation or Proceedings for an Offence

The first measure can be found in the Criminal Justice and Public Order Act 1994.

OFFENCE: **Intimidating Witnesses and Jurors—*Criminal Justice and Public Order Act 1994, s. 51***
- Triable either way • Five years' imprisonment and/or a fine on indictment
- Six months' imprisonment and/or a fine summarily

The Criminal Justice and Public Order Act 1994, s. 51 states:

(1) A person commits an offence if—
  (a) he does an act which intimidates, and is intended to intimidate, another person ('the victim'),
  (b) he does the act knowing or believing that the victim is assisting in the investigation of an offence or is a witness or potential witness or a juror or potential juror in proceedings for an offence, and
  (c) he does it intending thereby to cause the investigation or the course of justice to be obstructed, perverted or interfered with.
(2) A person commits an offence if—
  (a) he does an act which harms, and is intended to harm, another person or, intending to cause another person to fear harm, he threatens to do an act which would harm that other person,
  (b) he does or threatens to do the act knowing or believing that the person harmed or threatened to be harmed ('the victim'), or some other person, has assisted in an investigation into an offence or has given evidence or particular evidence in proceedings for an offence, or has acted as a juror or concurred in a particular verdict in proceedings for an offence, and
  (c) he does or threatens to do it because of that knowledge or belief.
(3) For the purposes of subsections (1) and (2) it is immaterial that the act is or would be done, or that the threat is made—
  (a) otherwise than in the presence of the victim, or
  (b) to a person other than the victim.
(4) The harm that may be done or threatened may be financial as well as physical (whether to the person or a person's property) and similarly as respects an intimidatory act which consists of threats.
(5) The intention required by subsection (1)(c) and the motive required by subsection (2)(c) above need not be the only or the predominating intention or motive with which the act is done or, in the case of subsection (2), threatened.

KEYNOTE

As discussed above, this section is aimed at protecting people involved in the investigation or trial of criminal offences.

These offences are designed to exist alongside the common-law offence of perverting the course of justice, and there will be circumstances which may fall under both the statutory and the common-law offences.

This is an offence of 'specific intent' or perhaps even multiple intent as it must be shown that the act was done with the intentions set out in s. 51(1)(a) and (c). It must also be shown that the defendant knew or believed the other person to be assisting in the investigation of an offence or that he/she was going to testify/appear on the jury in proceedings for an offence.

In a decision which appears to contradict the specific wording of the statute (s. 51(1)(a), 'he does an act which intimidates, and is intended to intimidate, another person') the Court of Appeal has confirmed that 'an act which intimidates' does not have to result in the victim *actually* being intimidated; so no intimidation 'result' from the defendant's actions is required even though the statute appears to require one. Therefore if a defendant seeks to deter a witness from giving evidence by intimidating him/her, the offence could be made out even if the victim was not actually in fear.

In *R* v *Patrascu* [2004] EWCA Crim 2417, the court provided further detail with regard to interpretation of the term 'intimidation'. The court held that a person did an act which intimidated another within the meaning of s. 51(1) if he/she put that other person in fear, or sought by threat or violence to deter him/her from some relevant action such as giving evidence. However, mere pressure which did not put the victim in fear or contained no element of threat or violence was insufficient. In other words, whilst not requiring an intimidation 'result', the defendant must do something more than just pressurising a victim to be guilty of the offence.

'Harm' for the purposes of s. 51(2) means physical harm and not simply an assault or battery. Therefore spitting at a person does not amount to 'harm' for these purposes (even though it would amount to other public order or assault offences) (*R* v *Normanton* [1998] Crim LR 220).

Section 51(2) provides a similar offence for acts done or threatened in the knowledge or belief that the person, *or another person*, has so assisted or taken part in proceedings. Doing acts to third parties in order to intimidate or harm the relevant person is also covered by this offence (s. 51(3)). Making threats by telephone will amount to 'doing an act to another' (*DPP* v *Mills* [1997] QB 300).

Section 51(8) creates a statutory presumption under certain circumstances that the defendant had the required motive at the time of his/her actions or threats.

Making a *threat* via a third person knowing it will be passed on and that the ultimate recipient would be intimidated by it amounts to an offence under s. 51(1) (*Attorney-General's Reference (No. 1 of 1999)* [1999] 3 WLR 769).

The intention to obstruct, pervert or interfere with the course of justice need not be the only or even the main intention (s. 51(5)).

1.16.5.2 Intimidation of Witnesses in Other Proceedings

In addition to the measures aimed at protecting those involved in the investigation and trial of criminal offences, there are further statutory measures designed to protect witnesses and others who are (or may become) involved in other proceedings.

OFFENCE: **Intimidation of Witnesses—*Criminal Justice and Police Act 2001, s. 39***
- Triable either way • Five years' imprisonment on indictment • Six months' imprisonment and/or fine summarily

The Criminal Justice and Police Act 2001, s. 39 states:

(1) A person commits an offence if—
  (a) he does an act which intimidates, and is intended to intimidate, another person ('the victim');
  (b) he does the act—
    (i) knowing or believing that the victim is or may be a witness in any relevant proceedings; and
    (ii) intending, by his act, to cause the course of justice to be obstructed, perverted or interfered with;
    and
  (c) the act is done after the commencement of those proceedings.

KEYNOTE

This offence has some similarities to the Criminal Justice and Public Order Act 1994 offence in the earlier paragraph. References to doing an act include threats—against a person and/or their property—and the making of any other statement (s. 39(6)). The key difference is that this offence is concerned with protecting people who are in some way connected with 'relevant proceedings' which are '*any proceedings in or before the Court of Appeal, the High Court, the Crown Court or any county or magistrates' court which are not proceedings for an offence*' (s. 41(1)). This means that the offence will be relevant if the proceedings involved are civil proceedings in the higher courts or the county court or if they are non-offence proceedings in the Crown Court or magistrates' court. Examples of the latter would be a hearing to deal with a breach of a community order or an application for an anti-social behaviour order. You must show that the relevant proceedings had already commenced by the time of the offence.

Note that some proceedings, such as inquests or police conduct hearings, will not be covered by the s. 41 definition and therefore the offences above.

As with the Criminal Justice and Public Order Act offence, this requires proof of 'multiple' intent in that, as well as showing the intimidatory act, it must also be shown that the elements set out at s. 39(1)(a)–(c) are present. However, if you can prove that the defendant:

- did any act that intimidated, and was intended to intimidate, another person, and
- that he/she did that act knowing or believing that that other person was or might be a 'witness' in any relevant proceedings that had already commenced,

there will be a presumption that the defendant did the act with the intention of causing the course of justice to be obstructed, perverted or interfered with (s. 39(3)). This presumption is, however, rebuttable. 'Witness' here is a very wide expression and extends to anyone who provides, or is able to provide, any information, document or other thing which might be used in evidence in those proceedings (see s. 39(5)).

In proving the offence it is immaterial whether the act:

- is done in the presence of the victim
- is done to the victim himself/herself or to another person

or whether or not the intention to obstruct, pervert or interfere with the course of justice is the main intention of the person doing it (s. 39(2)).

This offence is intended to exist alongside the common law offence of perverting the course of justice.

1.16.6 Harming Witnesses

OFFENCE: **Harming Witnesses—*Criminal Justice and Police Act 2001, s. 40***
- Triable either way • Five years' imprisonment on indictment • Six months' imprisonment and/or fine summarily

The Criminal Justice and Police Act 2001, s. 40 states:

(1) A person commits an offence if in circumstances falling within subsection (2)—
    (a) he does an act which harms, and is intended to harm, another person; or
    (b) intending to cause another person to fear harm, he threatens to do an act which would harm that other person.
(2) The circumstances fall within this subsection if—
    (a) the person doing or threatening to do the act does so knowing or believing that some person (whether or not the person harmed or threatened or the person against whom harm is threatened) has been a witness in relevant proceedings; and
    (b) he does or threatens to do that act because of that knowledge or belief.

KEYNOTE

A distinction between this and the s. 39 offence is that the offence above refers to someone who *has been* (or is believed to have been) a witness in relevant proceedings. Again, 'witness' is very wide and extends to anyone who has provided any information, document, etc. which was (or might have been) used in evidence in those proceedings (see s. 40(7)). For 'relevant proceedings' see the s. 39 offence. This offence is aimed at the general protection of people who have been involved in relevant proceedings. Therefore there is no requirement here for any intention to pervert or interfere with the course of justice. The harm caused or threatened does not have to be directed towards the witness themselves; the key element is the motivation of the defendant. In relation to that motivation, the Act creates a presumption as follows. If you can prove that, between the start of the proceedings and one year after they are concluded, the defendant:

- did an act which harmed, and was intended to harm, another person, or

- threatened to do an act which would harm another person intending to cause that person to fear harm

with the knowledge or belief required by s. 40(2)(a) above, he/she will be presumed to have acted because of that knowledge or belief (s. 40(3)). Again, this is rebuttable. It is immaterial whether the act or threat is made (or would be carried out) in the presence of the person who is or would be harmed, or of the person threatened or whether the motive mentioned in s. 40(2)(b) is the main motive. The harm done or threatened can be physical or financial and can be made to a person or property (s. 40(4)).

1.16.7 Assisting Offenders

OFFENCE: **Assisting Offenders—*Criminal Law Act 1967, s. 4***
- Triable on indictment; either way if original offence is either way • Where sentence for original offence is fixed by law, ten years' imprisonment and/or a fine on indictment; six months' imprisonment and/or a fine summarily • Where sentence for original offence is 14 years' imprisonment, seven years' imprisonment and/or a fine on indictment; six months' imprisonment and/or a fine summarily • Where sentence for original offence is ten years imprisonment, five years' imprisonment and/or a fine on indictment; six months' imprisonment and/or a fine summarily • Otherwise three years' imprisonment and/or a fine on indictment; six months' imprisonment and/or a fine summarily

The Criminal Law Act 1967, s. 4 states:

(1) Where a person has committed a relevant offence, any other person who, knowing or be-lieving him to be guilty of the offence or of some other relevant offence, does without lawful authority or reasonable excuse any act with intent to impede his apprehension or prosecution shall be guilty of an offence.

(1A) In this section and section 5 below, 'relevant offence' means—

    (a) an offence for which the sentence is fixed by law,

    (b) an offence for which a person of 18 years or over (not previously convicted) may be sen-tenced to imprisonment for a term of five years (or might be so sentenced but for the restrictions imposed by section 33 of the Magistrates' Courts Act 1980).

KEYNOTE

This offence must involve some positive act by the defendant; simply doing or saying nothing will not suffice.

Although there is no duty on people to assist the police in their investigations generally, this offence and the one below create a negative duty not to interfere with investigations after an offence has taken place.

For there to be an offence under ss. 4 or 5 there must first have been a relevant offence committed by someone. That relevant offence must, in the case of the above offence, have been committed by the 'assisted' person.

The defendant can commit the offence before the person he/she has assisted is convicted of committing the relevant offence.

It must be shown that the defendant knew or believed the person to be guilty of that, *or some other* relevant offence. Therefore, if the defendant believed that the 'assisted' person had committed a robbery when in fact he/she had committed a theft, that mistaken part of the defendant's belief will not prevent a conviction for this offence.

Mere *suspicion*, however strong, that the 'assisted' person had committed a relevant offence will not be enough.

This offence requires the consent of the DPP before a prosecution is brought (s. 4(4)).

This offence cannot be 'attempted' (Criminal Attempts Act 1981, s. 1(4)).

1.16.8 Concealing Relevant Offences

OFFENCE: **Concealing Relevant Offences—*Criminal Law Act 1967, s. 5***

- Triable on indictment; either way if original offence is triable either way
- Two years' imprisonment on indictment • Six months' imprisonment and/or a fine summarily

The Criminal Law Act 1967, s. 5 states:

(1) Where a person has committed a relevant offence, any other person who, knowing or believing that the offence or some other relevant offence has been committed, and that he has inform-ation which might be of material assistance in securing the prosecution or conviction of an offender for it, accepts or agrees to accept for not disclosing that information any consider-ation other than the making good of loss or injury caused by the offence, or the making of reasonable compensation for that loss or injury, shall be liable . . .

KEYNOTE

This offence also requires the consent of the DPP before a prosecution can be brought (s. 5(3)).

It is also excluded from the provisions of the Criminal Attempts Act 1981 (s. 1(4)).

Again, someone must have committed a relevant offence before this particular offence can be committed. The main focus of this offence is:

- the acceptance of, or agreement to accept 'consideration' (i.e. anything of value)
- beyond reasonable compensation for loss/injury *caused by the relevant offence*
- in exchange for not disclosing material information.

'Disclosure' does not appear to be confined to information passed to the police. It would probably extend to other agencies with a duty to investigate offences but is perhaps even wider than that.

This offence requires proof, not only of the defendant's knowledge or belief that a relevant offence had been committed, but also that he/she has information that might be of material assistance in securing the *prosecution or conviction* of *an offender* for it. Given this very broad wording, the possession of information that might provide useful intelligence in an investigation into relevant offences may meet the requirements of s. 5, although *proving* that the defendant had the required knowledge or belief presents considerable practical problems.

1.16.9 Miscellaneous Offences Relating to Offenders

OFFENCE: **Escaping—*Common Law***
- Triable on indictment • Unlimited punishment

It is an offence at common law to escape from legal custody.

KEYNOTE

The 'custody' from which a person escapes must be shown to have been lawful. The offence applies to both police custody (or police detention—see the Police and Criminal Evidence Act 1984, s. 118) or custody following conviction.

Whether a person was 'in custody' is a question of fact and the word 'custody' is to be given its ordinary and natural meaning—*E* v *DPP* [2002] EWHC 433 (Admin). (See also *Richards* v *DPP* [1988] QB 701.) In proving that a person was in custody at a particular time it should be shown that his/her liberty was restricted in a way that meant that he/she was confined by another and that his/her freedom of movement was controlled; it is not necessary, however, to show that the person's actual ability to move around was physically impeded, e.g. in secure accommodation (*E* v *DPP* above).

People may be in lawful custody even if not directly in the custody of a sworn police officer, for example those people who are being dealt with by an investigating officer or escort officers under sch. 4 to the Police Reform Act 2002.

People detained under the Mental Health Act 1983, s. 136, are also in lawful custody.

If a defendant uses force to *break out* of a prison or a police station, he/she may commit an offence of prison breach, again at common law and attracting the same punishment and mode of trial as escaping.

Under the Prisoners (Return to Custody) Act 1995, s. 1, a person who has been temporarily released under the Prison Act 1952 commits a summary offence if he/she remains unlawfully at large or fails to respond to an order of recall to prison.

Escort officers designated under sch. 4 to the Police Reform Act 2002 have a duty to prevent the escape of people in their charge who they are escorting in accordance with their statutory powers (see the Police Reform Act 2002, sch. 4, part 4, para. 35).

OFFENCE: **Assisting Escape—*Prison Act 1952, s. 39***
- Triable on indictment • Ten years' imprisonment

The Prison Act 1952, s. 39 states:

(1) Any person who
    (a) assists a prisoner in escaping or attempting to escape from a prison, or
    (b) intending to facilitate the escape of a prisoner
        (i) brings, throws or otherwise conveys anything into prison,
        (ii) causes another person to bring, throw or otherwise convey anything into prison, or
        (ii) gives anything to a prisoner or leaves anything in any place (whether inside or outside a prison),
    is guilty of an offence.

OFFENCE: **Harbouring Offenders—*Criminal Justice Act 1961, s. 22(2)***
- Triable either way • Ten years' imprisonment and/or a fine on indictment
- Six months' imprisonment and/or a fine summarily

The Criminal Justice Act 1961, s. 22 states:

(2) If any person knowingly harbours a person who has escaped from a prison or other institution to which the said section thirty-nine applies, or who, having been sentenced in any part of the United Kingdom or in any of the Channel Islands or the Isle of Man to imprisonment or detention, is otherwise unlawfully at large, or gives to any such person any assistance with intent to prevent, hinder or interfere with his being taken into custody, he shall be liable...

KEYNOTE

The offences under s. 39 of the 1952 Act and s. 22 of the 1961 Act do not apply to a prisoner who escapes while in transit to or from prison (*R* v *Moss and Harte* (1986) 82 Cr App R 116).

There is a particular offence, punishable by two years' imprisonment, of inducing or assisting a patient detained in a mental hospital to escape or to absent themselves without leave (Mental Health Act 1983, s. 128).

1.16.10 Wasting Police Time

OFFENCE: **Wasting Police Time—*Criminal Law Act 1967, s. 5(2)***
- Triable summarily • Six months' imprisonment and/or a fine

The Criminal Law Act 1967, s. 5 states:

(2) Where a person causes any wasteful employment of the police by knowingly making to any person a false report tending to show that an offence has been committed, or to give rise to apprehension for the safety of any persons or property, or tending to show that he has information material to any police inquiry, he shall be liable...

1.16.11 Contempt of Court

Acts which amount to contempt of court can be divided into criminal and civil contempt. Criminal contempt is defined at common law as 'behaviour involving interference with the due administration of justice' (*Attorney-General* v *Newspaper Publishing plc* [1988] Ch 333 and see Blackstone's Criminal Practice 2010, section B14.69).

Contempt can be committed in many different ways including misbehaviour in court, publication of matters prejudicial to a trial and taking photographs inside a court building. For a full explanation of the subject together with the extensive powers of courts to deal with contempt, see *Blackstone's Criminal Practice 2010,* para. B14.69 *et seq.*

1.17 Offences Arising from Immigration, Asylum and People Exploitation

1.17.1 Introduction

Immigration, asylum and the criminal exploitation of people has become an increasingly significant area of criminal activity in England and Wales. As a result, the government's legislative programme has made important amendments to the law governing this area of policing, including the introduction of a number of serious criminal offences. The key aspects of the legislation are the subject of this chapter.

1.17.2 Illegal Entry into the United Kingdom

Illegal Entry into the United Kingdom is a controversial and pressing police issue. The law regulating immigration is substantial, extending far beyond the scope of this Manual. That legislation was itself reinforced by a raft of additional measures contained in the Immigration and Asylum Act 1999 designed to address the issues arising from asylum-seekers and also from those criminals who specialise in smuggling illegal entrants into the country. Then came 11 September 2001, prompting swift and significant changes to legislation in a number of jurisdictions throughout the world. As well as bringing changes in other areas of law, the Anti-terrorism, Crime and Security Act 2001 made several amendments in relation to immigration and asylum.

1.17.2.1 Nationality, Immigration and Asylum

While most of the relevant legislation is still contained in the Immigration Act 1971, that Act has been amended in relation to offences and powers, while the whole framework for nationality and asylum was created by the Nationality, Immigration and Asylum Act 2002.

The Act is split into seven parts, each addressing a different aspect of this vast subject. The more important aspects of the Act for the police can be found in part 7 which sets out a number of offences, the key aspects of which are set out in the remainder of this chapter. The 2002 Act has been reinforced and extended by the Asylum and Immigration (Treatment of Claimants etc.) Act 2004 which creates a number of significant criminal offences, some of which are addressed throughout this chapter.

In addition, the Home Office has published a Circular (HOC 70/2004) reminding police officers of the availability of deportation orders which are available on the recommendation of a court (see s. 3(6) of the Immigration Act 1971). Before a court can make such a recommendation the person to be deported must have been served with a warning notice at least seven days before sentence is imposed. Responsibility for service of such notices will usually fall to the police, and the Home Office Immigration and Nationality Directorate advises that such a notice should normally be served where a person who appears to be eligible for deportation is charged with an offence punishable by imprisonment.

1.17.2.2 Illegal Entry

OFFENCE: **Illegal Entry—*Immigration Act 1971, s. 24***

- Triable summarily • Six months' imprisonment and/or fine

The Immigration Act 1971, s. 24 states:

(1) A person who is not a British citizen shall be guilty of an offence . . . in any of the following cases—

(a) if contrary to this Act he knowingly enters the United Kingdom in breach of a deportation order or without leave;

(aa) . . .

(b) if, having only a limited leave to enter or remain in the United Kingdom, he knowingly either—

 (i) remains beyond the time limited by the leave; or

 (ii) fails to observe a condition of the leave;

(c) if, having lawfully entered the United Kingdom without leave by virtue of section 8(1) above, he remains without leave beyond the time allowed by section 8(1);

(d) if, without reasonable excuse, he fails to comply with any requirement imposed on him under Schedule 2 to this Act to report to a medical officer of health or to attend, or submit to a test or examination, as required by such an officer;

(e) if, without reasonable excuse, he fails to observe any restriction imposed on him under Schedule 2 or 3 to this Act as to residence, as to his employment or occupation or as to reporting to the police or to an immigration officer or to the Secretary of State;

(f) if he disembarks in the United Kingdom from a ship or aircraft after being placed on board under Schedule 2 or 3 to this Act with a view to his removal from the United Kingdom;

(g) if he leaves or seeks to leave the United Kingdom through the tunnel system in contravention of a restriction imposed by or under an Order in Council under section 3(7) of this Act.

1.17.2.3 Use of Deception to Enter or Remain

OFFENCE: **Use of Deception—*Immigration Act 1971, s. 24A***

- Triable either way • Two years' imprisonment on indictment • Six months' imprisonment and/or a fine summarily

The Immigration Act 1971, s. 24A states:

A person who is not a British citizen is guilty of an offence if, by means which include deception by him—

(a) he obtains or seeks to obtain leave to enter or remain in the United Kingdom; or

(b) he secures or seeks to secure the avoidance, postponement or revocation of enforcement action against him.

KEYNOTE

The first offence above (s. 24) is concerned generally with non-British citizens who enter the UK illegally or who 'overstay' having been granted only limited leave to be here; it also addresses occasions where such people disregard some other lawful requirements placed upon them. The reference in s. 24(1)(c) to 'section 8(1)' refers to the special provisions made for seamen, aircrew, etc. landing lawfully in the United Kingdom.

The second offence (s. 24A) is broadly aimed at the more calculated actions by non-British citizens to get (or try to get) leave to enter or stay in the United Kingdom, or to evade deportation. 'Deception' here would appear to have its ordinary meaning and is not defined within the 1971 Act. It is worth noting that the relevant criminal conduct by the defendant here can be *any means which include deception by him/her*. Therefore, although the entire course of conduct by the defendant need not amount to a deception, it will be necessary to show that the defendant himself/herself carried out some act of deception (e.g. giving false details, providing misleading information, etc.). It will not be enough for this offence to show that someone else practised a deception in order to bring about the consequences at s. 24A(1)(a) and (b) for another person (but see below for further offence of assisting and harbouring).

1.17.3 People Trafficking and Exploitation

A very specific and increasingly prevalent form of offence involving unlawful immigration is that falling under the general heading of 'people trafficking'.

1.17.3.1 Assisting Unlawful Immigration and Asylum-seekers

OFFENCE: **Assisting Unlawful Immigration to Member State— *Immigration Act 1971, s. 25***

- Triable either way • 14 years' imprisonment on indictment • Six months' imprisonment and/or a fine summarily

The Immigration Act 1971, s. 25 states:

(1) A person commits an offence if he—
  (a) does an act which facilitates the commission of a breach of immigration law by an individual who is not a citizen of the European Union,
  (b) knows or has reasonable cause for believing that the act facilitates the commission of a breach of immigration law by the individual, and
  (c) knows or has reasonable cause for believing that the individual is not a citizen of the European Union.

KEYNOTE

This very broadly worded offence requires that the defendant facilitated the commission of any breach of immigration law by someone who is not an EU citizen. 'Immigration law' means a law in a Member State and which controls, in respect of some or all people who are not nationals of the State, entitlement to enter, travel across or be in the State (s. 25(2)). The above section has been amended to allow the Secretary of State to make an order prescribing additional States which are to be regarded as 'Member States' for the purposes of the section if he/she considers it necessary for the purpose of complying with the United Kingdom's EU obligations (see s. 25(7)). A document issued by the relevant government of a Member State will be conclusive in certifying any matter of law in this regard (s. 25(3)).

You must show that, in doing so, the defendant knew or had reasonable cause for believing that both his/her act facilitated the commission of the breach of immigration law *and* also that the person was not an EU citizen.

This offence can be committed outside the United Kingdom by British citizens and others with relevant forms of British citizenship (see s. 25(4)).

It is worth noting the Court of Appeal's observations that drivers and others involved in these types of offences are often of good previous character—in fact that is one of the criteria by which they are selected by the main organisers so as not to arouse suspicion of the authorities (*R* v *Salem* (2003) LTL 5 February).

The courts' powers to order forfeiture of vehicles, ships and aircraft under s. 25C apply to this offence (see below).

OFFENCE: **Helping Asylum-seeker to Enter United Kingdom—**
Immigration Act 1971, s. 25A

- Triable either way • 14 years' imprisonment on indictment • Six months' imprisonment and/or a fine summarily

The Immigration Act 1971, s. 25A states:

(1) A person commits an offence if—
    (a) he knowingly and for gain facilitates the arrival in the United Kingdom of an individual, and
    (b) he knows or has reasonable cause to believe that the individual is an asylum-seeker.

KEYNOTE

In order to prove this particular offence you must show that the defendant acted in the knowledge that he/she was facilitating the arrival in the United Kingdom of a person whom he/she knew was (or had reasonable cause to believe to be) an asylum-seeker *and* that, in so doing, that he/she acted 'for gain'.

'Asylum-seeker' means a person who intends to claim that to remove him/her from, or require him/her to leave the United Kingdom would be contrary to the United Kingdom's obligations under the Refugee Convention or the Human Rights Convention (in each case as defined under s. 167(1) of the Immigration and Asylum Act 1999) (s. 25A(2)).

The above offence does not apply to anything done by a person acting on behalf of an organisation which aims to assist asylum-seekers and *does not charge for its services* (s. 25A(3)).

The courts' powers to order forfeiture of vehicles, ships and aircraft under s. 25C apply to this offence (see below). For the specific provisions setting out the penalties for operators of vehicles (including rail freight wagons), see the Immigration and Asylum Act 1999, s. 32.

OFFENCE: **Assisting Entry to United Kingdom in Breach of Deportation**
Order—_Immigration Act 1971, s. 25B_

- Triable either way • 14 years' imprisonment on indictment • Six months' imprisonment and/or a fine summarily

The Immigration Act 1971, s. 25B states:

(1) A person commits an offence if he—
    (a) does an act which facilitates a breach of a deportation order in force against an individual who is a citizen of the European Union, and

(b) knows or has reasonable cause for believing that the act facilitates a breach of the deportation order.

(2) ...

(3) A person commits an offence if he—

(a) does an act which assists the individual to arrive in, enter or remain in the United Kingdom,

(b) knows or has reasonable cause for believing that the act assists the individual to arrive in, enter or remain in the United Kingdom, and

(c) knows or has reasonable cause for believing that the Secretary of State has personally directed that the individual's exclusion from the United Kingdom is conducive to the public good.

KEYNOTE

As with the earlier offences under s. 25 and 25A, the state of mind here is important to note.

For the first offence, there must be a deportation order in force and this will need to be proved before someone can be convicted. Additionally, the defendant must have known or had reasonable cause for believing that his/her act facilitated a breach of that order (therefore he/she must have known/had reasonable cause to believe that there was such an order in existence). This offence also applies where the Secretary of State personally directs that the exclusion from the United Kingdom of an individual who is a citizen of the European Union is conducive to the public good (an exclusion order) (s. 25B(2)).

The second offence is broader in scope than the offence under s. 25A (see above) and applies to acts that assist the person to arrive in, enter or remain in the United Kingdom. Again, however, the relevant knowledge or cause for belief are crucial.

The courts' powers to order forfeiture of vehicles, ships and aircraft under s. 25C apply to this offence (see below).

1.17.3.2 Powers of Seizure and Forfeiture

Where a person has been arrested for an offence under ss. 25, 25A or 25B, a police officer may detain any vehicle or certain smaller ships and aircraft where he/she has reasonable grounds for believing that:

- the vehicle, ship or aircraft has been used or was intended to be used in carrying out the arrangements in respect of the offence, and
- the person arrested is the owner, driver or, in the case of a ship or aircraft, the captain (see generally s. 25D).

Extensive powers for entry and search under warrant are made for immigration officers and the police under ss. 28A and 28B.

Following the conviction of a defendant for a relevant offence, a court may order the forfeiture of any vehicle used or intended to be used in connection with the offence if the person owned or was driving the vehicle at the time the offence was committed, or was a director, manager or secretary of a company that owned the vehicle at the time (see s. 25C).

This power will extend to ships and aircraft but there are minimum requirements in relation to the size of the vessel or aircraft and to the number of illegal entrants carried on board.

1.17.3.3 Trafficking People for Exploitation

In addition to the more general immigration offences and provisions discussed elsewhere in this chapter, there are specific statutory measures designed to increase the effectiveness of the police and other agencies in this area.

OFFENCE: **Trafficking People for Exploitation—*Asylum and Immigration (Treatment of Claimants etc.) Act 2004, s. 4***
- Triable either way • On indictment 14 years' imprisonment and/or fine
- 12 months, and/or fine summarily (unless committed before the commencement of s. 154 of the Criminal Justice Act 2003, in which case the reference to 12 months is six months)

The Asylum and Immigration (Treatment of Claimants etc.) Act 2004, s. 4 states:

(1) A person commits an offence if he arranges or facilitates the arrival in, or the entry into the United Kingdom of an individual (the 'passenger') and—
  (a) he intends to exploit the passenger in the United Kingdom or elsewhere, or
  (b) he believes that another person is likely to exploit the passenger in the United Kingdom or elsewhere.
(2) A person commits an offence if he arranges or facilitates travel within the United Kingdom by an individual (the 'passenger') in respect of whom he believes that an offence under subsection (1) may have been committed and—
  (a) he intends to exploit the passenger in the United Kingdom or elsewhere, or
  (b) he believes that another person is likely to exploit the passenger in the United Kingdom or elsewhere.
(3) A person commits an offence if he arranges or facilitates the departure from the United Kingdom of an individual (the 'passenger') and—
  (a) he intends to exploit the passenger outside the United Kingdom, or
  (b) he believes that another person is likely to exploit the passenger outside the United Kingdom.

KEYNOTE

The above offence covers arranging or facilitating the arrival in, departure from or travel within the United Kingdom of a whole series of different vulnerable categories of person, in each case with the relevant intention or belief with regard to that person's exploitation. For the purposes of this section a person is exploited if:

- they are the victim of behaviour that contravenes Article 4 of the European Convention on Human Rights (slavery and forced labour);
- they are encouraged, required or expected to do anything as a result of which they (or another person) would commit an offence under the Human Organ Transplants Act 1989;
- they are subjected to force, threats or deception designed to induce them to provide services, to provide another person with benefits or to enable another person to acquire benefits of any kind;
- they are requested or induced to undertake *any activity*, having been chosen on the grounds that they are mentally or physically ill or disabled, young or have a family relationship with a person and a person without the illness, disability, youth or family relationship would be likely to refuse the request or resist the inducement (s. 4(4)).

Where the offence is committed within the context of employment there are further considerations and offences and the advice of the Home Office Immigration and Nationality Directorate should be sought.

Sections 25C and 25D of the Immigration Act 1971 (forfeiture or detention of vehicle etc.) apply in relation to an offence under s. 4 above.

The Gangmasters (Licensing) Act 2004

The Gangmasters (Licensing) Act 2004 establishes a regulatory body (the Gangmasters Licensing Authority—GLA) whose remit includes the issuing and inspection of licences and the provision of information held by it to specified persons in accordance with the Act.

The definition of a gangmaster is very wide. In summary a gangmaster is a person who supplies a worker to do work to which the Act applies for another person (s. 4). The 'work' to which the Act applies is essentially agricultural work and gathering shellfish and includes processing or packaging any produce derived from agricultural work, shellfish, fish or products derived from shellfish or fish (s. 3). It does not matter whether the worker supplied in this way is supplied directly or indirectly or whether the work done is for the purposes of a business carried on by the recipient of the worker or in connection with services provided by him/her to another person. Similarly, it does not matter whether the gangmaster supplies the worker him/herself or procures that the worker is supplied, whether the worker works under a contract or whether the work is done under the control of the gangmaster, recipient or an intermediary (see generally s. 4(3)). A person will still be a 'worker' for the purposes of the Act even if he/she has no right to be, or to work, in the United Kingdom (s. 26).

OFFENCE: **Acting as a Gangmaster without Licence etc.—**
Gangmasters (Licensing) Act 2004, s. 12
- Triable either way • 10 years' imprisonment and/or a fine on indictment
- 12 months' imprisonment and/or a fine summarily; if committed before the commencement of s. 154(1) of the Criminal Justice Act 2003, six months

The Gangmasters (Licensing) Act 2004, s. 12 states:

(1) A person commits an offence if he acts as a gangmaster in contravention of section 6 (prohibition of unlicensed activities)...
(2) A person commits an offence if he has in his possession or under his control—
  (a) a relevant document that is false and that he knows or believes to be false,
  (b) a relevant document that was improperly obtained and that he knows or believes to have been improperly obtained, or
  (c) a relevant document that relates to someone else,
  with the intention of inducing another person to believe that he or another person acting as a gangmaster in contravention of section 6 is acting under the authority of a licence.

KEYNOTE

Section 6 of the Act provides for the issuing of licences as monitored by the GLA. A person acting as a gangmaster does not contravene s. 6 by reason only of the fact that he/she breaches a condition of the licence (s. 12(1)).

A relevant document is a licence or any document issued by the GLA in connection with a licence (s. 12(6)).

The offence at subs. (2) requires both the possession/control of the relevant document *and* the intention set out above.

The concept of 'false' documents is the same as that used in the wider legislation relating to forgery (see para. 1.14.11.4).

It is a further summary offence to enter into an arrangement with a gangmaster where, in supplying the workers or services, the gangmaster contravenes s. 6 (s. 13(1)).

The Act makes provision for the appointment of enforcement officers and extends certain powers of arrest and enforcement to those officers; it also allows for the appointment of compliance officers (s. 15).

Intentional obstruction of these officers in the exercise of their functions is a summary offence, as is failure without reasonable cause to comply with their proper instructions (s. 18).

1.17.4 Registration Cards

OFFENCE: **Misuse etc. of Registration Card—***Immigration Act 1971, s. 26A*
* Triable either way • Ten years' imprisonment on indictment • Six months' imprisonment and/or a fine summarily

The Immigration Act 1971, s. 26A states:

> (3) A person commits an offence if he—
>> (a) makes a false registration card,
>> (b) alters a registration card with intent to deceive or to enable another to deceive,
>> (c) ...
>> (d) uses or attempts to use a false registration card for a purpose for which a registration card is issued,
>> (e) uses or attempts to use an altered registration card with intent to deceive,
>> (f) makes an article designed to be used in making a false registration card,
>> (g) makes an article designed to be used in altering a registration card with intent to deceive or to enable another to deceive ...
>> (h) ...

KEYNOTE

A registration card here is a document which:

* carries information about a person (whether or not wholly or partly electronically), and
* is issued by the Secretary of State to the person wholly or partly in connection with a claim for asylum (whether or not made by that person) (s. 26A(1)).

These offences require different degrees of intent and the wording of each needs to be considered carefully.

'False registration card' means a document which is designed to appear to be a registration card (s. 26A(4)).

OFFENCE: **Possession of Registration Card or Immigration Stamp—***Immigration Act 1971, s. 26A(3)(c) and (h) and s. 26B*
* Triable either way • Two years' imprisonment on indictment • Six months' imprisonment and/or a fine summarily

The Immigration Act 1971, s. 26A states:

> (3) A person commits an offence if he—
>> ...
>> (c) has a false or altered registration card in his possession without reasonable excuse,
>> ...
>> (h) has an article within paragraph (f) or (g) in his possession without reasonable excuse.

The Immigration Act 1971, s. 26B states:

(1) A person commits an offence if he has an immigration stamp in his possession without reasonable excuse.
(2) A person commits an offence if he has a replica immigration stamp in his possession without reasonable excuse.

KEYNOTE

These lesser offences should be read in conjunction with the other s. 26A offences (see above).

As with the other offences, 'false registration card' here means a document which is designed to appear to be a registration card (s. 26A(4)).

'Immigration stamp' means a device which is designed for the purpose of stamping documents in the exercise of an immigration function; 'replica immigration stamp' means a device which is designed for the purpose of stamping a document so that it appears to have been stamped in the exercise of an immigration function; and 'immigration function' means a function of an immigration officer or the Secretary of State under the Immigration Acts (s. 26B(3)).

An immigration officer may arrest without warrant a person who has committed, or whom he/she has reasonable grounds for suspecting has committed an offence under ss. 26A or 26B (s. 28A(9A)).

1.17.5 Passport Offences

OFFENCE: **Making Untrue Statement to Procure Passport—*Criminal Justice Act 1925, s. 36***
   • Triable either way • Two years' imprisonment on indictment • Six months' imprisonment and/or a fine summarily

The Criminal Justice Act 1925, s. 36 states:

(1) The making by any person of a statement which is to his knowledge untrue for the purpose of procuring a passport, whether for himself or any other person, shall be [an offence].

OFFENCE: **Entering United Kingdom without Passport etc.—*Asylum and Immigration (Treatment of Claimants etc.) Act 2004, s. 2***
   • Triable either way • Two years' imprisonment on indictment • 12 months' imprisonment and/or a fine summarily if after the commencement of s. 154 of the Criminal Justice Act 2003, otherwise six months

The Asylum and Immigration (Treatment of Claimants etc.) Act 2004, s. 2 states:

(1) A person commits an offence if at a leave or asylum interview he does not have with him an immigration document which—
   (a) is in force, and
   (b) satisfactorily establishes his identity and nationality or citizenship.
(2) A person commits an offence if at a leave or asylum interview he does not have with him, in respect of any dependent child with whom he claims to be travelling or living, an immigration document which—
   (a) is in force, and
   (b) satisfactorily establishes the child's identity and nationality or citizenship.

KEYNOTE

'Immigration document' means a passport or a document which relates to a national of a state other than the United Kingdom and which is designed to serve the same purpose as a passport (s. 2(12)).

Section 2 creates two offences. Subsection (8) provides that a person shall be presumed for the purposes of this section not to have a document with them if they fail to produce it to an immigration officer or official of the Secretary of State on request. Therefore the first offence is effectively committed where a person is unable to produce a current passport or similar document at a 'leave' or 'asylum' interview. The second offence applies where the person at such an interview is unable to produce a current passport or similar document in respect of a dependent child with whom he/she claims to be living or travelling.

The person does not commit the offences if the interview takes place *after* the person has entered the United Kingdom and within the period of three days (beginning with the date of that interview) the person provides a passport or similar immigration document to an immigration officer or to the Secretary of State (s. 2(3)).

A document which purports to be, or is designed to look like, a passport or relevant immigration document, is a false immigration document. In addition, if a passport (or document) is used outside the period for which it is expressed to be valid, if it is used by or in respect of a person other than the person to or for whom it was issued or it is used contrary to any formal provisions for its use, it will be regarded as a false immigration document (see s. 2(13)). There are several specific defences to these offences. In addition to the more obvious ones (e.g. having a reasonable excuse for not being in possession of a passport being a European Economic Area national exercising a right in respect of entry/residence in the United Kingdom) it is also a defence to some of the above offences for a person to produce a *false passport or immigration document* and to prove that he/she used it as an immigration document for all purposes in connection with his/her journey to the United Kingdom (see s. 2(4)). This is both important and unusual in that the defence to the offence above is itself an offence (see para. 1.14.11.5).

The section makes other detailed provisos as to when this specific defence will apply and what will amount to a 'reasonable excuse' in relation to the more general defence.

1.17.6 Suspected International Terrorists

Under the Anti-terrorism, Crime and Security Act 2001, the Secretary of State may issue a certificate in respect of a person suspected of being a terrorist where the Secretary of State believes that the person's presence in the United Kingdom is a risk to national security. Broadly, a terrorist for this purpose is a person who:

- is or has been concerned in the commission, preparation or instigation of international terrorism; or
- is a member of, supports or assists an international terrorist group.

Terrorism is defined in s. 1 of the Terrorism Act 2000 (**see General Police Duties**). Generally, this means the use or threat of action which:

- involves serious violence against a person
- involves serious damage to property
- endangers another person's life
- creates a serious risk to the health or safety of the public
- is designed seriously to interfere with or seriously to disrupt an electronic system, and
- the use or threat is designed to influence the government or to intimidate the public or a section of the public, and

- the use or threat is made for the purpose of advancing a political, religious or ideological cause.

The Court of Appeal has held that the power to detain foreign nationals on the ground that they pose a risk to national security under these provisions does not breach Article 14 of the European Convention on Human Rights (see *A v Secretary of State for the Home Department* [2002] EWCA Civ 1502).

There are, however, several legal restrictions on the powers under the 2001 Act in relation to suspected international terrorists.

Index

A

Abduction of children
  appropriate consent 1.12.3.1
  consent of victim 1.12.3.1, 1.12.3.3
  Convention 1.12.3
  defences
    person connected with
        child 1.12.3.2
    person not connected with
        child 1.12.3.4
  Director of Public Prosecutions,
      consent for prosecution
      of 1.12.3.1
  firearms 1.7.9.5
  person connected with the
      child 1.12.3.1, 1.12.3.2
  person not connected with
      child 1.12.3.3, 1.12.3.4
  removal, meaning of 1.12.3.3
  sampling 1.12.3.3
Abetting
  conspiracy 1.3.3.1
  meaning 1.2.6
  perjury 1.16.2.1
Absolute liability *see* Strict liability
Abstracting electricity 1.13.11
Abuse of position of trust
  allegations 1.10.5.5
  fraud 1.14.2, 1.14.5
  Local Safeguarding Children Boards
      (LSCBs) 1.10.5.5
  teachers and support staff,
      allegations against 1.10.5.5
Accessories
  absence, crime committed in
      co-defendant's 1.2.6.2
  agreements 1.2.6
  aid, abet, counsel and procure 1.2.6
  beyond what was agreed,
      going 1.2.6.2
  complete departure 1.2.6.2
  contraception, provision of 1.2.6.1
  foreseeability 1.2.6.2
  harassment, protection from 1.2.6.1
  intention to aid principal 1.2.6.1
  joint enterprise 1.2.6.2
  mens rea 1.2.6.1, 1.2.6.2
  offensive weapons, knowledge of
      possession of 1.2.6.2
  presence at scene 1.2.6
  preliminary stages, participation
      in 1.2.6.2
  public order 1.2.6.2
  repentance 1.2.6.2
  sexual intercourse, girls under 16
      having 1.2.6.2
  state of mind 1.2.6.1
  trace the principal, failure to 1.2.6.2
  watching the offence 1.2.6
  withdrawal 1.2.6.2

Accounts
  bank accounts, deception
      and 1.13.14
  building society accounts 1.13.2.4
  false accounting 1.2.3, 1.14.11.1
  theft 1.13.2.4
Accredited persons, assault or
      obstruction of 1.7.3.5
Actual bodily harm
  assault occasioning ABH 1.8.6.1
  charging standards 1.8.6.1
  examples 1.8.6.1
  hair, cutting a person's 1.8.6.1
  intent 1.8.2.5, 1.8.3.2
  meaning 1.8.6.1
  psychiatric injury 1.8.6.1
  recklessness 1.1.4.2, 1.8.2.5
  types of injuries 1.8.6.1
Actus reus
  mens rea, contemporaneity
      with 1.2.2, 1.2.2.1, 1.2.2.2
  voluntary act 1.2.2.1
Administering poisons 1.9.3
Administration of justice offences
  assisting offenders 1.16.7
  concealing arrestable offences 1.16.8
  contempt of court 1.16.11
  escape
    assisting 1.16.9
    prison escape 1.16.9
  false statements
    criminal proceedings 1.16.3
    oath, on 1.16.3
  false testimony by unsworn
      child 1.16.3
  harbouring offenders 1.16.9
  harming witnesses 1.16.6
  intimidation of witnesses 1.16.5
  perjury 1.16.2
  perverting the course of
      justice 1.16.4
  prison escape 1.16.9
  unsworn child, false testimony
      by 1.16.3
  wasting police time 1.16.10
Adopted children, sexual offences
      and 1.10.5.7
Advertisements
  prostitutes near public phones,
      placing advertisement
      for 1.10.12.6
  rewards 1.13.12
Aerosol paint to children, sale of 1.15.7
Age
  criminal responsibility, of 1.1.4.2,
      1.4.10
  firearms 1.7.12
Agents provocateur 1.3.6.2
Aggravated burglary 1.13.4–1.13.4.1
  'at the time', meaning of 1.13.4
  explosives 1.13.4, 1.13.4.1

  firearms 1.13.4, 1.13.4.1
  'has with him', meaning of 1.13.4
  imitation firearms 1.13.4, 1.13.4.1
  instant arming 1.13.4
  knowledge of WIFE item,
      requirement of 1.13.4
  weapons 1.13.4, 1.13.4.1
  WIFE (weapons of offence, imitation
      firearms, firearms and
      explosives) 1.13.4, 1.13.4.1
Aggravated damage 1.15.2.1
Aggravated
      vehicle-taking 1.13.6–1.13.6.1
Aggravating factors *see also* Racially
      aggravated offences; Religiously
      aggravated offences
  burglary 1.13.4, 1.13.4.1
  criminal damage 1.15.2.1
  drug offences 1.6.5.5
  firearm 1.7.5.2, 1.7.9, 1.13.4,
      1.13.4.1
  school premises, drug offences
      committed on, in or in vicinity
      of 1.6.5.5
Aiding and abetting 1.3.3.1, 1.7.9.5
Air weapons
  age restrictions 1.7.12
  beyond premises, firing
      weapons 1.7.7.1
  dangerousness 1.7.7
  definition 1.7.7
  exemptions 1.7.4.4
  face to face sales 1.7.7.1
  gas cartridges 1.7.7
  lethal barrelled weapons 1.7.2.1
  public place, in a 1.7.10.1
  sale 1.7.12
Alternative verdicts 1.5.1
Ambulance services, assaults on 1.8.4.1
Ammunition
  definition 1.7.2.3
  loss, notice of 1.7.15
  possession 1.7.4.3
  section 1 firearms 1.7.5
Animals
  criminal damage 1.15.2.3
  cruelty 1.15.2.3
  firearms
    humane killng 1.7.4.4
    slaughtering 1.7.4.4
    tranquilising 1.7.4.4
    vermin 1.7.4.4
  going equipped 1.13.8
  humane killng 1.7.4.4
  property 1.13.2.4, 1.15.2.3
  sexual offences on 1.10.12
  slaughtering 1.7.4.4
  theft 1.13.2.4
  tranquilising 1.7.4.4
  vermin 1.7.4.4
  wild creatures 1.13.2.4